SNAKE

CHRIS MATTISON

DK LONDON
Editor Kaiya Shang
Project Art Editor Duncan Turner
Project Editor Miezan van Zyl
New Photography Gary Ombler
Jacket Designer Natalie Godwin
Jacket Editor Claire Gell
Jacket Design Development Manager Sophia MTT
Pre-production Producer Nadine King
Producer Mary Slater
Managing Art Editor Michael Duffy
Managing Editor Angeles Gavira
Art Director Karen Self
Design Director Phil Ormerod
Publisher Liz Wheeler
Publishing Director Jonathan Metcalf

DK DELHI
Senior Editor Dharini Ganesh
Project Art Editor Vaibhav Rastogi
Art Editor Anjali Sachar
Assistant Editor Isha Sharma
Managing Art Editor Sudakshina Basu
Managing Editor Rohan Sinha
Picture Researcher Sumedha Chopra
Picture Research Manager Taiyaba Khatoon
Jacket Designer Suhita Dharamjit
Managing Jackets Editor Saloni Singh
Pre-production Manager Balwant Singh
Production Manager Pankaj Sharma
Senior DTP Designer Harish Aggarwal
DTP Designers Rajesh Singh Adhikari, Jaypal Chauhan

First published in Great Britain in 1999
This revised edition published in 2015 by
Dorling Kindersley Limited, 80 Strand, London WC2R 0RL
Copyright © 1999, 2015 Dorling Kindersley Limited
A Penguin Random House Company

Text copyright © 1999, 2015 Chris Mattison
The right of Chris Mattison to be identified as Writer of this
Work has been asserted by him in accordance with the Copyright,
Designs and Patents Act 1998

2 4 6 8 10 9 7 5 3 1

001–253282–March/2016

A CIP catalogue record for this book is available from the British Library.

ISBN: 978-0-2412-2624-7

Printed in China

A WORLD OF IDEAS:
SEE ALL THERE IS TO KNOW
www.dk.com

CONTENTS

Introduction 6

The Essential Snake
Introduction.. 7
Evolution 8
Environment... 10
Size and Shape.. 12
Scales... 16
Anatomy and Movement 18
Skull and Teeth.. 20
Sense Organs.. 22
Hunting and Feeding.. 24
Venomous Snakes... 28
Passive Defence... 30
Active Defence.. 32
Reproduction 36
Conservation 38
Classification of Snakes 40

Snake Gallery
Introduction.. 41
Haitian Dwarf Boa 42
Cuban Dwarf Boa 43
Neotropical Sunbeam Snake..................................... 44
Asian Sunbeam Snake 45
Children's Python 46
Spotted Python... 47

Reticulated Python 48
Carpet Python 50
Green Tree Python 52
Burmese Python 54
Blood Python 56
Royal Python 58
Dumeril's Ground Boa 60
Common Boa...62
Calabar Ground Python 64
Emerald Tree Boa 66
Rainbow Boa 68
Green Anaconda 70
Rosy Boa 72
Brown House Snake 74
Trans-Pecos Ratsnake..76
Mangrove Snake..78
Green Catsnake 79
Common Egg-eater..80
Boomslang...82
Eastern Indigo Snake...84
Mandarin Ratsnake..86
Red-tailed Racer..88
Plains Hog-nosed Snake 90
Grey-banded Kingsnake...92
Mexican Kingsnake..93
California Kingsnake 94
Sonoran Mountain Kingsnake................................96
Milksnake 98
Grass Snake... 100
Banded Water Snake.. 102
Rough Green Snake 104
Baird's Ratsnake 106
Corn Snake 108
Pine Snake... 110
Chequered Garter Snake...................................... 112
San Francisco Garter Snake.................................. 114
Leopard Snake 116
Northern Death Adder.. 118
West African Green Mamba 120
Chinese Cobra 122
Monocled Cobra... 123
Red Spitting Cobra 124
Collett's Snake 126

Copperhead.. 128
Puff Adder 130
Gaboon Viper 132
Jararaca 134
Desert Horned Viper.. 136
Saw-scaled Viper.. 138
White-lipped Tree Viper.. 140
Nose-horned Viper 142
Adder 144
Western Diamondback Rattlesnake....................... 146
Neotropical Rattlesnake.. 148
Sidewinder 150

Snake Directory

Introduction.. 151
Snake Directory 151
Glossary 196
Index 197
Acknowledgments 200

INTRODUCTION

There has always been something of a mystery about snakes. How can they move so quickly without legs? How can they kill prey with only a single bite, delivered in the blink of an eye? And how do they swallow prey whole when it may be several times bigger than their jaws? It is little wonder that so many myths and legends have grown up around these amazing creatures.

Snakes can be frightening as well as fascinating. They are predators, like eagles, sharks, and tigers and, although we may have a sneaking admiration for their stealth and cunning, we know that some can be dangerous. For the snakes themselves, this has unfortunate consequences since, due to fear and ignorance, they are often killed on sight. In reality, however, only a small number of species can harm humans and, of these, the number that can actually kill us is even smaller.

There are many other interesting aspects to snakes' lives – their different forms, behaviours, defences, habitats, and their feeding and breeding habits. These are the subjects that have been emphasized in this book, and wherever possible, rather than merely describing snakes, the evolutionary reasons behind their development have also been given.

Much of this information is quite new, since snakes, being secretive, are among the most difficult animals to study in their own habitat. In recent years, professional biologists have pioneered new techniques for tracking and monitoring snakes in the wild, showing that snakes have an important role to play in the natural order. At the same time, amateur naturalists, perhaps alarmed by the rate at which flora and fauna are disappearing from our lives, are beginning to notice and appreciate their beauty.

Snake is written in the hope that the information provided by the text, combined with the stunning photographs, will give you a greater appreciation of snakes and will stimulate your interest in their lives. I hope it will answer some of your questions. Most importantly, I hope you will be convinced that "the only good snake is a live snake".

RHINOCEROS VIPER
One of the most flamboyant snakes, the Rhinoceros Viper becomes almost invisible when lying among the leaf-litter of its African rainforest home, hidden from predators and waiting for prey.

THE ESSENTIAL SNAKE

Over the course of millennia, thousands of species of snakes have evolved and dispersed throughout the world. The 3,500 or more species of existing snakes are all different, yet all have several physical characteristics in common, such as a scaly covering, lack of functional limbs, a long, forked tongue, and lidless eyes. In addition, and perhaps more importantly, all snakes have to interact with their environment, they all have to find enough food to eat, while avoiding being eaten themselves, and, if they are to pass on their successful qualities and features, they all have to reproduce. The following introductory section concentrates on these themes, cutting across the boundaries that distinguish one family or species from another, and looks at aspects of their lifestyles that affect them all. It also gives a comprehensive explanation of how snakes are classified into families.

Form

Snakes have, down the ages, been shaped by natural selection. This has resulted in some species that are very large and others that are very small. Large snakes are in the minority, although they attract the most attention. The vast majority of snakes are less than 1 m (3 ft 3 in) long. Other variations in shape have also evolved to allow snakes to succeed in a range of different environments – snakes may be fat or thin, rounded or flattened, and so on.

The same selective pressures that have caused snakes to evolve into elongated, tube-like animals have also moulded their internal organs to fit the shape of their bodies. It might be surprising to learn that snakes have, fundamentally, the same set of organs as humans. However, these are arranged rather differently to fit into the available space. Many organs are elongated, and the paired organs are often staggered rather than positioned side by side.

Behaviour

The need to survive has as strong an influence on snakes' behaviour as on their shape and appearance. Indeed, the way in which a species behaves is often linked to the way it looks. It is no surprise, therefore, that snakes have diverse methods of hunting, subduing prey, defence, and reproduction. These strategies are also influenced by natural selection, although the reason why one species lays eggs while another gives birth to live young, for example, is not always obvious. Finding the answers to questions such as this provides a continually absorbing challenge for zoologists.

The links between snakes' appearance and their activities are not always clear, nor do we fully understand why they behave as they do. Some of the questions often asked about snakes can be answered quite simply, but other answers are speculative. For, no matter how much we continue to learn, we will never know all the answers.

The future

Sadly, snakes are disappearing from many parts of the globe where they used to be common, just when we are starting to understand their place in our world. Snakes cannot respond quickly enough to the habitat destruction caused by encroaching urban development, intensive agriculture, and pollution, so they need human help if they are to survive. This section includes an exploration of the many threats snakes face today, as well as some examples of successful conservation in action.

EVOLUTION

To the best of our knowledge, snakes first appeared 100–150 million years ago, during the early Cretaceous period. Today, there are nearly 3,000 distinct species, which have evolved over millennia, perhaps from just one group of lizards. The evolution and spread of snakes has been highly successful – different species survive in a remarkable range of habitats and climatic conditions, and snakes have established themselves in almost every country in the world.

Origins

Within the diverse assemblage of animals known as reptiles, snakes are most closely related to lizards and amphisbaenians (burrowing reptiles that superficially resemble worms), all of which are subdivisions of the order Squamata.

The first snakes are thought to have arisen from a group of lizards that gradually lost their legs in response to a burrowing lifestyle – a subterranean habitat makes legs redundant; in fact, they get in the way. Lizards belonging to several surviving families still have a tendency to lose their legs for the same reason, but it is unlikely that snakes evolved from any of the legless lizards that exist today.

The earliest known snake is a terrestrial species called *Lapparentophis defrennei*, which lived in the region that is now North Africa between 100 and 150 million years ago. The next fossil record is that of a marine snake, *Simoliophis*, whose remains are about 100 million years old and occur in parts of Europe and North Africa that were once the sea bed. The fossil records are intermittent after this, but fossils that have been found all over the world and that date from about 65 million years ago show that, by this time, many more species of snakes were present. Some fossils belong to species that later became extinct, but a number are evidently closely related to living species belonging to a couple of the older families, the pipe snakes and the boas. There are no existing fossil records representing the most primitive living snakes, the thread and blind snakes, since the skeletons of their predecessors were too small and fragile to survive.

Dispersal

At the same time that snakes were evolving, Earth was undergoing dramatic changes (see "Land drift", above right), with the continental land masses separating and joining together. Because the vast majority of snakes are land creatures, with little chance of dispersing across the oceans, these land movements had important implications for their distribution. The earliest, most primitive snake families were able to disperse across continents that were still joined to one another, while the spread of more recent snake families was limited by the barriers of surrounding seas.

By looking at the present-day distribution of snakes, therefore, it is possible to tell, to a large extent, when they evolved and how they spread. It is clear, for example, that snakes in North America have more in common with those in Europe and Asia than with those in South America, and that South American snakes have affinities with species in Africa and Madagascar. These snakes were probably actively dispersing when the ancient southern continent, Gondwanaland, was separate from the northern continent, Laurasia.

LEGLESS LIZARD
With no front legs and only vestigial hind legs, this legless Glass Lizard is believed to resemble the earliest ancestors of today's snakes. Living a largely subterranean existence, the burrowing forms of snakes that evolved with no legs may have been better equipped to survive than limbed forms.

LAND DRIFT

The shape and position of Earth's land masses have altered radically during the evolution of snakes. After the formation of the supercontinent Pangaea, the land mass split into two vast continents and continued to drift to form the map of Earth known today.

Laurasia

Gondwanaland

200 MILLION YEARS AGO

Asian landmass

African landmass

75 MILLION YEARS AGO

North America

Asia

Africa

Australia

Antarctica

PRESENT DAY

Similarly, vipers, generally considered to be the most recently evolved family of snakes, are found throughout the warmer regions of the world except Australia, suggesting that they evolved after Australia separated from the large land masses.

Some species have made remarkable journeys. The boas on New Guinea and neighbouring South Pacific islands arrived from the west coast of South America. They may have been transported on an uprooted vegetable raft, their ability to go for long periods without food being essential to their survival. Perhaps a single pregnant female was washed ashore, and from this small beginning a new colony arose.

Radiation

The evolution of snakes into creatures with a wide variety of behaviours and anatomies has been largely influenced by changes in their environment, due either to their spread into new territories, or to changes in the environment itself. Snakes finding themselves in new or changing habitats need to adapt, either to avoid direct competition with another species, or to exploit a resource, such as a food source or living space. They may change physically, for instance, growing longer, shorter, stouter, or more slender, or their coloration may be modified to blend in with the new habitat.

In this way, snakes "radiate", reinventing themselves in new forms over thousands of generations. Although the vast majority of species do not adapt in time and die out, those that do adapt become successful and may eventually oust other species. This situation remains dynamic today, with populations expanding into and withdrawing from their geographical ranges, so that the existing set of species is in constant flux, with some increasing and others dwindling in number.

EVOLUTIONARY CONVERGENCE

The environment in which any species lives presents it with a series of challenges to its survival – how to find enough food, avoid being eaten by predators, find a mate, and produce offspring. Through the evolutionary process, each species arrives at distinct solutions to these problems. Sometimes, different species in distant yet similar habitats face almost identical problems, and have developed parallel solutions.

These pairs, or sets, of species typically have a similar appearance and behaviour pattern – known as evolutionary convergence – even though they may live thousands of miles apart.

There are numerous examples of this fascinating aspect of evolution. For example, the Green Tree Python of New Guinea and Australia and the Emerald Tree Boa of South America look so similar that they are hard to tell apart. Both are arboreal snakes living in forest habitats and, in response to similar conditions, they have both evolved with bright green colouring and white markings. They even drape themselves over boughs in exactly the same way.

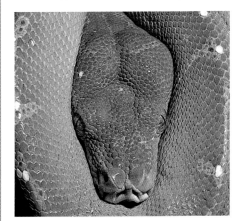
GREEN TREE PYTHON

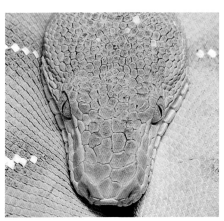
EMERALD TREE BOA

FILLING A NICHE
Some species have only evolved because of a vacant ecological niche. There are no vipers in Australia, but the Death Adder, a member of the cobra family, has come to look and behave like one, using its thick, heavy body to ambush prey.

ENVIRONMENT

In contrast to birds and mammals, snakes are unable to migrate or move over long distances and are, therefore, very much at the mercy of conditions in their immediate surroundings. Because every environment is different, each snake species has, over time, evolved various ways of adapting in order to survive. The most important environmental components that affect snakes are temperature, light, and water.

Regulating body temperature

Unlike mammals and birds, which generate body heat internally, snakes are ectotherms. This means that their body temperatures are determined by outside sources, such as the heat of the sun, and can only be adjusted by basking or seeking shade. For most species, the ideal temperature is around 30°C (85°F). At lower temperatures, snakes become sluggish, and body functions slow down or cease. At higher temperatures, they suffer heat exhaustion and eventually die.

How snakes regulate body heat depends on where they live. In the tropics, temperatures are usually stable, so snakes rarely need to bask. In very cold or cool places, they may frequently need to change position. This is partly why snakes are more numerous in warm regions, and why species diversity falls off towards the poles.

Only highly specialized snakes can survive in extreme conditions, so there are few species living in regions far from the equator or at high altitudes. In these places, temperatures do not rise much above freezing for most of the year. Snakes here are invariably small so that they can warm up quickly, and they are often dark for the same reason. They

LIVING IN WARM CLIMATES

Many snake species, including Dumeril's Ground Boa, inhabit warm parts of the world where there is little climatic variation. Snakes thrive in these regions because it is easy for them to maintain body temperature.

hibernate in winter, and most give birth to live young because, by basking, they can use their bodies to provide a better environment for the developing embryos than if they were to lay eggs (see p.37).

Snakes from deserts have also adapted their behaviour patterns to cope with extreme conditions. They may be active for only part of the year, hiding in burrows

ADAPTING TO THE DESERT

Many desert snakes shuffle down below the surface of the sand during the day to escape the lethally hot temperatures. Where traction is a problem, they may move across the surface by sidewinding (see p.19).

KEEPING COOL IN ARID REGIONS

Snakes from arid regions are often pale in colour to reflect heat and to merge with the sand, soil, or rock on which they live. These snakes shelter in burrows to avoid extremes of temperature.

HIBERNATING IN COLD CONDITIONS

The few species of snake that occupy mountainous regions with harsh environments often hibernate for up to eight months. For the rest of the year they are active only during the middle of the day.

during the hottest season or becoming active for a few short hours in the middle of the night. During winter, these same species may become active only during the day to avoid cold night temperatures. Desert snakes tend to live near rocky outcrops or in canyons and gullies, where they can find water and gain protection from extremes of temperature.

Burrowing and aquatic snakes have little opportunity to regulate their body temperatures, and so they typically live in places such as tropical forests and swamps, where temperatures are warm and even.

Surviving cold
Snakes in high latitudes hibernate in burrows and underground chambers to escape the worst of winter. But in late autumn and early spring they may be caught out above ground by a sudden drop in the air temperature. At these times, some species, including some North American garter snakes, produce

substances to prevent damage if ice crystals form inside their cells. For a short period, as much as 40 per cent of the fluid in their cells may turn to ice.

Saving energy
Ectotherms have the ability to exploit scarce or seasonal food sources because they do not need to use their metabolic energy for heat production, as mammals do. It is estimated that snakes can survive on less than ten per cent of the food needed by birds or mammals of equivalent size. Furthermore, when food is scarce, they can shut down their systems, for months if necessary, until food sources improve.

Balancing moisture
A scaly skin is only one of the methods snakes use to resist dehydration. The skin's degree of impermeability depends on the snake's origins. Those from dry, desert regions are often very efficient at conserving moisture, whereas those from humid or wet habitats quickly dehydrate

without access to water. Snakes also minimize water loss by excreting their nitrogenous waste as uric acid, a white, crystalline substance needing very little water to carry it out of the body.

Some snakes conserve water by coiling to reduce the surface area from which water can evaporate. Certain desert species avoid hissing so that valuable water vapour is not exhaled. Instead, these species have specialized scales that they rub together (stridulation), or tails that rattle to sound a warning to other creatures (see p.33).

Sea and wart snakes live in salt water and feed on marine animals that contain a high proportion of salt. This creates an imbalance in the ratio of salt to water in their bodies, which they correct by using a special gland on the floor of the mouth. Concentrated salty water collects here and is transferred to the sheath surrounding the tongue. When a snake flicks out its tongue underwater, it pushes out a small quantity of this solution, keeping the balance within acceptable limits.

WARMING UP IN TEMPERATE REGIONS
In temperate regions, where the weather is often cool, snakes exploit periods of sunshine by basking on open ground or rocks, which retain the heat of the sun, to raise their body temperatures.

THRIVING IN THE TROPICS
Tropical regions are host to a rich diversity of snake species because they provide ideal conditions – warm temperatures with little fluctuation and a humid atmosphere that prevents dehydration.

MAINTAINING BODY HEAT IN WATER
In an aquatic habitat, it is hard for snakes to adjust their body temperatures by moving position, so these snakes are rare outside tropical regions, which are usually consistently warm all year.

SIZE AND SHAPE

All snakes have fundamentally the same form, being long and thin with no limbs. Yet, different species can vary considerably in size, and there is even some difference in shape. The smallest snakes may be barely longer than a human finger, while the largest can extend to five or six times the height of a person. These variations are a result of natural selection as evolving species have adapted to different environments and ways of life.

SOUTHERN RUBBER BOA

LARGE AND SMALL
Even within a single group snakes may range in size from gigantic to tiny. Among boas, anacondas can grow to over 10 m (33 ft) long, while the Southern Rubber Boa, *Charina bottae*, reaches no more than 75 cm (2 ft 5 in). Here, a young Southern Rubber Boa is shown in true proportion to a Green Anaconda.

GREEN ANACONDA

Large snakes

The six largest snakes belong to just two families, the boas and the pythons. The two largest species are the Green Anaconda and the Reticulated Python. The python is usually regarded as the longest, growing to about 10 m (33 ft), but the Green Anaconda is far heavier. Not surprisingly, wild stories about the sizes of both species abound. In 1907 the explorer Sir Percy Fawcett claimed to have killed an anaconda in Brazil measuring 18.9 m (62 ft).

Somewhat smaller are the giant pythons from India and Burma, *Python molurus*, and from Africa, *Python sebae*.

Both species grow to 6 m (20 ft) or slightly more, although large specimens are becoming rarer as their habitats dwindle. The equivalent snake in Australia is the Scrub Python, *Simalia kinghorni*, which has been reliably recorded at over 8 m (26 ft), although it is more usually 3–4 m (9 ft 8 in–13 ft).

The smallest of the "Big Six" is the Common Boa. This has only once been reliably recorded at over 4 m (13 ft) and usually grows to about 3 m (9 ft 8 in).

There are few species of large snakes for two main reasons. First, such snakes need to eat a lot, but their size restricts them to

hunting by ambush, which can limit the food available to them. Second, snakes rely on outside sources to raise their body temperatures, and large snakes take a long time to warm up. All activity, whether

TYPES OF BODY SHAPE

A snake's shape gives clues to its lifestyle. Burrowing snakes are mostly cylindrical (A), while ground-dwellers have a flattened underside (D) to give the body purchase over irregular surfaces. The flat underside is also seen in species that climb, such as ratsnakes, which are loaf-shaped in cross section (C) with a corner at the bottom of each flank to grip bark. Some arboreal snakes are flattened from side to side (D) for rigidity as they cantilever their bodies out, supporting their own weight, to cross from branch to branch; steel girders are shaped like this for the same reason. Aquatic snakes may also have flattened sides (E) to enable them to propel their bodies through water. A few snakes, such as the kraits, are triangular (F), but the reason for this is not clear.

A   B   C   D   E   F

SHEDDING SKIN

Even small snakes never stop growing. Throughout their lives, all snakes regularly shed the outer layer of skin to allow for growth. A snake will rub its snout on a rough surface to free the skin, then crawl forward to pull the skin off, leaving it intact. Young snakes grow more quickly than adults, so shed most often.

hunting, breeding, or self-defence, is curtailed until they can do so. It is significant that the six largest snakes, as well as several other large species, including the King Cobra, *Ophiophagus hannah*, the Taipan, *Oxyuranus scutellatus*, and the Gaboon Viper, all live in or near the tropics. Towards the poles, the average size of snakes decreases, as does the number of species.

Small snakes

In contrast, there are many species so small that they are often overlooked. Snakes in the five most primitive families, anomalepids, gerrhopilids, typhlopids, leptotyphlopids, and xenotyphlopids, rarely grow to more than 30 cm (12 in). These families total about 300 species – over ten per cent of all snakes. The smallest may be *Tetracheilostoma carlae*, from Barbados, which is less than 10 cm (4 in) in length.

Small snakes require little food – most eat ants or termites and their larvae – and their bodies warm up quickly. However, their size makes them easy prey.

Shape

Snakes vary in shape, depending on how each species has evolved in relation to its environment. Snakes that are long and thin tend to be tree-dwellers or to rely on speed to hunt down prey. Arboreal snakes must be light in weight so that branches will support them. Most have long, prehensile tails to enable them to hang down and

pluck lizards and birds from the tree. Snakes that live in open country, such as whipsnakes, racers, and sand snakes, are also long and thin. They use their large eyes to spot prey at a distance and then chase it. The long tail is used as a counterbalance when the snake is flashing through grasses or low vegetation.

Short, thick snakes, such as many vipers and a number of pythons, do not chase prey or climb trees. Instead, they ambush their food. The heavy body is used to anchor the snake firmly to the ground as it lunges its head forwards to strike its prey.

FAT AND THIN

A snake's shape and weight often reveal how it hunts. Thin snakes can stalk prey, while thick, heavy species may rely on camouflage to ambush prey.

GREEN CATSNAKE

GABOON VIPER

BUILT TO CLIMB
Climbing snakes, such as this Green Vine Snake
(*Oxybelis fulgidus*), are usually long and slender.
This way their bodies can be supported when
they need to move among thin branches. Most
of them are coloured so that they can blend in
with their surroundings.

SCALES

Like chain mail worn by medieval crusaders, the scaly skin of the snake combines protection with flexibility, being formed from plate-like scales connected by an elastic skin. Snakes have different types of scale on different parts of the body. Each type serves a specific purpose, and each one varies according to the snake's habitat and lifestyle. The pigment in the scales gives the snake its colour and markings and provides another key element in its armoury, whether for camouflage in its habitat or as a warning to potential predators.

Functions of scales

A snake's skin is made up of two distinct parts: thickened areas, which are the scales, and the thinner, flexible areas between the scales, the interstitial skin. Unlike fish scales, the scales of snakes cannot be scraped off, but the outer layer of skin is shed regularly to allow for growth (see p.13).

Scales protect the snake from injury as it moves over rough ground. They also provide some defence against attack from parasites, biting insects, small predators, and from the snakes' own prey, which often fights back.

Scales may also help locomotion. Irregularities in the scales, especially along the trailing edges of those on the underside, help the snake to grip the surface and pull itself forward horizontally or vertically.

Scales help to minimize water loss through evaporation. This feature is most important in desert species, and

Head scales vary in shape according to their position

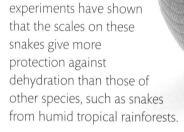
Ventral scales occur on the underside, from the chin to the cloaca

experiments have shown that the scales on these snakes give more protection against dehydration than those of other species, such as snakes from humid tropical rainforests.

Types of scale

A snake may have three or more types of scale on different parts of its body, each with a particular form and function.
Dorsal scales Found on the back and sides, these are usually arranged in rows, the number of which can identify a species. Dorsal scales may be keeled, as in most vipers, or smooth, as in burrowing snakes.
Ventral scales Located on the underside, these are smooth to aid locomotion. The last one, the pre-anal scale, may be single or paired. Entirely aquatic snakes have greatly reduced ventral scales, sometimes visible only as a narrow ridge along the

RELAXED SKIN   **STRETCHED SKIN**

INTERSTITIAL SKIN
Unlike the thickened areas, or scales, the thinner interstitial, or interscalar, skin is able to stretch. This gives the whole skin elasticity and flexibility of movement, while, at the same time, the snake benefits from the shield-like rigidity of the scales.

MODIFIED SCALES

The Madagascan Vine Snake, *Langaha madagascariensis*, demonstrates a unique and remarkable example of modification of the head scales. Its snout ends in a long protuberance, but while the male's is straight, the female's is broad and ornamented with numerous small spines. The purpose of this is unclear.

FEMALE MADAGASCAN VINE SNAKE

MALE MADAGASCAN VINE SNAKE

SCALE LOCATION
Snakes have different types of scale covering the back and sides, underside, head, and underside of the tail. They protect the snake from the elements and predators and help it to move.

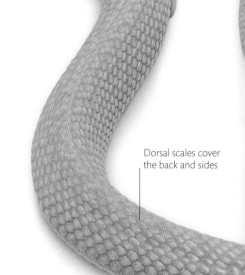
Dorsal scales cover the back and sides

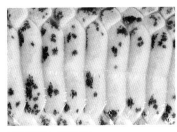

VENTRAL SCALES
The ventral scales of Dumeril's Ground Boa are typical of most snakes, forming a single row of short, wide, overlapping scales. They are always smooth to facilitate movement over the ground.

SMOOTH DORSAL SCALES
Triangular, overlapping dorsal scales, such as those seen on Baird's Ratsnake, create a smooth, polished surface. Snakes with smooth scales include the majority of boas and pythons.

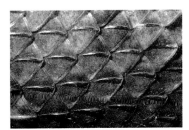

KEELED DORSAL SCALES
The Pacific Boa is one of a number of species that have keeled dorsal scales. This type of scale has a ridge, or a pair of ridges, along its centre, giving the snake a rough appearance.

GRANULAR DORSAL SCALES
Small and conical in shape and rough in texture, granular dorsal scales occur in only a few species of snake, including the aquatic wart, or file, snakes, which use them to grip fish.

LARGE HEAD SCALES
Seen here on the American Ratsnake, large head scales are arranged in distinctive patterns that help identify the snake. They occur in most colubrids, cobras, and some vipers.

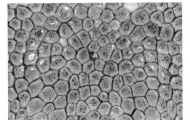

SMALL HEAD SCALES
The Emerald Tree Boa is one of many species of boa to have a large number of small, fairly uniform scales covering the top of the head. Such scales are also found in vipers.

SINGLE SUBCAUDAL SCALES
Subcaudal scales are similar to ventral scales. Here, the underside of a Rosy Boa's tail shows typical single subcaudal scales. In some species of snake these scales are paired.

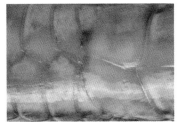

PAIRED SUBCAUDAL SCALES
Certain species, including Baird's Ratsnake, have paired subcaudal scales. Occasionally, however, single subcaudal scales may be found scattered among the double scales.

belly. This may be because these snakes do not haul their full body weight over rough surfaces.

Head scales These are large and plate-like in many species. They include the rostral scale, at the tip of the snout, the subocular scales, immediately below the eyes, and the labial scales, bordering the mouth. Some snakes, notably most boas and many vipers, have large labial scales, with small scales covering the upper surfaces of the head. These probably evolved from larger scales that became fragmented over time.

Subcaudal scales Found beneath the snake's tail, these scales are similar to the ventral scales, but may be either single or paired. In some snakes, single scales appear in places among the paired scales.

Scale coloration
The cells containing pigments are located in the scales and give each species its characteristic pattern and coloration. Snakes may be a single, uniform colour or, more frequently, patterned with spots, blotches, saddles, bands, or stripes, which often help them merge with their surroundings (see pp.30–31). In some species, such as the Rainbow Boa, the surface structure of the cells reflects and refracts the light, creating a shifting, iridescent effect.

Some species change colour during their lifetime. Newborn Emerald Tree Boas, for example, are yellow or red but turn green after about a year. A few species can change shade within minutes

(usually becoming paler at night), although this ability is less well developed than in many lizards.

Specialized scales
Some snakes have evolved specialized scales, such as the thorn-like projections on the Horned Adder, *Bitis caudalis*, or the short, fleshy horns or tentacles on the snout of the aquatic Asian Tentacled Snake, *Erpeton tentaculatum*.

In a few species, the tail ends in a sharp, pointed tip that can be pressed into the flesh of a predator. By contrast, shield-tailed snakes have obliquely truncated tails covered with small spines at the ends. These burrowing snakes are thought to use their tails to plug their burrows and so protect themselves from pursuing predatory snakes.

Some species, such as rattlesnakes, have modified scales on the tail that stay in place when the snake sheds its skin, forming a chain that can be vibrated to produce a warning sound (see p.33).

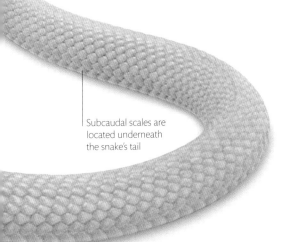

Subcaudal scales are located underneath the snake's tail

ANATOMY AND MOVEMENT

Despite its elongated shape, the anatomy of the snake has much in common with other vertebrates, including humans. It relies on the same systems to support life and shares many of the same organs, such as a heart, lungs, liver, and kidneys. The main differences lie in the shape and arrangement of these, determined by the snake's narrow body. A snake's skeleton looks complex, with hundreds of ribs, but is very simple in comparison with that of lizards and other reptiles.

Internal systems

Most of a snake's organs are contained inside its long ribcage, and together they make up the various systems for breathing, circulation, digestion, excretion, and reproduction.

Respiratory system Snakes inhale and exhale via their mouths and trachea. All snakes, except boas and pythons, lack a functional left lung. In every species, the right lung is greatly enlarged in order to compensate. The right lung is especially large in aquatic snakes, and the lower end is modified so that it is able to control the snake's buoyancy in water.

In some species, the lack of a left lung is also compensated for by a tracheal lung, which is an extension of the right lung. It provides extra capacity and may help the snake breathe while swallowing large prey. To prevent choking, snakes also have a muscular windpipe that they can push forward, forcing it under the prey so that they can continue breathing.

Circulatory system The snake's circulatory system is similar to that of most other animals (without the branches that extend into limbs, of course), except that the heart has only three chambers instead of four. It has only a single ventricle, which is partly divided, and the bloodstreams that pass through it do not mix.

Digestive system The digestive process begins in the snake's mouth, where oral glands secrete digestive juices while it is

THE SKELETON

Made up of a skull, spine, and ribs, the snake skeleton's most notable features are the strength and flexibility of the spine and the unusually large number of vertebrae – up to 400 in some species, although even small snakes may have 180.

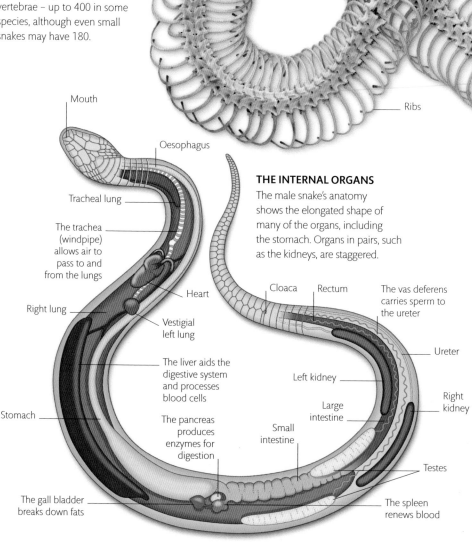

Neck vertebrae

Skull

Trunk vertebrae

Ribs

Mouth

Oesophagus

THE INTERNAL ORGANS

The male snake's anatomy shows the elongated shape of many of the organs, including the stomach. Organs in pairs, such as the kidneys, are staggered.

Tracheal lung

The trachea (windpipe) allows air to pass to and from the lungs

Heart

Right lung

Cloaca

Rectum

The vas deferens carries sperm to the ureter

Vestigial left lung

Ureter

The liver aids the digestive system and processes blood cells

Left kidney

Right kidney

Stomach

Large intestine

The pancreas produces enzymes for digestion

Small intestine

Testes

The gall bladder breaks down fats

The spleen renews blood

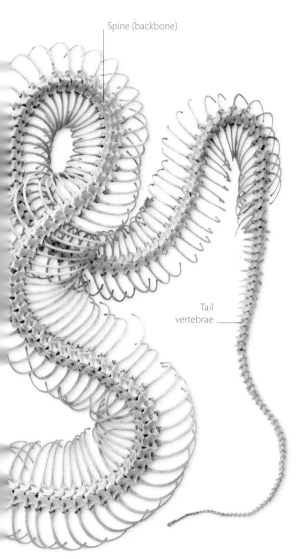

Spine (backbone)

Tail vertebrae

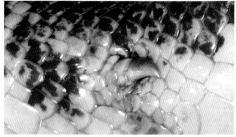

VESTIGIAL LIMBS
Members of the most primitive snake families have pelvic girdles, and, in some cases, vestigial hind limbs, retaining the link between snakes and their lizard ancestors.

organs, the hemipenes, although only one is used during mating. Sperm is carried from the testes to the hemipenes via the ureter. Females usually have staggered ovaries, but some species have no left ovary.

Nervous system This is made up of the brain and spinal cord, which extends along the entire backbone. The lack of limbs means that the nerve network is simplified, although snakes have additional nerves that serve the Jacobson's organ (see p.22), and, in some species, the heat-sensitive pits (see p. 23). The function of nerve endings below the pits and tubercles in the scales is unclear, but the pits may be sensitive to touch, heat, or light, or they may be used in some form of chemical communication.

Internal structure

Skeleton Since a snake has no limbs, its skeleton consists only of a skull (see pp.20–21), spine (backbone), ribs, and sometimes a vestigial pelvic girdle. The numerous vertebrae that make up the highly flexible spine are especially strong to cope with the strain imposed by the muscles. There is one pair of ribs attached to each of the neck and trunk vertebrae, but not to the tail vertebrae. The ribs are not joined along the snake's belly and are easily able to expand when the snake swallows large prey.

Muscles Animating the skeleton are many muscles attached to each vertebra and rib. It is the coordination of these muscles, coupled with the spine's flexibility, that gives a snake its characteristic weaving action.

feeding. In venomous species, these substances incapacitate the prey as well as aid digestion (see pp.24–25). The throat and oesophagus are muscular and help the snake push food into its stomach, which is merely a wide section of the gut. Due to the snake's narrow shape, the large and small intestines are less coiled, and so shorter overall, than in other creatures. Food that is undigested is expelled by snakes through the rectum and the cloaca.

Excretory system Snakes do not have a bladder. Waste filtered through the kidneys is excreted as uric acid, a white, crystalline material that contains very little water, enabling the snake to conserve moisture.

Reproductive system Like mammals and other reptiles, snakes use internal fertilization (see pp.36–37). Males have elongated testes and a pair of copulatory

LOCOMOTION

Snakes owe their efficient locomotion to their complex system of muscles. They use four principal types of motion, which they vary primarily according to the kind of terrain they have to traverse. Most marine snakes have a flattened, paddle-like tail to assist them in swimming.

LINEAR PROGRESSION
Waves of muscle contractions along the length of its body move the snake directly forward. The trailing edges of its large ventral scales provide grip.

LATERAL UNDULATION
This is the most common type of motion. The snake moves forward by pushing the sides of its body against rocks or other ground irregularities.

CONCERTINA MOVEMENT
In a tight space, the snake proceeds by bunching its muscles in turn, first at the rear as it extends its front, then at the front as it draws up the rear.

SIDEWINDING
On loose sand or a smooth surface, the snake lifts loops of its body clear as it moves sideways, creating downward pressure as it lifts to prevent sliding.

SKULL AND TEETH

Vital clues to understanding the relationships between snake families, genera, and species can be found in their skulls. As different species have evolved, their changing feeding habits have brought about changes to the shape and relative positions of the bones in the skull. The construction of the jaw and the arrangement of the teeth have been most affected. More advanced snakes, which swallow large prey whole, have jaws that expand, and even temporarily dislocate.

EATING LARGE PREY
Many snakes have jaws that are highly mobile, with some bones that can move away from each other. This allows a snake to eat prey that is considerably broader than its own head.

The skull

Unlike most carnivores, which can chew their prey, tear it apart, or hold it while they feed, snakes have no limbs and so have to swallow their food whole.

In the most primitive snakes, the jaws have only limited movement, if any. These species feed mainly on ants and termites, so a large gape is unnecessary. The more advanced snakes eat larger prey, so the capacity to open the jaws wide is essential. To do this, they have evolved skulls that are only loosely articulated. Bones that, in other animals, would normally be heavily built and solidly fused together are delicate and able to

move apart from each other when the jaws are stretched. The skulls in these species are constructed so that the upper and lower jawbones can move backwards, forwards, and outwards independently of each other or the rest of the skull. Further flexibility is provided by the lower jawbones, which are not joined at the chin but can stretch apart or be thrust forwards one side at a time. This allows the snake to hook its teeth into the prey and drag it into its gullet.

The teeth

Snakes have either hardly any teeth, or a large number, depending on their feeding habits. The teeth are arranged along the lower jaws, the outer set of upper jaws (the maxilla), and an inner set of upper jawbones (the palatine bones). Further back, the palatine bones are fused to the pterygoid bones, which also usually have teeth.

Instead of being rooted in a socket, the teeth of snakes are loosely attached to the surface of the jawbone on its inner edge. They are easily dislodged but are

THE EVOLVING SKULL

The evolution of flexible jaws resulted in changes to other parts of the skull. Some bones became smaller, while others grew larger or longer. The skulls of five different families of snake, from the earliest to the most recently evolved, show how the shapes of different bones have changed.

The most notable changes are to the jawbones. A small maxilla in primitive thread snakes becomes elongated in pythons and colubrids, then shortens again in cobras and vipers. The compound bone lengthens, while the tooth-bearing lower jawbone (the dentary) becomes shorter.

RIGID SKULL
The skulls of primitive snakes such as thread snakes are rigid and heavy, and the jawbones are very short.

FIXED FRONT FANGS
Mambas and other cobras have short, hollow, fixed front fangs with no teeth immediately behind them.

ELONGATED JAWS
Pythons have elongated jaws. The upper jawbones can spread apart, although the lower jaw is still relatively rigid.

HINGED FRONT FANGS
The fangs are very long and, by rotating the maxilla to which they are attached, the snake can fold them away until needed.

LIGHTWEIGHT SKULL
The skull and lower jaw of colubrids are reduced in size but are highly mobile. Some species have large fangs below the eyes.

KEY TO EVOLVING BONES

MAXILLA
DENTARY BONE
COMPOUND BONE
QUADRATE BONE
STAPES

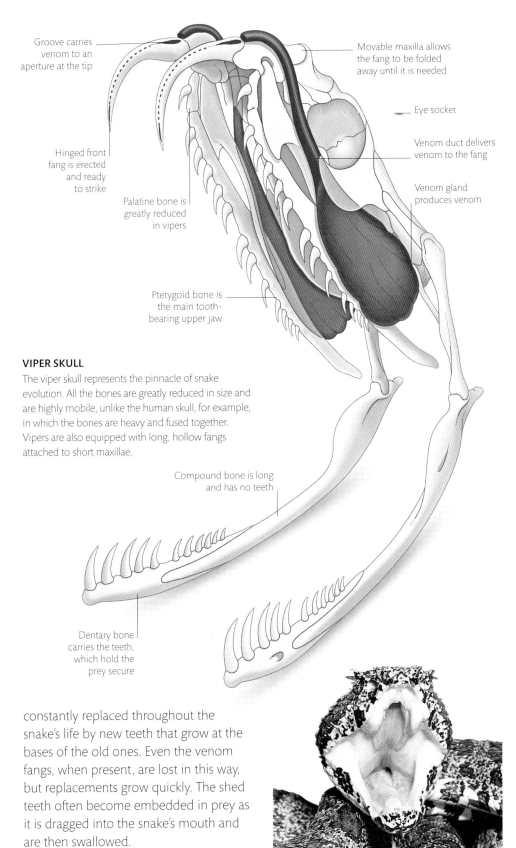

Groove carries venom to an aperture at the tip

Movable maxilla allows the fang to be folded away until it is needed

Eye socket

Hinged front fang is erected and ready to strike

Venom duct delivers venom to the fang

Venom gland produces venom

Palatine bone is greatly reduced in vipers

Pterygoid bone is the main tooth-bearing upper jaw

VIPER SKULL

The viper skull represents the pinnacle of snake evolution. All the bones are greatly reduced in size and are highly mobile, unlike the human skull, for example, in which the bones are heavy and fused together. Vipers are also equipped with long, hollow fangs attached to short maxillae.

Compound bone is long and has no teeth

Dentary bone carries the teeth, which hold the prey secure

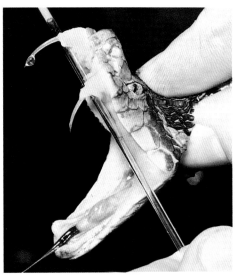

FLEXIBLE SKULL

The extent to which the whole skull can flex in the more advanced families of snakes is shown here. The fleshy sheath that normally covers the fangs has been pushed back and a drop of venom can be seen at the tip of one of the fangs. The snake's tongue and windpipe are on the floor of its mouth.

constantly replaced throughout the snake's life by new teeth that grow at the bases of the old ones. Even the venom fangs, when present, are lost in this way, but replacements grow quickly. The shed teeth often become embedded in prey as it is dragged into the snake's mouth and are then swallowed.

Fangs

Some snakes have teeth of several different types, notably enlarged fangs for injecting venom. These snakes are divided into two groups, opistoglyphous, or

FANGS AT REST

Vipers inject venom deep into prey with their long fangs to kill it before it has had time to stagger far. The fangs are attached to short bones, the maxillae, which can rotate through an angle of about 90 degrees so that they can be folded away when not in use.

rear-fanged, snakes, and proteroglyphous, or front-fanged, snakes. Within these categories, there are many variations (see pp.28–29).

Rear-fanged snakes These comprise about one-third of species in the colubrid family. They may have a single pair of fangs towards the backs of their mouths, or there may be two on each side. In some snakes, the enlarged fangs are grooved to facilitate the delivery of the venom to their tips. In a few species, the rear fangs are relatively close to the front of the snake's jaws, so they are capable of injecting venom even with a single bite. Only a few rear-fanged snakes are harmful to humans.

Front-fanged snakes Snakes with front fangs belong to the burrowing asps, cobra, and viper families. Cobra and viper fangs are hollow so that the venom can flow along their lengths, exiting near their tips, and penetrating deep into prey. An important difference between the cobra and viper families is the ability of vipers to fold their fangs against the roof of the mouth when not in use (see "Viper skull", above left).

SENSE ORGANS

Because the evolutionary history of snakes includes a long period when they lived underground, their sense organs have evolved in different ways to most other animals. Most importantly, many species of snake have poor eyesight, and many, especially the burrowing species, are almost blind. To compensate, some of their other senses are very highly developed, and some species have evolved systems for exploring their surroundings that are not found in other animals.

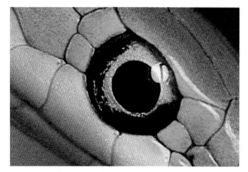

ROUND PUPIL (ROUGH GREEN SNAKE)

VERTICAL PUPIL (COMMON BOA)

HORIZONTAL PUPIL (LONG-NOSED TREE SNAKE)

PUPIL SHAPES
The shape of a snake's pupil indicates the probable period of its hunting activity. Generally, snakes with round pupils hunt by day, and snakes with vertical pupils hunt by night. Horizontal pupils occur only in some species of tree and twig snake. These snakes have good binocular vision and are able to judge distances between branches accurately.

Seeing
Many burrowing snakes have eyes that have degenerated to the point where they are only able to distinguish light from dark. This is true for almost all the species in the most primitive families – leptotyphlopids, anomalepids, and typhlopids – as well as burrowing snakes in other families.

The eyes of the remaining species have one of three pupil shapes: round, vertical, or horizontal. Most species of snake have round pupils. Snakes with small, round pupils tend to be secretive and are nocturnal hunters. Snakes with large, round pupils are usually diurnal (day) hunters and have good eyesight, although they find it difficult to see stationary objects clearly. To give them a better view when they are hunting, they may raise their heads and necks off the ground. All the water snakes, garter snakes, whipsnakes, and racers of North America, Europe, and Asia have eyes with large, round pupils.

Vertical pupils are typical of nocturnal species, such as vipers and tropical colubrids. These species have adapted to poor light conditions. In bright light, their pupils contract to slits to protect their retinas.

Horizontal pupils occur in only a few species: the eight Asian tree snakes in the genus *Ahaetulla* and the four African species of twig snake, *Thelotornis*. Because of the shape of the pupils and the size and position of the eyes, these snakes have good binocular vision – something that is not possible for snakes with eyes situated on the sides of the head. Binocular vision allows snakes to judge distances very accurately. This is important for species that use their bodies to bridge gaps between branches or need to reach out to pluck their prey from leaves and twigs.

Smelling
Like other vertebrates, snakes have nostrils that are connected to the olfactory parts of the brain. They also have an extra organ called the Jacobson's organ, consisting of a pair of depressions, or sacs, in the roof of the snake's mouth into which it inserts the tips of its forked tongue. The snake extends and flickers its tongue briefly, searching for scent molecules in the atmosphere. It brings its tongue back inside its mouth, to the Jacobson's organ, where the molecules are analysed and the information passed to the brain. This is why a snake will flicker its tongue repeatedly when disturbed or exploring new surroundings.

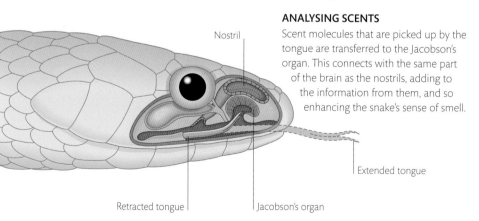

ANALYSING SCENTS
Scent molecules that are picked up by the tongue are transferred to the Jacobson's organ. This connects with the same part of the brain as the nostrils, adding to the information from them, and so enhancing the snake's sense of smell.

Nostril

Extended tongue

Retracted tongue

Jacobson's organ

Hearing

Although snakes have no external ears, vestiges of the internal structure of the ear are still present in the form of a small bone, the stapes, which transmits vibrations to the inner ear. To detect these, the lower jaw must be in contact with the ground. The vibrations are then transmitted via the jawbones, the stapes, and the quadrate bone to the inner ear. In addition to the footsteps of enemies and the scurryings of potential meals, snakes can almost certainly pick up low-frequency airborne sounds.

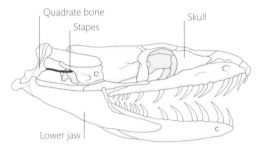

THE HEARING SYSTEM
A system of small bones in the skull allows the snake to "hear" vibrations that are picked up by the lower jawbone. This articulates with the stapes, which transmits the vibrations to the quadrate bone.

Sensing heat

Certain snakes have unique sense organs called heat pits. These are found in the members of three families: the boas, pythons, and pit vipers. Where present, boas have rows of pits between the scales that border the jaws, while those of pythons are within the scales. Pit vipers have a pair of pits between their eyes and nostrils – some of them are called *cuatro natrices* (four nostrils) in parts of Latin America for this reason.

In all species, the heat pits are lined with a layer of cells that contain many thermoreceptors, each of which is linked to the brain. Using these cells, snakes can detect minute rises in temperature, such as those radiated by the small, warm-blooded creatures that are their prey. (Even lizards, despite being cold-blooded, radiate some heat, because basking in the warm sun raises their body temperature above that of their

PIT VIPER HEAT PITS
The Red Diamond Rattlesnake, *Crotalus ruber*, like all pit vipers, has a pair of heat pits situated just below the level of its eyes. They act in stereo to pinpoint the direction and range of their target.

surroundings.) The heat pits allow snakes to detect changes in temperature as small as 0.2°C (0.4°F).

The heat pits are directed forwards, and by analysing the heat messages received on either side of its head, the snake can work out its prey's position and range. This means it can strike out accurately, even in total darkness. In experiments, a blind rattlesnake scored a direct hit on its prey 98 per cent of the time, but when its pits were covered, its success rate dropped to 27 per cent.

Other senses

Many snakes have small tubercles or pits in their scales, just visible to the naked eye. Tubercles are the most common and seem to be present in every species, even though they are sparse and localized in some. Although their exact function is not clear, it seems most likely that they have some sensory purpose because there is always a concentration of nerve endings in the region immediately below them. They may, for instance, be associated with touch, since they tend to be more numerous on parts of the body that come into contact with the substrate when the snake moves around.

Not all species of snake have pits. When present, the pits are most numerous on the snake's head, but they are also found in pairs at the tip of each dorsal (back) scale. The pits may possibly be light-sensitive, letting the snake know if any part of its body is still exposed when it shelters under a rock or enters a burrow.

Alternatively, the pits may play a role in chemical communication. Little is known about this form of communication in snakes, but it is likely that individual snakes can sense the presence of other members of the same species (and perhaps other species) by scent. This would help them to find mates, for instance, or to follow trails to mass hibernation sites.

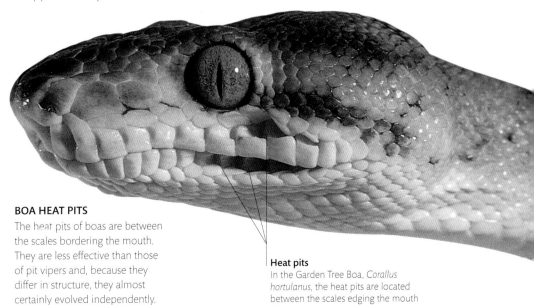

BOA HEAT PITS
The heat pits of boas are between the scales bordering the mouth. They are less effective than those of pit vipers and, because they differ in structure, they almost certainly evolved independently.

Heat pits
In the Garden Tree Boa, *Corallus hortulanus*, the heat pits are located between the scales edging the mouth

HUNTING AND FEEDING

All snakes are carnivores, but different species eat a huge variety of prey, from ants to antelopes and almost anything in between, as long as it is alive or has only recently died. Despite their lack of limbs, snakes are impressive hunters, whether they hunt by stealth, scent, or speed. All must swallow their prey whole, eating small or helpless creatures alive, and killing larger prey first by constriction or by venom.

EATING LIVE PREY
Snakes, such as the Grass Snake, that eat frogs, toads, and fish, all of which are defenceless, have few problems in overpowering their prey. They do not need to kill it first and can swallow it alive, although they may turn it around in their mouths so that it goes down headfirst.

Types of prey

Some snakes are specialists, feeding only on one group of animals, such as slugs or snails, or even on just a single species. Others are generalists and eat more or less anything they can swallow – a kingsnake, for instance, may eat frogs and toads, lizards, small birds, mammals, and other snakes.

Freshwater fish are eaten by many aquatic and semi-aquatic snakes, including a few vipers, such as the Cottonmouth, whose Latin name, *Agkistrodon piscivorus*, means "fish-eater". Three species of sea snake feed only on fish eggs along coral reefs. As a result, they have effectively lost their venom apparatus through evolution.

Many species eat frogs, toads, and salamanders. Hog-nosed snakes, for example, use their plough-shaped snouts to root out toads that have burrowed down into the soil to escape summer drought. Other species hunt frogs at night when they are feeding or calling for mates. A Central American snake, *Leptodeira septentrionalis*, eats frogs' eggs that have been stuck to leaves. Ironically, the frogs place them there to keep them safe from predatory fish.

Passive hunters

Some snakes do not actively look for food but wait for it to come to them. These snakes are found in several families, especially among the vipers and some of the larger boas and pythons. Sit-and-wait predators typically have thick-set, heavy bodies that anchor them firmly when they strike. They are well camouflaged so that prey may come close without detecting them. Certain species sense the presence of prey with their heat-sensitive facial pits (see p.23), and they can strike accurately, even on dark nights. Despite this, many snakes have to wait for long periods of time, often returning to the same spot on several successive nights, before they successfully ambush a meal.

Snakes increase their chances of a kill by waiting in a spot where prey, often small mammals, is likely to pass by. They can probably identify these places by scent. Others use the tip of the tail to lure prey close. Often, the tip is coloured differently from the rest of the snake so that it resembles a worm or a caterpillar. Typically, the snake lies with its body partially hidden in sand or among vegetation and curls its tail around so that the lure is close to the snake's head. If a likely target appears, the snake wriggles its tail enticingly. When the prey moves closer to investigate, the snake strikes.

FEEDING ON SNAKES
Most snakes will tackle and eat other reptiles, including snakes, which are an easy shape to swallow. Some species specialize in eating lizards and snakes, while others, such as the Common Kingsnake, eat them only as part of a varied diet, which may also include frogs, birds, and mammals.

Active hunters

Other snakes go looking for their food. Nocturnal species may search rock crevices or among vegetation for sleeping lizards. Some species investigate rodent burrows, tree holes, and other refuges. Snail- and slug-eating snakes track their victims by following their distinctive slime trails, and many others also hunt by scent.

Snakes with large eyes tend to hunt by day, using their vision to detect prey. They are often long and slender in shape, and many raise their heads off the ground to survey their surroundings. If they see or sense a potential victim, they usually approach stealthily at first, then make a short, fast dash. These snakes are often known as whip-snakes or racers in their countries of origin, even though they may not belong to these genera.

FEEDING ON LARGE PREY
A Thompson's Gazelle makes a large meal for an African Rock Python, *Python sebae*, and may last for several weeks, or even months. Prey as large as this may be too much to handle, and pythons sometimes have to release a prospective meal.

KILLING BY CONSTRICTION
Constrictors such as the African Python loop their bodies around the prey and tighten their coils as it breathes out. The prey dies from restricted blood flow and asphyxiation rather than being crushed. The coils may also hasten the process by restricting blood flow to parts of the body.

Constrictors

Although small prey, such as frogs, may be picked up and swallowed alive, larger prey may put up more of a struggle or fight back, so must be despatched before being eaten. Some snakes kill using venom (see pp.28–29), while others use constriction.

Constrictors are found in several families but are most often associated with boas, pythons, and several groups of colubrids, notably ratsnakes and their relatives. A constrictor kills its prey by coiling its body around the victim, then squeezing until it prevents it from breathing and cutting off its blood circulation at the same time.

SWALLOWING CONSTRICTED PREY
Like all constrictors, the Common Boa does not begin to swallow until it is sure its prey is dead. Once struggling has ceased, the snake slackens its coils and begins to search for the head. It starts to loosen its hold so that it can swallow the prey more easily. As it swallows it pulls the body from its coils, which are now relatively loose.

EATING EGGS

A number of snakes eat soft-shelled eggs, such as those laid by lizards or other snakes, and a few also eat birds' eggs as part of a varied diet. The African egg-eating snakes, however, feed exclusively on birds' eggs and have evolved unique characteristics to deal with their hard shells.

These snakes, of which there are 12 species, lack functional teeth but have tooth-like spines in their throats, on the underside of the neck vertebrae. They use these to saw through the top of the egg-shell. This allows the snake to swallow the contents of the egg without the shell, which would otherwise take up valuable space in its stomach.

ENGULFING THE EGG
The egg-eater opens its jaws widely and pushes slightly downwards as it begins to engulf an egg at least twice the diameter of its head and body.

CRACKING THE SHELL
In the snake's throat the egg is forced against the bony spines that project downwards. These move back and forth to saw through the top of the egg.

SWALLOWING THE CONTENTS
As soon as the shell begins to collapse, the snake's throat muscles work in waves to squeeze out the contents, which run down into its stomach.

DISPOSING OF THE REMAINS
Once the shell is empty the snake forces it back into its mouth and regurgitates it in the form of a boat-shaped pellet, held together by sticky membrane.

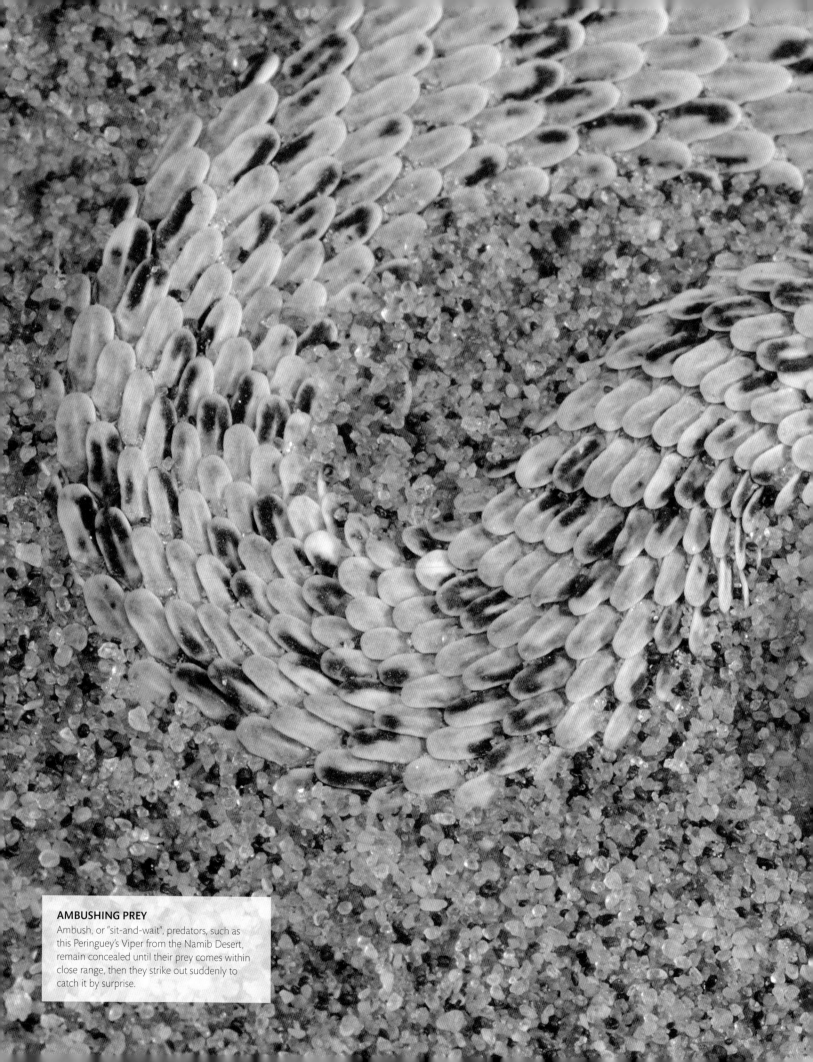

AMBUSHING PREY
Ambush, or "sit-and-wait", predators, such as this Peringuey's Viper from the Namib Desert, remain concealed until their prey comes within close range, then they strike out suddenly to catch it by surprise.

VENOMOUS SNAKES

Although venomous snakes are notorious, they make up only a small minority. About 250 species are considered to be dangerous to humans – less than one-tenth of all species – and only about 50 are potentially lethal. Venomous snakes occur in several families. All elapids (cobras and their relatives) and vipers are venomous. In addition, a significant number of species in the Colubridae and the Lamprophiidae have modified salivary glands that produce a type of venom.

Producing venom

Snakes' ability to produce venom evolved primarily as a means of subduing prey, although they also use it as a defence. Venom is formed from modified saliva, a mixture of proteins and enzymes that originally served to aid digestion of the prey. The stronger these digestive juices, the more powerful the venom, so the distinction between venomous and non-venomous snakes is blurred. Generally, snakes classified as venomous are those with specialized teeth that deliver venom deep into the body of their prey, although there are some species without modified teeth that also produce venom.

FAST-ACTING VENOM
The world's longest venomous snake, the King Cobra, produces a particularly potent venom and feeds almost exclusively on other snakes (its Latin name, *Ophiophagus hannah*, means "snake-eater"). By the time the meal reaches its stomach, the venom will already have started the digestive process.

Toxicity

The potency of venom varies from species to species, the most potent being produced by those that feed on fast-moving prey. The venom of some marine elapids, for example, is among the most toxic in the world, since they eat reef fish, which would elude them if the venom did not act rapidly. Certain snakes have specialized venom, adapted to a particular prey – it will affect a lizard, for example, but not a similar-sized bird.

Among land snakes, the Australian Inland Taipan, *Oxyuranus microlepidotus*, the Black Mamba, *Dendroaspis polylepis*,

PREPARING TO STRIKE
A viper erects its long front fangs as soon as its mouth is open, ready to strike at enemies or prey and deliver its venom deep into its victim.

PREYING ON LIZARDS

Although there are plenty of exceptions, lizards are often the preferred prey of rear-fanged snakes, which hold on to them while their venom takes effect. Lizards can be worked into the back of the mouth easily and are unlikely to do much damage to the snake in the struggle to escape.

and the King Cobra, *Ophiophagus hannah*, are considered to be the most venomous, although they kill only a handful of people each year, since they are rare and are not very aggressive unless cornered. In contrast, saw-scaled, or carpet, vipers have less toxic venom, but account for several thousand human deaths a year.

Not all venom has the same effect. Cobra venom typically acts on the nervous system (neurotoxic venom), and that of vipers on the blood cells (haemotoxic venom). Neurotoxic venom acts fastest, paralysing the victim. Haemotoxic venom acts more slowly, causing death by haemorrhaging or blood clotting. Sea snakes and a few Australian land elapids have myotoxic venom, which affects muscles.

A single species may have more than one type of venom – some populations of the Mojave Rattlesnake, *Crotalus scutulatus*, have a largely neurotoxic type, for example, while in others it is mainly haemotoxic.

Striking at prey

The way venomous snakes strike their prey varies from species to species. Members of the viper family usually draw back the front part of the body into an S-shaped loop, then straighten out suddenly to strike. At the same time, they open their jaws wide and swing their fangs down so that they point forwards. Snakes in the cobra family make short, fast strikes, while some snakes strike sideways (see "Side strike", right).

Injecting venom

Most venomous snakes are equipped with enlarged fangs, which may be hollow or grooved, for delivering venom into their prey quickly and effectively. The fangs may be situated at the rear or at the front of the snake's mouth (see p.21).

Snakes with rear fangs need to have a good grip on their victims in order to inject their venom. They work the prey into the back of the mouth, then bite down on it to produce a deep wound into which the venom runs. If the prey struggles, the snake may bite repeatedly, as though chewing, until it is dead. Because of this method of killing prey, these snakes are not often a threat to humans. However, a few species, including twig snakes and the Boomslang, have been known to cause deaths. Rear-fanged colubrids produce venom in modified salivary glands, known as the Duvernoy's glands.

SIDE STRIKE

Some burrowing asps, *Atractaspis*, which are members of the Lamprophiidae, hunt their prey in narrow tunnels where there is insufficient space for a normal strike. These species have specialized front fangs that they can pivot to the side and expose without opening their mouths. The snake slides its head alongside its victim, then stabs it with a rapid sideways or backwards motion.

BURROWING ASP

Front-fanged snakes are highly adapted to their method of hunting. They may strike the prey then release it at once to avoid the risk of injury as it struggles. The prey succumbs quickly and cannot travel far, so the snake is able to track it by following the scent trail it leaves behind.

SWALLOWING DEAD PREY
The Adder kills its prey with its venom before eating it. Like most snakes, whether venomous or non-venomous, it swallows its victim headfirst, using its tongue to locate the head. The limbs of prey such as lizards fold backwards, allowing the body to slide easily down the snake's gullet.

ATTACKING WITH FRONT FANGS
Vipers have long, hinged front fangs, which they use to inject venom and to pull their prey into the mouth. The snake uses them alternately, like mobile hooks, working first on one side and then the other.

PASSIVE DEFENCE

Snakes are undoubtedly fearsome predators, but they are also regarded as a potential meal by numerous creatures. These range from birds of prey to carnivorous mammals, and even include some types of snake. All snakes prefer to avoid direct conflict and rely on passive strategies as a first line of defence, although some species actively defend themselves against predators (see pp.32–33). Passive defences include concealment, camouflage – helping the snake merge with its surroundings – and mimicry, in which a harmless snake looks like a venomous species, deterring potential predators.

Predators of snakes

Snakes, especially small ones, have many enemies. Several birds of prey, such as hawks, eagles, hornbills, storks, roadrunners, and secretary birds, feed on them extensively, while smaller birds, such as members of the crow family, are opportunist predators and will prey on snakes if they have the chance. Other predators include small mammals, for example, mongooses, raccoons, hedgehogs, skunks, and foxes. Large lizards, frogs, toads, insects, and even spiders also feed on snakes.

In many areas, however, snakes are often the most efficient hunters of other snakes. A long, thin body shape means that they are easy to swallow and fit neatly inside each other. Snakes are also able to follow one another into small spaces. Some snakes are well able to defend themselves actively against predators. Others rely entirely on a range of subtle defences.

Camouflage

The body shape of snakes is important in helping them to stay camouflaged. Snakes can easily change from being stretched out to coiling up tightly, and forming any shape in between, making it difficult for predators to build up an image. This allows many snakes to go undetected unless they move. Most snakes are coloured to match the rock, vegetation, or other substrate on which they live. Where a species occurs over a wide geographic range and the substrate varies, its coloration is also likely to vary. This often accounts for differences in colour between populations of the same species.

However, few species use colour alone to produce their camouflaged effect. A plain brown snake, for example, would not be well camouflaged on dead leaves. Nearly all snakes have dark or light markings, in the form of spots or blotches, that help to disguise their outlines. Some species are marked with a spectacular arrangement of geometrical shapes in different colours, which, while conspicuous on a plain background, make the snake disappear in its preferred habitat. Many camouflaged species have lines passing through their eyes to help to disguise a feature that can often give away their location to a predator.

Warning coloration

Some species use the very opposite strategy to that of camouflage: bold coloration helps protect them. These snakes are brightly coloured to warn predators that they are venomous, so avoiding confrontation and conserving venom. The most common colour scheme is red, black, and white (or yellow), usually arranged in rings. Snakes of this type are generally called coral snakes. All belong to the Elapidae, or cobra, family.

DISAPPEARING ACT
Lying still in the leaf litter of the forest floor in tropical Africa, the Gaboon Viper is almost invisible, especially in dappled light and shade.

MILKSNAKE

CORAL SNAKE

MIMICKING VENOMOUS SNAKES

With its bands of red, black, and white, this harmless Milksnake is strikingly similar in appearance to the unrelated, and highly venomous, coral snakes, providing it with a measure of protection against predators. Mimicry of this kind is also seen in other snakes. As their name suggests, Viper Boas, *Candoia aspera*, resemble vipers.

Some non-venomous species, the harmless "false" coral snakes, protect themselves with the same defensive coloration. These snakes include mountain kingsnakes and other members of the genus *Lampropeltis*.

Warning colours are not restricted to coral snakes and their mimics. A number of snakes from around the world have brightly coloured undersides, for instance, which they display when they are alarmed.

DIFFERING FORMS
In polymorphic species such as the Garden Tree Boa, two or more colours or patterns occur within the same population. Several distinct colour forms can even be present in a single litter, as here. This phenomenon is a means of defence, helping to confuse predators, which tend to recognize only one form.

Polymorphism

Snake species in which two or more distinct colours or patterns occur in the same population, irrespective of the substrate on which the snakes live, are known as polymorphic. This is another defence strategy based on the way predators build up search images of their prey. Since only one of the polymorphic forms will fit this image, the other is likely to be overlooked by predators, and thus improve its survival rate. When the most common form has been preyed on so heavily that it becomes the less common of the two, predators' attention switches to the other form.

Polymorphic species may occur in striped or blotched forms, as in the European Leopard Snake, or banded and striped forms, as in some populations of the California Kingsnake. Other species exhibit a bewildering variety of colour forms. The Garden Tree Boa, *Corallus enhydris*, for example, occurs in a variety of colours from mottled grey to orange.

CONCEALMENT

Snakes are expert at squeezing into tight spaces, such as cavities under rocks and logs, burrows made by themselves or other animals, rocky crevices, and, in areas inhabited by humans, holes in walls. Desert species, such as the Desert Horned Viper, often bury themselves in the sand to avoid detection by potential predators or prey, as well as to escape from the scorching heat of the midday sun. The snake wriggles and rocks its body downwards, shovelling sand upwards and over its back.

THE VIPER RETREATS INTO THE SAND

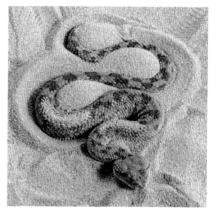

IT FLICKS SAND OVER ITS BACK

SOON, ONLY THE TOP OF ITS HEAD IS VISIBLE

ACTIVE DEFENCE

If passive defences such as concealment or camouflage fail to deter a predator, a snake must defend itself actively. Different species employ a variety of strategies, ranging from playing dead to drawing attention away from the snake's vulnerable head by feigning a counter-attack with the tail. Many snakes make a ferocious display to intimidate predators, inflating their bodies, hissing, or lunging in mock strikes. Some snakes have specialized defences. They include the rattlesnakes, which vibrate their tails to create an alarming buzz, and the spitting cobras of Africa and Asia, which can spray venom over a long distance.

FEIGNING DEATH
If intimidation fails to ward off a predator, the Hog-nosed Snake plays dead, rolling on to its back and writhing to imitate death throes. It then lies completely still with its tongue hanging out.

Balling and tail loss

A number of snakes, such as the Royal Python and some West Indian dwarf boas, react to danger by balling, or hiding their heads in their coils. Other snakes conceal the head but raise the tail above their coils, diverting the predator's attention and reducing the risk of life-threatening damage to the head. Species that do this have blunt tails, which may be marked to mimic their heads. For example, some Calabar Ground Pythons have imitation eye markings.

Some snakes are even able to discard part of the tail, as lizards do, to escape from their predators. The South American snakes *Pliocercus elapoides* and *Scaphiodontophis venustissimus* have fracture planes across the tail vertebrae to help them break easily.

HEAD OR TAIL?
Certain snakes, such as the Common Pipe Snake, *Cylindrophis ruffus*, protect themselves by concealing their heads, the most vulnerable part of the body. They also draw attention towards their blunt tails, which they move in a head-like manner, sometimes even using them to make false strikes.

Certain African snakes, such as *Psammophis* and *Natriciteres* species, spin their bodies rapidly if grasped, so the tail may break off even though it has no fracture planes.

Playing dead

A few species of snake feign death as part of their defensive repertoire. These include the Grass Snake, hog-nosed snakes, and the Ring-necked Spitting Cobra, or Rinkhals, *Hemachatus haemachatus*. The snake flips over on to its back with its mouth gaping open and its tongue lolling out. A foul-smelling secretion is often produced at the same time, which may contribute to the effect by suggesting decomposition. This is still a risky strategy, however, for, although many predators avoid prey that is already dead, some are not averse to eating carrion. For this reason, it is possible that snakes play dead only as a last resort.

Intimidation

Many snakes, including those that are actually harmless, try to intimidate attackers. Some inflate the body to make themselves look less like easy prey. This is often accompanied by hissing as the snake expels air forcibly through its windpipe. African twig snakes and Boomslangs puff up their throats, revealing bold markings or colours between their scales, while parrot snakes gape their jaws, displaying bright mouths quite unlike their camouflaged scales.

Defensive displays are sometimes followed by mock strikes in which the snake lunges but does not make contact. Only if this fails does it launch into a real attack. Even non-venomous snakes may

BALLING
The Royal Python, here emerging to check if danger is past, frequently uses the strategy of balling, protecting its head in the centre of its coils. For this reason, it is also called the Ball Python.

INTIMIDATION STRATEGIES
Snakes such as the Reticulated Python have a whole repertoire of intimidating behaviour, including hissing, inflating the body in order to look threatening, and opening the mouth wide as if about to strike.

WARNING RATTLE
Rather than waste venom in a strike, the Western Diamondback Rattlesnake first uses its rattle as a deterrent if threatened. It raises its tail and vibrates the tip rapidly, making a buzzing noise.

inflict a painful bite, since many have long, curved teeth that penetrate deeply. This is often enough to deter all but the most persistent predator.

Warning signals
Many snakes hiss when disturbed, but some make more unusual warning sounds, such as the rattling or buzzing produced by rattlesnakes. The rattle consists of segments of old scales that clatter together when the snake vibrates its tail. The segments are formed from the hardened remains (epidermis) of the scale at the tip of the tail. Like an hour-glass, this scale is constricted around the middle, so the epidermis is trapped loosely at the tip each time the snake sheds its skin, and another segment is added. Adult snakes may accumulate ten segments or more, but six or seven is more usual because the oldest part is brittle and periodically breaks off.

Desert vipers in Africa and the Middle East also use audible warnings. The Desert Horned Viper and the carpet vipers have serrated scales on their flanks that may be rubbed together like pieces of sandpaper to make a warning rasp. These snakes coil in a characteristic horse-shoe shape and move different parts of their bodies in opposite directions to create the sound.

the fangs have a sharp kink near the end. The opening at the front of the fang is so tiny that venom is forced through it under pressure and may land over 1 m (3 ft 3 in) away. To improve the trajectory, the snake raises its front half as it spits. When hunting, spitting cobras inject their venom by biting in the same way as other front-fanged snakes (see p.29).

SPRAYING VENOM
The venom from a spitting cobra is aimed at the eyes and other mucous membranes of any creature regarded as a potential threat. It causes instant pain but is not fatal to humans.

THREATENING POSTURE
One of a number of snakes that enlarge their bodies to deter attackers, the King Cobra, *Ophiophagus hannah*, rears its head and flattens its neck to form the characteristic hood. Some cobras have a large, eye-like marking, seen when the hood is spread, that also intimidates the aggressor.

Spitting
The spitting cobras of Africa and Asia can defend themselves by spraying venom. In these species, the venom canals in

REPRODUCTION

Most snakes lead a solitary lifestyle and may not come into contact with a suitable mate very often. To increase their chances of breeding successfully, snakes have the highly unusual capability of delaying fertilization after mating. Females can store sperm until conditions are favourable for the young to develop, giving the offspring a good chance of survival. While most species are egg-layers, some are live-bearers, with the young being incubated inside the mother's body.

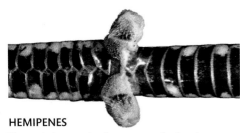

HEMIPENES
The male has a pair of sex organs, the hemipenes. Only one of these is used at each mating, but they may be alternated in subsequent matings.

Courtship

Although some species of snake mate several times with the same partner, in most cases the male departs immediately after mating to look for other females. The female may then also mate with other males and eventually produce offspring from several different fathers.

Snakes find their mates during the breeding season in a number of ways. Some species hibernate communally in a den that may contain several hundred snakes. These species tend to mate in early spring, almost as soon as they emerge from hibernation and before they disperse. In certain species, including mambas, most vipers, and the most northerly-occurring rattlesnakes, males fight for the privilege of mating with females. In male-to-male combat, two rivals rear up and entwine the front parts of their bodies, trying to push each other to the ground.

These movements are so graceful that early observers thought they were witnessing a courtship dance. Eventually, one snake, usually the larger, succeeds in driving away the other and can then mate with the female, who has usually remained coiled quietly nearby.

It is thought that tropical species, which do not hibernate in a group, may find each other by chance, probably using chemical clues, such as scent to track each other down.

Fertilization

Fertilization may take place shortly after mating, or the sperm may be stored in the female's oviduct. Certain species that, because of climatic conditions, have a very brief period of activity, will mate one year and produce young the next. The New Mexican Ridge-nosed Rattlesnake, *Crotalus willardi*, for example, mates in summer, but the eggs do not begin to develop until the next spring. These species therefore breed only every other year, or even less often. The aquatic and slow-moving file snakes, *Acrochordus* species, probably the slowest breeders, have ten years or more between

MATING BALL
Some northern populations of garter snake, notably those of the Red-sided Garter Snake, *Thamnophis sirtalis parietalis*, form huge mating balls, with numerous males all trying to mate with a smaller number of females.

ENTWINED MATES
When mating, snakes start by lying side by side, then the male crawls along the female's back, flicking his tongue over her and twitching as he goes. If receptive, she may also twitch before raising her tail so that they can mate. They often remain joined for several minutes or even hours.

litters. Species from regions with markedly distinct seasons, such as summer and winter, wet and dry, ensure that the young emerge at a favourable time, usually when food is in abundance, while many tropical species may breed almost continually through the year.

Egg-laying snakes

Most species lay eggs. The eggs are left to the mercy of the weather, developing best in a warm environment, so egg-laying species are usually found in tropical and subtropical locations.

Snakes lay their eggs in sites that are likely to provide stable conditions for their development, which can take up to three months. Some species burrow in sand or sandy soil, or make an egg chamber beneath a rock. Dead vegetation or rotting wood is favoured because it is easy to dig into, has good insulating properties, often generating its own heat, and retains moisture. The eggs need a moist place because the shells are soft and permeable and can absorb water and oxygen as the embryo develops.

BROODING EGGS
Once snakes have laid their eggs, they usually take no further interest in them, although pythons coil around their eggs throughout the incubation period to regulate their temperature, and cobras and a few other species stay nearby to guard their clutches.

Clutches vary in size, depending on the species and size of the mother. They range from one or two to up to 100 eggs in the case of the large pythons, including the Indian Python, *Python molurus*, African Rock Python, *Python sebae*, and Reticulated Python.

Live-bearing snakes

Live-bearers carry their developing young inside them. They do not nourish them via a placenta as mammals do, but retain the eggs in their oviducts rather than laying them. The young develop inside a thin membrane, instead of a shell, from which they break out around the time of birth.

By basking to raise its body temperature, the female can hasten the development of the unborn young, making successful breeding less dependent on the external temperature. It is no coincidence that vipers, many of which are live-bearers, thrive in mountain habitats or at extreme latitudes too cold for other snakes. Aquatic snakes, including most of the sea snakes, are live-bearers because they rarely come ashore. Similarly, many arboreal snakes bear live young, avoiding the need to descend to ground level, where many of them are defenceless.

The most prolific live-bearers include two vipers, the Puff Adder and the Fer-de-Lance, and three non-venomous snakes, the Common Garter Snake, the Mississippi Green Water Snake, *Nerodia cyclopion*, and the African Mole Snake, *Pseudaspis cana*. Each of these has been known to produce litters of over 100 young, the Puff Adder holding the record at 156.

BEARING LIVE YOUNG
In the majority of cases, live-bearing snakes give birth in a secluded place – a space underneath a rock, for example – usually during warm weather. Even though a birth occasionally takes place in the open, this has rarely been observed.

SINGLE-SEX SNAKE

Not all snakes need to mate in order to reproduce their species successfully. The Brahminy Blind Snake, a native of India and Southeast Asia but now found in many other warm countries, including South Africa and Australia, is the only parthenogenetic (female-only) species. As soon as each snake is mature, it begins to lay fertile eggs, without having mated. All of these eggs subsequently hatch into females that are clones of their mother. In general, parthenogenetic species tend to be very successful for a while but, in the long term, they lack the variability that would allow them to adapt to changing conditions.

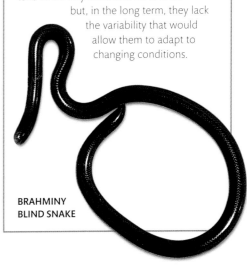

BRAHMINY BLIND SNAKE

BREAKING THE SHELL

TASTING THE AIR

STARTING TO EMERGE

LEAVING THE EGG

CONSERVATION

Snakes spend much of their lives hidden from view, so their increasing rarity may easily pass unnoticed. Yet unless conservation is made an urgent priority, hundreds of species are likely to become extinct in the near future. The most serious threat comes from humans and is mainly due to habitat destruction. Snakes are also killed out of fear, and many fall prey to traffic and the skin trade.

PRODUCTS OF THE SNAKE TRADE
Snakes have long been prized for their skins, used for the manufacture of boots, shoes, belts, handbags, wallets, and other goods. Over one million snakes are killed each year for the skin trade, especially pythons and other species from the Far East.

Threats to snakes

The natural habitats of snakes, like those of many other creatures, have been ravaged by the activities of man. The effects have been most devastating in the rainforests of Central and South America and Southeast Asia, where land clearance for agriculture involves logging and burning. The situation is made worse by erosion and climatic changes that arise from these and other human activities.

Many snake species in these areas have already been exterminated, often partly because they cannot escape from threatened habitats as easily as mammals and birds. In some cases, species have become extinct even before we knew they existed.

Some species are killed by introduced predators, including cats, dogs, mongooses, and rats, that have been released either deliberately or accidentally by man. Island species are especially vulnerable. On Round Island, in the Indian Ocean, for example, both members of the family Bolyeriidae are threatened by non-indigenous predators. Rats and cats have preyed on snakes, while goats have eroded their habitat. The Round Island Burrowing Boa has not been seen since

1975 and is probably extinct. The other species, *Casarea dussumieri*, has only been brought back from the brink of extinction by drastic conservation measures.

Other human activities have contributed to the decline of snakes. Industrial and commercial development often drives out their prey, depriving them of food. Snakes are killed on sight in many countries, whether venomous or not, and thousands

DEFORESTATION
Vast tracts of tropical forest have been cleared for the timber trade and for mining, agriculture, and cattle ranching. Irreplaceable trees have been felled, destroying the habitats of snakes and numerous other species.

die on the roads. Snakes are also deliberately exploited, principally for the skin trade. Smaller numbers are captured for the pet trade, zoos, and research. In parts of North America, rattlesnakes are even killed as a recreational activity, in "rattlesnake roundups".

Conservation measures

There is no doubt that snakes need immediate help if they are to survive. For many species, it is already too late, but the growing interest in saving and protecting endangered species is now filtering through to include snake conservation.

Research A vital priority is more funding for research to fill in the many gaps in our knowledge of snakes. Some snake species are known from only a handful of preserved specimens, making it difficult for conservationists to provide appropriate help.

Nature reserves The development of reserves dedicated to snakes is still a long way off, but snakes do gain some incidental protection where they share habitats with other endangered species. For this reason, national parks and nature reserves are of great value in helping to conserve species.

Captive breeding For some species, captive breeding programmes may be the only answer as conservationists, including enthusiastic amateurs, race against time to save them from extinction.

SAVING THE MILOS VIPER

The Milos Viper, also known as the Cyclades Blunt-nosed Viper, lives on four small Greek islands. On the largest of these islands, its existence was threatened by gypsum mining, and research was undertaken to monitor and assess its population. As a result, several measures have been proposed to protect it, including the establishment of protected areas, construction of barriers and underground tunnels to allow the viper to cross roads more safely, the eradication of feral cats, and stricter controls on the illegal collection of the snakes.

FITTING A RADIO TRANSMITTER FOR RESEARCH

A MILOS VIPER KILLED BY QUARRY TRAFFIC

For example, many American and European zoos have cooperated in breeding three threatened boa species of Madagascar, while colonies of several other endangered snake species are maintained and bred in zoos throughout the world. The aim of captive breeding should be to release snakes back into the wild, but if a species is rare due to habitat destruction, effective conservation measures need to be put in place first.

On Round Island, the goats and rabbits introduced by man, which were eating the vegetation, were eradicated in the 1970s and 1980s. This allowed trees and undergrowth to recover, benefiting the lizards that are the boas' main prey. As a result, the island is now better able to support snakes than at any time in the past 100 years.

Education The best conservation tool is education, and people in many countries are starting to appreciate the value of their wildlife. While snakes are not the main focus of attention, they do benefit from a more tolerant approach to wildlife, a move against the use of animal products in the fashion industry, and the growth of eco-tourism in places that previously attracted few visitors.

Legislation Many snake species around the world now enjoy some measure of legal protection: there are laws that restrict and regulate the collection, trade, and export of rare snakes (or products made from snakes), and, in a few cases, even protect native snake species from interference by man.

ANTIGUAN RACER
Numbers of the critically endangered Antiguan Racer, *Alsophis antiguae*, have risen from about 60 in 1995 to more than 300 in 2009, following the eradication of introduced rats and mongooses from a small island where it still existed. The species was also reintroduced to another island, providing an additional safeguard.

ORNATE GROUND SNAKE
The Ornate Ground Snake, *Erythrolamprus ornatus*, a Caribbean species that was previously declared extinct, has been rediscovered on a tiny islet off St Lucia. With an estimated population of just 18, it is the world's rarest snake. Its continued survival depends on the measures taken to preserve its fragile habitat.

CLASSIFICATION OF SNAKES

The science of establishing relationships between different organisms and arranging them in a way that reflects these relationships is called classification. Snakes belong to the class Reptilia, or reptiles. The reptiles are divided into four orders: the Testudines (turtles and tortoises), the Crocodylia (crocodiles and alligators), the Rhynchocephalia (tuataras), and the Squamata. The Squamata are divided into three suborders: the Serpentes (snakes), Sauria (lizards), and Amphisbaenia (amphisbaenians, or worm lizards).

WHITE-LIPPED TREE VIPER
The arrangement of the fangs and the numerous small head scales identify this species as a member of the Viperidae, or viper, family. Heat pits place it in the subfamily Crotalinae, or pit vipers. It is not always this easy to classify snakes on the basis of its external characteristics.

Families

Within the suborder Serpentes, the 27 families of snakes are arranged into six major groups, or superfamilies. Each of these contains a set of families that are thought to be closely related in an evolutionary sense. At present, these groupings are tentative and research is ongoing, and therefore it is difficult to arrive at a definitive family tree.

Five families of blind snakes form a natural group that is clearly separate from the other families. This is traditionally known as the Scolecophidia. The remaining superfamilies consist of the file snakes (Acrochordoidea); the pipe and shield-tailed snakes (Uropeltoidea); the pythons and their relatives (Pythonoidea); the boas (Booidea); and the colubrids and their relatives (Colubroidea), sometimes known as "typical" snakes.

Within each superfamily, snakes are grouped into families, then genera, and then species. In some cases, species are further divided into subspecies, although the definition of subspecies is not universally agreed.

Several questions remain unanswered at this time. Four families are not currently assigned to any of the superfamilies as their relationships are not fully understood. These are the South American pipe snakes (Aniliidae); Round Island boas (Bolyeriidae); dwarf boas (Tropidophiidae); and the spine-jawed snakes (Xenophidiidae). Some classification schemes do not recognize the Dipsadidae, Natricidae, or the Pseudoxenodontidae, preferring to treat them as subfamilies of the Colubridae. The family tree shown here treats them as separate families. Finally, the Calabar Ground Boa is sometimes placed in a family of its own, the Calabaridae, but here it is treated as a member of the Boidae.

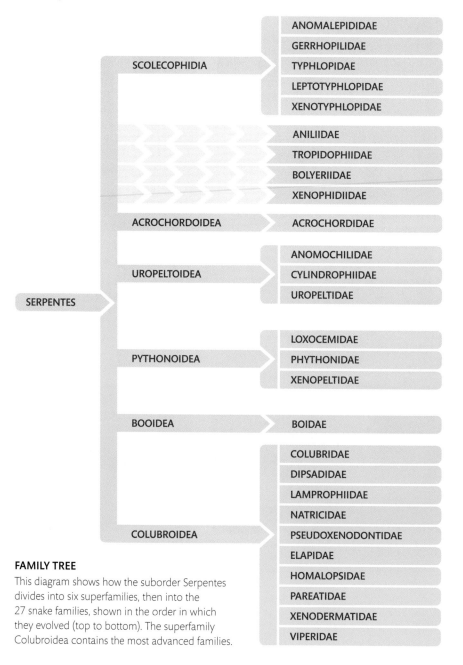

FAMILY TREE
This diagram shows how the suborder Serpentes divides into six superfamilies, then into the 27 snake families, shown in the order in which they evolved (top to bottom). The superfamily Colubroidea contains the most advanced families.

SERPENTES

SCOLECOPHIDIA
- ANOMALEPIDIDAE
- GERRHOPILIDAE
- TYPHLOPIDAE
- LEPTOTYPHLOPIDAE
- XENOTYPHLOPIDAE

- ANILIIDAE
- TROPIDOPHIIDAE
- BOLYERIIDAE
- XENOPHIDIIDAE

ACROCHORDOIDEA
- ACROCHORDIDAE

UROPELTOIDEA
- ANOMOCHILIDAE
- CYLINDROPHIIDAE
- UROPELTIDAE

PYTHONOIDEA
- LOXOCEMIDAE
- PHYTHONIDAE
- XENOPELTIDAE

BOOIDEA
- BOIDAE

COLUBROIDEA
- COLUBRIDAE
- DIPSADIDAE
- LAMPROPHIIDAE
- NATRICIDAE
- PSEUDOXENODONTIDAE
- ELAPIDAE
- HOMALOPSIDAE
- PAREATIDAE
- XENODERMATIDAE
- VIPERIDAE

SNAKE GALLERY

The Snake Gallery illustrates 61 species of snake, chosen to reflect the fantastic diversity of size, shape, colour, and markings found among these remarkable creatures. Some species have also been included for their fascinating behaviour. Together they represent all major regions of the world. The species have been arranged according to the most recent system of classification, with the primitive families at the beginning and the more recently evolved towards the end. Snakes in some families are either extremely rare or seldom seen and are not often photographed, so not all the snake families are represented. Each snake is introduced with a description of its most interesting features. Captions, annotations, and boxes explain important aspects of behaviour, physical characteristics, camouflage, and unusual methods of locomotion, providing fascinating and, in some cases, little-known facts.

GALLERY DETAILS

Each spread features one or two species of snake. This annotated example shows how the information on each spread is organized.

ICONS USED IN THIS BOOK

- Species
- Family
- Habitat
- Breeding
- Diet
- Distribution
- Size
- Reproduction
- Notes

Species name
This gives the common name of the species that is being described

Main characteristics
The most useful pointers in helping to identify the featured species are given here

Footprint
The footprint shows the relative size of the snake. It is equivalent to 25 cm (10 in)

Average adult length
The dark grey snake indicates the typical length reached by an adult of the species

Record length
Four of the six snake species that reach a noteworthy length are featured. The pale grey snake gives the largest recorded size

Additional pictures
These show particular features or behavioural practices that help identify the featured snake

Box
This covers a topic relevant to the featured snake – from conservation issues to other species with similar characteristics

Fact file
This gives key information about the species: its Latin name, family, natural habitat, breeding details, preferred food, and distribution

World map
The approximate geographic range of the species is shown in red

Dark colours
The brown background, seen here in its darkest phase, may become paler at night

HAITIAN DWARF BOA
A small head, supple body, and mottled coloration all help this little snake to avoid detection. Moderately large eyes enable the Haitian Dwarf Boa to see at night, when it is out hunting for food.

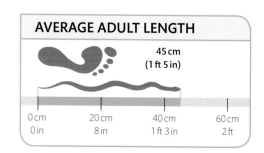

HIDING PLACES
Dwarf boas coil up in small spaces when they rest during the day. The rolled-up stems of palm fronds and the "vases" of air plants are favourite hiding places, but they may also crawl under logs, boards, or pieces of rubbish. When exposed, they tend to remain still at first and can easily be overlooked.

HAITIAN DWARF BOA

Previously considered to be members of the boa family, the dwarf boas now comprise a family in their own right. The Haitian Dwarf Boa feeds almost exclusively on lizards, which it stalks at night while they are asleep, and which it constricts. When disturbed, it may roll itself into a ball and produce a foul-smelling fluid from its cloaca.

Main characteristics

The Haitian Dwarf Boa is slender and has smooth scales, a small head with large scales covering the top, and an unusual coloration of dark green blotches on a brown background. No other snake has the same colour pattern, but in some cases dark individuals can be mistaken for other species. Unusually among snakes, it sometimes undergoes a colour change, during which its dark background turns yellow.

AVERAGE ADULT LENGTH

45 cm
(1 ft 5 in)

0 cm	20 cm	40 cm	60 cm
0 in	8 in	1 ft 3 in	2 ft

FACT FILE

- *Tropidophis haetianus*
- Tropidophiidae (dwarf boas)
- Woods
- Live-bearers, producing 5–10 young
- Lizards and small mammals
- Cuba, Hispaniola, and Jamaica

CUBAN DWARF BOA

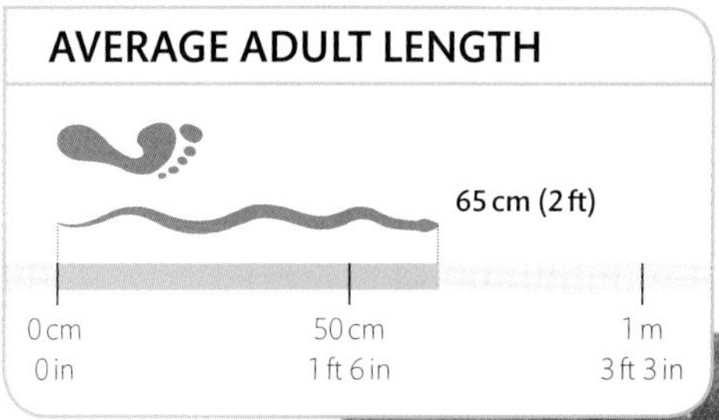

The most common species of dwarf boa, the Cuban Dwarf Boa is found in a wide variety of habitats, including rainforests, rocky hillsides, and plantations. It lives mostly on the ground, but also climbs into shrubs and up rocks in search of prey. Its diet includes tree frogs, lizards, small mammals, and, occasionally, birds. It never bites but releases a foul-smelling slime from its cloaca when threatened.

Main characteristics

The Cuban Dwarf Boa is the largest of the dwarf boas. It has a stocky body, small head, small eyes with vertical pupils, and a short tail. The tail tip may be black or yellow, contrasting with the rest of the body. Its scales are smooth with a satin-like sheen.

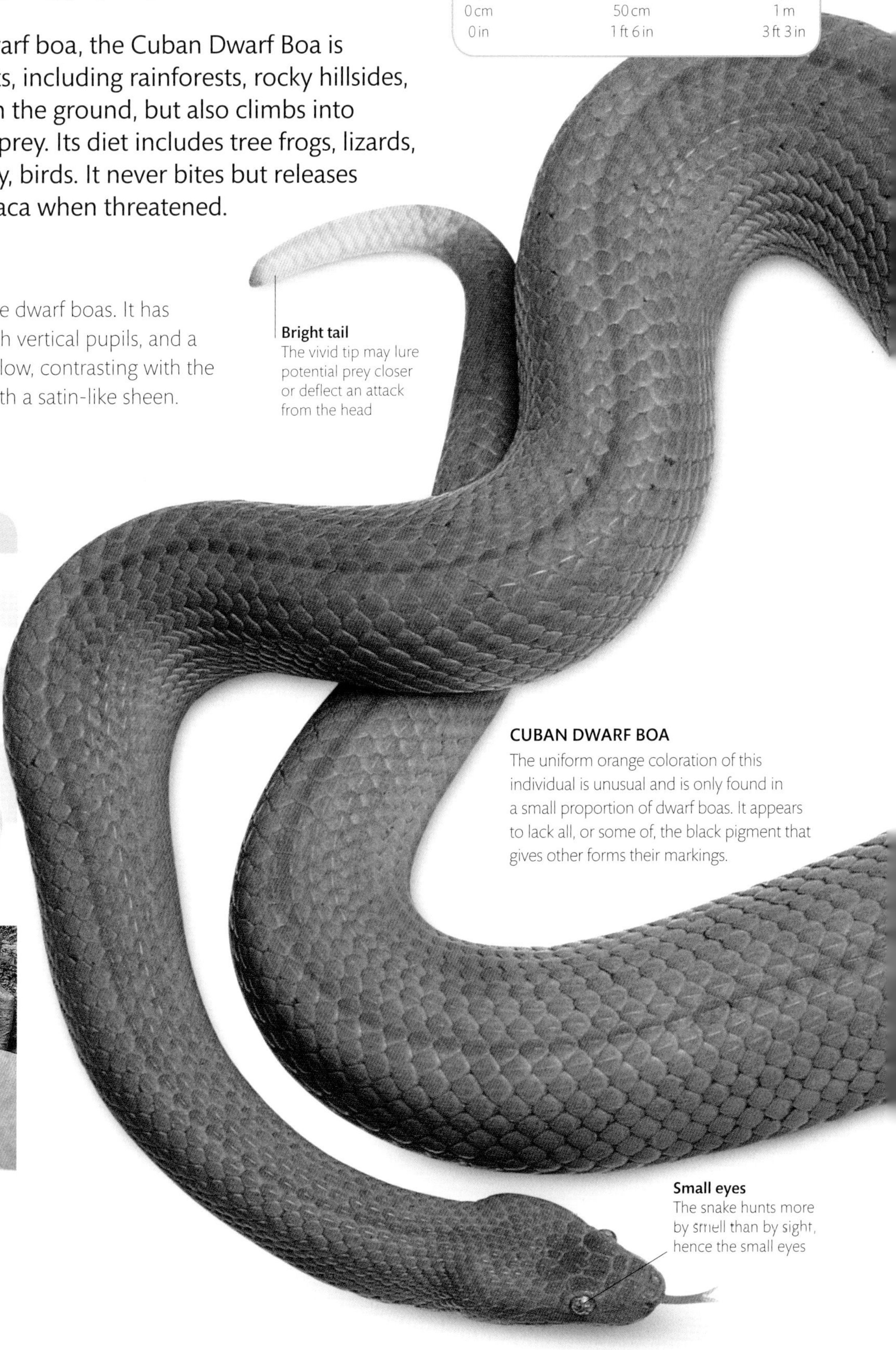

AVERAGE ADULT LENGTH

65 cm (2 ft)

0 cm	50 cm	1 m
0 in	1 ft 6 in	3 ft 3 in

FACT FILE

- *Tropidophis melanurus*
- Tropidophiidae (dwarf boas)
- Deciduous forests
- Live-bearers, producing about 8 young
- Frogs, reptiles, and small mammals
- Cuba

Bright tail
The vivid tip may lure potential prey closer or deflect an attack from the head

CUBAN DWARF BOA
The uniform orange coloration of this individual is unusual and is only found in a small proportion of dwarf boas. It appears to lack all, or some of, the black pigment that gives other forms their markings.

Small eyes
The snake hunts more by smell than by sight, hence the small eyes

COLOUR DIFFERENCES

This species is highly variable in colour. The most common form is tan, grey, or buff with irregular dark blotches along the back. This combination means that the snake is well camouflaged when it is resting among dead leaves or other forest debris.

NEOTROPICAL SUNBEAM SNAKE

The Neotropical Sunbeam Snake is something of a mystery. It is the sole member of its family, and it is not fully understood how its characteristics relate to those of other snakes. It shares some features with pythons, for instance, although pythons are not found in the Americas. Its burrowing habits and secretive lifestyle make it difficult to study. However, it has been observed eating iguana eggs.

FACT FILE

- *Loxocemus bicolor*
- Loxocemidae
- Tropical, moist, dry, and arid forests
- Egg-layers, producing small clutches of eggs
- Rodents, lizards, and lizard eggs
- Southern Mexico to Costa Rica

AVERAGE ADULT LENGTH

1 m (3 ft 3 in)

0 cm	50 cm	1 m	1.5 m
0 in	1 ft 6 in	3 ft 3 in	5 ft

Main characteristics

This species is stout with a very muscular body. Its small, shiny body scales are mostly dark grey, with white patches. The narrow head, spade-shaped snout, and small eyes are all adaptations to its burrowing lifestyle, helping it to tunnel through loose soil.

HEAD SCALES
Large scales cover the top of the head, unlike most other primitive snakes. Its shallow shape is an adaptation to a burrowing lifestyle.

Small eyes
The eyes are small, and the snake is thought to rely on its sense of smell when hunting

NEOTROPICAL SUNBEAM SNAKE
The adult *Loxocemus* has irregular patches of white scales on the body. These appear as the snake ages, and the pale neck collar typical of the hatchling snakes disappears.

COLOUR CHANGE
This unusual specimen lost all its grey pigment after shedding its skin, apart from a small patch on the head.

ASIAN SUNBEAM SNAKE

Although they are only distantly related, this species is the Asian counterpart of the Neotropical Sunbeam Snake (see opposite). It too comes from a very small family, which contains just one other similar species from China. Like the Neotropical Sunbeam Snake, the Asian Sunbeam Snake spends most of its life below the ground, feeding on rodents and other burrowing vertebrates, including other snakes.

Main characteristics
The most obvious distinguishing feature of the Asian Sunbeam Snake is its highly polished, iridescent scales; no other species of snake shines so brightly. It has a thickset, powerful body with a narrow head, which is scarcely distinct from its neck.

FACT FILE
- *Xenopeltis unicolor*
- Xenopeltidae (sunbeam snakes)
- Forest clearings, plantations, gardens, and parks
- Egg-layers, producing up to 10 eggs
- Almost anything, but especially frogs, reptiles, and small mammals
- Southern China, eastern and West Malaysia, Philippines, and Southeast Asia

AVERAGE ADULT LENGTH

1 m (3 ft 3 in)

| 0 cm | 50 cm | 1 m | 1.5 m |
| 0 in | 1 ft 6 in | 3 ft 3 in | 5 ft |

Iridescence
A layer of dark pigmentation just below the surface of each scale enhances the iridescence

Narrow neck
The narrow head blends almost imperceptibly into the slender neck

ASIAN SUNBEAM SNAKE
Shimmering scales give this snake its common name. It is also known occasionally as the Iridescent Earth Snake. Its Latin name, *Xenopeltis*, means "strange covering".

WEDGE-SHAPED HEAD
The shape of the head enables the snake to push through loose soil. The eyes are small.

Head scales
Large, iridescent scales completely cover the top of the head

CHILDREN'S PYTHON

Named in honour of JG Children, who was in charge of the zoological collection at the British Museum, London, in the first half of the nineteenth century, Children's Python lives in a variety of habitats, usually on the ground but sometimes climbing into trees. This species is active at night, hunting lizards, small birds, and mammals.

Main characteristics

The young Children's Python is heavily blotched, then becomes brown or reddish brown as it grows. Large scales on the top of the head contrast with small, smooth ones on the body. This characteristic is typical of the species and its close relatives; most pythons have small head scales. There are heat pits in some of the scales bordering the mouth.

EGG INCUBATION

Like all pythons, the female Children's Python broods her eggs by coiling herself around them throughout the incubation period, which lasts for nearly two months. This behaviour helps to hide and protect the eggs from the snake's predators. It also maintains constant temperature and humidity levels around the eggs.

FACT FILE

- *Antaresia childreni*
- Pythonidae (pythons)
- Woodlands, monsoon forests, and dry scrub, usually among rocks
- Egg-layers, producing up to 15 eggs
- Reptiles, birds, and small mammals
- Northern Australia

CHILDREN'S PYTHON

The Children's Python is among the smallest species of python, never exceeding 1 m (3 ft 3 in) in length. Despite its small size, it is a powerful constrictor. This snake is half-grown but will become less marked as it ages.

Prominent eyes
The eyes are prominent and have the vertical pupils of a nocturnal hunter

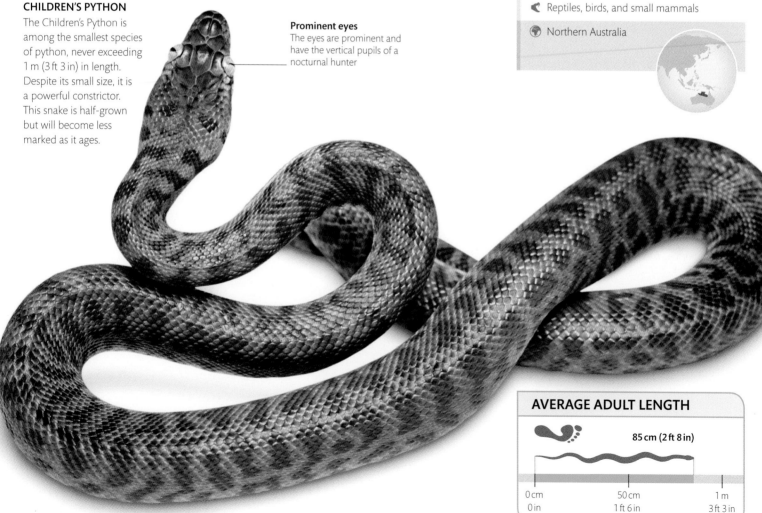

AVERAGE ADULT LENGTH

85 cm (2 ft 8 in)

0 cm	50 cm	1 m
0 in	1 ft 6 in	3 ft 3 in

SPOTTED PYTHON

This small python occurs in most types of habitat, but is especially fond of rocky hillsides and outcrops with crevices and caves. It is active at night, when it goes in search of prey. Insect-eating bats, which it catches at cave entrances, are a favourite food.

FACT FILE

- *Antaresia maculosa*
- Pythonidae (pythons)
- Moist and dry forests, grasslands, and rocky outcrops
- Egg-layers, producing up to 15 eggs
- Reptiles, birds, and small mammals, including bats
- Australia (eastern Queensland and extreme northeastern New South Wales)

Main characteristics

The Spotted Python has a slender, cylindrical body covered with smooth, iridescent scales. It keeps this irregularly blotched pattern throughout its life, but the size of the blotches and their contrast with the background colour can vary. In some individuals the spots join together in places to produce a ragged zigzag pattern along the back.

Large scales
There are large scales on top of the head and shallow heat pits in some of the scales bordering the mouth

KILLING PREY
A powerful constrictor, the Spotted Python wraps several coils of its body around the prey and squeezes, starting to swallow only when it is sure that the prey is dead. Even then, the snake does not release its quarry, but pulls the body through its coils as it swallows.

Irregular pattern
The characteristic blotches have ragged edges, like a rug or tapestry. This is because the dark pigmentation is restricted to complete scales

SPOTTED PYTHON
Formerly classified with Children's Python (see opposite), the Spotted Python was recognized as a separate species only in 1985. Distinguishing the two species can be difficult, especially in juveniles, although the more heavily spotted pattern, larger size, and darker overall coloration of the Spotted Python are usually good identification characteristics.

AVERAGE ADULT LENGTH

90 cm (3 ft)

0 cm	50 cm	1 m
0 in	1 ft 6 in	3 ft 3 in

RETICULATED PYTHON

Thought to be the world's longest snake, the Reticulated Python is an inhabitant of the steamy tropical rainforests of Asia. It leads a secretive life, well camouflaged among forest vegetation. Occasionally, it strays into villages and the outskirts of large towns, probably attracted by potential prey in the form of rats and domestic animals. It is one of only a handful of snakes that are known to have eaten humans, although cases are exceptionally rare.

Main characteristics

The Reticulated Python has a complex, geometric pattern, which incorporates a number of different colours. A series of irregular diamond shapes along the back is flanked with smaller markings, which often have light centres. Its size and unmarked head are usually enough to identify this species, even though there is some variation in pattern. Despite its wide distribution and the variation in size, colour, and markings, no subspecies has been described so far. This is partly due to the difficulties involved in capturing, preserving, and transporting a snake of this size.

Plain head
A conspicuous line running from each eye to the angle of the jaw, and another running from the snout to the nape of the neck, are the only markings on an otherwise plain head

FOREST CAMOUFLAGE
Despite its massive size, the Reticulated Python is surprisingly hard to spot, even in places where it is common. This is partly due to excellent camouflage and partly because it is not very active during the day, when it rests in thick vegetation, in a hollow tree, or lies partially buried in forest debris.

FACT FILE

- 〰 *Malayopython reticulatus*
- Pythonidae (pythons)
- Rainforest
- Egg-layers, producing around 60 eggs, occasionally up to 100
- Birds and mammals, including, on rare occasions, people
- Southeast Asia, Bangladesh, Borneo, and Indonesia

AVERAGE ADULT LENGTH

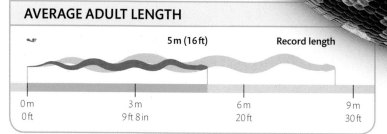

5 m (16 ft)   Record length

| 0 m | 3 m | 6 m | 9 m |
| 0 ft | 9 ft 8 in | 20 ft | 30 ft |

RETICULATED PYTHON
A reticulated, or net-like, pattern gives this snake its common and Latin names. A broad head and a huge gape enable it to swallow large prey and make it an efficient hunter. Long, curved teeth ensure that the snake rarely loses its grip on its victim, once caught.

Large body
A powerful constrictor, the adult snake's size allows it to easily overpower and kill animals as large as deer, pigs, and dogs

NIGHT VISION
The Reticulated Python has vertical pupils with bright orange irises. It is a nocturnal hunter, which relies heavily on ambush tactics to catch prey.

Smooth scales
This species has smooth scales. Most are of a single colour, so that the markings appear ragged at the edges

Geometric markings
There are irregular diamond shapes along the back

CARPET PYTHON

This slender, graceful python occurs in many colour forms throughout its wide geographic range in Australia and New Guinea. It occupies a number of different types of habitat and is usually nocturnal but, depending on the climate, it can also be diurnal. The Carpet Python is often found around human habitations, where it does a useful job eating rats and other vermin.

Triangular head
The distinctive shape of the head is characteristic of this species

Main characteristics

Most forms have intricate markings consisting of light and dark bands, or reticulations, on a background of grey, brown, or reddish brown. They all have triangular heads, which are distinct from the neck and covered with many small scales. There is a conspicuous row of heat pits in the scales bordering the mouth, and the eyes are moderately large with vertical pupils.

HUNTING METHODS

The Carpet Python uses its heat-sensitive pits to locate warm-blooded prey, such as rodents. Once it has pinpointed the prey's whereabouts, it strikes rapidly, throwing a number of coils around the creature and then tightening them until the victim stops breathing. The snake only begins to swallow its meal when the prey has been squeezed to death.

FACT FILE

- ⚮ *Morelia spilota*
- ⛓ Pythonidae (pythons)
- ⌂ Dry forests, rocky scrublands, along river courses, and rainforests
- ● Egg-layers, producing 10–50 eggs
- ◖ Reptiles, birds, and small mammals
- ⊕ New Guinea and most of Australia (but not in deserts)

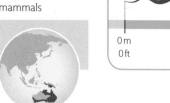

AVERAGE ADULT LENGTH

2 m (6 ft 6 in)

| 0 m | 1 m | 2 m | 3 m |
| 0 ft | 3 ft 3 in | 6 ft 6 in | 9 ft 8 in |

Exotic markings
Light and dark bands on
a pale background give the
effect of an Oriental carpet,
hence the common name

CENTRAL AUSTRALIAN CARPET PYTHON

The Central Australian Carpet Python, *Morelia bredli*,
is a close relative of the Carpet Python, although it is
slightly smaller. Also known as the Desert Carpet
Python, it was not considered to be a distinct species
until 1981. It differs mainly in having smaller (and
therefore more numerous) scales on the top of the
head. *Morelia bredli* occurs in the central Australian
deserts, where it lives among rocky outcrops or near
trees and shrubs. Its reddish brown coloration is a
perfect match with the red earth and rock of its
habitat. In most other respects, this species is similar
to the Carpet Python.

**ADULT ON CLIFF LEDGE, CAMOUFLAGED
AGAINST THE ROCK**

Strong body
Powerful body muscles prevent the
heart and lungs of the snake's prey
from functioning, thus causing rapid
unconsciousness and a quick death

Effective camouflage
The irregular pattern serves
to conceal the snake's
outline from predators

CARPET PYTHON
Carpet Pythons' markings are intricate
and often spectacular, but in their
natural habitat these markings make
them easy to overlook, whether they
are coiled among rocks or vegetation,
or in the branches of trees.

GREEN TREE PYTHON

A beautiful snake that conforms to the popular vision of a jungle serpent, the Green Tree Python is found only in the rainforests of New Guinea and extreme northern Queensland. It spends its entire life in the canopy, draped spectacularly over boughs during the day and hunting for its prey of arboreal mammals and roosting birds by night.

GREEN TREE PYTHON
This is the only python that is predominantly green in colour. It is also more slender than most other pythons. Both characteristics are adaptations to living in the forest canopy.

Main characteristics

The Green Tree Python is similar in appearance to the Emerald Tree Boa (see pp.66–67), which comes from South America. The adult snake is bright green and usually has a broken line of white markings along the midline of the back. Juveniles are bright sulphur yellow or, rarely, red; the young become green when they are about a year old. Other important distinguishing characteristics of the Green Tree Python are the small scales on the head and the heat pits situated in the scales bordering the mouth.

Strong muscles
The greater part of the snake's weight is supported by powerful muscles. The ability to stretch out unsupported helps this snake move efficiently from branch to branch

Head bulges
The bulges conceal powerful jaw muscles. A firm grip is important for an arboreal species because it would be unlikely to recover dropped animals

AVERAGE ADULT LENGTH

1.2 m (4 ft)

| 0 cm | 50 cm | 1 m | 1.5 m |
| 0 in | 1 ft 6 in | 3 ft 3 in | 5 ft |

SCALY HEAD
The head is covered with numerous small, granular scales. The nasal scales are large. Adults have uniform green heads with pale green, yellowish, or white lips. Occasional specimens have scattered blue scales on their heads.

Heat pits
These are situated in the scales, whereas those of the Emerald Tree Boa are situated between the scales

Large eyes
Vertical pupils and large eyes identify this snake as a nocturnal hunter. Adults have cream eyes, while those of juveniles are white with a dark line passing through their centres

FACT FILE

- *Morelia viridis*
- Pythonidae (pythons)
- Rainforests
- Egg-layers, producing up to 25 eggs
- Reptiles, birds, and small mammals
- New Guinea and surrounding islands, extreme northern Queensland, Australia

YELLOW YOUNG
Like all female pythons, the Green Tree Python coils around her eggs throughout the incubation period to protect them from predators and extremes of temperature. The young hatch after about two months and are usually brilliant yellow. This coloration is paralleled in the Emerald Tree Boa, but the reason for it is still unknown to zoologists.

BURMESE PYTHON

Commonly found near villages, and even cities, the Burmese Python performs a useful function by eating rats and other vermin. Unfortunately, it is not always welcome because it also takes chickens and other domestic animals. All pythons coil around their eggs, but the Burmese Python is able to raise its body temperature by a process known as shivering thermogenesis.

Main characteristics

Apart from its large size – commonly up to 3–4 m (9 ft 8 in–13 ft), and occasionally longer – the Burmese Python can be distinguished by its rich chestnut and tan coloration, smooth scales, large scales on the top of the head, and the presence of heat pits. Out of its habitat, it could be confused with the African Rock Python, which is similar in size and coloration but has a different pattern.

ALBINO FORM
Through a genetic anomaly, some Burmese Pythons lack the dark pigments that give them their rich coloration. These albinos are selectively bred in captivity to produce pure strains, called golden pythons.

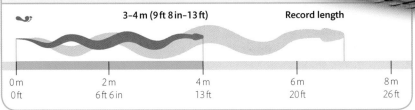

AVERAGE ADULT LENGTH

3–4 m (9 ft 8 in–13 ft)   Record length

0 m	2 m	4 m	6 m	8 m
0 ft	6 ft 6 in	13 ft	20 ft	26 ft

BURMESE PYTHON

This richly coloured form has a geographic range centred around Myanmar (Burma), as its name suggests. The large, interlocking blotches along the back are always present, even in paler forms. Its markings blend perfectly with the flecked light of its natural habitat.

FACT FILE

- *Python bivittatus*
- Pythonidae (pythons)
- Rainforests, plantations, and fields
- Egg-layers, producing up to 50 eggs
- Birds and mammals
- Northeastern India, Nepal, Bangladesh, Indonesia, Southeast Asia, introduced to Florida, USA

Desirable skin
Rich colours and smooth scales have resulted in the Burmese Python being widely hunted for the skin trade. Exterminated in several regions, it is now rare in many of the places where it was formerly common

Prominent heat pits
Heat pits help the snake to pinpoint its prey, even in total darkness

HEAD MARKINGS

Dark arrowhead markings help to identify this species. A wedge-shaped mark runs from each eye to the angle of the jaw, with another immediately below each eye.

BLOOD PYTHON

A stocky snake, the Blood Python is at home in the soggy jungles of Southeast Asia. It leads a sedentary lifestyle, hiding among the leaf-litter and forest debris and waiting for its next meal to come within range. Its great bulk provides a firm anchor from which it can launch a sudden strike, taking its victim completely by surprise.

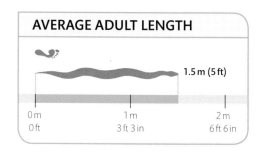

AVERAGE ADULT LENGTH

1.5 m (5 ft)

| 0 m | 1 m | 2 m |
| 0 ft | 3 ft 3 in | 6 ft 6 in |

Main characteristics

The Blood Python is the most thickset of the pythons, and it is quite easy to identify by its proportions alone. The head is light on top and dark at the sides, while the eyes are small. The scales are smooth and shiny, and the body is invariably marked with large, dark blotches on a lighter background. The colours of the different forms can be highly variable.

Swivelling eyes
Unusually, the eyes swivel, enabling this snake to observe prey or predators without turning its head. The eyes are small and brightly coloured, with orange irises and vertical pupils

EMERGING FROM THE EGG
The young python uses an egg tooth, a small, horny appendage on the tip of the snout, to make one or two slashes in the shell, through which it emerges. The egg tooth soon falls off.

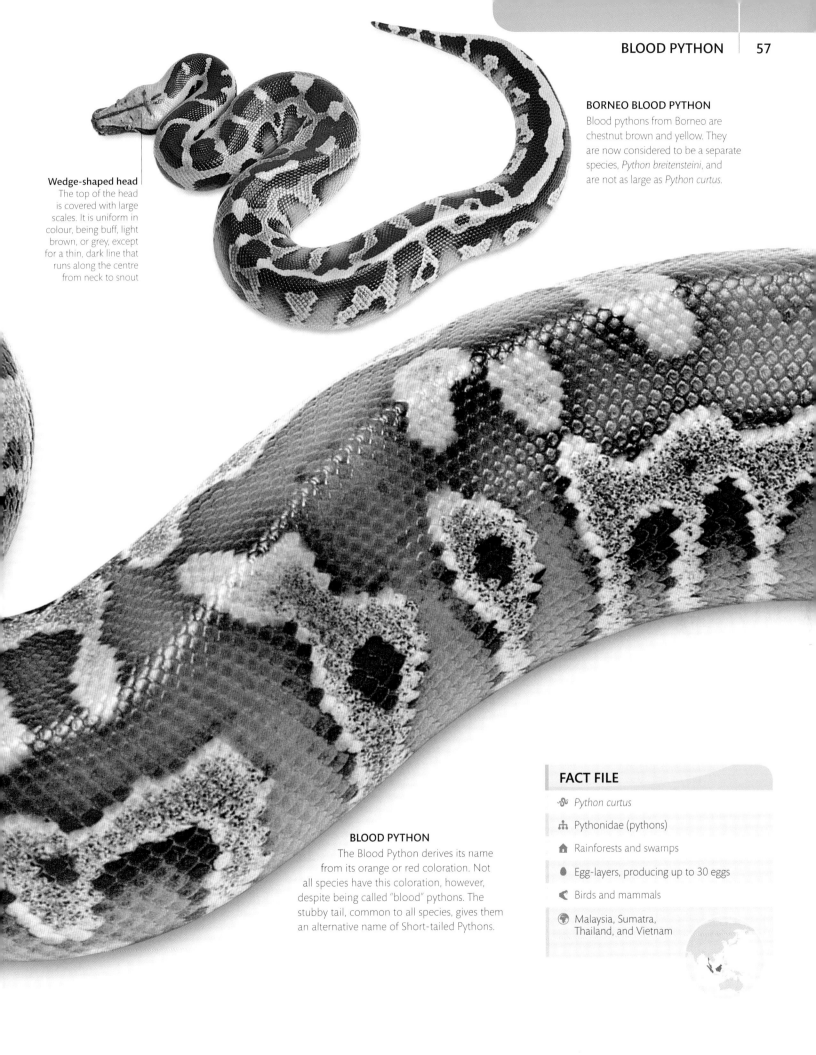

Wedge-shaped head
The top of the head is covered with large scales. It is uniform in colour, being buff, light brown, or grey, except for a thin, dark line that runs along the centre from neck to snout

BORNEO BLOOD PYTHON
Blood pythons from Borneo are chestnut brown and yellow. They are now considered to be a separate species, *Python breitensteini*, and are not as large as *Python curtus*.

BLOOD PYTHON
The Blood Python derives its name from its orange or red coloration. Not all species have this coloration, however, despite being called "blood" pythons. The stubby tail, common to all species, gives them an alternative name of Short-tailed Pythons.

FACT FILE

- *Python curtus*
- Pythonidae (pythons)
- Rainforests and swamps
- Egg-layers, producing up to 30 eggs
- Birds and mammals
- Malaysia, Sumatra, Thailand, and Vietnam

ROYAL PYTHON

Inoffensive to humans, the Royal Python is the smallest of the four African pythons. Its home is the grasslands and sparse woodlands of the West African savanna, where it spends much of its life in underground burrows. It is active mainly by night, although during the long dry season it may remain permanently in hiding.

Main characteristics

A short, stocky snake, the Royal Python is strongly marked in black and tan, which makes it hard to see when it is nestled among short vegetation. It has a short tail and a powerful, muscular body, which it uses to constrict prey. Its scales are small and shiny and do not overlap. It grows to a maximum length of about 2 m (6 ft 6 in).

Saddle variation
Slight variations in the shape and number of the saddles make each one individual

TIGHT DEFENCE
The Royal Python rolls itself into a ball whenever it feels threatened, hiding its head in the centre of the coils and exposing only its scaly armour to enemies.

ROYAL PYTHON
Dark brown and tan markings make this one of the most attractive pythons. Small scales and a handsome pattern make it a favourite in the skin trade, leading to large-scale slaughter.

Sturdy body
The body is short and stout. It is slightly triangular when seen in cross-section

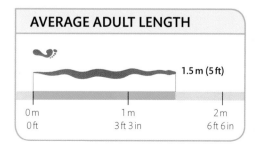

AVERAGE ADULT LENGTH

1.5 m (5 ft)

0 m	1 m	2 m
0 ft	3 ft 3 in	6 ft 6 in

Eye stripe
The stripe on each side of the Royal Python's eye helps to disguise the outline of the head, making it difficult for a predator to spot the snake

Powerful coils
Like other pythons, this species uses powerful muscles to constrict warm-blooded prey, such as rodents

FACT FILE

- *Python regius*
- Pythonidae (pythons)
- Grassland and dry forests
- Egg-layers, producing about 4–8 eggs
- Birds and small mammals
- West Africa

Visible heat pits
The heat pits, used for detecting prey, are well-developed and clearly visible

BROAD HEAD
This species has a rounded snout and small scales covering the top of the broad head. The eyes are large and the pupils are vertical, as in most snakes that are active by night.

DUMERIL'S GROUND BOA

Habitat destruction and collection for the pet trade have much reduced the numbers of Dumeril's Ground Boa, a species that lives among the leaf-litter on the forest floor of southern and southwestern Madagascar. However, it is being widely bred by zoos, which are cooperating in a captive breeding programme. A supply of captive-bred Dumeril's Ground Boas should ensure that collecting for the pet trade is no longer necessary.

CAMOUFLAGE
Dumeril's Ground Boa's markings in shades of brown, tan, orange, and olive-green are a good match for the mosaic of leaves and other debris covering the forest floor.

Main characteristics

A stocky snake, Dumeril's Ground Boa starts life with a pinkish flush to its markings, but this soon fades. Adults display an intricate brown and tan pattern in different shades. The inky black blotches on the scales bordering the mouth are characteristic.

Changing colours
The scales of the adult snake have lost the red, pink, or orange flush which is present on the juvenile Dumeril's Ground Boa

CHIN GROOVE
There is a conspicuous groove under the chin of all snakes, known as the mental groove. It marks a particularly elastic area of skin, which allows the lower jaw to expand during swallowing.

Head scales
There are many small scales on the top of the head

Cylindrical body
The thick, stocky body is roughly cylindrical in shape

FACT FILE

- 🐍 *Acrantophis dumerili*
- 🔬 Boidae (boas)
- 🏠 Dry forests
- ● Live-bearers, producing typically up to 15, exceptionally to 20
- 🦅 Birds and mammals
- 🌍 Southern and southwestern Madagascar

AVERAGE ADULT LENGTH

2 m (6 ft 6 in)

| 0 m | 1 m | 2 m | 3 m |
| 0 ft | 3 ft 3 in | 6 ft 6 in | 9 ft 8 in |

DEFORESTATION

Dumeril's Ground Boa is only one of many unique reptiles, amphibians, mammals, and plants on Madagascar that are endangered by the destruction of their habitat. All are in grave danger of extinction if deforestation continues at its present rate. Only a small proportion of Madagascar's forests remain. Felling trees to provide agricultural land not only removes the forest cover but also results in soil erosion and the subsequent silting up of rivers.

LAND CLEARED FOR AGRICULTURE, MADAGASCAR

DUMERIL'S GROUND BOA
Like most other boas, Dumeril's Ground Boa has a powerful, muscular body, which it uses to constrict prey, and a short tail. This shape limits the speed of its movements, but it can strike quickly at prey, which it usually ambushes. Its coloration, small scales, and heavy body are similar to the Common Boa.

Unique markings
The markings are highly variable, and no two snakes are exactly alike. The saddles along the midline form perfect ovals in places, while in others, the halves of the saddles do not match

COMMON BOA

Probably among the most widely known of snake species, the Boa Constrictor, as it is popularly known, is a magnificent predator from the jungles of Central and South America that has adapted itself to a wide range of different habitats and lifestyles. It has few enemies once it reaches its adult length of 3 m (9 ft 8 in) or more.

Main characteristics

The Common Boa has a relatively small head in comparison to its stout, powerful body. Owing to its wide geographic range, the colour and markings vary greatly, being either silver, grey, or tan, with large blotches, or saddle-shaped markings, which may be dark red or brown. Some forms are suffused with black, while others are a pale, greyish pink.

AT RISK

Although the Common Boa is widespread, some local populations are endangered. Among these is a small form, living on two small islands off the north coast of Honduras, whose numbers have been greatly reduced due to collection for the pet trade and habitat destruction. They may already have been exterminated from other islands where they previously occurred.

COMMON BOA FROM HOG ISLAND

Narrow head
The head is thin, with a squared-off snout, and is covered with many small scales. The markings emphasize the shape and break up the outline

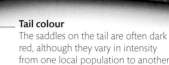

Tail colour
The saddles on the tail are often dark red, although they vary in intensity from one local population to another

FACT FILE

- *Boa constrictor*
- Buidae (boas)
- Varied, from semi-arid scrub to rainforests
- Live-bearers, producing up to 50 young
- Birds and small mammals
- Central and South America

VARIED HABITATS

Although the Common Boa is usually found in rainforests, it also occurs in drier environments in Mexico and on the grasslands of northern Argentina. It lives in trees or on the ground, but becomes increasingly terrestrial as it gets larger.

Expanding scales
The skin on the neck and throat is very elastic, allowing the snake to swallow prey that is relatively large

AVERAGE ADULT LENGTH

	3 m (9 ft 8 in)	Record length
0 m	2 m	4 m	6 m
0 ft	6 ft 6 in	13 ft	20 ft

SWALLOWING PREY

The Common Boa begins to swallow its meal once the prey is dead. The snake gradually spreads its jaws as it slowly pulls the corpse through the coils and down the throat.

Thick body
The Common Boa has a thick, muscular body, used for gripping branches while it is climbing and for constricting its prey

COMMON BOA

The formidable size and powerful body of the Common Boa allow it to feed easily on a variety of warm-blooded prey. It may be active by day or by night, depending on the climate and time of year.

CALABAR GROUND PYTHON

Very little is known about the natural history of the Calabar Ground Python, which leads a hidden existence in tunnels beneath the soil. It lives in tropical forests and probably feeds mainly on nestling rodents, which it tracks down in their burrows. Inoffensive to humans, it never attempts to bite. Calabar was the former name for the part of West Africa in which this snake lives.

Main characteristics

The Calabar Ground Python appears to have two heads. Both head and tail are blunt, and the tail is short. Its body is almost perfectly cylindrical and has smooth scales. All these characteristics are found in several other species of burrowing snake, but the Calabar Ground Python is probably the most perfect example, making it easily identifiable.

Varied coloration
This individual has many red or orange patches, whereas the coloration of others is uniform. The reddish scales are scattered randomly over the entire body

DECEPTIVE TAIL
The tail is clearly intended to imitate the head of the snake. It is the same shape and colour, and even has similar white scales under the "chin." Many individuals have scars on their tails, where they have been attacked by predators who mistook the snake's tail for its head.

Blunt head
Used as a ram, the blunt head moves from side to side as the snake progresses, compacting displaced soil against the walls of its burrow

Heavy body
Unlike many other heavy-bodied snakes, this species does not crawl on its belly, but braces part of its body against the burrow walls while it pushes or pulls another part forward

CALABAR GROUND PYTHON

The blunt snout, thick neck, cylindrical body, and short tail of the Calabar Ground Python are all the result of its burrowing lifestyle, helping it to force its way through soil.

DEFENSIVE POSTURE

When threatened, the Calabar Ground Python hides its head in its coils and raises its tail. It may even make mock strikes with the tail, deflecting the attack away from the vulnerable head.

AVERAGE ADULT LENGTH

1.1 m (3 ft 6 in)

0 cm	50 cm	1 m	1.5 m
0 in	1 ft 6 in	3 ft 3 in	5 ft

FACT FILE

🐍 *Calabaria reinhardtii*

🔗 Boidae (boas)

🌲 Forests

⬤ Egg-layers, producing 1–4 moderately large eggs

🐁 Small mammals

🌍 West Africa

EMERALD TREE BOA

This bright green snake lives in the dense rainforests of South America, where it spends its days coiled inconspicuously over a horizontal bough. At night, it hangs downward in the hope of ambushing prey – usually a bird, bat, or small arboreal mammal. It never descends to the ground, and even gives birth to live young in the canopy. Totally undisturbed forest habitats are essential for its survival.

Main characteristics

Bright green coloration and white markings along the back make the Emerald Tree Boa unmistakable among South American snakes, although the Green Tree Python (see p.52), from Southeast Asia and the northern tip of Australia, is almost identical. Differences include the larger scales on the top of the Emerald Tree Boa's head and the position of the heat pits between scales bordering the mouth; those of the python are within the scales.

BROAD HEAD

Like most boas, the broad head is covered with small scales. The muscles around the jaws are large, enabling the snake to clamp down firmly on its prey as it plunges long, curved teeth deeply into the victim's body.

Heat pits

These are deep and very conspicuous. They are most useful for a nocturnal hunter, enabling the snake to strike accurately at prey

Ambush position

When hunting, this species hangs down in a loose, S-shaped coil, which enables it to extend the head and neck rapidly

Stable anchor

The tail curls around a branch, providing an anchor for the hanging snake

JUVENILE COLORATION

A newborn Emerald Tree Boa is usually brick red, but can also be tan or yellow in colour. Its scales change gradually as the snake grows and are usually green by the time it is about 1 m (3 ft 3 in) long.

AVERAGE ADULT LENGTH

0 m	1 m	2 m	3 m
0 ft	3 ft 3 in	6 ft 6 in	9 ft 8 in

2 m (6 ft 6 in)

FACT FILE

- *Corallus caninus*
- Boidae (boas)
- Rainforest
- Live-bearers, producing up to 20 young
- Birds and small mammals
- Northern South America

White patches
The characteristic white markings vary a little in size and distinctness

Typical coloration
The adult is always green, although the shade can vary slightly

EMERALD TREE BOA

Bright green coloration and slender body proportions reflect the Emerald Tree Boa's arboreal habits. White crossbars help to break up the snake's outline and camouflage it when it is coiled at rest.

GARDEN TREE BOA

The Emerald Tree Boa's closest relative is the Garden Tree Boa, which is found in South America and on some West Indian islands. This species is shorter, more slender, and occurs in a variety of colours – but not bright green. A light body enables it to crawl onto thin twigs to prey on its favourite diet of sleeping lizards.

JUVENILE HUNTING FOR LIZARDS

RAINBOW BOA

The Rainbow Boa occurs in several distinct forms, or subspecies, each varying slightly in size and coloration. All, however, have a dazzling, iridescent skin. Rainbow Boas are primarily arboreal but may also be found on the ground.

Large eyes
Rainbow Boas have moderately large eyes because they hunt by sight on occasion

BRAZILIAN RAINBOW BOA
The Brazilian Rainbow Boa is the most colourful of the various species. Its orange or rich red background is decorated with black circles and a row of eyespot markings along the flanks.

Main characteristics

The Rainbow Boa is slender and muscular. It has a narrow head, often with a dark line down the centre and another over each eye. There is a row of shallow heat pits along the upper jaw. Juvenile Rainbow Boas are even more brightly more brightly coloured than the adults, and this is also characteristic of closely related species.

Shimmering scales
The smooth, iridescent scales shimmer and appear to change colour as the snake moves

AVERAGE ADULT LENGTH

2 m (6 ft 6 in)

0 m	1 m	2 m	3 m
0 ft	3 ft 3 in	6 ft 6 in	9 ft 8 in

LIVE YOUNG
Rainbow Boas give birth to live young, which develop inside a thin membrane. They break out just before or just after they are born. The Argentine Rainbow Boa is shown here.

PARAGUAYAN RAINBOW BOA
The Paraguayan Rainbow Boa, *Epicrates crassus*, is heavy-bodied. It has bold circles down the back and very dark lines running down the narrow head.

ARGENTINE RAINBOW BOA
The appearance of the Argentine Rainbow Boa, *Epicrates alvarezi*, is very distinctive. The scales are less shiny than other forms, with a complex pattern of light circles and semi-circles on a dark background.

Dark eyespots
Lateral rings, or eyespots, are more pronounced in juveniles, but are always dark in colour

FACT FILE

- *Epicrates cenchria*

- Boidae (boas)

- Rainforest and forest clearing

- Live-bearers, producing up to 25 young

- Birds and small mammals

- Northern and central South America

GREEN ANACONDA

Native to South America, this gigantic snake is thought to grow to a greater size than any other species, once its weight and girth are taken into account. Because it becomes so heavy, it has to live partially in water to support its weight, and must catch its prey by ambush. Early accounts by Victorian explorers of anacondas measuring up to 18 m (59 ft) long were certainly exaggerations, but even so, adult anacondas are impressive. They have few enemies other than humans, and their life span can exceed 20 years.

Main characteristics

The Green Anaconda is a massive olive-green or brown snake, which has a number of circular, or oval, black blotches scattered at random over the entire body. There are very few similar snakes anywhere in the world, so its size, coloration, and habitat make this species easy to identify.

High-set eyes
The Green Anaconda's eyes are set towards the top of the head, which allows the snake to submerge its body, leaving little more than the eyes above the surface

GREEN ANACONDA
A supple, sinuous body helps to propel the Green Anaconda through swamps and shallow water, and also to constrict its prey. On land, however, its heavy body makes the snake sluggish, especially as it ages and its length and girth increase.

LARGE HEAD
The thick, powerful neck merges with the large head. A dark stripe passes from each eye to the angle of the jaw, although this can be obscured in old snakes since they darken over the whole body.

Aquatic camouflage
Dappled markings provide camouflage when the snake lies among vegetation in shallow water

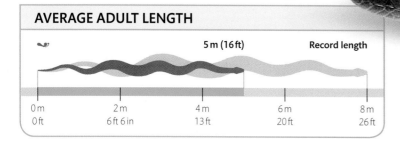

AVERAGE ADULT LENGTH

	5 m (16 ft)	Record length

0 m	2 m	4 m	6 m	8 m
0 ft	6 ft 6 in	13 ft	20 ft	26 ft

YELLOW ANACONDA

The Yellow Anaconda, *Eunectes notaeus*, is a much smaller species than the Green Anaconda, growing to "only" 2–3 m (6 ft 6 in–9 ft 8 in). It is more colourful, being yellow or ochre with bold, black blotches on the body. The behaviour and habits of the Yellow Anaconda are similar to those of the Green Anaconda. Both species, for instance, are aquatic and bear live young. Juvenile Yellow Anacondas frequently feed on fish.

A JUVENILE LYING IN SHALLOW WATER

FACT FILE

- *Eunectes murinus*

- Boidae (boas)

- Swamps and flooded forests

- Live-bearers, producing up to 40 young

- Almost anything, including fish, reptiles, birds, and mammals

- South America, primarily the Amazon basin and Trinidad

Mighty body
The powerful coils rarely allow the snake's prey to escape once captured

FORMIDABLE PREDATOR

Apart from mammals and birds, this snake also eats freshwater turtles and even caimans, a type of alligator. Tussles with such formidable adversaries can take several hours, but the snake rarely loses. There have been a few authenticated reports of anacondas eating children.

ROSY BOA

The Rosy Boa is an attractive but secretive inhabitant of the deserts of southwestern North America. It frequents rocky places, hiding by day in crevices and burrows, and emerging at night to hunt for rodents and other small mammals. The movements of the Rosy Boa are slow and deliberate, although it can strike quickly. Like all boas, it is a powerful constrictor. It is completely inoffensive towards humans, and is frequently kept as a pet.

Main characteristics

A thick-bodied snake, the Rosy Boa has a small head and a short tail. The small scales are smooth and glossy. The body is cylindrical in shape, with a pattern consisting of three broad, longitudinal stripes on a light background. The colour of the stripes varies from one form to another.

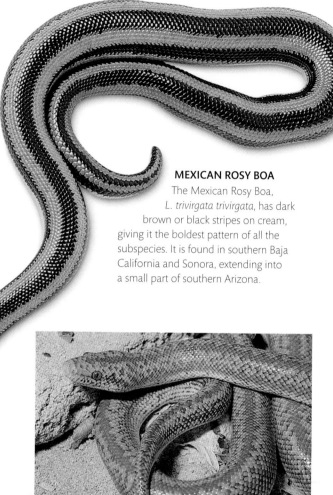

MEXICAN ROSY BOA
The Mexican Rosy Boa, *L. trivirgata trivirgata*, has dark brown or black stripes on cream, giving it the boldest pattern of all the subspecies. It is found in southern Baja California and Sonora, extending into a small part of southern Arizona.

LONG HEAD
The head is elongated and covered with many small scales. The eye is small with a vertical pupil, which is typical of nocturnal foragers. The Rosy Boa does not have heat-sensitive pits.

COASTAL ROSY BOA
The stripes of the Coastal Rosy Boa, *L. trivirgata roseofusca*, have ragged edges, especially in old adults. This species lives along the coastal region of southern California and adjacent parts of Baja California.

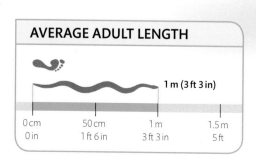

AVERAGE ADULT LENGTH

1 m (3 ft 3 in)

0 cm	50 cm	1 m	1.5 m
0 in	1 ft 6 in	3 ft 3 in	5 ft

Thick neck
The thick, powerful neck is only barely distinct from the snake's head

CENTRAL BAJA ROSY BOA
This form of Rosy Boa, *L. trivirgata saslowi*, has orange stripes, which are usually well-defined with straight edges, and its eyes have orange irises. It occurs in central Baja California.

FACT FILE

- *Lichanura trivirgata*

- Boidae (boas)

- Deserts and rocky outcrops

- Live-bearers, producing up to 8 young

- Small mammals

- USA (southern California and southwest Arizona); Mexico (Baja California and Sonora)

NORTHERN ROSY BOA

The Northern Rosy Boa, *Lichanura orcutti*, comes from parts of California and northern Arizona. Its orange-brown stripes have ragged edges and are not as well-defined as those of the Rosy Boa, *Lichanura trivirgata*.

Variable coloration
This form, like most of the others, does not live up to its common name, since it is rarely "rosy" in colour. Only a few individuals have an orange or pinkish hue

BROWN HOUSE SNAKE

An elegant and graceful species, the Brown House Snake is found in a wide range of habitats, including farm buildings and the outskirts of towns, where it is often tolerated for its beneficial effects on rodent populations; its ability to enter narrow burrows and crevices makes it a formidable rodent hunter. It has an extensive geographic range, but in the driest deserts it is restricted to the vicinity of oases.

Smooth scales
The body scales are smooth and, instead of being glossy, have a silky texture

Main characteristics

The Brown House Snake is usually reddish brown in colour, but is sometimes dark brown or olive. Very occasionally individuals are orange. The two cream stripes through the eyes, which sometimes extend onto the neck, help to identify this species. Young snakes have indistinct blotches along the flanks, which are sometimes also visible in mature specimens.

AVERAGE ADULT LENGTH

95 cm (3 ft)

0 cm	50 cm	1 m
0 in	1 ft 6 in	3 ft 3 in

Eye shape
The eyes are prominent, and vertical pupils indicate a nocturnal hunter

BROWN HOUSE SNAKE

The long, curved, boa-like teeth at the front of the upper jaw of this species, and other members of the genus, give these snakes their scientific generic name of *Boaedon*. This species' slender, supple body enables it to crawl into small spaces and, therefore, to be an effective hunter. The Brown House Snake is the most widespread of the eight species in its genus.

EATING HABITS

The Brown House Snake is an efficient hunter that can tackle moderately large prey. The skin of the throat is especially elastic, allowing it to stretch its mouth wide. A large meal may take four or more days to digest, after which the snake will be ready for another one.

FACT FILE

- *Boaedon fuliginosus*
- Colubridae (colubrids)
- Scrub, grassland, and rocky places
- Egg-layers, producing up to 15 eggs
- Small mammals, including bats
- Africa south of the Sahara, and western Morocco

Pale coloration
The scales pale in colour low down on the flanks and become creamy white underneath the snake

Strong muscles
Powerful muscles are used to constrict prey. The strength of the Brown House Snake is at least equal, size for size, to that of boas and pythons

DESERT FORM

Brown House Snakes from the deserts of Namaqualand, South Africa, tend to be pale and have large eyes. Bright streaks run from the snout through the eyes and along the side of the head above the jaw. These snakes are sometimes considered to be a separate subspecies, *Boaedon fuliginosus mentalis*.

TRANS-PECOS RATSNAKE

Inhabiting the dry mountains and valleys of the Chihuahuan Desert in southern Texas and northeastern Mexico, the Trans-Pecos Ratsnake hunts at night for the small rodents on which it feeds. During the day it hides among rocks or in rodent burrows, avoiding the lethally high temperatures. Because of its secretive habits it is rarely seen, even though it can be present in large numbers in favourable habitats.

Main characteristics

Two types of pattern occur on this snake, the typical form and the "blonde" form, but both are essentially yellow or tan with darker blotches. The head is unmarked, and the margins of the large scales covering it are easily seen. The prominent eyes with their round pupils are very distinctive and are unlike those of any other American ratsnake.

FACT FILE

- 🐍 *Bogertophis subocularis*
- ⚏ Colubridae (colubrids)
- 🏠 Rocky, semi-arid valleys and gullies
- ● Egg-layers, producing up to 12 eggs
- ◀ Small mammals, lizards, and birds
- 🌐 USA (extreme southern Texas, and New Mexico); northeastern Mexico (Coahuila)

AVERAGE ADULT LENGTH

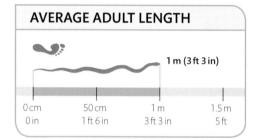

1 m (3 ft 3 in)

0 cm	50 cm	1 m	1.5 m
0 in	1 ft 6 in	3 ft 3 in	5 ft

TRANS-PECOS RATSNAKE
Among the longest and most slender species of ratsnake, the Trans-Pecos Ratsnake occasionally grows to a length of nearly 2 m (6 ft 6 in).

Large eyes
Large eyes help this species hunt at night

"BLONDE" FORM
This coloration is less common than that of the typical form. The markings are smaller and have a washed-out appearance, and the background colour is lighter.

TYPICAL FORM
The most common form of this species has dorsal blotches arranged as a series of H-shaped markings down the back, often touching, or nearly touching, each other. The markings tend to be most concentrated and darkest towards the snake's tail.

Ridged body
The Trans-Pecos Ratsnake has flattened flanks, which form a pair of ridges where they join the underside and help the snake to climb over rock faces

Dorsal blotches
Distinctive blotches form a series of H-shaped markings down the back

Back scales
The back scales are slightly keeled, but those on the flanks are smooth. They all have a velvety sheen. The belly scales are silvery white and perfectly smooth

MANGROVE SNAKE

Living in trees, including mangroves, and shrubs near water, the brilliantly coloured Mangrove Snake is a rear-fanged species, with long fangs below each eye, and it bites readily in self-defence. Although this can cause humans some pain and discomfort, the venom is mild, and the bites are unlikely to have serious consequences.

FACT FILE

- *Boiga dendrophila*
- Colubridae (colubrids)
- Lowland rainforests and mangrove swamps
- Egg-layers, producing 4–15 eggs
- Reptiles, birds, and small mammals
- Indonesia, Southeast Asia, Borneo, and Philippines

AVERAGE ADULT LENGTH

2.5 m (8 ft 2 in)

| 0 m | 1 m | 2 m | 3 m |
| 0 ft | 3 ft 3 in | 6 ft 6 in | 9 ft 8 in |

Shiny scales
The scales are large, distinct, smooth, and very shiny

Main characteristics

The Mangrove Snake is unlikely to be confused with any other snake because of its glossy scales and distinctive coloration. The only other similar species from the same region is the Banded Krait, which, in contrast, has wide yellow bands, a triangular cross-section, and rarely climbs.

Spade-shaped head
The wide, spade-shaped head is very distinct from the slender neck. The top of the head has no markings

THREATENING POSTURE
When annoyed, the Mangrove Snake flares its lips to display bright yellow and black scales. It may also open its mouth wide in an attempt to intimidate enemies.

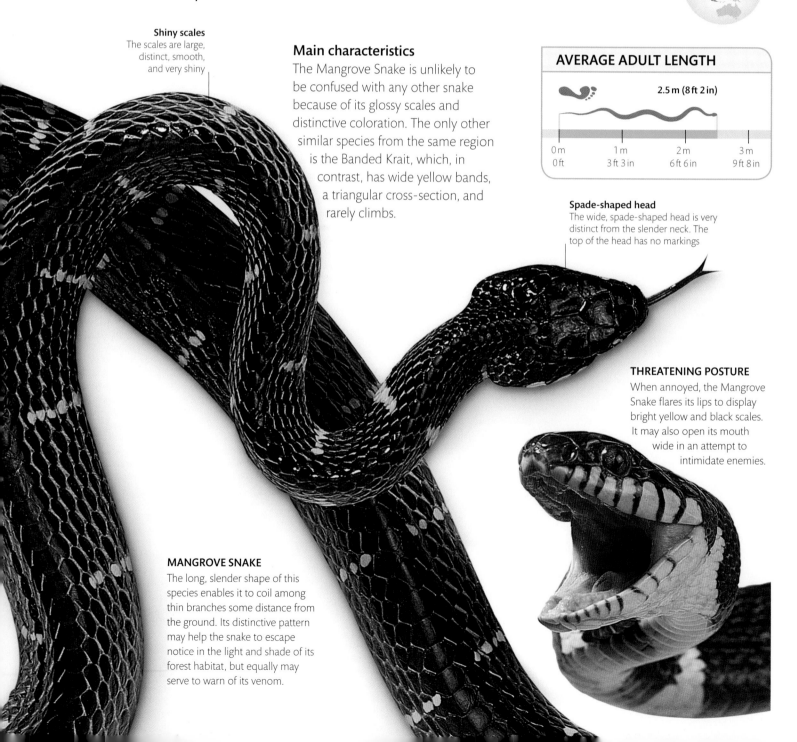

MANGROVE SNAKE
The long, slender shape of this species enables it to coil among thin branches some distance from the ground. Its distinctive pattern may help the snake to escape notice in the light and shade of its forest habitat, but equally may serve to warn of its venom.

GREEN CATSNAKE

The Green Catsnake is at home in trees and bushes, where its green coloration and slow movements make it difficult to distinguish from vines and creepers. Its main defence is intimidation, opening its mouth wide so that the black lining shows. Although it is a rear-fanged species, its venom is mild and harmless to humans.

Main characteristics

Bright green coloration and a slender body distinguish this species from most others. Its body is deeper than it is wide and is slightly triangular in cross-section, with a ridge along the dorsal midline. The head is very wide in comparison with the neck. The Green Catsnake has an unusual row of very large scales along the centre of the back. It is sometimes confused with the Green Tree Viper, from the same habitat and region, but this species is more heavily built and has a deeper head covered with small scales.

FACT FILE

- *Boiga cyanea*
- Colubridae (colubrids)
- Forests, especially near water
- Egg-layers, producing fewer than 10 eggs
- Frogs, reptiles, small birds, and mammals
- Northeast India, Nepal, Southeast Asia, and southern China

GREEN CATSNAKE
The bright green colour of this species is unique among catsnakes, although its build and habitat are similar. Distinctive, large eyes with vertical pupils give the snakes of this genus their common name. They are also known as cat-eyed snakes.

Centre scales
A row of very large scales covers a ridge running along the centre of the back

AVERAGE ADULT LENGTH

1.5 m (5 ft)

0 m	1 m	2 m
0 ft	3 ft 3 in	6 ft 6 in

Slender body
The long, thin body is flattened from side to side. This high, narrow shape helps the snake to span large gaps between branches

Big eyes
Huge eyes and vertical pupils immediately identify this as a species that is active at night

WIDE HEAD
The pear-shaped head of the Green Catsnake is much wider than the slender neck. The large scales covering the top of the head are well defined.

Protruding eyes
Large eyes and a narrow snout give this species good forward vision

COMMON EGG-EATER

An anatomically modified head and 30 specialized vertebrae enable the Common Egg-eater to feed on birds' eggs. It lays its own eggs and devours most of its food in the spring when birds are nesting. For the rest of the year it fasts and is rarely seen, despite being a common species. Hatchlings, which are only about 20 cm (8 in) long, must find small eggs such as those of weaver birds, tits, and finches.

Main characteristics

The Common Egg-eater can grow to about 1 m (3 ft 3in), but is usually smaller. The combination of a narrow head, rounded snout, and very rough scales makes it easily identifiable. It may be grey, light brown, or olive, but there is always a series of irregular dark blotches along the back. The top of the head is marked with a dark chevron pointing forwards. There is a similar marking on the back of the neck.

Expanding jaw
The snake's jaw can easily accommodate an egg four to five times the size of its head

THE SNAKE STRETCHES ITS JAW AND NECK

THE EGG IS ALMOST ENTIRELY ENGULFED

Distinctive marking
There is a dark chevron on the top of the head and a similar marking on the neck

CONSUMING AN EGG

An egg-eater engulfs whole eggs by wedging them against a firm object before forcing them into its throat. The 22nd and 28th vertebrae then penetrate the shell, while vertebrae 29 and 30 prevent the egg from moving, and vertebrae 1 to 21 prevent it from slipping out of the snake's mouth. The egg is crushed by vertebrae 23 to 27. The contents of the egg are swallowed, but the shell, folded into a characteristic pellet, is regurgitated.

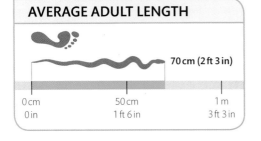

AVERAGE ADULT LENGTH

70 cm (2 ft 3 in)

0 cm	50 cm	1 m
0 in	1 ft 6 in	3 ft 3 in

COMMON EGG-EATER
Heavily keeled scales give the Common Egg-eater a superficial similarity to the carpet and saw-scaled vipers. This deception is even extended to the obliquely arranged keels on its flanks, enabling it to imitate the rasping sound these vipers make.

Varying coloration
The background colour is usually grey, but this may vary in other individuals to match the soil on which they live

Back markings
A series of irregular dark blotches run along the snake's back

Keeled scales
The scales along the centre of the snake's back are elongated and heavily keeled

DEFENCE

The Common Egg-eater, which has no functional teeth, is harmless to humans. To protect itself from its potential predators, such as birds of prey and mammals, it mimics the venomous vipers that live in the same part of the world. A grey individual, for instance, looks like a night adder or a carpet viper. The Common Egg-eater may even imitate the defensive behaviour of the viper by forming semi-circular coils, rasping the rough scales on its flanks together, and spreading its jaws to make its head look as broad as possible.

COMMON EGG-EATER

CARPET VIPER

FACT FILE

- *Dasypeltis scabra*
- Colubridae (colubrids)
- Savannas, scrub, and open woodlands
- Egg-layers, producing up to 18 eggs
- Birds' eggs
- Africa, south of the Sahara

BOOMSLANG

The Boomslang hunts chameleons, birds, and other small animals during the day, using camouflage and a stealthy approach to get within striking distance, and then snatching its prey in a sudden rush. It kills with venom delivered through fangs that are situated below the eyes and is one of the few colubrids that can kill humans, although it only bites when cornered.

Main characteristics

An elongated shape and arboreal habits help to identify this snake, but its variable colour and markings can cause confusion. Juveniles are grey or greyish brown, and females are usually uniform olive-brown. Males, however, may be uniform brown or black, or they may be bright green, reddish, or even bluish green in colour, often with dark edges to the scales. The eye is thought to be larger, relative to the size of its head, than that of any other species.

AVERAGE ADULT LENGTH

1.4 m (4 ft 6 in)

1.5 m	5 ft
1 m	3 ft 3 in
50 cm	1 ft 6 in
0 cm	0 in

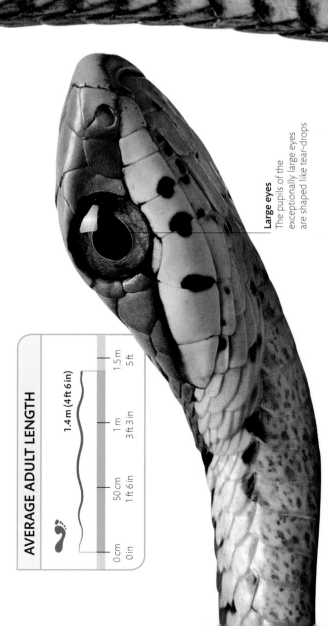

POINTED HEAD
The huge eyes – which are green in juveniles – and sharply angled snout are the most conspicuous features of this head. The scales are very well defined and may be outlined with black in older individuals.

Large eyes
The pupils of the exceptionally large eyes are shaped like tear-drops

Ventral scales
Wide ventral scales with free trailing edges grip rough bark and tree branches, helping to move the snake forwards

BOOMSLANG
The Boomslang's elongated shape and large eyes are directly linked to its lifestyle. It lives in trees and shrubs, gliding easily through the branches while looking for the lizards that are its favourite prey. "Boomslang" is the Afrikaans word for tree snake.

FACT FILE

- *Dispholidus typus*
- Colubridae (colubrids)
- Open scrub and lightly wooded grassland
- Egg-layers, producing up to 25 eggs
- Lizards and small birds
- Africa, south of the Sahara, but not in the most extreme deserts and rainforests

Pointed snout
The narrow, pointed snout enhances the snake's ability to see objects in the foreground

Binocular vision
The eyes are positioned towards the front of the head, and the pupils are slightly elongated. This allows the snake to focus both eyes on an object and thus to judge distances accurately

JUVENILE SNAKE

The juvenile Boomslang is greyish in colour with a head that is darker than its body, a white lower lip, and a yellow throat. It retains this coloration until it is about 1 m (3 ft 3 in), usually at about a year old.

FAVOURITE FOOD

Chameleons are the Boomslang's most common prey. They are numerous throughout the snake's geographic range and are also slow to escape once they have been detected. The Boomslang grips its prey, making a deep wound and working venom into the bite via its enlarged rear fangs. It holds on until struggling ceases and may bite repeatedly, as though chewing, until the prey is dead.

EASTERN INDIGO SNAKE

The Eastern Indigo Snake is found only in Florida and adjacent parts of neighbouring states. It lives in dry, sandy places, especially oak and pinewoods, and is active by day. It is an alert, fast-moving hunter, feeding on a wide variety of vertebrate prey such as fish, mammals, birds and their eggs, and other reptiles, including venomous snakes. It does not constrict its prey but pins it down with its body. Despite its large size, it is inoffensive and never attempts to bite, although it may hiss and flatten its neck when alarmed. Related species in Central and South America are brown rather than glossy black, and live in a wider variety of habitats.

Glossy scales
The large scales are very glossy and are a distinctive feature of the snake's appearance

Main characteristics

The largest colubrid in North America, the Indigo Snake is jet black with large scales and a glossy sheen. Its chin may be cream or deep red and its body is somewhat triangular in cross-section. It normally lives in oak woods, pine hammocks, and other slightly raised, dry habitats, but it may also occur near canals and streams. It sometimes uses the burrows of gopher tortoises to shelter in, to avoid very cold or very hot weather.

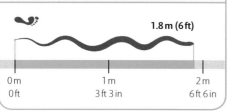

AVERAGE ADULT LENGTH

1.8 m (6 ft)

0 m	1 m	2 m
0 ft	3 ft 3 in	6 ft 6 in

Contrasting chin
In dramatic contrast to the jet black body, the chin may be deep red or cream

EASTERN INDIGO SNAKE
This is the longest species of snake in North America, often exceeding 2 m (6 ft 6 in). There are records of specimens measuring over 2.5 m (8 ft 2 in), but these are rare.

FACT FILE

- *Drymarchon couperi*
- Colubridae (colubrids)
- Varied, often dry forests
- Egg-layers, producing up to 14 eggs
- Fish, amphibians, reptiles, birds, eggs, and small mammals
- Southeastern North America (Florida and parts of Georgia, Alabama)

FOREST CAMOUFLAGE
Snakes belonging to the same genus from Central America are known by the local name of *Cribo*. Their colouring gives them excellent camouflage on the floor of their tropical forest habitat.

Dark coloration
The black scales of the Eastern Indigo Snake help it absorb heat efficiently

Unique markings
The bull's-eye markings may help to break up the snake's outline when it is lying among leaf-litter in patches of light and shade

MANDARIN RATSNAKE

Unusual colours and markings distinguish this Far Eastern ratsnake from other members of the genus. It usually lives in cool montane habitats up to 3,000 m (9,800 ft), such as forests and rocky scrub, but it also occurs at lower elevations, where it may be found in agricultural settings, such as rice fields, probably attracted by the large populations of small rodents that frequent such areas.

Main characteristics
The yellow bull's-eye body markings, surrounded by black circles or triangles, and the boldly marked head, are unique among snakes. The background colour may be grey, brown, or reddish brown. The size and shape of the dorsal blotches varies slightly.

MANDARIN RATSNAKE
Contrasting black and yellow markings on this snake, especially on the head, give it a unique and very exotic appearance.

AVERAGE ADULT LENGTH

1.3 m (4 ft 3 in)

1.5 m
5 ft

1 m
3 ft 3 in

50 cm
1 ft 6 in

0 cm
0 in

FACT FILE

- *Euprepiophis mandarinus*
- Colubridae (colubrids)
- Lightly wooded and scrub-covered mountain slopes
- Egg-layers, producing 3–8 eggs
- Rodents, especially nestlings
- Northeastern India, eastern Myanmar (Burma), northern Laos, northern Vietnam, southeastern China, and Taiwan

Scale variation
Individual scales can be smooth or slightly keeled

Slender shape
The cross-section of the body is more cylindrical than that of most ratsnakes, especially those species that climb

Background coloration
The background colour may vary

Black eye stripes
Radiating, dense black lines help to disguise the eyes from predators

NARROW HEAD

The head is barely wider than the neck and is boldly marked in black and yellow. The narrow head shape and rounded snout may enable the ratsnake to poke about in small crevices and burrows in search of nestling rodents.

RED-TAILED RACER

Long and slender, this snake is at home among the rainforests of Southeast Asia. It spends most of its time in trees, among shrubs, and in understorey vegetation, where it is well camouflaged. Active during the day, the Red-tailed Racer is a quick, powerful constrictor, feeding on birds, arboreal mammals, and lizards. Although harmless, it is an aggressive species that is always ready to defend itself by biting.

RED-TAILED RACER
A long, slender body, smooth scales, and long tail allow this snake to move swiftly through bushes and shrubs. The contrasting colour on its tail is never red, despite its name.

Main characteristics

The Red-tailed Racer is usually bright green in colour, although it can also be brown, grey, or reddish brown. The scales bordering the mouth are usually lighter than those on the rest of the body and are yellow or yellowish green. Its tail coloration contrasts with the body and can be brown, grey, rust, or orange.

Good vision
Large eyes enable this snake to hunt birds, mammals, and lizards during the day

Compressed body
In cross-section, the slender body is compressed from side to side to give it more rigidity when the snake stretches out

FACT FILE

- 🐍 *Gonyosoma oxycephalum*

- 🔱 Colubridae (colubrids)

- 🏠 Primary and secondary rainforests, mangrove swamps, and plantations

- ● Egg-layers, producing 5–12 eggs

- ◗ Lizards, birds, and small mammals, especially bats

- 🌍 Indonesia, Philippines, Southeast Asia, and Andaman Islands

AVERAGE ADULT LENGTH

1.7 m (5 ft 6 in)

0 m	1 m	2 m
0 ft	3 ft 3 in	6 ft 6 in

RED MOUNTAIN RACER

Several other Asian snakes are known as racers or ratsnakes, many of them in the genera *Elaphe*, *Gonyosoma*, or *Oreocryptophis*, for instance. They include the Red Mountain Racer (*Oreocryptophis porphyraceus*), also known as the Red Bamboo Snake, which comes from montane habitats in the same region as the Red-tailed Racer. There is little or no competition between them, however, as one in from the lowlands and is arboreal whereas the other is from mountains and foothills and is terrestrial.

ADULT CAMOUFLAGED AMONG DEAD LEAVES

DEFENCE POSTURE

When threatened, the Red-tailed Racer flattens its throat from side to side and raises its head and neck and the front part of its body off the ground. This posture is intended to intimidate the snake's enemies, making it appear larger.

Smooth scales
The smooth, shiny scales are easily differentiated as their edges are often picked out in black

Striped marking
A dark eye-stripe divides the dark green area from the lighter colour of the lip scales

Blue tongue
This is one of several related Asian species that have blue tongues. The tongue is often protruded for several seconds at a time. The purpose of this display is not known

PLAINS HOG-NOSED SNAKE

A skilled exponent of the art of bluffing, the Plains Hog-nosed Snake puffs up its body and hisses loudly when confronted by an enemy. If this tactic fails, it rolls over and pretends to be dead. It is perfectly harmless and spends its time searching for frogs and toads on the prairies and in woodlands. It is one of the few species of snake that will eat dead prey that is beginning to decompose.

Main characteristics

There are five species of hog-nosed snake, all with similar physical and behavioural characteristics. The Plains Hog-nosed Snake is a short, stout species with rough scales, a blotched pattern down the back, and an unmistakable, upturned snout. It is usually brown in colour, although it can also have a greenish or reddish tinge. In addition, some forms have blotches on their backs that are not sharply defined.

STAPLE FOOD

All hog-nosed snakes prefer to eat toads rather than small mammals. They are efficient, diurnal burrowers, rootling out any buried prey they find. It is thought that the snakes are immune to the poisons that the toads produce in the warty glands on their heads and backs. Because toads puff themselves up, the hog-nosed snake has to be capable of stretching its mouth to an enormous extent in order to swallow them.

EASTERN HOG-NOSED SNAKE SWALLOWING A TOAD

Rostral scale
The sharp-edged, shovel-shaped rostral scale at the tip of the snout is used to dig up toads, which form the bulk of its diet

CHUNKY HEAD
Hog-nosed snakes have broad, chunky heads. There is a bar of colour stretching across the snout from eye to eye. This helps to break up the outline, protecting the snake from the attention of predators.

Rough scales
Hog-nosed snakes have heavily keeled scales, perhaps to provide a firm grip when digging

AVERAGE ADULT LENGTH

50 cm (1 ft 6 in)

0 cm	50 cm	1 m
0 in	1 ft 6 in	3 ft 3 in

HATCHING OUT

The young hatch about two months after the eggs are laid. They immediately shed their skins and begin to search for food, in the shape of juvenile frogs and toads, and lizards.

Short tail
This snake has a short tail, which is typical of species that burrow

FACT FILE

- *Heterodon nasicus*

- Colubridae (colubrids)

- Dry sandy prairies, sand bushlands, and farms

- Egg-layers, producing up to 4–23 eggs; average 10.5

- Amphibians, lizards, and small birds and mammals

- Central North America, from southern Canada to northern Mexico

Western coloration
The Plains Hog-nosed Snake is lighter in colour than its eastern relatives

PLAINS HOG-NOSED SNAKE

This form has a row of well-defined blotches down the back, which alternate with smaller ones on the flanks. The blotches are usually brown, but are sometimes olive or reddish in colour. Other forms have less obvious markings.

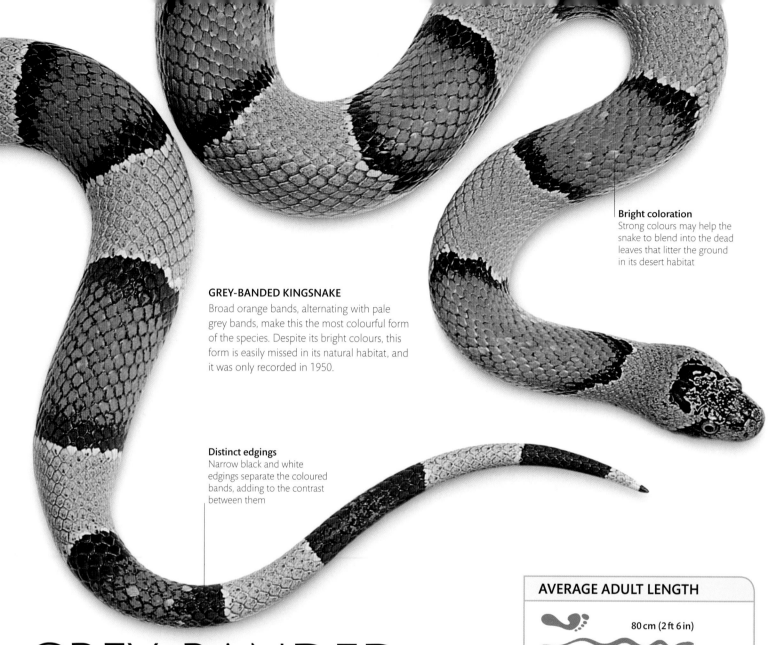

GREY-BANDED KINGSNAKE
Broad orange bands, alternating with pale grey bands, make this the most colourful form of the species. Despite its bright colours, this form is easily missed in its natural habitat, and it was only recorded in 1950.

Bright coloration
Strong colours may help the snake to blend into the dead leaves that litter the ground in its desert habitat

Distinct edgings
Narrow black and white edgings separate the coloured bands, adding to the contrast between them

GREY-BANDED KINGSNAKE

A colourful snake that is native to south Texas and adjacent parts of Mexico, this species lives in the Chihuahuan Desert, where the underlying limestone provides the crevices and subterranean cavities in which it hides. It seldom ventures out, except in the spring, when males search for mates and, even then, only at night.

Main characteristics
The Grey-banded Kingsnake is highly variable in colour – even offspring from the same clutch of eggs can differ markedly. The dorsal bands may be orange, red, or brownish red, or they may be absent altogether, leaving only narrow black bars. It has a small head with small eyes. The smooth scales have a texture that is satin-like rather than glossy.

AVERAGE ADULT LENGTH

80 cm (2 ft 6 in)

0 cm	50 cm	1 m
0 in	1 ft 6 in	3 ft 3 in

FACT FILE

- *Lampropeltis alterna*
- Colubridae (colubrids)
- Rocky deserts with underlying limestone
- Egg-layers, producing 3–13 eggs; average 7.5
- Reptiles, small birds, and mammals
- North America (extreme southwestern Texas and southeastern New Mexico, and adjacent states of northeastern Mexico)

MEXICAN KINGSNAKE

Although several other kingsnakes occur in Mexico, this is one of the few endemic species. It inhabits the mountainous northeast, where it hunts for lizards and small rodents among the rocks in valleys and on hillsides. At least three subspecies are recognized; all forms are very colourful, but both colour and markings vary considerably.

FACT FILE

- *Lampropeltis mexicana*
- Colubridae (colubrids)
- Rocky deserts and valleys
- Egg-layers, producing up to 12 eggs
- Reptiles, small birds, and mammals
- Northeast and central Mexico

Main characteristics

The Mexican Kingsnake has a cylindrical body, a small head, and smooth scales. The red or orange markings are shaped like large saddles or narrow crossbars. All markings are invariably edged in black. The background colour may be grey, cream, or pinkish. Of the three forms, one, the San Luis Potosí Kingsnake, has a distinctive red marking on the head, which is lacking in the other two forms.

COLOUR VARIATION
The Mexican Kingsnake from Nuevo Leon belongs to the subspecies *Lampropeltis mexicana thayeri*. It is often cream with narrow slashes of red edged in black, but individuals from the same region may have varied patterns.

MEXICAN KINGSNAKE
The large red saddles and intricate head marking immediately identify *Lampropeltis mexicana mexicana* as belonging to the population from San Luis Potosí.

AVERAGE ADULT LENGTH

80 cm (2 ft 6 in)

0 cm	50 cm	1 m
0 in	1 ft 6 in	3 ft 3 in

Saddle markings
These cover the top of the body only and are therefore known as saddles, despite looking like bands from above

CALIFORNIA KINGSNAKE

Familiar throughout the American southwest, the boldly marked California Kingsnake lives in deserts, arid shrubby hillsides, and chaparrals. Closely related kingsnakes are found throughout North America. Their adaptability is reflected in their diet, which includes almost any animal, including fish, frogs, lizards, and rodents. The California Kingsnake also eats other snakes, including venomous species.

Main characteristics

The California Kingsnake has a cylindrical body, smooth, shiny scales, and a narrow head. The head is approximately the same diameter as the rest of the body. Coloration varies from one locality to another, but it is usually black or dark brown with white or cream markings in a variety of patterns. Individuals from northeast Mexico are sometimes plain black as adults.

Round pupils
The eyes have round pupils and are set further forward than those of many other species of snake

NARROW HEAD
The head ends in a blunt snout. The California Kingsnake usually has white spots on the front of the head. White bars on the scales bordering the mouth are common to many of the subspecies.

Shiny scales
The scales are smooth and shiny. The Latin name, *Lampropeltis*, means "shiny-shields"

FACT FILE

- *Lampropeltis californiae*
- Colubridae (colubrids)
- Deserts, other arid places, rocky hillsides, forests, meadows, and land used for agriculture
- Egg-layers, producing up to 20 eggs
- Reptiles, birds, and mammals
- USA (California; western parts of neighbouring states) and Mexico (Baja California; Sonora)

SNAKE EATS SNAKE
California Kingsnakes eat a large variety of prey, including other snakes. Some prey species, such as rattlesnakes, are venomous, but the California Kingsnake has some immunity to the venom. When a rattlesnake is approached, it arches its body off the ground so as to look bigger. This strategy has only a limited success, however, and most are quickly overpowered by the California Kingsnake's powerful coils. The form illustrated here may belong to a more easterly occurring population, sometimes known as the Desert Kingsnake.

Distinctive markings
This snake is boldly marked with wide, contrasting bands, or rings. In some individuals, a number of the bands are broken, or divided, usually near the dorsal midline

AVERAGE ADULT LENGTH

1.1 m (3 ft 6 in)

| 0 cm | 50 cm | 1 m | 1.5 m |
| 0 in | 1 ft 6 in | 3 ft 3 in | 5 ft |

CALIFORNIA KINGSNAKE
This species is among the most distinctive of the kingsnakes, with wide, pale bands on a darker background. The black and white coloration is typical of inland individuals, but on the coast they are brown and cream. In some populations the markings of some individuals consist of stripes instead of bands.

SONORAN MOUNTAIN KINGSNAKE

Formerly known as the Arizona Mountain Kingsnake, this species' name has been changed so that it more accurately describes its natural geographic range, which extends to the north, east, and south of Arizona. However, it is restricted exclusively to mountainous areas within this region. It is thought to undergo long periods of hibernation. When active, it feeds on lizards and small mammals.

Main characteristics

Striking markings make this snake easy to identify. The white rings, which are always complete, alternate with the red rings, which may sometimes be reduced to wedges along the flanks where the black bands widen as they reach the dorsal midline. The red rings lack the black tips that are typical of most forms of the Milksnake (see pp.98–99), which have similar markings. The snout is always white, in contrast to the California Mountain Kingsnake (see opposite), which has a black snout.

Alternating bands
The red-black-white-black-red combination of bands is known as triads. The number of body triads can vary from one population of the Sonoran Mountain Kingsnake to another

SONORAN MOUNTAIN KINGSNAKE
The bright red, black, and white stripes that are characteristic of this snake seem to flicker when it moves quickly among rocks or vegetation and may serve to distract a predator's attention for long enough to enable the snake to reach cover.

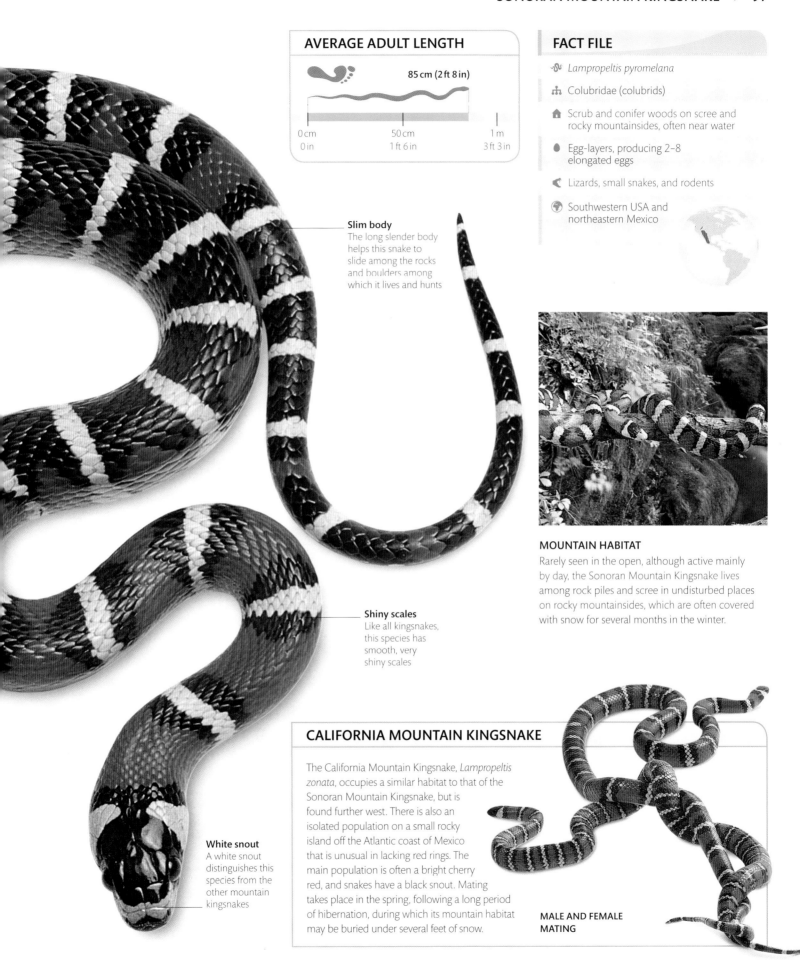

AVERAGE ADULT LENGTH

85 cm (2 ft 8 in)

0 cm	50 cm	1 m
0 in	1 ft 6 in	3 ft 3 in

FACT FILE

- *Lampropeltis pyromelana*
- Colubridae (colubrids)
- Scrub and conifer woods on scree and rocky mountainsides, often near water
- Egg-layers, producing 2–8 elongated eggs
- Lizards, small snakes, and rodents
- Southwestern USA and northeastern Mexico

Slim body
The long slender body helps this snake to slide among the rocks and boulders among which it lives and hunts

Shiny scales
Like all kingsnakes, this species has smooth, very shiny scales

White snout
A white snout distinguishes this species from the other mountain kingsnakes

MOUNTAIN HABITAT
Rarely seen in the open, although active mainly by day, the Sonoran Mountain Kingsnake lives among rock piles and scree in undisturbed places on rocky mountainsides, which are often covered with snow for several months in the winter.

CALIFORNIA MOUNTAIN KINGSNAKE

The California Mountain Kingsnake, *Lampropeltis zonata*, occupies a similar habitat to that of the Sonoran Mountain Kingsnake, but is found further west. There is also an isolated population on a small rocky island off the Atlantic coast of Mexico that is unusual in lacking red rings. The main population is often a bright cherry red, and snakes have a black snout. Mating takes place in the spring, following a long period of hibernation, during which its mountain habitat may be buried under several feet of snow.

MALE AND FEMALE MATING

MILKSNAKE

The milksnakes consist of a group of seven species previously considered to be forms of a single species. Collectively, they have a wide geographical range, from Canada in the north to Ecuador in the south. They occupy a range of habitats, from forests to mountains and rainforests to deserts, although they avoid the most arid regions. The species featured here is the Atlantic Central American Milksnake, *Lampropeltis polyzona*, which comes from Mexico.

Wide neck band
The Pueblan form is distinguished by a wide white neck band and black snout

Main characteristics

Milksnakes have slender, cylindrical bodies, smooth shiny scales, and a narrow head, which is barely wider than their neck. Most forms have red, white, and black bands around the body; these may be approximately equal in width, or the red bands may be widest. Some forms have saddles rather than complete bands. Hatchlings are especially brightly coloured, but their markings dull slightly as they become older, and small dusky areas develop on the scales.

SINALOAN MILKSNAKE
The Sinaloan form, from parts of northwestern Mexico, is distinct from most other forms of the Milksnake because it has extremely wide, red bands and narrow, black-white-black bands. It is more slender and slightly shorter than the Pueblan form.

Flickering colours
The red, white, and black coloured bands flicker when the snake moves quickly, confusing predators and making it difficult to follow

LAYING EGGS
The Milksnake lays between three and 24 eggs (average 7.6) in the spring or early summer. The young hatch about ten weeks later and measure 20–30 cm (8–12 in).

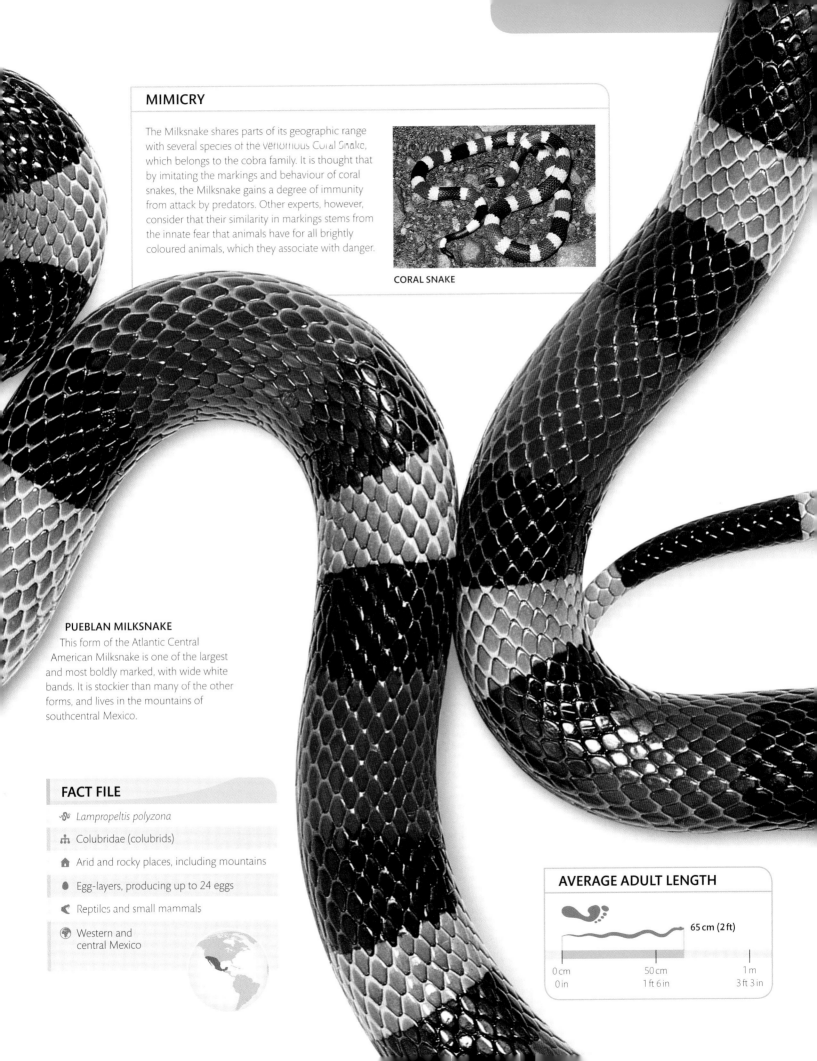

MIMICRY

The Milksnake shares parts of its geographic range with several species of the venomous Coral Snake, which belongs to the cobra family. It is thought that by imitating the markings and behaviour of coral snakes, the Milksnake gains a degree of immunity from attack by predators. Other experts, however, consider that their similarity in markings stems from the innate fear that animals have for all brightly coloured animals, which they associate with danger.

CORAL SNAKE

PUEBLAN MILKSNAKE

This form of the Atlantic Central American Milksnake is one of the largest and most boldly marked, with wide white bands. It is stockier than many of the other forms, and lives in the mountains of southcentral Mexico.

FACT FILE

- Lampropeltis polyzona
- Colubridae (colubrids)
- Arid and rocky places, including mountains
- Egg-layers, producing up to 24 eggs
- Reptiles and small mammals
- Western and central Mexico

AVERAGE ADULT LENGTH

65 cm (2 ft)

0 cm	50 cm	1 m
0 in	1 ft 6 in	3 ft 3 in

GRASS SNAKE

Semi-aquatic, this species is found in a variety of damp habitats. When it swims, it usually stays on the surface with the head well out of water. It feeds largely on frogs, but also takes toads, newts, tadpoles, and fish. It is inoffensive to humans and never attempts to bite. Within its huge geographic range, it is one of the most common and adaptable of species. Females are larger than males, and individuals from the south are larger than those of northerly populations.

GRASS SNAKE

Narrow, heavily keeled scales may help to propel this snake through the water, and its sinuous body enables it to work its way through reeds, rushes, and other dense aquatic vegetation.

AVERAGE ADULT LENGTH

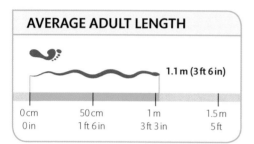

1.1 m (3 ft 6 in)

0 cm	50 cm	1 m	1.5 m
0 in	1 ft 6 in	3 ft 3 in	5 ft

Main characteristics

The Grass Snake is generally easily identifiable by the distinctive collar behind the head, which is usually yellow, but may be orange, cream, or white, and has a pair of black crescents immediately behind it. The snake's coloration varies from brown or greenish grey to olive-green and, sometimes, black. The members of some populations from southeastern Europe and northern Italy have two pale lines running down their bodies. Spanish specimens are often more uniform in coloration and lack the light-coloured collar and the bars on the flanks. The Grass Snake's distinctive collar can be obscure in very dark specimens.

FACT FILE

- 🐍 *Natrix natrix*
- 🔗 Colubridae (colubrids)
- 🏠 Marshes and the edges of streams, ponds, lakes, and canals
- ● Egg-layers, producing up to 30 eggs
- 🦎 Fish, amphibians, and tadpoles
- 🌍 Most of Europe, parts of North Africa, Middle East, and Central Asia

Plain head
The top of the head is covered with large scales, and is usually plain in colour

Distinctive marking
The bright collar, together with the two black patches behind it, is a good distinguishing characteristic

Orange irises
This species has average-sized eyes with round pupils and orange irises

Flank markings
The dark crossbars down the flanks are nearly always present, except in black specimens

Defence mechanism
This snake has puffed up its body to make itself look bigger and intimidate enemies

EGG INCUBATION

Because they tend to live in cold places, female Grass Snakes search out decaying vegetation in which to lay eggs. The heat generated by the process of decomposition speeds up the development of the eggs. Several females may lay eggs together in a particularly favourable site.

DEFENCE

If cornered, the Grass Snake may play dead by lying upside down with its mouth open and tongue hanging out. At the same time, it secretes a foul-smelling fluid from the cloaca. After a while it rights itself and makes off. Otherwise, it tries to escape by taking cover in water or in dense vegetation.

BANDED WATER SNAKE

Inhabiting the swamps, lake edges, rivers, and wetlands of the American southeast, the Banded Water Snake feeds on fish and amphibians, and basks on branches and riverbanks. It is often bad-tempered, striking and biting vigorously in self-defence. Although it is harmless, it is sometimes killed in the belief that it is a venomous Cottonmouth – a pit viper with which it shares its habitat. There are a number of forms, or subspecies.

Main characteristics

A narrow head distinguishes this species from the venomous Cottonmouth with which it is sometimes confused; the Cottonmouth has a broad, triangular head. Unlike the viper, the Banded Water Snake is slender, although females can become very bulky, especially when pregnant. A banded pattern is common to the species, although the width and coloration may vary.

MATING BALL
Water snakes sometimes form a mating ball as several males try to mate with the same female. In snakes with this breeding system, males are often significantly smaller than females because they do not need to fight to win a mate. Females give birth to young about three to four months after mating.

BANDED WATER SNAKE
Broad bands distinguish this form, which occurs throughout the Mississippi basin. It can be difficult to see the banded pattern, especially if the snake has been swimming in muddy water.

Flattened body
The body is slightly flattened towards the tail, which helps to propel the snake through water

FACT FILE

- *Nerodia fasciata*

- Colubridae (colubrids)

- All types of freshwater habitats, including ponds, lakes, swamps, and streams

- Live-bearers, producing 10–20 young (exceptionally over 50)

- Fish and amphibians

- Southeastern North America

ENDANGERED HABITAT

In southern Florida, the Banded Water Snake's preferred habitat is cypress swamps. However, the demands of a rapidly expanding human population are steadily reducing water levels in the swamps. As a result, the plants and wildlife of the swamps are now seriously endangered.

CYPRESS SWAMP IN SOUTHERN FLORIDA

Camouflage markings
Irregular, blotchy markings disguise the snake's outline when it lies motionless in mud and vegetation at the water's edge

AVERAGE ADULT LENGTH

65 cm (2 ft)

0 cm	50 cm	1 m
0 in	1 ft 6 in	3 ft 3 in

Keeled scales
The scales are keeled, perhaps as an aid to pushing the snake through water

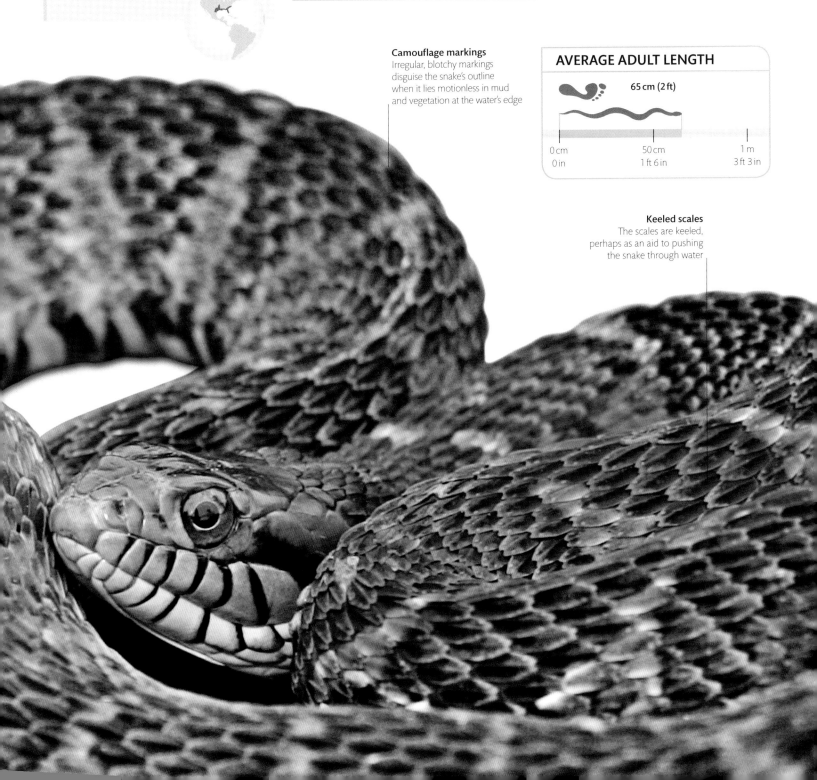

ROUGH GREEN SNAKE

A dainty, slender species, the Rough Green Snake lives in shrubs and thickets close to water, particularly favouring the lush growth around the margins of streams and lakes. It frequents branches that overhang the water's edge and may even enter the water on occasion. It is largely insectivorous, living primarily off crickets, grasshoppers, grubs, caterpillars, and spiders.

Main characteristics

The Rough Green Snake is long and very thin with a bright green upper surface and a white or pale green underside. Its scales are keeled, giving it a rough appearance. This characteristic separates it from the only other similar species in North America, the Smooth Green Snake.

Large eyes
This species has relatively large eyes with round pupils. It hunts by sight during the day.

NARROW HEAD
The head is only just wider than the neck. The snout is pointed. This species eats small items of food and does not need a large gape.

Rough scales
Each scale has a distinct keel, giving the snake's skin a rough texture

ROUGH GREEN SNAKE
The bright green coloration and slender shape of this species camouflage it well. As long as it remains still, it is hard to find, and it is probably more common than rare sightings suggest.

Head scales
Large scales cover the head. The dark colour of the top scales gives good camouflage

FACT FILE

- *Opheodrys aestivus*
- Colubridae (colubrids)
- Thick vegetation, often near lakes, rivers, and streams
- Egg-layers, producing 3–12 eggs
- Insects, such as crickets, grasshoppers, butterfly and moth caterpillars, spiders, and occasionally, small frogs
- North America (southeastern USA and extreme northeastern Mexico)

AVERAGE ADULT LENGTH

80 cm (2 ft 6in)

1 m
3 ft 3 in

50 cm
1 ft 6 in

0 cm
0 in

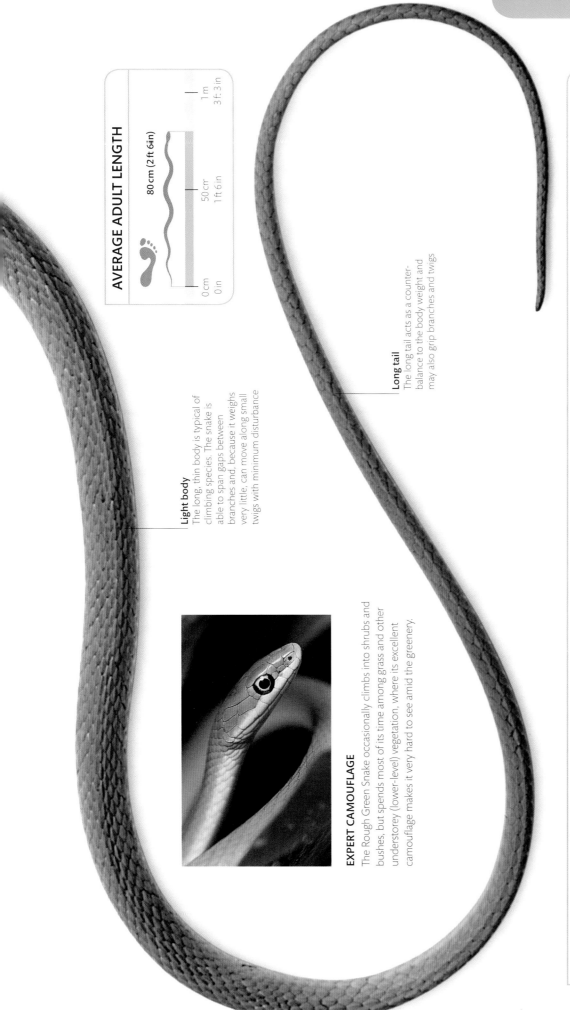

Light body
The long, thin body is typical of climbing species. The snake is able to span gaps between branches and, because it weighs very little, can move along small twigs with minimum disturbance

Long tail
The long tail acts as a counter-balance to the body weight and may also grip branches and twigs

EXPERT CAMOUFLAGE

The Rough Green Snake occasionally climbs into shrubs and bushes, but spends most of its time among grass and other understorey (lower-level) vegetation, where its excellent camouflage makes it very hard to see amid the greenery.

WESTERN SHOVEL-NOSED SNAKE

BLACK-BANDED SNAKE

BLUNT-HEADED SLUG SNAKE

INVERTEBRATE EATERS

The Rough Green Snake is one of a large number of snakes that prey primarily on invertebrates, but it has been documented eating small frogs. They include specialized feeders, such as the Blunt-headed Slug Snake, *Aplopeltura boa*, and the centipede-eating Black-banded Snake, *Scolecophis atrocinctus*, as well as generalized feeders, such as the Western Shovel-nosed Snake, *Chionactis occipitalis*, which eats scorpions, spiders, cockroaches, and larvae.

BAIRD'S RATSNAKE

A long, slender, elegant snake, Baird's Ratsnake was named in honour of Spencer Fullerton Baird, a nineteenth-century zoologist. It is found in the rocky deserts of Texas and adjacent parts of northeastern Mexico. It is seldom seen, hiding by day and emerging at night, especially after rain, to hunt for small rodents and birds.

Main characteristics

Baird's Ratsnake changes colour as it grows. Juveniles are grey with dark crossbars. These fade with age, and the snake turns first plain grey, then orange and grey, as each scale develops an orange crescent at its base. There is often, though not always, a pair of dusky lines along the back.

Juvenile coloration
The typical crossbars have faded, but the adult orange coloration of this Texas form has not yet appeared

Smooth scales
Most scales are only lightly keeled and the snake has a satin-like sheen

JUVENILE BAIRD'S RATSNAKE
Like many young snakes, juvenile Baird's Ratsnakes are relatively slender and become more thickset as they grow. Their coloration changes at the same time. The reason for this is not fully understood but may be related to their changing lifestyle.

AVERAGE ADULT LENGTH

1.3 m (4 ft 3 in)

0 cm	50 cm	1 m	1.5 m
0 in	1 ft 6 in	3 ft 3 in	5 ft

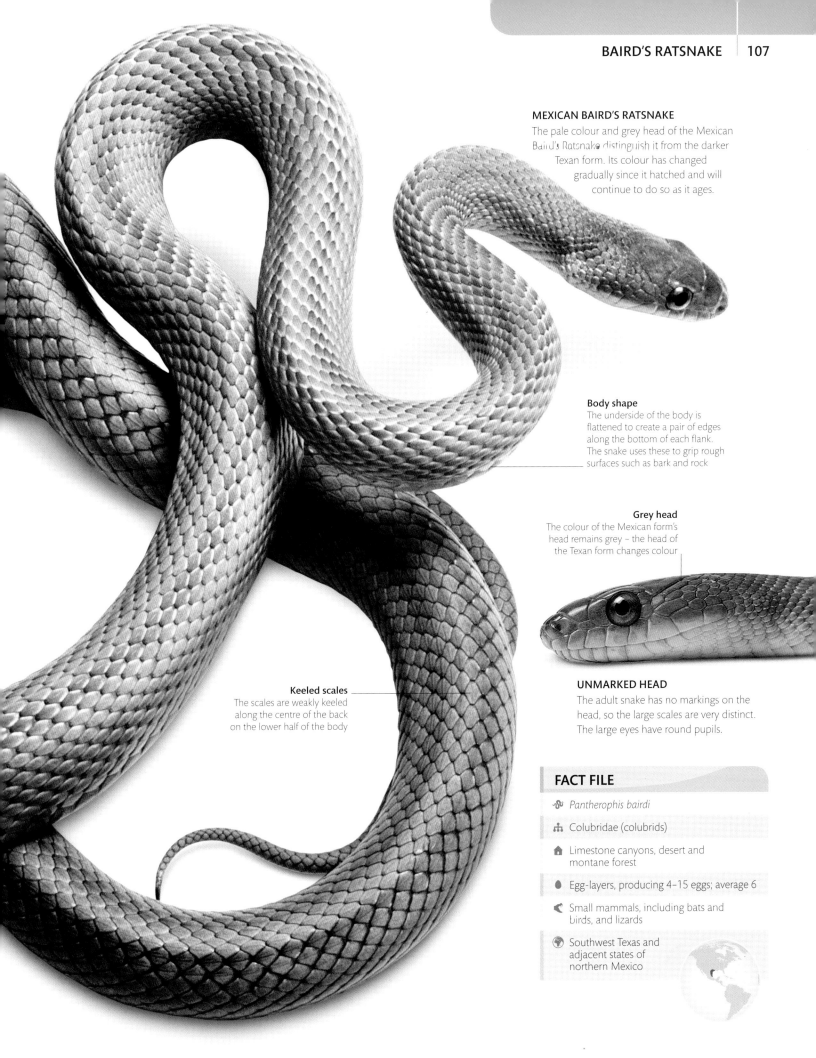

MEXICAN BAIRD'S RATSNAKE

The pale colour and grey head of the Mexican Baird's Ratsnake distinguish it from the darker Texan form. Its colour has changed gradually since it hatched and will continue to do so as it ages.

Body shape

The underside of the body is flattened to create a pair of edges along the bottom of each flank. The snake uses these to grip rough surfaces such as bark and rock

Grey head

The colour of the Mexican form's head remains grey – the head of the Texan form changes colour

Keeled scales

The scales are weakly keeled along the centre of the back on the lower half of the body

UNMARKED HEAD

The adult snake has no markings on the head, so the large scales are very distinct. The large eyes have round pupils.

FACT FILE

- *Pantherophis bairdi*
- Colubridae (colubrids)
- Limestone canyons, desert and montane forest
- Egg-layers, producing 4–15 eggs; average 6
- Small mammals, including bats and birds, and lizards
- Southwest Texas and adjacent states of northern Mexico

CORN SNAKE

Also known as the Red Ratsnake, the Corn Snake is a common and beautiful species native to the southeastern region of the USA. It is found around houses and gardens as well as in natural habitats. The Corn Snake has become a very popular domestic pet, and selective breeding has produced forms that bear little resemblance to their wild ancestors. All, however, belong to the same species.

Main characteristics

Corn Snakes are slender, with narrow heads and well-defined neck regions. The number and size of the saddles, or blotches, down the back can vary, as can the colour, although the differences are less extreme in snakes from the wild. In some forms the blotches merge to form a broad stripe or an irregular zigzag.

FACT FILE

- *Pantherophis guttatus*
- Colubridae (colubrids)
- Old fields, open woodlands, and pine barrens
- Egg-layers, producing up to 30 eggs
- Lizards, birds, and small mammals
- Southeastern USA

AVERAGE ADULT LENGTH

1 m (3 ft 3 in)

0 cm	50 cm	1 m	1.5 m
0 in	1 ft 6 in	3 ft 3 in	5 ft

CORN SNAKES
These captive-bred Corn Snakes display some of the many variations in colour and pattern that are the result of many years of selective breeding from occasional, naturally occurring mutations.

Wild coloration
The coloration and pattern of this form are the same as those of the wild form of the Corn Snake

TREE CLIMBER
A wild Corn Snake climbs well, although it is not classified as an arboreal species. It climbs in order to search for prey. Here, it is searching for birds' nests containing unguarded eggs and nestlings.

Large eyes
The Corn Snake has large eyes and round pupils. It has moderately good daytime vision, even though it is mainly active at night

Plate-like scales
Like nearly all colubrids, the Corn Snake has large, plate-like scales on the top of the head

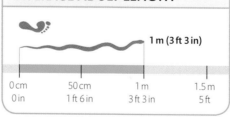

Amelanistic form
When a form lacks black pigment, it is known as amelanistic. Only shades of red and orange remain, and the eyes are pink

Snow Corn Snake
Individuals lacking black and red pigmentation are known as Snow Corns. They are almost pure white, with just a faint tinge of pink

Dorsal markings
These are usually square and well separated but become elongated and may touch each other towards the snake's neck

PINE SNAKE

The Pine Snake is a large, powerful snake that constricts its prey. It intimidates enemies by gaping, hissing loudly, and striking vigorously. It is a good burrower, especially in the sandy soil typical of much of its geographic range, often seeking its prey underground. The Pine Snake eats large numbers of rats and mice, which makes it a useful farmyard visitor. It also occasionally takes birds and their eggs, unfortunately including those of domestic fowl.

NORTHERN PINE SNAKE
This northern subspecies has large dark blotches on a white or ivory coloured background and is more boldly marked than other forms. As with all Pine Snakes, the snake is most heavily pigmented at the front of the body.

Main characteristics
Depending on the subspecies, the Pine Snake has variable markings. It may have black or brown blotches on a white background, be plain beige, or have colours which blend together. One form, the Black Pine Snake, is a uniform black. All have sharply pointed snouts and heavily keeled scales. Over most of its geographic range, the adult Pine Snake can be readily identified by its large size.

Camouflage coloration
Pale coloration helps the snake to avoid detection by potential predators when on pale, sandy soil

MANY-SCALED HEAD
The Pine Snake has more scales on top of the head than most other colubrids, with four prefrontal scales (those immediately in front of the large scale between the eyes). It also has relatively large eyes, typical of snakes that are mostly active in the day.

PINEWOOD HABITAT
As its name suggests, the Pine Snake is most at home among pinewoods, although it also occurs in fields, around human dwellings, and along rocky ridges. Its main requirement is some loose, sandy soil in which to dig a burrow.

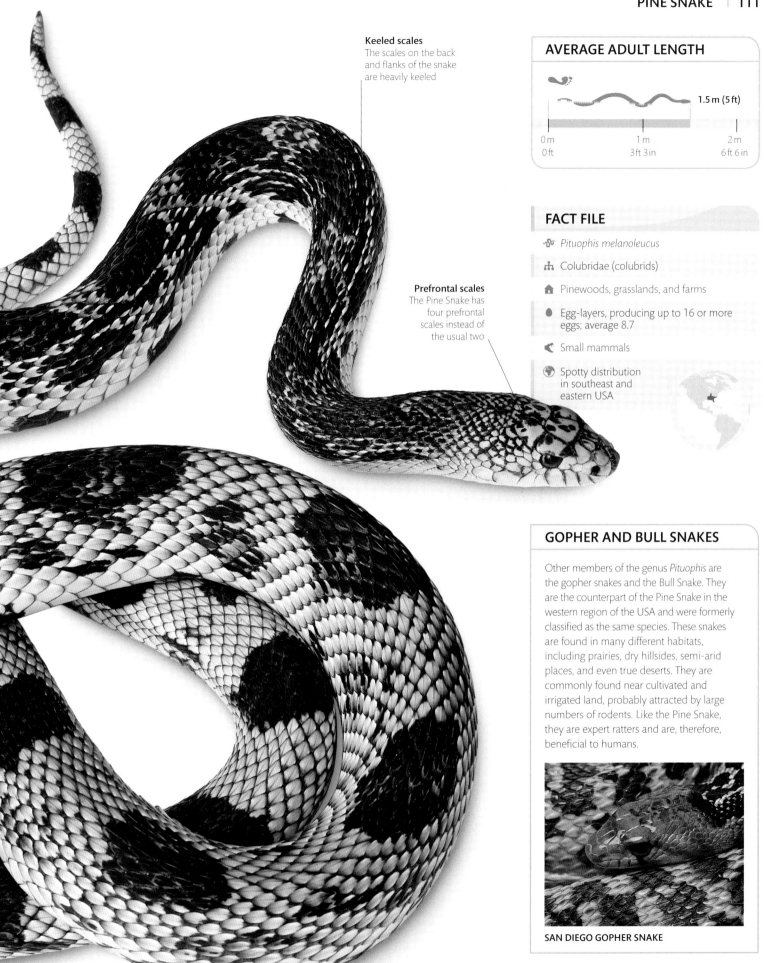

Keeled scales
The scales on the back and flanks of the snake are heavily keeled

Prefrontal scales
The Pine Snake has four prefrontal scales instead of the usual two

AVERAGE ADULT LENGTH

1.5 m (5 ft)

0 m	1 m	2 m
0 ft	3 ft 3 in	6 ft 6 in

FACT FILE

- *Pituophis melanoleucus*
- Colubridae (colubrids)
- Pinewoods, grasslands, and farms
- Egg-layers, producing up to 16 or more eggs; average 8.7
- Small mammals
- Spotty distribution in southeast and eastern USA

GOPHER AND BULL SNAKES

Other members of the genus *Pituophis* are the gopher snakes and the Bull Snake. They are the counterpart of the Pine Snake in the western region of the USA and were formerly classified as the same species. These snakes are found in many different habitats, including prairies, dry hillsides, semi-arid places, and even true deserts. They are commonly found near cultivated and irrigated land, probably attracted by large numbers of rodents. Like the Pine Snake, they are expert ratters and are, therefore, beneficial to humans.

SAN DIEGO GOPHER SNAKE

CHEQUERED GARTER SNAKE

One of the most adaptable species of garter snake, the Chequered Garter Snake never occurs far from water, and it has extended its geographic range into deserts and semi-arid regions by living alongside seasonal streambeds and irrigation ditches. Usually diurnal, in such places it sometimes become nocturnal in order to avoid high daytime temperatures. It also reduces its dependency on fish and amphibians for food by adding nestling rodents to its diet.

Main characteristics

This is the only garter snake with a pattern of bold, squarish blotches on either side of a cream mid-dorsal stripe. The dark collar marking just behind the head is also characteristic. The head is uniform in colour with the exception of a small light-coloured marking on the top. Like all garter snakes, this species has heavily keeled scales and a slender body shape, although it is more stocky than many of the other species.

HEAD COLOUR
The head is invariably olive on top. The light-coloured lip scales often have short, dark bars along the edges, and these radiate out from the region of the eyes.

Large eyes
The Chequered Garter Snake has large eyes with round pupils and hunts by day

Tapering snout
The snout is long and tapering, like that of all garter snakes

Slender tail
The tail is long and slender. The thickness of the tail towards the base shows that this is a male snake – in females it is thinner

AVERAGE ADULT LENGTH

75 cm (2 ft 5 in)

0 cm		50 cm		1 m
0 in		1 ft 6 in		3 ft 3 in

CHEQUERED GARTER SNAKE
The chequerboard pattern is distinctive enough to give this species its common name; other garter snakes are boldly striped.

Head scales
Large plate-like scales cover the head. There is a small marking on the top of the head

GARTER SNAKE WITH STRIPED PATTERN

PLAINS GARTER SNAKE

The Plains Garter Snake is found further north than the Chequered Garter Snake. It is one of several garter snakes with a striped pattern, but the bright orange, mid-dorsal stripe is a reliable identification characteristic. More dependent on water than the chequered species, it is only common in river valleys and around the edges of ponds.

FACT FILE

- *Thamnophis marcianus*

- Colubridae (colubrids)

- Ponds, streams, rivers, and ditches, often in otherwise arid places

- Live-bearers, producing 5–31 young; average 14.9

- Fish, frogs, toads, tadpoles, lizards, and small mammals

- North and Central America, from Kansas, New Mexico, and Arizona, into northern Mexico; spotty distribution in Central America

SAN FRANCISCO GARTER SNAKE

The San Francisco Garter Snake is a subspecies of the Common, or Eastern, Garter Snake. The species is widely distributed over North America, where it occurs in several colour forms and subspecies. Many of these forms are quite common, but this particular one is critically endangered because most of its habitat has already been destroyed, and the remaining portions are threatened by encroaching development and channelling of water sources underground.

BASKING IN SUNSHINE
The San Francisco Garter Snake is most active in the afternoon, after the typical San Francisco morning mist has cleared and the sun has broken through.

Main characteristics

Two broad red stripes on either side of a greenish yellow or bluish stripe along the centre of the back, all edged in black, make this one of the most distinctive garter snakes. The top of the head is also red. A slender body shape and heavily keeled scales distinguish the San Francisco Garter Snake from all other striped snakes found in the region.

IDENTIFYING GARTER SNAKES

Garter snakes can be very difficult to identify, especially if several species occur in the same area. One of the most reliable guides to identification is the position of the stripes along the centre of the snake's back and along the flanks. Species tend to be highly consistent in the arrangement of these stripes and the scale rows on which they occur. The two species illustrated demonstrate this point: note the differences in the width and coloration of the stripes.

SAN FRANCISCO GARTER SNAKE

PLAINS GARTER SNAKE

SAN FRANCISCO GARTER SNAKE
The uninterrupted, bright red stripes along the San Francisco Garter Snake's body contrast strongly with the wide bluish mid-dorsal stripe. It is one of North America's most beautiful snakes, as well as being one of its rarest, despite being protected.

Striking coloration
Bright stripes edged in black cover the upper part of the body

AVERAGE ADULT LENGTH

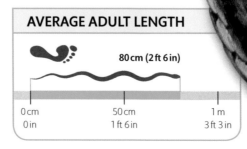

80 cm (2 ft 6 in)

0 cm	50 cm	1 m
0 in	1 ft 6 in	3 ft 3 in

FACT FILE

- *Thamnophis sirtalis tetrataenia*

- Colubridae (colubrids)

- Ponds, marshes, roadside ditches, and streams

- Live-bearing, producing 12–24 young

- Frogs and toads, fish, and small mammals. Invertebrates on occasion

- Western parts of the San Francisco Peninsula, California, USA

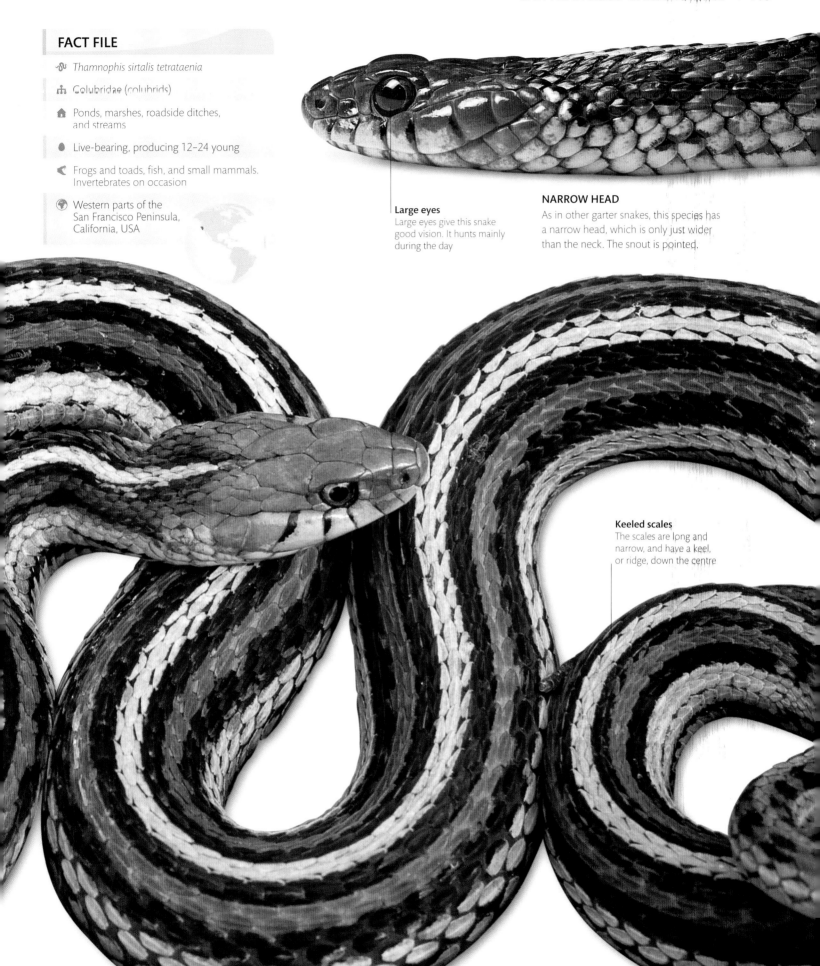

Large eyes
Large eyes give this snake good vision. It hunts mainly during the day

NARROW HEAD
As in other garter snakes, this species has a narrow head, which is only just wider than the neck. The snout is pointed.

Keeled scales
The scales are long and narrow, and have a keel, or ridge, down the centre

LEOPARD SNAKE

This small ratsnake is arguably the most attractive of all the European snakes. It lives among rocks and dry stone walls, often near fields and human dwellings, where it hunts for mice. Because it is active mainly at night, it is rarely seen, even in places where it is common. Although there is considerable variation in its markings, it is always brightly coloured. It is sometimes mistaken for a viper and therefore killed needlessly, despite its beneficial feeding habits.

Main characteristics

The Leopard Snake is slender and dainty in appearance. It is usually cream, yellowish, or light grey with dark red or reddish brown markings finely outlined in black. These markings may be arranged in a number of different ways, depending on the snake's geographic origins. The bold markings on its head are characteristic.

AVERAGE ADULT LENGTH

70 cm (2 ft 3 in)

0 cm	50 cm	1 m
0 in	1 ft 6 in	3 ft 3 in

Smooth scales
Unlike most ratsnakes, the Leopard Snake has smooth scales

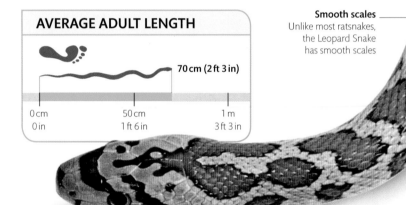

Narrow head
The slim head restricts the size of prey the snake can consume

Large eyes
The large eyes have orange irises and round pupils. Their outlines are disguised by several dark markings, which radiate outwards

HEAD MARKINGS
The head is light in colour with a bold, black marking between the eyes, and another running from the top of each eye to the angle of the jaw. The head is covered in large scales.

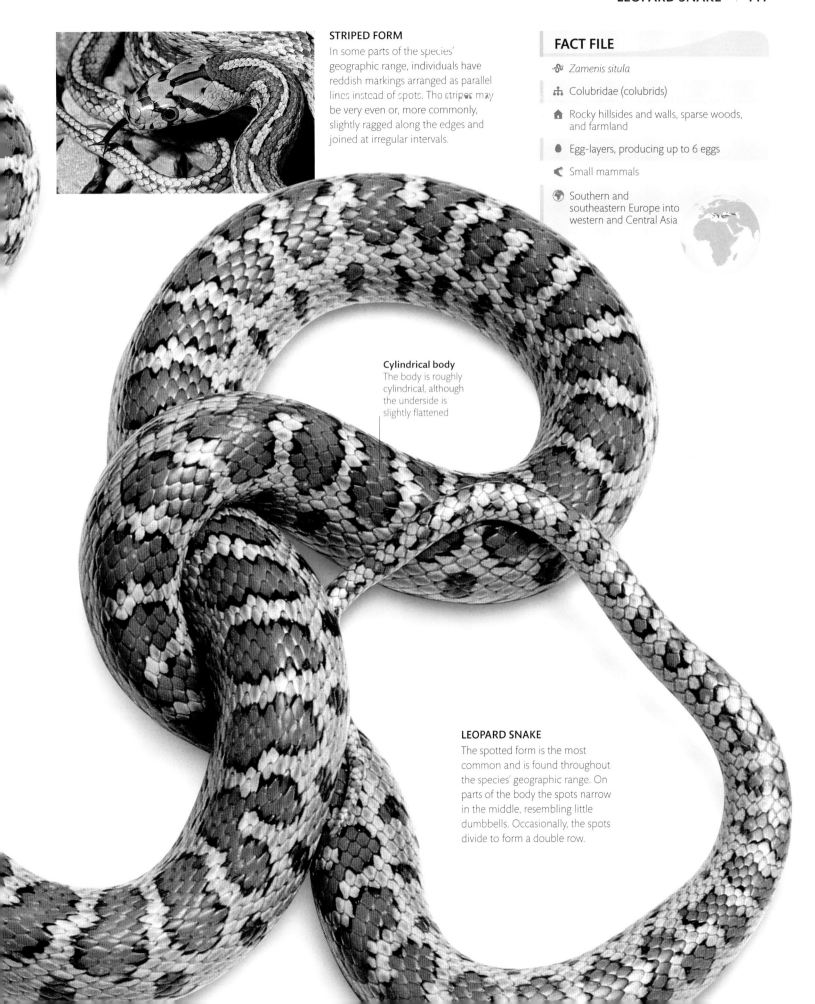

STRIPED FORM
In some parts of the species'
geographic range, individuals have
reddish markings arranged as parallel
lines instead of spots. The stripes may
be very even or, more commonly,
slightly ragged along the edges and
joined at irregular intervals.

Cylindrical body
The body is roughly
cylindrical, although
the underside is
slightly flattened

LEOPARD SNAKE
The spotted form is the most
common and is found throughout
the species' geographic range. On
parts of the body the spots narrow
in the middle, resembling little
dumbbells. Occasionally, the spots
divide to form a double row.

NORTHERN DEATH ADDER

Although death adders look and behave like vipers, they are members of the cobra family. Because there are no vipers in Australasia, death adders have evolved to fill their ecological niche (see p.8). Their potent, fast-acting venom and sluggish habits make them responsible for a high proportion of Australia's serious snakebites.

ENTICING LURE
The snake rests with the body well hidden and its curled tail exposed near its head. The tail tip is a different colour from the body and is twitched enticingly if potential prey appears.

Main characteristics

A thickset body, superficially more like that of a viper than a member of the cobra family, and colours and markings that closely match those of its surroundings, make the death adders unmistakable in Australia and New Guinea. The Northern Death Adder can be identified by raised edges along the scales over the eyes (known as the supraocular scales).

FACT FILE

- *Acanthophis praelongus*
- Elapidae (cobras and their relatives)
- Wet and dry forests
- Live-bearers, producing up to 20 young
- Lizards and mammals
- Northern Australia and New Guinea

TRIANGULAR HEAD
The head is short and triangular with a sloping snout. The head scales are smaller than those of other members of the cobra family, but not fragmented like those of true vipers.

Raised edges
These horn-like structures directly above the eyes give the Northern Death Adder its characteristic profile. Their function is still unknown

Thin tail
The tail tip is thin and roughened, and may look like a caterpillar or a worm to a foraging lizard or mouse. Jerky movements enhance the effect

AVERAGE ADULT LENGTH

50 cm (1 ft 6 in)

| 0 cm | 50 cm | 1 m |
| 0 in | 1 ft 6 in | 3 ft 3 in |

NORTHERN DEATH ADDER

Its dark coloration, thick body, and chunky head give the Northern Death Adder a rather sinister appearance. Although it is highly venomous, it never bites unless provoked and prefers to avoid confrontation.

DESERT DEATH ADDER

The Desert Death Adder, *Acanthophis pyrrhus*, occurs in the remote desert regions of central Australia, where its striking reddish coloration matches the red soil and rock on which it lives. Its natural history is not as well known as that of the other species of death adder, but it is presumed to have a similar lifestyle.

RED COLORATION PROVIDES IDEAL DESERT CAMOUFLAGE

WEST AFRICAN GREEN MAMBA

The West African Green Mamba is one of three green species of mamba. All belong to the genus *Dendroaspis* (tree asp) and are similar in appearance. Mambas are among the most notorious of the venomous African snakes, even though bites are rare. If disturbed, they will try to escape and will only bite if cornered. The bite is highly dangerous, often proving fatal if not treated immediately.

Main characteristics

A brightly coloured snake with large scales, the West African Green Mamba has an elegant, pointed head and conspicuous eyes. It is primarily green in colour, but the scales on the long tail are yellow and edged in black, giving the impression of a braided rope. Its large dorsal scales are arranged in 13 rows, far fewer than are present on most snakes.

BLACK MAMBA

At a length of up to 3.5 m (11 ft), the Black Mamba, *Dendroaspis polylepis*, is the longest venomous – and probably the most feared – snake in Africa. It rears up when threatened, and a large one could easily look a human in the face! At breeding time, males entwine their bodies and attempt to force each other to the ground. The Black Mamba varies in colour from brown to grey or olive, but is never black.

MALES IN COMBAT

Large scales
The scales are huge, especially down the centre of the back. They are smooth, but not particularly shiny

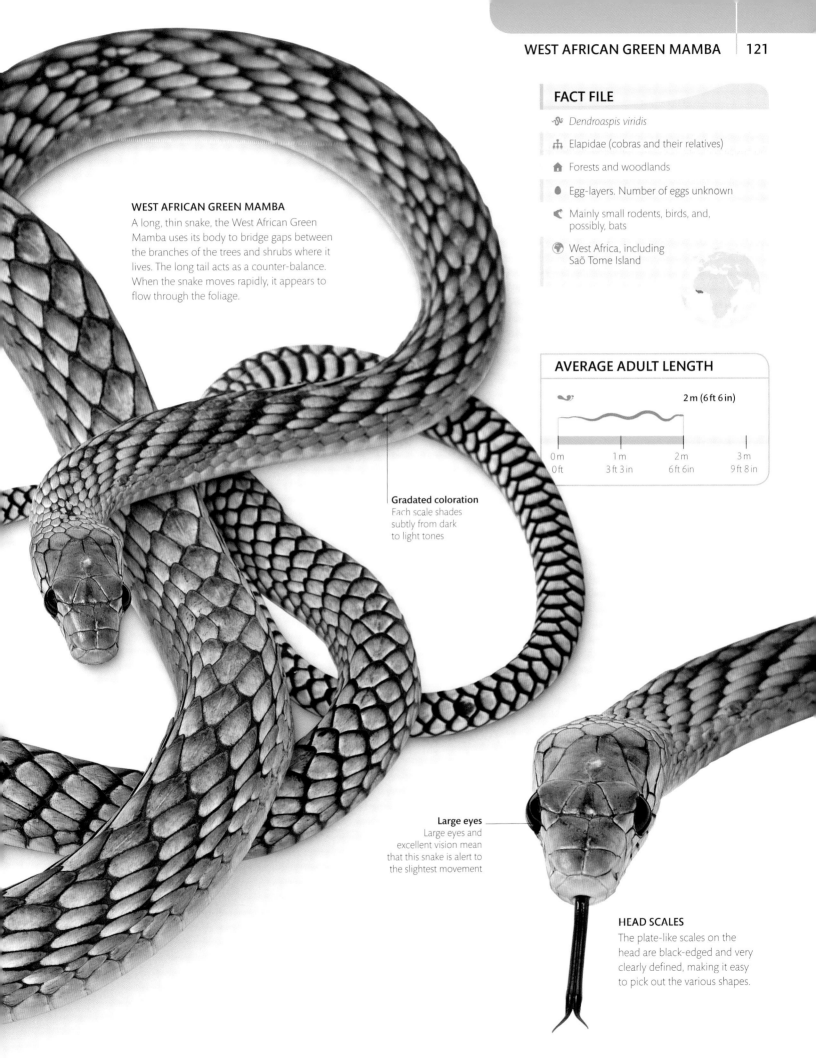

WEST AFRICAN GREEN MAMBA

A long, thin snake, the West African Green Mamba uses its body to bridge gaps between the branches of the trees and shrubs where it lives. The long tail acts as a counter-balance. When the snake moves rapidly, it appears to flow through the foliage.

FACT FILE

- *Dendroaspis viridis*
- Elapidae (cobras and their relatives)
- Forests and woodlands
- Egg-layers. Number of eggs unknown
- Mainly small rodents, birds, and, possibly, bats
- West Africa, including Saõ Tome Island

AVERAGE ADULT LENGTH

2 m (6 ft 6 in)

0 m	1 m	2 m	3 m
0 ft	3 ft 3 in	6 ft 6 in	9 ft 8 in

Gradated coloration
Each scale shades subtly from dark to light tones

Large eyes
Large eyes and excellent vision mean that this snake is alert to the slightest movement

HEAD SCALES
The plate-like scales on the head are black-edged and very clearly defined, making it easy to pick out the various shapes.

CHINESE COBRA

The most common species of cobra over much of southern China and adjoining countries, this snake lives mostly in open areas, such as grasslands, fields, and lightly wooded areas. It feeds on a variety of prey, including fish, amphibians, birds, and mammals. It is not an aggressive species, although its potentially lethal venom and habit of living in close proximity to humans make it a constant threat wherever it is found.

FACT FILE

- *Naja atra*
- Elapidae (cobras and their relatives)
- Grasslands, fields, and lightly wooded areas
- Egg-layers. Clutch size is unknown
- Fish, amphibians, birds, and mammals
- Southern China, Thailand, Vietnam, and Taiwan

Main characteristics

Thickset for a cobra, this species is usually dark brown or black. Occasional specimens are lighter in colour. It has a number of widely spaced, indistinct, light bands, one scale wide, around the body. There is an eyespot marking on the back of the hood, but this is also true of the Monocled Cobra (see opposite), and the two species may be confused: until recently, they were classified as a single species.

CHINESE COBRA
This classic cobra rears up when alarmed and spreads its hood by altering the position of its ribs. The spreading of the hood is intended to intimidate prey by making the snake look larger. It may also serve to indicate its venomous nature to potential predators.

AVERAGE ADULT LENGTH

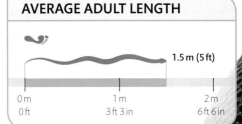

1.5 m (5 ft)

0 m	1 m	2 m
0 ft	3 ft 3 in	6 ft 6 in

Heavy body
This species is heavily built, although many members of the cobra family are slender

HOODED HEAD
The hood widens just behind the head and is marked with a conspicuous eyespot. Large scales cover the top of the head.

Dull scales
The scales are smooth, but appear dull rather than shiny

Eyespot marking
On top of the neck is a light circle with a black centre and black edging

MONOCLED COBRA

Snake charmers often choose to work with the Monocled Cobra because, although it is instantly recognizable as a venomous snake, it normally has a placid disposition. Its name refers to the single eyespot marking on the hood, which looks like a monocle.

Main characteristics

Like the Chinese Cobra (see opposite), this species is heavily built and has a single eye-spot on the hood. However, on average, the Monocled Cobra is slightly smaller than the Chinese Cobra. In addition, it is lighter in colour, and the pale flecks on the back, if present, are more randomly scattered. The light coloured head is devoid of any markings.

FACT FILE

- *Naja kaouthia*
- Elapidae (cobras and their relatives)
- Fields and sparse forests
- Egg-layers. Clutch size is unknown
- Fish, amphibians, birds, and mammals
- Northern and northeastern India, southern China, and Southeast Asia

Large eyes
The eyes are moderately large and, being dark, contrast strongly with the scales around them

Light coloration
This snake is light brown, with pale flecks

MONOCLED COBRA
The Monocled Cobra spreads its hood to look larger and thus intimidate enemies. It does not spread its hood when hunting, although it may raise its head to obtain a better view of its surroundings.

AVERAGE ADULT LENGTH

1.3 m (4 ft 3 in)

| 0 cm | 50 cm | 1 m | 1.5 m |
| 0 in | 1 ft 6 in | 3 ft 3 in | 5 ft |

HOOD MARKS
Eyespot markings such as this serve as a warning signal throughout the animal kingdom. The marking also gives the snake its name.

Smooth scales
This species has the typical smooth scales of the genus *Naja*

Distinctive monocle
This is usually white or cream with a black border and two or three black spots

RED SPITTING COBRA

A small cobra from the dry grasslands and scrubby habitats of East and northeastern Africa, the Red Spitting Cobra is set apart from other cobras by its reddish brown colour. This species defends itself from a distance by squirting jets of venom at high pressure through small apertures located in the front of each fang. If the venom enters the human eye, it is extremely painful. When hunting, the snake injects venom through biting. As a last resort, it will also defend itself in this way. However, bite victims usually recover quickly.

RED SPITTING COBRA
The deep red coloration of this individual is related to its maturity – juveniles are a brighter red and gradually become darker as they grow. The Red Spitting Cobra's scales will also become dull when it is about to shed its skin.

Main characteristics

This cobra is moderately slender with smooth, shiny scales. It has a narrow hood, unlike the Asian cobras, which have wide, pear-shaped hoods. It is usually red or reddish brown, but can sometimes be olive or grey. It has a broad, dark band on the throat, which is plainly visible when the snake rears up. The hood is erected only when an individual feels threatened.

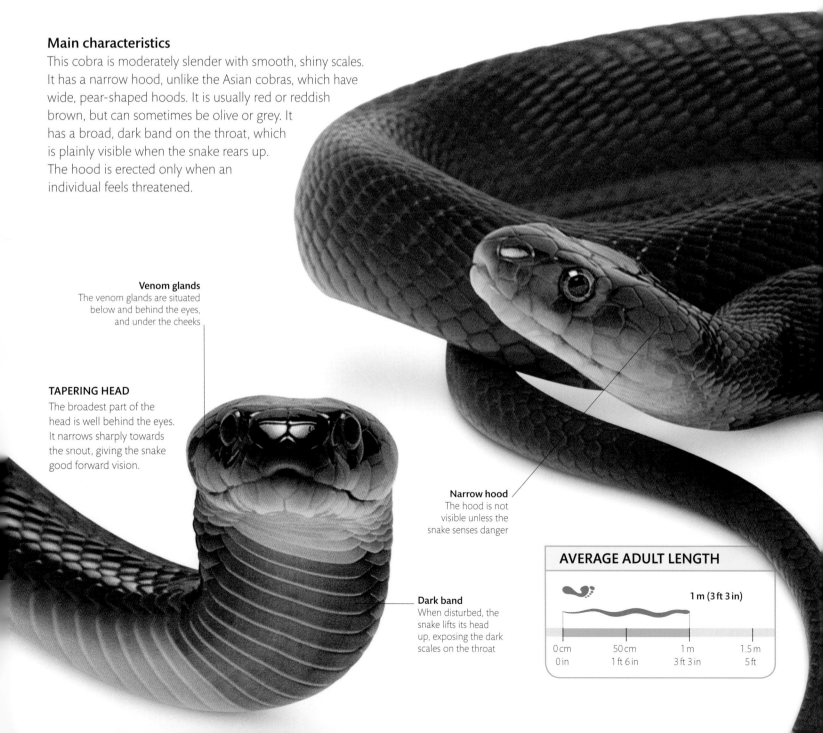

Venom glands
The venom glands are situated below and behind the eyes, and under the cheeks

TAPERING HEAD
The broadest part of the head is well behind the eyes. It narrows sharply towards the snout, giving the snake good forward vision.

Narrow hood
The hood is not visible unless the snake senses danger

Dark band
When disturbed, the snake lifts its head up, exposing the dark scales on the throat

AVERAGE ADULT LENGTH

1 m (3 ft 3 in)

0 cm	50 cm	1 m	1.5 m
0 in	1 ft 6 in	3 ft 3 in	5 ft

FACT FILE

- *Naja pallida*
- Elapidae (cobras and their relatives)
- Dry grassland and semi-desert
- Egg-layers, producing up to 15 eggs
- Other snakes, birds, and small mammals
- East and northeastern Africa

ARID HABITAT

This snake lives among the sparse vegetation of oases, hillsides, and riverbanks. Adults hide among piles of vegetation or in burrows. They are predominantly nocturnal, but juveniles are sometimes active by day. If disturbed the Red Spitting Cobra will move away rapidly.

Camouflage colours
The reddish brown coloration blends into dry vegetation, but looks conspicuous when the snake is seen out of habitat

Shiny scales
This species has smooth, glossy scales

COLLETT'S SNAKE

A handsome Australian cobra, living in an isolated region of semi-arid grasslands and lightly wooded places, Collett's Snake is thought to adapt its lifestyle to the seasons, being active by day during the winter and nocturnal during the hotter parts of summer. Little is known about its natural habits. Although, as a venomous species, it is potentially dangerous, it is unlikely to have caused human fatalities.

Main characteristics

Collett's Snake is a stocky species with a distinctive colour pattern in which dark brown and reddish scales combine to create a coppery overall coloration. The scales on the lower flanks are often arranged in irregular patches, and sometimes suggest a cross-banded arrangement. The body may be speckled.

COLLETT'S SNAKE

This snake is undoubtedly one of the more colourful Australian species. Although it only occurs with dark brown and reddish coloration, Collett's Snake belongs to a genus, *Pseudechis*, whose members are sometimes known collectively as black snakes.

AVERAGE ADULT LENGTH

1.5 m (5 ft)

| 0 m | 1 m | 2 m |
| 0 ft | 3 ft 3 in | 6 ft 6 in |

Smooth scales

The scales are smooth, but not very shiny. Each scale is a single colour, resulting in a mosaic-like pattern with jagged edges

Copper pattern

The dark brown and red pattern is thought to camouflage this species when it is resting on the dark red soils of its desert habitat

FACT FILE

- *Pseudechis colletti*

- Elapidae (cobras and their relatives)

- Grasslands and lightly wooded areas

- Egg-layers. Clutch size is unknown

- Probably amphibians, lizards, snakes, and small mammals

- Central Queensland, Australia

Large scales
Like most of the cobra family and the harmless colubrids, the scales on the snake's head are large and very well-defined

Cylindrical body
The body is roughly cylindrical in cross-section, indicating a burrowing or terrestrial lifestyle. Collett's Snake is thought to hide in burrows, or beneath dead vegetation and other debris, and hunts on the ground

TIGER SNAKES

Tiger snakes, which belong to the genus *Notechis*, are close relatives of Collett's Snakes. There are two species, both very dangerous, which are responsible for most snake-bite deaths in Australia. The Mainland Island Snake is found on the mainland, Tasmania, and many of the small islands in the Bass Straits. Some of these island populations, notably that of Chappel Island, are remarkable for their eating habits. The snakes gorge on mutton-bird chicks during the birds' nesting season, but for the rest of the year have little or no food, although juveniles eat small lizards. As an adaptation to this enforced feast and famine regime, the Chappel Island Tiger Snakes grow to roughly twice the size of tiger snakes on the mainland. This enables them to store fat efficiently, and thus to survive between nesting seasons.

MAINLAND ISLAND SNAKE

CHAPPEL ISLAND TIGER SNAKE

COPPERHEAD

Distinctively marked pit vipers, Copperheads are closely related to rattlesnakes. They live in a variety of habitats and can be quite common in places, although excellent camouflage and their habit of remaining motionless mean that they often go unnoticed. Although venomous, Copperheads try to avoid confrontation. Their bite is only rarely serious.

Main characteristics

A coppery coloured head and broad bands of chestnut brown and orange, tan, or grey combine to give the Copperhead its unmistakable appearance. The band colours vary between different populations, but always contrast sharply with the background colour. A number of subspecies are recognized. Some water snakes have similar markings, but seen at close quarters, the facial pits distinguish the Copperhead.

CHUNKY HEAD
The wide head ends in an upturned snout. Moderately large eyes and vertical pupils indicate that the snake is primarily nocturnal, although it can be active during the day in cool weather.

Faint markings
In contrast to the rest of the body, the head is uniform in colour, with only faint traces of the facial markings found in many other pit vipers

Matt scales
The matt texture of the scales, combined with pastel hues, enhances the snake's camouflage

FOREST CAMOUFLAGE
Although the Copperhead's markings appear gaudy when seen in isolation, they provide exceptionally good camouflage when the snake is resting among dead leaves. The banded markings also serve to break up the snake's outline, making it hard for predators to identify its shape.

TAIL TIP
The tip of a juvenile Copperhead's tail is bright yellow and is used as a lure to entice small frogs and lizards to come within striking range. As the snake matures, its hunting methods and choice of prey alter. Consequently, the bright coloration gradually fades. The Copperhead vibrates its tail when aroused to produce a warning rustling or rattling noise, especially where it makes contact with dead leaves.

COPPERHEAD

The wide head, tapering quickly to a narrow neck, gives the Copperhead its distinctive shape, and the coppery colour gives the snake its name. It is also known as the Moccasin, but this name is best avoided because it also applies to other snakes.

Varying band width
The dark bands widen on the flanks. Although the two halves of each band often correspond exactly, they are sometimes staggered or broken in places

Broad head
The venom glands behind the eyes give this viper a spade-shaped head

AVERAGE ADULT LENGTH

80 cm (2 ft 6 in)

0 cm	50 cm	1 m
0 in	1 ft 6 in	3 ft 3 in

FACT FILE

- *Agkistrodon contortrix*
- Viperidae (vipers and pit vipers)
- Rocky hillsides, semi-deserts, woodland, grassland, and swamps
- Live-bearers, producing 3–21 eggs; average 7
- Frogs, birds, and small mammals
- Central and Eastern USA; adjacent states of North Mexico

PUFF ADDER

A large, slow-moving viper, the Puff Adder is responsible for a significant number of snakebite accidents in Africa. It is not aggressive, but relies heavily on its camouflage, so it is easily overlooked by humans and can inadvertently be trodden upon. It strikes quickly, and its long fangs penetrate deeply. Its potent venom is produced in huge quantities. Although this snake kills many people in rural areas, death is usually preventable if suitable medical treatment is available.

Main characteristics

It would be difficult to mistake the Puff Adder for any other species. Despite variations in colour, the combination of wide body, broad head, and rounded snout, together with the pattern of clearly defined chevrons on the back, makes it instantly identifiable. Unless in a hurry, which is seldom, it moves slowly forward in a straight line.

Distinguishing pattern
A distinctive pattern of dark chevrons helps to identify the Puff Adder

PUFF ADDER
The Puff Adder's massive body becomes even larger when it is annoyed or cornered. It inflates itself with air, which it then releases, producing an intimidating, loud, low-pitched hiss or a drawn-out "sssssssh" sound. Puff Adders from desert regions tend to be paler than this more typically coloured individual.

BRIGHT COLORATION
Considering their large geographic range, Puff Adders vary little in coloration and markings. The most strikingly marked individuals come from the Cape region of South Africa, where males have bright yellow and sooty black markings.

Keeled scales
Heavily keeled scales are typical of most of the viper family. Their matt, roughened texture enhances the snake's camouflage when it is lying in vegetation

AVERAGE ADULT LENGTH

95 cm (3 ft)

0 cm	50 cm	1 m
0 in	1 ft 6 in	3 ft 3 in

FACT FILE

- *Bitis arietans*
- Viperidae (vipers and pit vipers)
- Grasslands, scrub, mountainsides, and semi-deserts
- Live-bearers, producing up to 50 young (exceptionally 100 and one record of 156)
- Mainly rodents
- Africa and southwestern Arabia

Small eyes
The eyes are small with vertical pupils. They are positioned towards the top of the head

Broad head
The head is broad in order to accommodate the huge venom glands

PEAR-SHAPED HEAD
The Puff Adder's broad, pear-shaped head is covered in numerous small scales. Its eyes are small and not immediately obvious, due to the dark stripe passing through them.

GABOON VIPER

Originally described from sightings in Gabon (hence the common and Latin names), the Gaboon Viper is a much feared snake, although bites are rare. It lurks among dead leaves in dappled light, its outline disguised by the geometric pattern of rectangles and triangles along its body. It hardly moves, preferring to wait for its prey to come within range, then it strikes with great speed, injecting venom with fangs that can be up to 4 cm (1^1/$_2$ in) long.

Textured scales
The large, keeled scales have a velvety texture, enhanced by their soft pastel shades

Main characteristics

The most obvious feature of this species is its impressive size, especially the thickness of the body and the width of the great, triangular head, the top of which is always pale in colour. Its geometric pattern, in shades of pastel grey, buff, and purple, is also distinctive. It would be difficult to mistake this snake for any other.

BROAD HEAD
Nearly as broad as it is long, the head widens considerably behind the eyes. The two horns at the tip of the snout vary in size. Those of the West African species, *Bitis rhinoceros*, are bigger, on average, than those specimens from the rest of the species' geographic range.

Venom gland
The width of the head is due to the venom glands, which are situated below and behind each eye. The glands are extremely large and produce and store huge quantities of venom

Prominent markings
There are prominent wedge-shaped markings on the side of the head

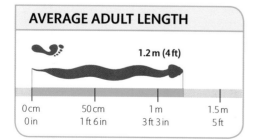

AVERAGE ADULT LENGTH

1.2 m (4 ft)

0 cm	50 cm	1 m	1.5 m
0 in	1 ft 6 in	3 ft 3 in	5 ft

FACT FILE

- *Bitis gabonica*
- Viperidae (vipers and pit vipers)
- Edges of forests and forest clearings
- Live-bearers, producing up to 60 young
- Small and medium-sized mammals
- Central and southern Africa

GABOON VIPER

A massive viper from the rainforests of West Africa, the coloration and markings seem garish when the snake is seen out of habitat. However, in its natural environment, the snake's camouflage is superb. Because of its markings, its sedentary lifestyle, and the sparse population of the area in which it lives, this snake is seldom seen.

Stout body
The stout body is typical of "sit-and-wait" predators, which do not need to chase after prey. When alarmed, the Gaboon Viper can puff up its body to an even greater girth. It produces a loud, low-pitched hiss when it exhales

Geometric markings
Grey, buff, and purple rectangles and triangles are arranged in a geometric pattern along the body

EXPERT CAMOUFLAGE

The ability of this species to blend into its forest surroundings is legendary. When lying on leaves, the Gaboon Viper's kaleidoscopic patches of different colours serve to break up its outline, and the eyes are disguised by the head markings.

JARARACA

The Jararaca belongs to the group of snakes commonly known as lanceheads. The snake's common name is derived from Amerindian; alternative versions are *Yararaca* and *Yarar*. Due to the Jararaca's excellent camouflage, abundance, and liking for cultivated areas and forest clearings, humans are frequently bitten. Although the venom is potent, medical intervention prevents most fatalities.

Main characteristics

It can be difficult to distinguish this species of viper from several other lanceheads that are found in the same part of the world. The triangular head and pointed snout are common to all lanceheads, and the Jararaca's coloration is too variable to be a good identification characteristic. Triangular blotches along the back are often obscured by dark pigmentation, especially in adults, and there is often more contrast in the markings of juveniles.

FACT FILE

- *Bothrops jararaca*
- Viperidae (vipers and pit vipers)
- Grasslands and forest clearings
- Live-bearers, thought to produce about 20 young
- Birds and small mammals
- Southern Brazil, northeastern Paraguay, and into northern Argentina

JARARACA

A long, dark body, obscure markings, and a preference for shady places make this snake hard to see and, therefore, dangerous to people working on the land. The triangular shape of its head is the result of large venom glands immediately behind its eyes.

Keeled scales
Dark coloration and heavily keeled scales give this snake a matt, almost sooty appearance

TRIANGULAR HEAD

The broad, triangular head and arrow-shaped marking are characteristic, and it is easy to see why this group of snakes has been given the common name of lancehead. The vertical pupils identify it as a nocturnal hunter.

Conspicuous heat pits
Heat pits enable the Jararaca to hunt effectively at night

AVERAGE ADULT LENGTH

1.5 m (5 ft)

| 0 m | 1 m | 2 m |
| 0 ft | 3 ft 3 in | 6 ft 6 in |

Geometric coloration
The tips of triangular blotches meet along the centre of the snake's back. However, these may be indistinct

FER-DE-LANCE

Other lanceheads are found throughout Central and South America. The most common, and therefore the most familiar, is *Bothrops asper*, from Central and northern South America. Like the similar *Bothrops atrox*, this species is sometimes known as a Fer-de-Lance, but its Spanish name of *Terciopelo*, meaning "velvet", is more appropriate. It is responsible for a large number of human fatalities.

JUVENILE EATING A TEIID LIZARD

DESERT HORNED VIPER

An inhabitant of the Sahara Desert, the Desert Horned Viper has made some interesting adaptations to its environment. To move across loose, windblown sand, it uses an unusual technique called sidewinding (see p.19). To escape the notice of predators and to ambush its prey, it conceals itself beneath the sand. It adjusts its period of activity according to the season: in the hot summer it becomes nocturnal, but at cooler times of the year it is diurnal. It is unusual among vipers in that it lays eggs.

Ridged horns
Each horn has a ridge running along it, and the horns may bend forwards slightly

Main characteristics

A short, stocky viper, this snake has rough scales and a distinctive "horn" over each eye. Its colour varies slightly but is usually dirty yellow, buff, cream, or light brown with scattered and irregular crossbars and blotches of a darker shade.

MYSTERIOUS HORNS
When the viper shuffles down into the sand, only the eyes and horns are visible. Each horn is a single scale, modified into a thorn-like structure. The function of the horns is not certain. They may help to reduce glare from the sun since they are found in other species of vipers from desert habitats.

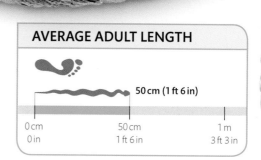

BLUNT HEAD
The Desert Horned Viper has the typical wide, blunt head found throughout the viper family. It has large eyes with vertical pupils. A covering of small, heavily keeled scales gives the head a rough texture.

AVERAGE ADULT LENGTH

50 cm (1 ft 6 in)

0 cm	50 cm	1 m
0 in	1 ft 6 in	3 ft 3 in

Keeled scales
The scales are all heavily keeled. Those on its flanks have oblique keels with serrated ridges

DESERT HORNED VIPER
When the Desert Horned Viper rubs its keeled scales together, they produce a loud rasping or "zizzing" noise. The snake uses this device to warn potential predators of its presence.

FACT FILE

- *Cerastes cerastes*
- Viperidae (vipers and pit vipers)
- Deserts
- Egg-layers, producing up to 23 eggs
- Lizards, birds, and small mammals
- North Africa

DESERT CAMOUFLAGE
The Desert Horned Viper is coloured to match the sand on which it lives. This can vary from pale yellow to brown. The snake's hunting strategy is to shuffle down until its body is covered with a fine layer of sand, with just the top of its head showing. From this position, it can strike at small lizards, which make up the bulk of its prey.

SAW-SCALED VIPER

Although small, the Saw-scaled Viper is extremely dangerous because of its venom and its readiness to bite if trodden on or otherwise disturbed. It is responsible for most of the snake-bite fatalities throughout its geographic range because of its abundance and habit of lying partially buried in the sand or soil. Its common name refers to the serrated keels on some of its scales, which are used to produce a hissing sound.

Main characteristics

This species is slender for a viper and has a very distinct, pear-shaped head. Its body pattern is intricate and varies according to the colour of the soil on which it lives, occurring in different shades of brown, beige, or grey, with brown or reddish brown blotches. However, all individuals have black and white spots along the back. There is usually a cross-shaped marking on the head.

Large eyes
The large eyes are positioned towards the top of the head

Complex coloration
The intricate markings break up the viper's outline when it is resting on gravelly sand or among dry vegetation

SAW-SCALED VIPER
Apart from producing a warning sound, the heavily keeled scales help this snake to shuffle down into the sand or soil where it remains motionless, and almost invisible, lying in wait for its prey.

PEAR-SHAPED HEAD
The Saw-scaled Viper has a pear-shaped head with a rounded snout that is covered with many small scales. The depth of the head and position of the eyes enable the snake to see when it is partially buried.

Distinctive spots
The indistinct black-edged white spots are a notable characteristic

FACT FILE

- 🐍 *Echis carinatus*

- 🔬 Viperidae (vipers and pit vipers)

- 🏠 Deserts, dry scrub forests, grasslands, and rocky places

- ● Live-bearers, producing up to 23 young

- 🌙 Most small creatures, from invertebrates to amphibians, reptiles, birds, and mammals

- 🌍 Arabia, Middle East, parts of Central Asia, India, and Sri Lanka

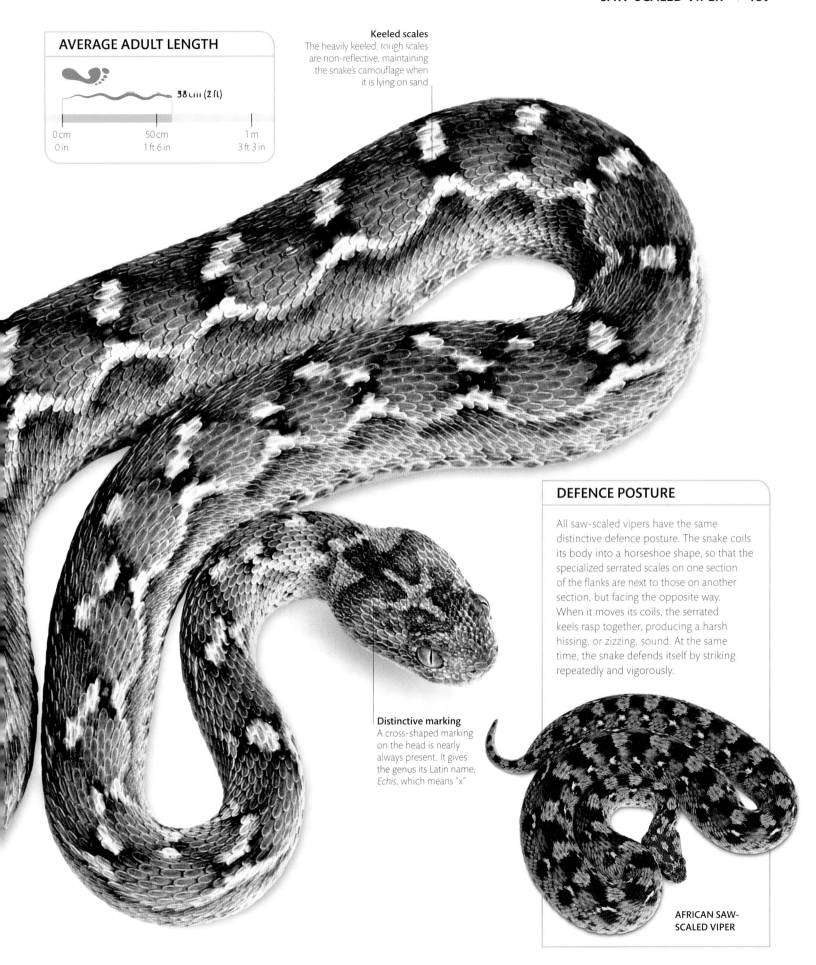

AVERAGE ADULT LENGTH

58 cm (2 ft)

0 cm	50 cm	1 m
0 in	1 ft 6 in	3 ft 3 in

Keeled scales
The heavily keeled, rough scales are non-reflective, maintaining the snake's camouflage when it is lying on sand

Distinctive marking
A cross-shaped marking on the head is nearly always present. It gives the genus its Latin name, *Echis*, which means "x"

DEFENCE POSTURE

All saw-scaled vipers have the same distinctive defence posture. The snake coils its body into a horseshoe shape, so that the specialized serrated scales on one section of the flanks are next to those on another section, but facing the opposite way. When it moves its coils, the serrated keels rasp together, producing a harsh hissing, or zizzing, sound. At the same time, the snake defends itself by striking repeatedly and vigorously.

AFRICAN SAW-SCALED VIPER

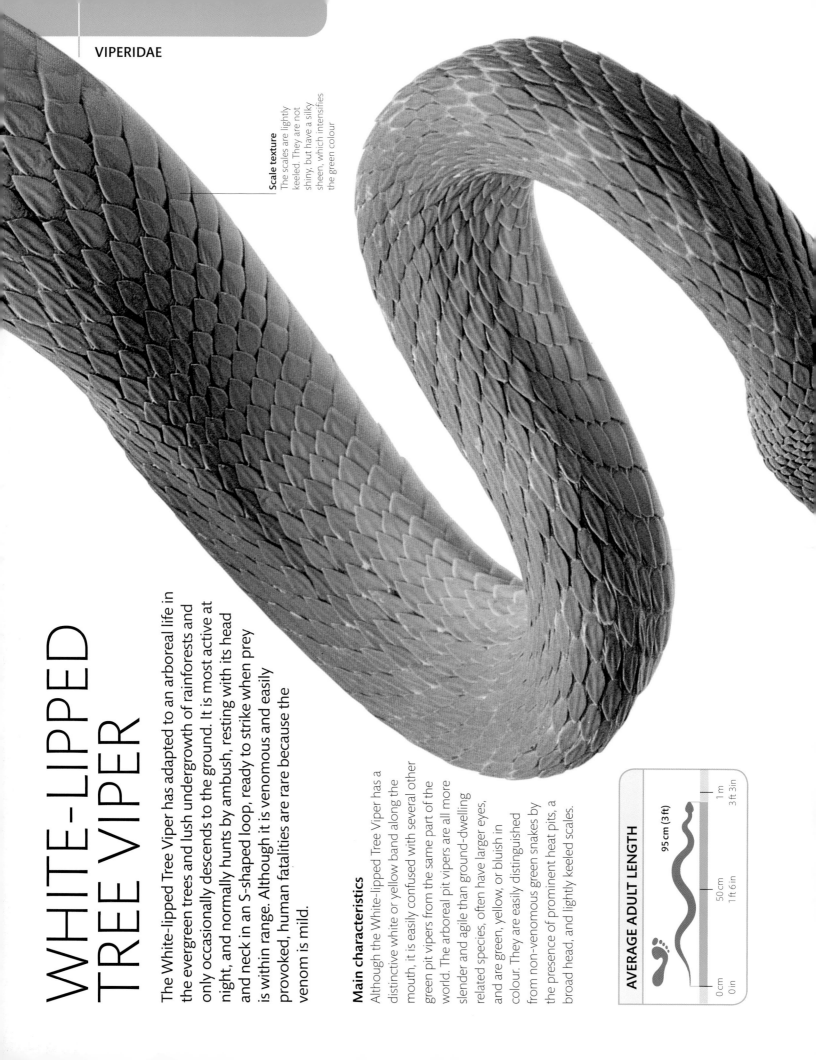

Scale texture
The scales are lightly keeled. They are not shiny, but have a silky sheen, which intensifies the green colour

WHITE-LIPPED TREE VIPER

The White-lipped Tree Viper has adapted to an arboreal life in the evergreen trees and lush undergrowth of rainforests and only occasionally descends to the ground. It is most active at night, and normally hunts by ambush, resting with its head and neck in an S-shaped loop, ready to strike when prey is within range. Although it is venomous and easily provoked, human fatalities are rare because the venom is mild.

Main characteristics

Although the White-lipped Tree Viper has a distinctive white or yellow band along the mouth, it is easily confused with several other green pit vipers from the same part of the world. The arboreal pit vipers are all more slender and agile than ground-dwelling related species, often have larger eyes, and are green, yellow, or bluish in colour. They are easily distinguished from non-venomous green snakes by the presence of prominent heat pits, a broad head, and lightly keeled scales.

AVERAGE ADULT LENGTH

95 cm (3 ft)

1 m
3 ft 3 in

50 cm
1 ft 6 in

0 cm
0 in

ISLAND PIT VIPERS

Pit vipers occur throughout the major archipelagos of the region, such as the Indonesian chain, the Philippines, and Celebes. Many island species, such as the Sumatran Pit Viper, have evolved in isolation from other mainland vipers. All of the island species are at home in rainforests, bamboo thickets, and plantations, where their predominantly green coloration provides excellent camouflage. Heat pits help them to find prey in poor light.

SUMATRAN PIT VIPER REARING UP

WHITE-LIPPED TREE VIPER

The long, slim body of this snake and its green coloration are evidence of an arboreal lifestyle. It can remain motionless, head down and ready to strike, for many minutes – or even hours – waiting for suitable prey to stray within range.

Large heat pits
The heat pits are set into the side of the head and are large. They point directly forwards and work as a pair

FACT FILE

- *Trimeresurus albolabris*
- Viperidae (vipers and pit vipers)
- Forests and plantations, especially near streams
- Live-bearers, producing 10–11 young
- Frogs, birds, and small mammals
- Southern China to India and south to the Indonesian Archipelago, but absent from the Malay peninsula

Yellow eye
The size of the eye and the vertical pupil mark this species as a nocturnal hunter. The eyes are one of its most conspicuous features

WIDE HEAD
The width of the White-lipped Tree Viper's head can be seen clearly from the front. The snake is poised to strike. Its head is drawn back, and the front of the body is tensed in readiness to straighten out suddenly.

NOSE-HORNED VIPER

The Nose-horned Viper inhabits the mountain slopes and hillsides of eastern Europe and Turkey. It may be active by day or by night and often lies, partially hidden, among a jumble of rocks, or at the base of a small bush. It forages for small rodents, lizards, and birds, and often climbs into low shrubs in search of the latter. Although it has fairly potent venom, it is generally inoffensive and reluctant to bite. The isolated populations of Switzerland and Austria have enjoyed full legal protection for many years.

Main characteristics

The horn on the snout and the bold zigzag dorsal marking are enough to distinguish the Nose-horned Viper from any other. Its colour can vary greatly, however. Apart from geographical differences, the sexes are dimorphic (different in appearance). Males are boldly marked with a dark brown or black zigzag on a pale background, whereas females tend to be brown or orange with less contrasting markings. The zigzag stripe often has a dark edging in both sexes. Occasional specimens have a yellowish or pinkish background colour and, very rarely, completely black specimens occur. This is the most common species of viper in the area where it occurs.

Zigzag pattern
A zigzag marking with dark edges running down the back is common to the female and male

GIVING BIRTH

All the members of the genus *Vipera*, to which the Nose-horned Viper belongs, give birth to live young, although a few closely related vipers lay eggs. The Nose-horned Viper mates in April or May, and the young are born the following August or September. They measure 16–18 cm (6–7 in) at birth, and are born with fangs and a small amount of venom. Young snakes take two to four years to reach breeding size.

FACT FILE

- *Vipera ammodytes*
- Viperidae (vipers and pit vipers)
- Dry, rocky, and sandy hillsides and valleys
- Live-bearers, producing 5–15 young
- Lizards, birds, and small mammals
- Southern Austria, northern Italy, the Balkan region, Turkey, and parts of the Middle East

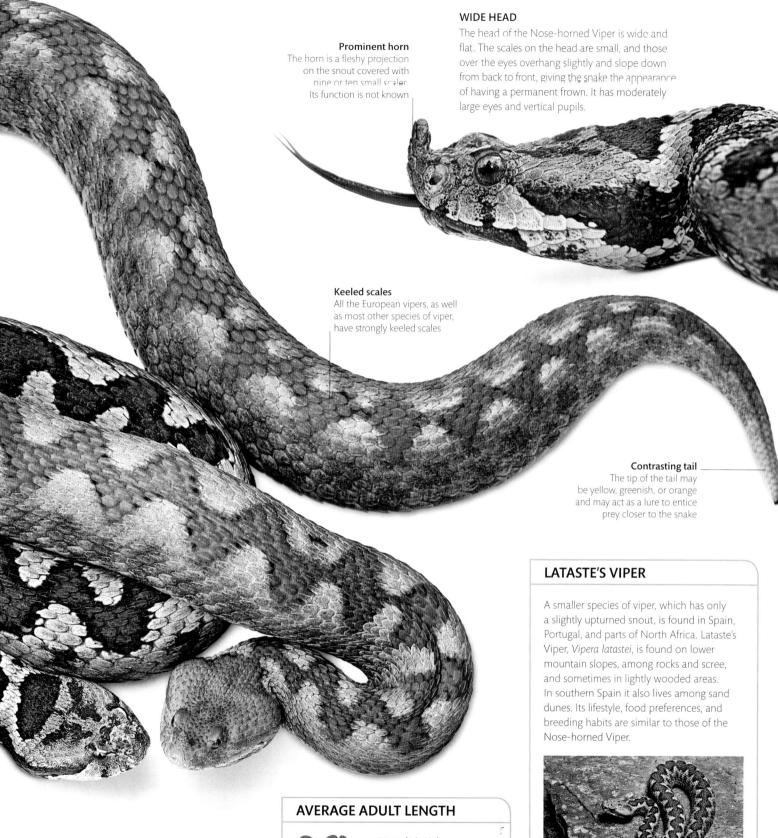

WIDE HEAD
The head of the Nose-horned Viper is wide and flat. The scales on the head are small, and those over the eyes overhang slightly and slope down from back to front, giving the snake the appearance of having a permanent frown. It has moderately large eyes and vertical pupils.

Prominent horn
The horn is a fleshy projection on the snout covered with nine or ten small scales. Its function is not known

Keeled scales
All the European vipers, as well as most other species of viper, have strongly keeled scales

Contrasting tail
The tip of the tail may be yellow, greenish, or orange and may act as a lure to entice prey closer to the snake

LATASTE'S VIPER

A smaller species of viper, which has only a slightly upturned snout, is found in Spain, Portugal, and parts of North Africa. Lataste's Viper, *Vipera latastei*, is found on lower mountain slopes, among rocks and scree, and sometimes in lightly wooded areas. In southern Spain it also lives among sand dunes. Its lifestyle, food preferences, and breeding habits are similar to those of the Nose-horned Viper.

ADULT ON A ROCKY SHELF

NOSE-HORNED VIPERS
Brown or orange individuals of this species are invariably females; males are normally silver-grey with a dark zigzag. There is also some variation from one population to another, possibly corresponding to differently coloured rocks or soils.

AVERAGE ADULT LENGTH

75 cm (2 ft 5 in)

0 cm	50 cm	1 m
0 in	1 ft 6 in	3 ft 3 in

ADDER

Known also as the Northern Viper, the Adder is a familiar species around which many folktales and superstitions have been created. Nearly all of them are inaccurate; the Adder does not swallow its young in times of danger, nor does it form itself into a hoop and roll away. It has the largest geographic range of any terrestrial snake, occurring from northern and central Europe, right across Central Asia to the Pacific coast. It is also found further north than any other species of snake.

Main characteristics

The Adder is a small snake with a narrow head and a distinctive zigzag pattern along the back. Unlike several other vipers, it does not have a darker edging to its dorsal marking, and additional blotches along the flanks alternate with the angles of the zigzag. There is nearly always a dark V- or X-shaped mark on the nape of the neck.

Colour variation
Dark markings on a light background are typical of males, whereas females have brown or reddish markings that contrast less with the background colour

AVERAGE ADULT LENGTH

50 cm (1 ft 6 in)

| 0 cm | 50 cm | 1 m |
| 0 in | 1 ft 6 in | 3 ft 3 in |

BLACK ADDER
A small proportion of adders are completely black. They are more frequent in the colder, more northerly parts of the species' geographic range, as well as on small islands, especially in the Baltic Sea. The black coloration helps this adder to warm up speedily, but it is not well camouflaged.

Dorsal pattern
The dorsal zigzag serves to camouflage the snake and to break up its outline. It is characteristic of most European vipers, although its appearance varies between species

FACT FILE

- Vipera berus
- Viperidae (vipers and pit vipers)
- Varied, including lightly wooded areas, heaths, grasslands, and bogs
- Live-bearers, producing 3–20 young
- Lizards and small mammals
- Northern and central Europe; across Central Asia to the Pacific coast

FOLDING FANGS
The Adder's fangs, like those of all vipers, are hinged and can be folded against the roof of the mouth when not in use. They are erected just before the snake strikes and directed forwards. Venom is forced out through small orifices located near the fang tips.

FIGHTING MALES

Males combat in the spring in order to win the right to mate. A pair of males intertwine the front parts of their bodies and try to wrestle each other to the ground; they do not bite. The loser makes off, and the victor often mates immediately with the female.

SURVIVING COLD TEMPERATURES

The Adder occurs as far north as 69 degrees latitude, which is well inside the Arctic Circle. The Adder's small size and predominantly dark coloration help it to heat up quickly in a cold environment, and its ability to hibernate for many months each winter enables it to survive conditions that would otherwise be fatal. Giving birth to live young is another adaptation to the cold environment.

Dark marking
There is always a dark line from the eye to the angle of the jaw

ADDER

The Adder's markings help it to hide in broken light, especially among fronds of bracken, which commonly grows in its habitat. The contrast between the zigzag and the background colour can vary but, otherwise, the Adder's markings are remarkably consistent across its wide geographic range.

WESTERN DIAMONDBACK RATTLESNAKE

A Western Diamondback Rattlesnake in defensive posture is an awesome spectacle, and very few predators are prepared to tackle it. The snake raises its tail and draws up its body into an S-shape, like a coiled spring, flickering its tongue and vibrating its rattle every time it senses movement that might spell danger. It is active mainly by night, although it may emerge from its hiding place during late afternoon. Large, heavy-bodied individuals often crawl in a straight line rather than wriggle from side to side.

Main characteristics

The Western Diamondback Rattlesnake is a large snake, which sometimes grows to over 1.5 m (5 ft). It is heavy-bodied, often becoming even more bulky with age. The head is wide and triangular, and there is nearly always a dark streak, bordered by a pair of lighter ones, passing from the eye to the angle of the jaw. An obvious identification feature is the black and white banding on the tail just before the rattle.

FACT FILE

- Crotalus atrox
- Viperidae (vipers and pit vipers)
- Deserts, scrub, and rocky hillsides
- Live-bearers, producing 4–21 young
- Birds and mammals
- Southwestern and southcentral USA, into Mexico

RATTLESNAKE ROUNDUPS

A few states in the USA still allow rattlesnake roundups, and the Western Diamondback is the species most affected. Large numbers are slaughtered for the amusement of spectators. As a result, some local populations of diamondback have been virtually eliminated.

AVERAGE ADULT LENGTH

1.3 m (4 ft 3 in)

1.5 m	5 ft
1 m	3 ft 3 in
50 cm	1 ft 6 in
0 cm	0 in

DIAMONDBACKS

Several large rattlesnakes have angular, blotched markings. Some common names reflect this, including those for the Western and Eastern Diamondbacks, and the Red Diamond Rattlesnake.

Banded tail
The stripes act as a visual warning to supplement the audible rattle

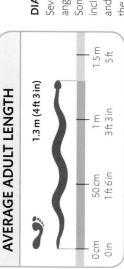

Poison glands
Plump cheeks accommodate large poison glands, situated behind the eyes

Sheathed fangs
When not in use, the fangs are covered with a pair of fleshy sheaths. These slide back out of the way when the fangs are erected and ready for action

FANG ACTION

The snake swings the fangs forward as it strikes so that they stab, rather than bite, their victim. The bones to which the fangs are attached are short and mobile, allowing the whole apparatus to move through 90 degrees.

Heat pits
The heat pits point forward and work together to pinpoint the snake's prey

Warning rattle
The rattle is raised, ready to sound a warning against any potential threat

WESTERN DIAMONDBACK RATTLESNAKE

This species comes in many colour variations to match the surface on which it lives. The rattle, which may have up to 16 segments, is used as a warning signal. It prevents large mammals from trampling the snake by accident, for instance. A new segment is added to the rattle every time the rattlesnake sheds its skin.

Speckled scales
A pattern of small speckles is superimposed over the large dorsal blotches

NEOTROPICAL RATTLESNAKE

Variable in appearance, the Neotropical Rattlesnake has the largest geographic range of any rattlesnake and is the only species found south of Mexico. It is probably responsible for more cases of serious snakebite in South America than any other species, and mortality is high without treatment. The snake's Spanish name, *Cascabel*, means little bell, which is a strangely inappropriate description of its rattle.

Main characteristics

The pair of parallel stripes down the neck make this species easy to identify. In addition, it has a pronounced ridge along the back, caused by spines on top of each vertebra and high keels on the scales covering this part of the body. The body scales are rougher than those of any other species of rattlesnake. Markings are extremely variable, and at least eight subspecies are recognized.

Identifying stripes
A pair of parallel stripes runs down the neck into the upper part of the body. These tend to be dark in colour

FACT FILE

- *Crotalus durissus*
- Viperidae (vipers and pit vipers)
- Dry tropical forests and clearings
- Live-bearers
- Birds and mammals
- Central and South America

NEOTROPICAL RATTLESNAKE
Pale markings in greenish grey are typical of the form of Neotropical Rattlesnake from Brazil. Like all snakes belonging to the species, it is easily provoked into using its rattle as a warning signal when it senses danger.

VENEZUELAN SUBSPECIES

Of all the subspecies of the Neotropical Rattlesnake, *Crotalus durissus vegrandis*, from Venezuela, is the most distinctive. The dorsal markings and the stripes on the neck are mostly obscured by speckles of dark grey and white. This form is sometimes considered to be a full species in its own right.

AVERAGE ADULT LENGTH

1 m (3 ft 3 in)

| 0 cm | 50 cm | 1 m | 1.5 m |
| 0 in | 1 ft 6 in | 3 ft 3 in | 5 ft |

Loud rattle
The rattle produces a loud buzzing sound when the snake becomes alert to danger

BREEDING HABITS

All rattlesnakes give birth to live young. They are born in a thin membrane, but soon break free and become fully independent. Neotropical Rattlesnakes probably breed every year, but other species from cooler climates may only breed every two or three years.

Keeled scales
This species has very heavily keeled scales, giving it the roughened texture and appearance of a pineapple

SIDEWINDER

The Sidewinder is a small rattlesnake that lives amidst dunes of loose, windblown sand. It moves rapidly over them in a looping motion, known as sidewinding (see p.19), mostly at night. Before morning, it digs itself into the sand, often at the base of a small bush, to escape from excessive heat. The Sidewinder is not as dangerous as its reputation suggests, although its bites require medical attention.

Main characteristics

The Sidewinder has raised scales over its eyes and a dark line through each eye. The head is much wider and flatter than that of other rattlesnakes. Its coloration varies to match the ground on which it lives, and can be yellow, grey, or orange, with indistinct spots of darker and lighter shades. Its method of locomotion is its most distinctive feature.

PARALLEL TRACKS

The Sidewinder's tracks consist of a series of unconnected imprints at about 45 degrees to the direction of travel. Each track shows a small hook at either end where the snake curls its head and tail.

FACT FILE

- *Crotalus cerastes*
- Viperidae (vipers and pit vipers)
- Deserts
- Live-bearers, producing 7–18 young
- Lizards and small mammals
- Extreme southwestern USA and adjacent Mexico

AVERAGE ADULT LENGTH

50 cm (1 ft 6 in)

0 cm	50 cm	1 m
0 in	1 ft 6 in	3 ft 3 in

Raised scales
The "horns" over its eyes are unique among rattlesnakes and immediately distinguish it from other small species

Small rattle
The rattle is small, compared with that of other species, but still acts as an effective warning to enemies

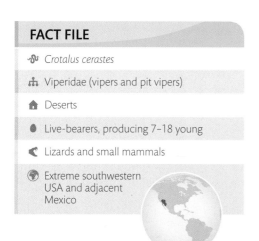

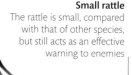

SIDEWINDER
The Sidewinder is, relatively, the stoutest species of rattlesnake and has a flattened head. The body shape, also flattened, helps the snake move across the sand, putting the greatest possible area into contact with the ground.

SNAKE DIRECTORY

Contents

Anomalepididae	p.151
Gerrhopilidae	p.151
Typhlopidae	p.151
Leptotyphlopidae	p.153
Xenotyphlopidae	p.154
Aniliidae	p.154
Tropidophiidae	p.155
Bolyeriidae	p.155
Xenophidiidae	p.155
Acrochordidae	p.155
Anomochilidae	p.155
Cylindrophiidae	p.155
Uropeltidae	p.156
Loxocemidae	p.156
Pythonidae	p.156
Xenopeltidae	p.157
Boidae	p.157
Colubridae	p.159
Dipsadidae	p.169
Lamprophiidae	p.176
Natricidae	p.181
Pseudoxenodontidae	p.184
Elapidae	p.184
Homalopsidae	p.189
Pareatidae	p.190
Xenodermatidae	p.191
Viperidae	p.191

SNAKE LENGTHS

The following categories have been used to indicate snake lengths:

small	to about 75 cm (2 ft 5 in)
medium	75–150 cm (2 ft 5 in–5 ft)
large	1.5–3 m (5 ft–9 ft 8 in)
very large	over 3 m (9 ft 8 in)

● Indicates species that are featured in the Snake Gallery section

The Snake Directory is the most complete listing of snake species possible at present – undoubtedly many more species are yet to be described.

Several species of snake are poorly known. Indeed, some are known from only a single individual, and it is not always feasible to give precise information about some species.

Families

Snakes are currently grouped into 27 families. Each family is divided into genera and these are further divided into species. Some families contain only one or a few species; in contrast, the largest family, the Colubridae, contains 844 species.

The five most primitive families – the Anomalepididae, Gerrhopilidae, Typhlopidae, Leptotyphlopidae, and Xenotyphlopidae – differ from other snakes in that their skulls are very rigid and their eyes are either small and covered with scales or lacking altogether. They are sometimes grouped as a superfamily, known as the Scolecophidia, or blind snakes.

Of the other 22 families, 12 contain relatively primitive snakes, although in some cases their relationships are not completely resolved. They are distributed around the world and reflect the first wave of diversification among snakes. These families tend to have fewer species and are thought to be in decline; they include the boas and pythons. Four families – Aniliidae, Tropidophiidae, Bolyeriidae, and Xenophidiidae – are not assigned to any superfamily and their relationships are unclear at present. They are, however, thought to be primitive families, having appeared before most other snakes.

The remaining ten families are the most advanced and are very diverse; they include the Colubridae, Viperidae, and Elapidae, and seven additional families recently separated from the Colubridae.

Some families, such as the Boidae and the Colubridae, are divided into subfamilies, and these are listed in the directory, although experts are not unanimously agreed on the placement of species within them. Families are arranged in order, from the most primitive to the most recently evolved, as currently understood. Within each family and subfamily (where present), the genera and species are arranged alphabetically.

ANOMALEPIDIDAE
Dawn Blind Snakes

4 GENERA CONTAINING 18 SPECIES

This is the most primitive snake family. Very little is known about its members, which are perhaps the least known of all vertebrates. All members are very small with smooth, shiny scales, slender, cylindrical bodies, and short tails. Most are brown or black, although some species have yellow or white heads and tails. Members of some genera have a pair of teeth on the lower jaw, whereas others have no teeth at all. The eyes are rudimentary.

Anomalepididae spend nearly all their time below ground and feed mostly on termites. Their method of reproduction is unknown, although it is assumed that they lay eggs. The family is restricted to tropical Central and South America.

GENUS: ANOMALEPIS

🐍 4
↔ Small and slender
🌍 Central America and northern South America
🏠 Subterranean, in forests
🦗 Termites
⚲ Thought to be egg-layers
📝 Poorly known

SPECIES:

Anomalepis aspinosus
Anomalepis colombia
Anomalepis flavapices
Anomalepis mexicanus

GENUS: HELMINTHOPHIS

🐍 3
↔ Small, to 30 cm (12 in)
🌍 Northern South America
🏠 Subterranean
🦗 Termites
⚲ Thought to be egg-layers
📝 Poorly known

SPECIES:

Helminthophis flavoterminatus
Helminthophis frontalis
Helminthophis praeocularis

GENUS: LIOTYPHLOPS

🐍 10
↔ Small
🌍 Central and northern South America
🏠 Subterranean
🦗 Termites
⚲ Thought to be egg-layers
📝 Poorly known

SPECIES:

Liotyphlops albirostris
Liotyphlops anops
Liotyphlops argaleus
Liotyphlops beui
Liotyphlops caissara
Liotyphlops haadi
Liotyphlops schubarti
Liotyphlops ternetzii
Liotyphlops trefauti
Liotyphlops wilderi

GENUS: TYPHLOPHIS

🐍 1
↔ Small
🌍 Central and northern South America
🏠 Subterranean
🦗 Termites
⚲ Thought to be an egg-layer
📝 Poorly known

SPECIES:

Typhlophis squamosus

GERRHOPILIDAE

1 GENUS CONTAINING 17 SPECIES

This contains a single genus (but see note below) of blind snakes from Asia and, possibly, Mauritius. They have small, gland-like structures over their rostral and nasal scales, and occasionally on other scales on their head and chin. Their natural history is poorly known.

GENUS: GERRHOPILUS

🐍 17
↔ Small
🌍 India, Southeast Asia, and New Guinea
🏠 Subterranean
🦗 Termites, ants and their larvae
⚲ Egg-layers, where known
📝 A second genus, *Cathetorhinus*, is sometimes included in this family. The single member, *Cathetorhinus melanocephalus*, is poorly known and even its distribution is uncertain

SPECIES:

Gerrhopilus andamanensis
Gerrhopilus ater
Gerrhopilus beddomii
Gerrhopilus bisubocularis
Gerrhopilus ceylonicus
Gerrhopilus depressiceps
Gerrhopilus floweri
Gerrhopilus fredparkeri
Gerrhopilus hades
Gerrhopilus hedraeus
Gerrhopilus inornatus
Gerrhopilus manilae
Gerrhopilus mcdowelli
Gerrhopilus mirus
Gerrhopilus oligolepis
Gerrhopilus thurstoni
Gerrhopilus tindalli

TYPHLOPIDAE
Blind Snakes

16 GENERA CONTAINING 262 SPECIES

Blind snakes are small with smooth, shiny scales, cylindrical bodies, and short tails, which often end in a small spine. Most are brown, black, or pinkish, but some species have faint stripes or blotches. They have teeth in the upper jaw only and rudimentary eyes.

Burrowing species that feed almost entirely on termites and ants, they are found in a variety of environments, but usually avoid very dry soils. Individuals may be found resting beneath partially buried logs or stones. They appear to be egg-layers, although the reproductive habits of the majority of species in this family are not known. Members are found in Central and South America, Africa, southern Asia, and Australasia, with one species in southeastern Europe.

GENUS: **ACUTOTYPHLOPS**

- 🐍 5
- ↔ Small
- 🌐 Bougainville Island, New Guinea, and the Solomon Islands
- 🏠 Subterranean
- 🦎 Unknown, but thought to be small invertebrates
- ⚥ Unknown, but thought to be egg-layers
- 📝 Poorly known; the genus was first described in 1995

SPECIES:

Acutotyphlops banaorum
Acutotyphlops infralabialis
Acutotyphlops kunuaensis
Acutotyphlops solomonis
Acutotyphlops subocularis

GENUS: **AFROTYPHLOPS**

- 🐍 26
- ↔ Small. One species, A. schlegelii, is the world's largest worm snake at nearly 1 m (3 ft 3 in)
- 🌐 Africa
- 🏠 Subterranean
- 🦎 Termites and ants
- ⚥ Egg-layers
- 📝 Previously placed in the genus Typhlops

SPECIES:

Afrotyphlops angeli
Afrotyphlops angolensis
Afrotyphlops anomalus
Afrotyphlops bibronii
Afrotyphlops blanfordii
Afrotyphlops brevis
Afrotyphlops congestus
Afrotyphlops decorosus
Afrotyphlops elegans
Afrotyphlops fornasinii,
    Fornasini's Blind Snake
Afrotyphlops gierrai
Afrotyphlops kaimosae
Afrotyphlops liberiensis
Afrotyphlops lineolatus
Afrotyphlops manni
Afrotyphlops mucruso
Afrotyphlops nanus
Afrotyphlops nigrocandidus
Afrotyphlops obtusus,
    Slender Blind Snake
Afrotyphlops punctatus
Afrotyphlops rondoensis
Afrotyphlops schlegelii,
    Schlegel's Blind Snake
Afrotyphlops schmidti
Afrotyphlops steinhausi
Afrotyphlops tanganicanus
Afrotyphlops usambaricus

GENUS: **AMEROTYPHLOPS**

- 🐍 15
- ↔ Small
- 🌐 South America, Trinidad (West Indies), and Grenada (Lesser Antilles)
- 🏠 Subterranean
- 🦎 Termites and ants
- ⚥ Egg-layers
- 📝 Previously placed in the genus Typhlops

SPECIES:

Amerotyphlops amoipira
Amerotyphlops arenensis
Amerotyphlops brongersmianus
Amerotyphlops costaricensis
Amerotyphlops lehneri
Amerotyphlops microstomus
Amerotyphlops minuisquamus
Amerotyphlops paucisquamus
Amerotyphlops reticulatus
Amerotyphlops stadelmani
Amerotyphlops tasymicris
Amerotyphlops tenuis
Amerotyphlops trinitatus
Amerotyphlops tycherus
Amerotyphlops yonenagae

GENUS: **ANILIOS**

- 🐍 46
- ↔ Small
- 🌐 Australia, New Guinea, and Indonesia
- 🏠 Subterranean
- 🦎 Termites and ants
- ⚥ Egg-layers
- 📝 Previously placed in the genus Typhlops

SPECIES:

Anilios affinis
Anilios ammodytes
Anilios aspinus
Anilios australis
Anilios batillus
Anilios bicolor
Anilios bituberculatus
Anilios broomi
Anilios centralis
Anilios chamodracaena
Anilios diversus
Anilios endoterus
Anilios erycinus
Anilios ganei
Anilios grypus
Anilios guentheri
Anilios hamatus
Anilios howi
Anilio insperatus
Anilios kimberleyensis
Anilios leptosomus
Anilios leucoproctus
Anilios ligatus
Anilios longissimus
Anilios margaretae
Anilios micrommus
Anilios minimus
Anilios nema
Anilios nigrescens
Anilios nigricaudus
Anilios nigroterminatus
Anilios pilbarensis
Anilios pinguis
Anilios polygrammicus
Anilios proximus
Anilios robertsi
Anilios silvia
Anilios splendidus
Anilios torresianus
Anilios tovelli
Anilios troglodytes
Anilios unguirostris
Anilios waitii
Anilios wiedii
Anilios yampiensis
Anilios yirrikalae

GENUS: **ARGYROPHIS**

- 🐍 12
- ↔ Small
- 🌐 India, Southeast Asia, and Indonesia
- 🏠 Subterranean
- 🦎 Termites and ants
- ⚥ Egg-layers
- 📝 Previously placed in the genus Typhlops

SPECIES:

Argyrophis bothriorhynchus
Argyrophis diardii
Argyrophis fuscus
Argyrophis giadinhensis
Argyrophis hypsobothrius
Argyrophis klemmeri
Argyrophis koshunensis
Argyrophis muelleri
Argyrophis oatesii
Argyrophis roxaneae
Argyrophis siamensis
Argyrophis trangensis

GENUS: **CYCLOTYPHLOPS**

- 🐍 1
- ↔ Small, to just over 14 cm (5½ in)
- 🌐 Southeastern Sulawesi and Indonesia
- 🏠 Clearings in secondary forests
- 🦎 Unknown, but thought to be ants and termites
- ⚥ Unknown, but thought to be an egg-layer
- 📝 The genus and species were first described in 1994; only two specimens are known

SPECIES:

Cyclotyphlops deharvengi

GENUS: **GRYPOTYPHLOPS**

- 🐍 1
- ↔ Small
- 🌐 India
- 🏠 Subterranean
- 🦎 Termites and ants
- ⚥ Egg-layer
- 📝 Previously placed in the genus Rhinotyphlops

SPECIES:

Grypotyphlops acutus

GENUS: **INDOTYPHLOPS**

- 🐍 23
- ↔ Small
- 🌐 India, Pakistan, Sri Lanka, Southeast Asia, and China, including Hong Kong and Taiwan
- 🏠 Subterranean
- 🦎 Termites and ants
- ⚥ Egg-layers. Indotyphlops braminus (see p.37) is unique among snakes, being the world's only parthenogenic (all-female) species
- 📝 Previously placed in the genus Typhlops

SPECIES:

Indotyphlops ahsanai
Indotyphlops albiceps
Indotyphlops braminus,
    Brahminy Blind Snake
Indotyphlops exiguus
Indotyphlops filiformis
Indotyphlops fletcheri
Indotyphlops jerdoni
Indotyphlops khoratensis
Indotyphlops lankaensis
Indotyphlops lazelli
Indotyphlops leucomelas
Indotyphlops loveridgei
Indotyphlops madgemintonae
Indotyphlops malcolmi
Indotyphlops meszoelyi
Indotyphlops ozakiae
Indotyphlops pammeces
Indotyphlops porrectus
Indotyphlops schmutzi
Indotyphlops tenebrarum
Indotyphlops tenuicollis
Indotyphlops veddae
Indotyphlops violaceus

GENUS: **LEMURIATYPHLOPS**

- 🐍 3
- ↔ Small
- 🌐 Madagascar
- 🏠 Subterranean
- 🦎 Termites and ants
- ⚥ Egg-layers
- 📝 A new genus described in 2014, previously placed in the genus Typhlops

SPECIES:

Lemuriatyphlops domerguei
Lemuriatyphlops microcephalus
Lemuriatyphlops reuteri

GENUS: **LETHEOBIA**

- 🐍 28
- ↔ Small
- 🌐 Africa
- 🏠 Subterranean
- 🦎 Termites and ants
- ⚥ Egg-layers
- 📝 Previously placed in the genus Rhinotyphlops

SPECIES:

Letheobia acutirostrata
Letheobia caeca
Letheobia crossii
Letheobia debilis

Letheobia episcopus
Letheobia erythraea
Letheobia feae
Letheobia gracilis
Letheobia graueri
Letheobia jubana
Letheobia kibarae
Letheobia largeni
Letheobia leucosticta
Letheobia lumbriciformis
Letheobia newtoni
Letheobia pallida
Letheobia pauwelsi
Letheobia pembana
Letheobia praeocularis
Letheobia rufescens
Letheobia simonii
Letheobia somalica
Letheobia stejnegeri
Letheobia sudanensis
Letheobia swahilica
Letheobia toritensis
Letheobia uluguruensis
Letheobia wittei

GENUS: **MADATYPHLOPS**

- 13
- Small
- Madagascar
- Subterranean
- Termites and ants
- Egg-layers
- A new genus described in 2014, previously placed in the genus *Typhlops*

SPECIES:

Madatyphlops andasibensis
Madatyphlops arenarius
Madatyphlops boettgeri
Madatyphlops calabresii
Madatyphlops comorensis
Madatyphlops cuneirostris
Madatyphlops decorsei
Madatyphlops leucocephalus
Madatyphlops madagascariensis
Madatyphlops mucronatus
Madatyphlops ocularis
Madatyphlops platyrhynchus
Madatyphlops rajeryi

GENUS: **MALAYOTYPHLOPS**

- 9
- Small
- Philippines, eastern Indonesia
- Subterranean
- Termites and ants
- Egg-layers
- A new genus described in 2014, previously placed in the genus *Typhlops*

SPECIES:

Malayotyphlops canlaonensis
Malayotyphlops castanotus
Malayotyphlops collaris
Malayotyphlops hypogius
Malayotyphlops koekkoeki
Malayotyphlops kraalii
Malayotyphlops luzonensis
Malayotyphlops ruber
Malayotyphlops ruficaudus

GENUS: **RAMPHOTYPHLOPS**

- 21
- Small, to about 20 cm (8 in), occasionally larger
- New Guinea, Solomon Islands, New Caledonia, and neighbouring Micronesian islands
- Subterranean, including in plantations
- Ants and termites
- Egg-layers, where known

SPECIES:

Ramphotyphlops acuticaudus
Ramphotyphlops adocetus
Ramphotyphlops angusticeps
Ramphotyphlops becki
Ramphotyphlops bipartitus
Ramphotyphlops conradi
Ramphotyphlops cumingii
Ramphotyphlops depressus
Ramphotyphlops exocoeti
Ramphotyphlops flaviventer
Ramphotyphlops hatmaliyeb
Ramphotyphlops lineatus
Ramphotyphlops lorenzi
Ramphotyphlops mansuetus
Ramphotyphlops marxi
Ramphotyphlops multilineatus
Ramphotyphlops olivaceus
Ramphotyphlops similis
Ramphotyphlops suluensis
Ramphotyphlops supranasalis
Ramphotyphlops willeyi

GENUS: **RHINOTYPHLOPS**

- 6
- Small, to about 30 cm (12 in)
- East and southern Africa
- Subterranean, usually found in dry soils
- Ants and termites
- Egg-layers

SPECIES:

Rhinotyphlops ataeniatus
Rhinotyphlops boylei,
Boyle's Blind Snake
Rhinotyphlops lalandei,
Delalande's Blind Snake
Rhinotyphlops schinzi,
Beaked Blind Snake
Rhinotyphlops scortecci
Rhinotyphlops unitaeniatus

GENUS: **TYPHLOPS**

- 49
- Small
- Predominantly the West Indies but two species, as currently recognized, occur in West Africa
- Subterranean
- Ants and termites, where known
- Egg-layers, where known

SPECIES:

Typhlops agoralionis
Typhlops anchaurus
Typhlops annae
Typhlops anousius
Typhlops arator
Typhlops biminiensis
Typhlops capitulatus
Typhlops cariei
Typhlops catapontus
Typhlops caymanensis
Typhlops coecatus
Typhlops contorhinus
Typhlops disparilis
Typhlops dominicanus
Typhlops epactius
Typhlops eperopeus
Typhlops geotomus
Typhlops golyathi
Typhlops gonavensis
Typhlops granti
Typhlops guadeloupensis
Typhlops hectus
Typhlops hypomethes
Typhlops jamaicensis
Typhlops leptolepis
Typhlops longissimus
Typhlops lumbricalis
Typhlops monastus
Typhlops monensis
Typhlops naugus
Typhlops notorachius
Typhlops oxyrhinus
Typhlops pachyrhinus
Typhlops paradoxus
Typhlops perimychus
Typhlops platycephalus
Typhlops proancylop
Typhlops pusillus
Typhlops richardi
Typhlops rostellatus
Typhlops satelles
Typhlops schwartzi
Typhlops silus
Typhlops sulcatus
Typhlops sylleptor
Typhlops syntherus
Typhlops tetrathyreus
Typhlops titanops
Typhlops zenkeri

GENUS: **XEROTYPHLOPS**

- 4
- Small
- North Africa, Iran, southeast Europe, and Socotra (Yemen)
- Subterranean
- Termites and ants
- Egg-layers
- A new genus described in 2014, previously placed in the genus *Typhlops*. *Xerotyphlops vermicularis* is the only blind snake occurring in Europe.

SPECIES:

Xerotyphlops etheridgei
Xerotyphlops socotranus
Xerotyphlops vermicularis,
European Blind Snake, or Worm Snake
Xerotyphlops wilsoni

LEPTOTYPHLOPIDAE
Slender Blind Snakes

2 SUBFAMILIES CONTAINING 12 GENERA AND 118 SPECIES

The members of this family are small and slender with smooth, shiny scales. Most individuals are pink or silvery grey, but some are darker. All have teeth in the lower jaw only, and the upper jaw is rigid. Slender blind snakes have well-developed pelvic girdles, and some have vestigial hind limbs in the form of small spurs. They do not have left lungs, and females do not have left oviducts. The rudimentary eyes are small, and each one is covered by a scale.

All slender blind snakes live underground, where they feed on termites and their larvae. They use their tiny mouths to grasp the soft-bodied insects and squeeze them dry. Some species (perhaps all of them) produce pheromones that protect them from attacks by soldier termites. These snakes appear to be egg-layers, although the reproductive method of several species has not been recorded. The family is found in practically all parts of the world where there are termites: North America, Central and South America, Africa, Arabia, and the Middle East.

SUBFAMILY: **LEPTOTYPHLOPINAE**
4 GENERA CONTAINING 51 SPECIES

African blind snakes with long tails. They live in forested habitats, or scrub, and only appear on the surface after heavy rain washes them out of their burrows.

GENUS: **EPACROPHIS**

- 3
- Small and slender
- East Africa
- Subterranean
- Termites
- Egg-layers, where known
- Previously placed in the genus *Leptotyphlops*

SPECIES:

Epacrophis boulengeri
Epacrophis drewesi
Epacrophis reticulatus

GENUS: **LEPTOTYPHLOPS**

- 23
- Small and slender
- Africa and Arabia
- Subterranean
- Termites
- Egg-layers

SPECIES:

Leptotyphlops aethiopicus
Leptotyphlops conjunctus,
Cape Thread Snake
Leptotyphlops distanti,
Distant's Thread Snake
Leptotyphlops emini
Leptotyphlops howelli
Leptotyphlops incognitus
Leptotyphlops jacobseni
Leptotyphlops kafubi
Leptotyphlops keniensis
Leptotyphlops latirostris
Leptotyphlops macrops
Leptotyphlops mbanjensis
Leptotyphlops merkeri
Leptotyphlops nigricans,
Black Thread Snake
Leptotyphlops nigroterminus
Leptotyphlops nursii
Leptotyphlops pembae
Leptotyphlops pitmani
Leptotyphlops pungwensis
Leptotyphlops scutifrons,
Peter's Thread Snake
Leptotyphlops sylvicolus

Leptotyphlops tanae
Leptotyphlops telloi,
   Tello's Thread Snake

GENUS: **MYRIOPHOLIS**

- 🐍 20
- ↔ Small and slender
- 🌍 Africa and Arabian Peninsula
- 🏠 Subterranean
- 🦗 Termites
- ⚲ Egg-layers
- ✎ Previously placed in the genus *Leptotyphlops*

SPECIES:

Myriopholis adleri
Myriopholis albiventer
Myriopholis algeriensis
Myriopholis blanfordi
Myriopholis boueti
Myriopholis braccianii
Myriopholis burii
Myriopholis cairi
Myriopholis erythraeus
Myriopholis filiformis
Myriopholis ionidesi
Myriopholis longicauda,
   Long-tailed Thread Snake
Myriopholis macrorhyncha,
   Beaked Thread Snake
Myriopholis macrura
Myriopholis narirostris
Myriopholis parkeri
Myriopholis perreti
Myriopholis rouxestevae
Myriopholis wilsoni
Myriopholis yemenica

GENUS: **NAMIBIANA**

- 🐍 5
- ↔ Small and slender
- 🌍 Southwest Africa. The name refers to the Namib Desert, not Namibia the country; some species are found only in neighbouring countries
- 🏠 Subterranean
- 🦗 Termites
- ⚲ Egg-layers
- ✎ Previously placed in the genus *Leptotyphlops*

SPECIES:

Namibiana gracilior,
   Slender Thread Snake
Namibiana labialis,
   Damara Thread Snake
Namibiana latifrons
Namibiana occidentalis,
   Western Thread Snake (Africa)
Namibiana rostrata

SUBFAMILY: **EPICTINAE**
8 GENERA CONTAINING 75 SPECIES

Blind snakes of this subfamily are found in the Americas and nearby Caribbean islands. They occur in forests and deserts, depending on the species, and are more likely to be seen on the surface than other blind snakes, but only at night.

GENUS: **EPICTIA**

- 🐍 32
- ↔ Small and slender
- 🌍 South America
- 🏠 Subterranean
- 🦗 Termites
- ⚲ Egg-layers
- ✎ Previously placed in the genus *Leptotyphlops*

SPECIES:

Epictia albipuncta
Epictia alfredschmidti
Epictia antoniogarciai
Epictia ater
Epictia australis
Epictia bakewelli
Epictia borapeliotes
Epictia clinorostris
Epictia collaris
Epictia columbi
Epictia diaplocia
Epictia goudotii
Epictia magnamaculata
Epictia melanura
Epictia munoai
Epictia nasalis
Epictia peruviana
Epictia phenops
Epictia rubrolineata
Epictia rufidorsa
Epictia septemlineata
Epictia signata
Epictia striatula
Epictia subcrotilla
Epictia teaguei
Epictia tenella
Epictia tesselata
Epictia tricolor
Epictia undecimstriata
Epictia unicolor
Epictia vanwallachi
Epictia vellardi

GENUS: **MITOPHIS**

- 🐍 4
- ↔ Small and slender
- 🌍 Hispaniola (Haiti and the Dominican Republic)
- 🏠 Subterranean
- 🦗 Termites
- ⚲ Egg-layers
- ✎ Previously placed in the genus *Leptotyphlops*

SPECIES:

Mitophis asbolepis
Mitophis calypso
Mitophis leptipileptus
Mitophis pyrites

GENUS: **RENA**

- 🐍 12
- ↔ Small and slender
- 🌍 Southern North America, Central America, and South America
- 🏠 Subterranean
- 🦗 Termites
- ⚲ Egg-layers
- ✎ Previously placed in the genus *Leptotyphlops*

SPECIES:

Rena affinis
Rena boettgeri
Rena bressoni
Rena dissecta
Rena dugesii
Rena dulcis,
   Texas Blind Snake
Rena humilis,
   Western Threadsnake (America)
Rena iversoni
Rena maxima
Rena myopica
Rena segrega
Rena unguirostris

GENUS: **RHINOLEPTUS**

- 🐍 1
- ↔ Small
- 🌍 Central Africa (Senegal and Guinea)
- 🏠 Subterranean
- 🦗 Thought to be ants and termites
- ⚲ Thought to be an egg-layer
- ✎ Poorly known

SPECIES:

Rhinoleptus koniagui

GENUS: **SIAGONODON**

- 🐍 4
- ↔ Small
- 🌍 South America
- 🏠 Subterranean, in forests
- 🦗 Presumably termites
- ⚲ Egg-layers
- ✎ Previously placed in the genus *Leptotyphlops*

SPECIES:

Siagonodon acutirostris
Siagonodon borrichianus
Siagonodon cupinensis
Siagonodon septemstriatus

GENUS: **TETRACHEILOSTOMA**

- 🐍 3
- ↔ Small
- 🌍 West Indies
- 🏠 Subterranean
- 🦗 Presumably termites
- ⚲ Egg-layers
- ✎ Previously included in the genus *Leptotyphlops*

SPECIES:

Tetracheilostoma bilineatum
Tetracheilostoma breuili
Tetracheilostoma carlae

GENUS: **TRICHEILOSTOMA**

- 🐍 5
- ↔ Small
- 🌍 Tropical Africa
- 🏠 Subterranean, in forests
- 🦗 Termites
- ⚲ Egg-layers
- ✎ Previously included in the genus *Leptotyphlops*

SPECIES:

Tricheilostoma bicolor
Tricheilostoma broadleyi
Tricheilostoma dissimilis
Tricheilostoma greenwelli
Tricheilostoma sundewalli

GENUS: **TRILEPIDA**

- 🐍 14
- ↔ Small and slender
- 🌍 Northern South America to eastern Brazil
- 🏠 Subterranean
- 🦗 Termites
- ⚲ Egg-layers
- ✎ Previously placed in the genus *Leptotyphlops*

SPECIES:

Trilepida anthracina
Trilepida brasiliensis
Trilepida brevissima
Trilepida dimidiatum
Trilepida dugandi
Trilepida fuliginosa
Trilepida guayaquilensis
Trilepida jani
Trilepida joshuai
Trilepida koppesi
Trilepida macrolepis
Trilepida nicefori
Trilepida pastusa
Trilepida salgueiroi

XENOTYPHLOPIDAE
1 GENUS CONTAINING 1 SPECIES

This family contains only one species – the poorly known *Xenotyphlops grandidieri*, from Madagascar. It is pink, with a large circular rostral scale, giving its head a "bulldozer-like" appearance. Specimens have been found only in the extreme north of the island, mostly under stones in sandy soil.

GENUS: **XENOTYPHLOPS**

- 🐍 1
- ↔ To about 26 cm (10¼ in)
- 🌍 Northern Madagascar
- 🏠 Subterranean
- 🦗 Probably termites
- ⚲ Egg-layer
- ✎ The species *X. mocquardi* has been synonymized with *X. grandidieri*

SPECIES:

Xenotyphlops grandidieri

ANILIIDAE
South American Pipe Snake

1 GENUS CONTAINING 1 SPECIES

The South American Pipe Snake is placed in a family of its own, although it was formerly included in Cylindrophiidae.

GENUS: **ANILIUS**

- 🐍 1
- ↔ Medium, to a maximum of 1 m (3 ft 3 in), but usually smaller

- South America (Amazon basin)
- Forests and swamps, where it burrows in mud
- Snakes and other burrowing reptiles, and amphibians
- Live-bearer
- A red and black false coral snake

SPECIES:
Anilius scytale

TROPIDOPHIIDAE
Dwarf Boas
2 GENERA CONTAINING 34 SPECIES

Although members of this family used to be placed within Boidae, they are now considered to form a separate family. They are small to medium-sized snakes and occur in a variety of colours and patterns. Some species are capable of limited physiological colour changes, often becoming paler at night. Their eyes have vertically elliptical pupils. Unlike the boas and pythons, they have a well-developed tracheal lung. Males of all species have pelvic girdles and vestigial legs in the form of small spurs. Females of some species also have pelvic girdles and spurs, but the spurs are smaller than those of the males. Females of other species lack pelvic girdles altogether.

These are secretive snakes, living among leaf-litter and under rocks and logs. They are active at night and feed on a variety of prey, including invertebrates, amphibians, lizards, and small mammals, which they may constrict. Some species are partially arboreal. They give birth to live young after a long gestation period.

They are found in the Caribbean region, and in Central and South America.

GENUS: **TRACHYBOA**
Eyelash Boas

- 2
- Small, to just over 30 cm (12 in)
- Central and northern South America
- Tropical forests
- Thought to be lizards and small mammals
- Live-bearers
- Secretive and not well known. Characterized by clusters of scales over each eye

SPECIES:
Trachyboa boulengeri
Trachyboa gularis

GENUS: **TROPIDOPHIS**
Dwarf Boas

- 32
- Small to medium, with fairly stout bodies
- West Indies (notably Cuba) and Central and South America

- Damp places, such as forests, plantations, and parks
- Invertebrates, amphibians, lizards, and small mammals
- Live-bearers

SPECIES:
Tropidophis battersbyi,
    Battersby's Dwarf Boa
Tropidophis bucculentus
Tropidophis canus,
    Bahamas Dwarf Boa
Tropidophis caymanensis,
    Cayman Islands Dwarf Boa
Tropidophis celiae
Tropidophis curtus
Tropidophis feicki,
    Feick's Dwarf Boa
Tropidophis fuscus,
    Brown Dwarf Boa
Tropidophis galacelidus
Tropidophis grapiuna
Tropidophis greenwayi,
    Turks and Caicos Dwarf Boa
- *Tropidophis haetianus*,
    Haitian Dwarf Boa (p.42)
Tropidophis hardyi
Tropidophis hendersoni
Tropidophis jamaicensis,
    Jamaican Warf Boa
Tropidophis maculatus,
    Spotted Dwarf Boa
- *Tropidophis melanurus*,
    Cuban Dwarf Boa (p.43)
Tropidophis morenoi
Tropidophis nigriventris
Tropidophis pardalis,
    Leopard Dwarf Boa
Tropidophis parkeri
Tropidophis paucisquamis
Tropidophis pilsbryi
Tropidophis preciosus
Tropidophis schwartzi
Tropidophis semicinctus
Tropidophis spiritus
Tropidophis stejnegeri
Tropidophis stullae
Tropidophis taczanowskyi
Tropidophis wrighti,
    Wright's Dwarf Boa
Tropidophis xanthogaster

BOLYERIIDAE
Round Island Boas
2 GENERA CONTAINING 2 SPECIES

This is a small family of only two species, one of which is thought to be extinct. They have no pelvic girdles, and it is this characterization that separates them from the true boas and tropidophids. The left lung is greatly reduced. They are small to medium-sized snakes, which probably feed exclusively on lizards. One species lays eggs; reproduction in the other species has not been confirmed.

Confined to the tiny island of Round Island in the Indian Ocean, north of Mauritius, these snakes have suffered greatly from habitat devastation, largely due to the activities of two introduced mammals: goats and rabbits.

GENUS: **BOLYERIA**

- 1
- Small
- Round Island
- Soil-filled, rocky fissures

- Thought to be lizards
- Unknown, but thought to have laid eggs
- Thought to be extinct; the last specimen was seen in 1975

SPECIES:
Bolyeria multocarinata,
    Round Island Burrowing Boa

GENUS: **CASAREA**

- 1
- Medium, with a flattened head
- Round Island
- Rocky places
- Thought to be lizards
- Egg-layer
- Very rare; its natural history is poorly known

SPECIES:
Casarea dussumieri,
    Round Island Keel-scaled Boa

XENOPHIDIIDAE
Spine-jawed Snakes
1 GENUS CONTAINING 2 SPECIES

Two species are known, each from a single specimen, one from Borneo and the other from the Malaysian Peninsula. These snakes are apparently small, forest-floor dwellers but very poorly known.

GENUS: **XENOPHIDION**

- 2
- Small
- Sabah, Borneo (*X. acanthognathus*) and Selangar, Malaysia (*X. schaeferi*)
- Primary rainforest
- Worms, insects, and their larvae
- Thought to be egg-layers
- Only described in 1995 and therefore poorly known as yet

SPECIES:
Xenophidion acanthognathus
Xenophidion schaeferi

ACROCHORDIDAE
File Snakes
1 GENUS CONTAINING 3 SPECIES

Three strange aquatic species comprise this family, which includes some primitive and some advanced characteristics. They have small granular scales and loose skin that hangs in folds around their bodies; out of the water they are effectively helpless. Two out of the three species are dull grey in colour, but *A. javanicus* has bold white bands, especially when young. They all catch small fish, eels, and crustaceans, using their rough, granular scales to grasp them between their coils.

File snakes are found in Southeast Asia, northern Australia, and Papua New Guinea.

GENUS: **ACROCHORDUS**

- 3
- Medium to large, to 2.5 m (8 ft 2 in) in *A. arafurae*, and very thickset
- Southeast Asia, northern Australia, and Papua New Guinea
- Aquatic, living in marine and brackish water, and freshwater
- Fish and crustaceans
- Live-bearers, only giving birth every 8–10 years

SPECIES:
Acrochordus arafurae,
    Arafura File Snake or
    Elephant Trunk Snake
Acrochordus granulatus,
    Small File Snake
Acrochordus javanicus,
    Javan File Snake

ANOMOCHILIDAE
Dwarf Pipe Snakes
1 GENUS CONTAINING 3 SPECIES

The three species belonging to the genus *Anomochilus* are very rare, very poorly known, and have only recently been placed in their own family. Superficially, they are similar to the members of the Cylindrophiidae family, with which they were formerly grouped. They are found in Malaysia, Sumatra, and Borneo.

GENUS: **ANOMOCHILUS**

- 3
- Small, not more than 40 cm (1 ft 3 in)
- Malaysia, Sumatra, and Borneo
- Subterranean
- Unknown
- Unknown

SPECIES:
Anomochilus leonardi
Anomochilus monticola
Anomochilus weberi

CYLINDROPHIIDAE
Asian Pipe Snakes
1 GENUS CONTAINING 13 SPECIES

Asian Pipe Snakes are small and dark with boldly marked, black and white undersides. The tail is waved in the air if the snake is disturbed. All burrow. They are found in Asia, from Sri Lanka and India, down into the Malay peninsula, Borneo, and parts of Indonesia.

GENUS: **CYLINDROPHIS**

- 13
- Small, to 70 cm (2 ft 3 in) at most
- Sri Lanka, India, and Southeast Asia
- Forests, in underground tunnels
- Eels, caecilians, and other snakes
- Live-bearers

SPECIES:

Cylindrophis aruensis
Cylindrophis boulengeri
Cylindrophis burmanus
Cylindrophis engkariensis
Cylindrophis isolepis
Cylindrophis jodiae
Cylindrophis lineatus
Cylindrophis maculatus
Cylindrophis melanotus
Cylindrophis mirzae
Cylindrophis opisthorhodus
Cylindrophis ruffus
Cylindrophis yamdena

UROPELTIDAE
Shield-tailed Snakes

8 GENERA CONTAINING 54 SPECIES

All individuals are small and cylindrical. Some have a pelvic girdle, but others do not, which suggests that the family represents an evolutionary stage in snakes' transition from primitive to more advanced characteristics. The left lung is either absent or greatly reduced in size. The snakes spend most of their time beneath the surface, in leaf-litter, soil, or mud, and many species are poorly known. All are thought to eat burrowing invertebrates and other small snakes. The family is restricted to southern India and Sri Lanka.

GENUS: **BRACHYOPHIDIUM**

- 1
- Very small
- Southern India
- Unknown
- Thought to be earthworms
- Thought to be a live-bearer

SPECIES:
Brachyophidium rhodogaster

GENUS: **MELANOPHIDIUM**

- 3
- Medium
- Southern India
- Montane forests
- Thought to be earthworms
- Thought to be live-bearers

SPECIES:
Melanophidium bilineatum
Melanophidium punctatum
Melanophidium wynaudense

GENUS: **PLATYPLECTRURUS**

- 2
- Small
- Southern India and Sri Lanka, although *P. madurensis* is known from only one specimen in Sri Lanka
- Montane forests
- Thought to be earthworms
- Live-bearers, producing small litters

SPECIES:
Platyplectrurus madurensis
Platyplectrurus trilineatus

GENUS: **PLECTRURUS**

- 4
- Small
- Southern India
- Unknown
- Thought to be earthworms
- Thought to be live-bearers

SPECIES:
Plectrurus aureus
Plectrurus canaricus
Plectrurus guentheri
Plectrurus perroteti

GENUS: **PSEUDOTYPHLOPS**

- 1
- Small, to about 50 cm (1 ft 6 in)
- Sri Lanka
- Fields, where it lives in humus
- Earthworms
- Live-bearer
- The specific name was given in error, because the species was thought to come from the Philippines

SPECIES:
Pseudotyphlops philippinus

GENUS: **RHINOPHIS**

- 16
- Small, to about 30 cm (12 in), except for *R. oxyrhynchus*, which grows to 57 cm (1 ft 8 in)
- Southern India and Sri Lanka
- Forests and plantations, where they burrow in soil and leaf-litter. Also under rotting logs and in silted-up drains
- Earthworms
- Live-bearers, where known
- Some species are rare, known from only a few specimens

SPECIES:
Rhinophis blythii
Rhinophis dorsimaculatus
Rhinophis drummondhayi
Rhinophis erangaviraji
Rhinophis fergusonianus
Rhinophis goweri
Rhinophis homolepis
Rhinophis lineatus
Rhinophis oxyrhynchus
Rhinophis philippinus
Rhinophis porrectus
Rhinophis punctatus
Rhinophis sanguineus
Rhinophis travancoricus
Rhinophis tricolorata
Rhinophis zigzag

GENUS: **TERETRURUS**

- 1
- Small
- Southern India
- Unknown
- Thought to be earthworms
- Thought to be a live-bearer
- Very rare, and poorly known

SPECIES:
Teretrurus sanguineus

GENUS: **UROPELTIS**

- 26
- Small
- Southern India and Sri Lanka
- Varied, but all are burrowers
- Thought to be earthworms
- Live-bearers
- Some species are rare; *U. ruhunae*, for instance, is known from a single specimen

SPECIES:
Uropeltis arcticeps
Uropeltis beddomii
Uropeltis bicatenata
Uropeltis broughami
Uropeltis ceylanicus
Uropeltis dindigalensis
Uropeltis ellioti
Uropeltis liura
Uropeltis macrolepis
Uropeltis macrorhyncha
Uropeltis maculata
Uropeltis madurensis
Uropeltis melanogaster
Uropeltis myhendrae
Uropeltis nitida
Uropeltis ocellata
Uropeltis petersi
Uropeltis phillipsi
Uropeltis phipsonii
Uropeltis pulneyensis
Uropeltis rubrolineata
Uropeltis rubromaculatus
Uropeltis ruhunae
Uropeltis shorttii
Uropeltis smithi
Uropeltis woodmasoni

LOXOCEMIDAE
Neotropical Sunbeam Snake

1 GENUS CONTAINING 1 SPECIES

A family of one species, from Central America, formerly thought to be a New World Python.

GENUS: **LOXOCEMUS**

- 1
- Medium, growing to just over 1 m (3 ft 3 in), and stocky
- Central America
- Scrub and deciduous dry forests
- Varied, including lizards, small rodents, and the eggs of lizards (iguanas in particular)
- Egg-layer

SPECIES:
- *Loxocemus bicolor* (p.44) Neotropical Sunbeam Snake

PYTHONIDAE
Pythons

8 GENERA CONTAINING 40 SPECIES

The python family contains a number of giant snakes. However, there are also small to medium-sized members in the family, including a few that do not exceed 1 m (3 ft 3 in) in length. Pythons may have large or small scales on the top of their heads and many species have heat pits along the margins of their jaws, although these are lacking in the two members of the genus *Aspidites*, the Papuan Olive Python, *Liasis papuana*, and the Ringed Python, *Bothrochilus boa* (which is a python, despite its specific name).

Like the boas, pythons have exploited a number of habitats, although there are no highly adapted burrowing species. All the pythons lay eggs, which they coil around and guard, or brood, for the duration of their development.

Pythons are found in Australia, Papua New Guinea, Indonesia, Timor, Africa, and southern and Southeast Asia. At present, there are 40 species grouped into 8 genera. This arrangement has been changed many times recently, so it is possible that there will be more changes in the future.

GENUS: **ANTARESIA**

Southern Pythons

- 4
- Small to medium, to about 1.5 m (5 ft). *A. perthensis*, with a maximum length of 60 cm (2 ft), is the smallest python
- Australia
- Deserts and wooded areas. *A. perthensis* often lives in termite mounds
- Lizards and small mammals
- Egg-layers
- All four species have heat pits

SPECIES:
- *Antaresia childreni*, Children's Python (p.46)
- *Antaresia maculosa*, Spotted Python (p.47)
- *Antaresia perthensis*, Anthill Python
- *Antaresia stimsoni*, Stimson's Python

GENUS: **ASPIDITES**

- 2
- Moderately large, to about 2.5 m (8 ft 2 in)
- Australia
- Varied, from humid forests to arid deserts
- Birds, small mammals, and other reptiles, including venomous snakes
- Egg-layers
- They have no heat pits

SPECIES:
Aspidites melanocephalus, Black-headed Python
Aspidites ramsayi, Woma

GENUS: **BOTHROCHILUS**

- 🐍 7
- ↔ Moderately large, to about 1.5 m (5 ft), and slender
- 🌐 Papua New Guinea
- 🏠 Forests and plantations, where they are secretive and semi-burrowing
- ◀ Lizards and small mammals
- ♀ Egg-layers
- ✎ Previously placed in the genus *Liasis*

SPECIES:

> *Bothrochilus albertisii,*
> D'Alberti's Python or
> White-lipped Python
> *Bothrochilus biakensis*
> *Bothrochilus boa,*
> Ringed Python
> *Bothrochilus fredparkeri*
> *Bothrochilus huonensis*
> *Bothrochilus meridionalis*
> *Bothrochilus montanus*

GENUS: **LIASIS**

- 🐍 4
- ↔ Medium to large
- 🌐 Australia, New Guinea, and some Indonesian islands
- 🏠 Open country, marshes, and forests
- ◀ Fish, amphibians, lizards, snakes, birds, and mammals
- ♀ Egg-layers
- ✎ Three species have heat pits. *L. fuscus* is sometimes considered to be a variant of *L. mackloti*

SPECIES:

> *Liasis fuscus,*
> Australian Water Python
> *Liasis mackloti,*
> Macklot's Python or Speckled Python
> *Liasis olivaceus,*
> Olive Python
> *Liasis papuana,*
> Papuan Olive Python

GENUS: **MALAYOPYTHON**

- 🐍 2
- ↔ Very large, to 8 m (26 ft) in the case of the Reticulated Python, *M. reticulatus*, which may be the world's longest snake
- 🌐 Southeast Asia and Indonesia
- 🏠 Forests, grasslands, and plantations, often common around human habitations
- ◀ Mammals, including humans on rare occasions
- ♀ Egg-layers
- ✎ Previously placed in the genus *Python*

SPECIES:

> ● *Malayopython reticulatus,*
> Reticulated Python (pp.48–49)
> *Malayopython timoriensis,*
> Timor Python

GENUS: **MORELIA**

- 🐍 4
- ↔ Medium to large
- 🌐 Australia, New Guinea, and neighbouring islands
- 🏠 Varied, including deserts, grasslands, and forests
- ◀ Reptiles, birds, and mammals up to the size of wallabies
- ♀ Egg-layers
- ✎ They have prominent heat pits. *M. viridis*, formerly *Chondropython viridis*, is totally arboreal, closely paralleling the South American Emerald Tree Boa in appearance and habits

SPECIES:

> *Morelia bredli,*
> Central Australian Carpet Python or Desert Carpet Python
> *Morelia carinata,*
> Rough-scaled Python
> ● *Morelia spilota,*
> Carpet Python or Diamond Python (pp.50–51)
> ● *Morelia viridis,*
> Green Tree Python (pp.52–53)

GENUS: **PYTHON**

- 🐍 10
- ↔ Medium to large, often heavily built
- 🌐 Africa, southern and Southeast Asia, and Australasia (Timor)
- 🏠 Varied, from rocky deserts (*P. anchietae*) to rainforests
- ◀ Almost exclusively warm-blooded prey, mostly mammals. Some are known to have eaten small humans
- ♀ Egg-layers
- ✎ There are no burrowing, aquatic, or highly arboreal species

SPECIES:

> *Python anchietae,*
> Angolan Python
> ● *Python bivittatus,*
> Burmese Python or Indian Python (pp.54–55)
> *Python breitensteini,*
> Borneo Blood Python
> *Python brongersmai,*
> Malaysian Blood Python or Sumatran Blood Python
> ● *Python curtus,*
> Blood Python or Short-tailed Python (pp.56–57)
> *Python kyaiktiyo*
> *Python molurus,*
> Asian Rock Python
> *Python natalensis,*
> Southern African Python
> ● *Python regius,*
> Royal Python or Ball Python (pp.58–59)
> *Python sebae,*
> African Rock Python

GENUS: **SIMALIA**

- 🐍 7
- ↔ Large, potentially to 5 m (16 ft) but usually smaller
- 🌐 Australia, Indonesia, and New Guinea
- 🏠 Forest, grasslands, and scrub
- ◀ Mammals
- ♀ Egg-layers
- ✎ Previously placed in the genus *Morelia*

SPECIES:

> *Simalia amethistina,*
> Amethystine Python, Scrub Python
> *Simalia boeleni,*
> Boelen's Python
> *Simalia clastolepis*
> *Simalia kinghorni,*
> Kinghorn's Python
> *Simalia nauta*
> *Simalia oenpelliensis,*
> Oenpelli Rock Python
> *Simalia tracyae*

XENOPELTIDAE
Sunbeam Snakes

1 GENUS CONTAINING 2 SPECIES

This family of two species from the Far East bears a superficial resemblance to *Loxocemus*. Both have a compressed, spade-shaped head for burrowing, and smooth, glossy, highly iridescent scales.

GENUS: **XENOPELTIS**

- 🐍 2
- ↔ Medium, to over 1 m (3 ft 3 in), and cylindrical
- 🌐 China and Southeast Asia
- 🏠 Lightly wooded areas and open ground, including plantations, gardens, and parks
- ◀ Reptiles and small mammals
- ♀ Egg-layers
- ✎ *X. hainanensis* was described only in 1972, and its natural history is poorly known in comparison to that of the other species

SPECIES:

> *Xenopeltis hainanensis*
> ● *Xenopeltis unicolor,*
> Asian Sunbeam Snake or Iridescent Earth Snake (p.45)

BOIDAE
Boas

5 SUBFAMILIES CONTAINING 14 GENERA AND 59 SPECIES

This family, which previously included the pythons, contains some of the world's largest snakes, such as the Anaconda and the Common Boa (*Boa constrictor*). They are not all large however, and the smallest species, the North American Rubber Boa, rarely grows to more than 60 cm (2 ft) in total length. Boas are characterized by small scales on the head and body. The body scales are usually smooth, but can occasionally be rough, as in the Rough-scaled Sand Boa, *Eryx conicus*.

All have muscular bodies that are used to constrict prey. Some species have heat pits bordering the mouth.

Boas have varied lifestyles, from burrowing to semi-aquatic to arboreal, and are found in most tropical and subtropical parts of the world. The greatest species diversity occurs in the West Indies, where there are many species of *Chilabothrus*, several of them restricted to one or two small islands.

Most boas are live-bearers, except the Calabar Ground Python, and one or possibly two sand boas, *Eryx*, which lay eggs.

SUBFAMILY: **BOINAE**
8 GENERA CONTAINING 39 SPECIES

This family includes the majority of species and all the largest boas. They are found throughout the West Indies, Central and South America, and in Madagascar, and some of the Pacific Islands. Most species are, to some extent, arboreal, although a number are also found on the ground. The anacondas, *Eunectes*, are aquatic. Boas mostly eat birds and mammals, although the small species also eat frogs and lizards. A number of species have heat-sensitive pits with which they can detect and hunt prey. All the members of this subfamily are live-bearers.

GENUS: **ACRANTOPHIS**

Madagascan Ground Boas

- 🐍 2
- ↔ Large, 2.5–3.2 m (8 ft 2 in–10 ft 5 in)
- 🌐 Madagascar
- 🏠 Rainforests, deciduous forests, grasslands, and agricultural areas
- ◀ Mammals and large birds, including domestic animals and chickens
- ♀ Live-bearers
- ✎ Placed in the genus *Boa* for a short time

SPECIES:

> ● *Acrantophis dumerili,*
> Dumeril's Ground Boa (pp.60–61)
> *Acrantophis madagascariensis,*
> Madagascan Ground Boa

GENUS: **BOA**

Boas

- 🐍 2
- ↔ Medium to very large. The Common Boa grows to more than 3 m (9 ft 8 in) in length
- 🌐 Central and South America (*B. constrictor*) and Madagascar. The Common Boa has one of the largest latitudinal geographic ranges of any snake, from Mexico in the north to Argentina in the south, and it also occurs on a number of Caribbean islands

- 🏠 Varied, from dry desert scrub to tropical rainforest
- 🦅 Birds and mammals
- ⚤ Live-bearers
- 📝 Until recently, the Madagascan species used to be placed in this genus

SPECIES:
- Boa constrictor, Common Boa (p.62–63)
  Boa imperator

GENUS: **CANDOIA**

Pacific Boas

- 🐍 5
- ↔ Medium to large, and stocky
- 🌍 New Guinea and neighbouring South Pacific islands
- 🏠 Forests
- 🦅 Lizards, birds, and mammals
- ⚤ Live-bearers
- 📝 Pacific boas are unusual among boas in having keeled scales. One species, C. bibroni, is long, slender, and highly arboreal, whereas the other four are stockier and live mostly on the ground. C. aspera, the smallest species, lives in leaf-litter and is often found near streams. Its shape and markings resemble those of vipers; it might be a mimic of the highly venomous Death Adder, Acantophis, from the same region

SPECIES:
- Candoia aspera
  Candoia bibroni
  Candoia carinata
  Candoia paulsoni,
    Solomon Island Ground Boa
  Candoia superciliosa

GENUS: **CORALLUS**

Tree Boas

- 🐍 9
- ↔ Large, to over 2 m (6 ft 6 in)
- 🌍 Central and South America
- 🏠 Forests
- 🦅 Lizards, birds, and mammals
- ⚤ Live-bearers
- 📝 C. cropanii is sometimes placed in a separate genus, Xenoboa. It is the world's rarest boa – only three known specimens have been collected to date, all from the vicinity of São Paulo, Brazil

SPECIES:
- Corallus annulatus,
    Annulated Boa
  Corallus batesii
  Corallus blombergi
- Corallus caninus,
    Emerald Tree Boa (pp.66–67)
  Corallus cookii,
    Cook's Tree Boa
  Corallus cropanii,
    Cropan's Tree Boa
  Corallus grenadensis,
    Grenada Tree Boa

Corallus hortulanus,
  Amazon Tree Boa
  or Cook's Tree Boa
Corallus ruschenbergerii

GENUS: **CHILABOTHRUS**

West Indian Boas

- 🐍 10
- ↔ Large, to 4.8 m (15 ft 7 in), but usually less than 3 m (9 ft 8 in)
- 🌍 West Indies
- 🏠 Forests, grasslands, and plantations
- 🦅 Lizards, frogs, and mammals
- ⚤ Live-bearers
- 📝 Previously placed in the genus Epicrates

SPECIES:
- Chilabothrus angulifer,
    Cuban Boa
  Chilabothrus chrysogaster,
    Turks Island Boa
  Chilabothrus exsul,
    Abaco Island Boa
  Chilabothrus fordii,
    Ford's Boa
  Chilabothrus gracilis,
    Vine Boa
  Chilabothrus inornatus,
    Puerto Rican Boa
  Chilabothrus monensis,
    Virgin Islands Boa or Mona Boa
  Chilabothrus striatus,
    Haitian Boa
  Chilabothrus strigilatus,
  Chilabothrus subflavus,
    Jamaican Boa

GENUS: **EPICRATES**

- 🐍 5
- ↔ Small to medium
- 🌍 Central and South America
- 🏠 Rainforests, grasslands, and plantations
- 🦅 Small mammals and birds
- ⚤ Live-bearers
- 📝 Previously classified as subspecies of E. cenchria, all these have now been elevated to species status

SPECIES:
- Epicrates alvarezi,
    Argentinian Rainbow Boa
  Epicrates assisi
- Epicrates cenchria,
    Rainbow Boa (pp.68–69)
  Epicrates crassus,
    Paraguayan Rainbow Boa
  Epicrates maurus,
    Brown Rainbow Boa

GENUS: **EUNECTES**

Anacondas

- 🐍 4
- ↔ Very large; E. murinus is the largest snake in the world
- 🌍 South America
- 🏠 Swamps and flooded forests
- 🦅 Turtles, crocodilians, birds, and mammals
- ⚤ Live-bearers

SPECIES:
- Eunectes beniensis
  Eunectes deschauenseei
- Eunectes murinus,
    Green Anaconda or Anaconda (pp. 70–71)
  Eunectes notaeus,
    Yellow Anaconda

GENUS: **SANZINIA**

Madagascar Tree Boas

- 🐍 2
- ↔ Large, 1.5–1.8 m (5–6 ft)
- 🌍 Madagascar
- 🏠 Arboreal by day, terrestrial by night, in forests and plantations
- 🦅 Small mammals
- ⚤ Live-bearers
- 📝 Previously placed in the genus Boa, as a single species, B. madagascariensis, with two subspecies

SPECIES:
- Sanzinia madagascariensis,
    Madagascan Tree Boa
  Sanzinia volontany

SUBFAMILY: **UNGALIOPHIINAE**
Dwarf Boas

2 GENERA CONTAINING 3 SPECIES

Three small boas from Central and South America make up this subfamily. They may be terrestrial or arboreal. The members of this subfamily are nocturnal.

GENUS: **EXILIBOA**

- 🐍 1
- ↔ Small
- 🌍 Southern Mexico
- 🏠 Montane cloud forests
- 🦅 Unknown
- ⚤ Thought to be a live-bearer
- 📝 Very rare, known from only a handful of specimens

SPECIES:
- Exiliboa placata,
    Oaxaca Boa

GENUS: **UNGALIOPHIS**

Banana Boas

- 🐍 2
- ↔ Small to medium, to about 50 cm (1 ft 6 in), and slender
- 🌍 Central America
- 🏠 Forests, partially arboreal
- 🦅 Frogs, lizards, and small mammals
- ⚤ Live-bearers
- 📝 They are sometimes accidentally transported in bunches of bananas

SPECIES:
- Ungaliophis continentalis
  Ungaliophis panamensis

SUBFAMILY: **CALABARIINAE**
1 GENUS CONTAINING 1 SPECIES

The Calabar Ground Boa (or Python) has been a problem for researchers for some years. A separate family, the Calabaridae, has been proposed for it but here it is retained within the Boidae, in a subfamily of its own.

GENUS: **CALABARIA**

- 🐍 1
- ↔ Medium, to 1 m (3 ft 3 in)
- 🌍 West Africa
- 🏠 Terrestrial, in tropical rainforest
- 🦅 Small mammals
- ⚤ Egg-layer
- 📝 The single member of the genus has, at various times, been placed in the Pythonidae and in a separate family, the Calabaridae. It was also placed in the genus Charina for a short time

SPECIES:
- Calabaria reinhardtii,
    Calabar Ground Python (pp. 64–65)

SUBFAMILY: **CHARININAE**
2 GENERA CONTAINING 4 SPECIES

This subfamily consists of four species of small boas from North America, previously associated with the sand boas, Eryx, but now considered separate enough to justify a subfamily of their own. They are ground and rock dwelling species, with small scales, small heads, and small eyes. They hunt for young mammals in burrows and nests, but sometimes take other prey.

GENUS: **CHARINA**

- 🐍 2
- ↔ Small to medium, with stocky bodies and short tails
- 🌍 North America
- 🏠 Pine woods and clearings, where it lives under logs, bark, and other forest debris
- 🦅 Small mammals
- ⚤ Live-bearers

SPECIES:
- Charina bottae,
    Rubber Boa
  Charina umbratica,
    Southern Rubber Boa

GENUS: **LICHANURA**

Rosy Boas

- 🐍 2
- ↔ Medium, to 1 m (3 ft 3 in), usually less
- 🌍 Western North America
- 🏠 Rocky deserts and scrub
- 🦅 Small mammals
- ⚤ Live-bearers

The rosy boas have been re-classified several times. For a short while they were placed in the genus *Charina*

SPECIES:
Lichanura orcutti,
Northern Three-lined (Rosy) Boa
- *Lichanura trivirgata,*
Rosy Boa (pp.72–73)

SUBFAMILY: ERYCINAE
1 GENUS CONTAINING 12 SPECIES

A single genus, *Eryx*, now remains in this previously more extensive subfamily. All have thickset, almost cylindrical bodies, with short tails and blunt heads. They occupy dry habitats and are burrowers, often found beneath rocks. They feed on small mammals, especially nestling rodents, and lizards.

GENUS: ERYX
Sand Boas

- 12
- Small to medium, with stout, cylindrical bodies
- North and East Africa, the Middle East, Central and southern Asia. One species, *E. jaculus*, is found just inside Europe, in the Balkan region
- Arid regions, beneath rocks or in burrows
- Lizards, small mammals, and ground-nesting birds
- Live-bearers, except, *E. jayakari,* which lays eggs
- Three of the species from northeast Africa are poorly known

SPECIES:
Eryx borrii
Eryx colubrinus,
Egyptian Sand Boa or Kenyan Sand Boa
Eryx conicus,
Rough-scaled Sand Boa
Eryx elegans
Eryx jaculus,
Turkish Sand Boa or Javelin Sand Boa
Eryx jayakari,
Arabian Sand Boa
Eryx johnii
Eryx miliaris
Eryx muelleri
Eryx somalicus
Eryx tataricus
Eryx whitakeri

COLUBRIDAE
Colubrids

4 SUBFAMILIES CONTAINING 121 GENERA AND 847 SPECIES

Containing more than 800 species, the Colubridae is a large family. These species all share a number of fundamental characteristics: they lack a pelvic girdle, a functional left lung, and a coronoid bone (a small bone in the lower jaw that is present in some of the more primitive snakes). With few exceptions, their heads are covered in large, symmetrical,

plate-like scales (like members of the cobra family, but unlike most boas, pythons, and vipers).

Despite these similarities, colubrids are enormously diverse. They range in size from tiny snakes less than 30 cm (12 in) long to large species measuring up to 3 m (9 ft 8 in) or more. They may be elongated or chunky, and may be coloured almost any hue. Colubrids may burrow, swim, or climb, and live in just about every habitat, from freshwater lakes and swamps to the most arid deserts. They eat a huge variety of prey, from small invertebrates up to moderately large mammals. Some species constrict their prey, whereas others merely grasp it and proceed to swallow; a relatively small number have venom-delivering fangs at the rear of their jaws with which they envenomate and subdue their prey. Most lay eggs, although a sizeable proportion, notably those from cooler environments, give birth to live young.

Members of this family are found in nearly every corner of the world, except in the very coldest places and in central and southern Australia. They are most common in warmer regions, with their numbers falling off towards the higher latitudes.

A number of subfamilies are recognized; some are well defined but, in others, there is considerable debate over the assignment of species.

SUBFAMILY: CALAMARIINAE
Reed Snakes

7 GENERA CONTAINING 87 SPECIES

The members of this subfamily are all small, and live in leaf-litter or under logs and other forest debris, where they feed on earthworms and other soft-bodied invertebrates. Their common name comes from their cylindrical body-shape and rather stiff bodies. They occur in India, Southeast Asia, China, and the Philippines.

GENUS: CALAMARIA
Reed Snakes and Worm Snakes

- 61
- Small
- India, southern and southwestern China, Southeast Asia, and the Indonesian archipelago
- Forests and damp places, where they live underground in burrows
- Earthworms and other soft-bodied invertebrates
- Egg-layers

SPECIES:
Calamaria abramovi
Calamaria abstrusa
Calamaria acutirostris
Calamaria albiventer
Calamaria alidae
Calamaria apraeocularis
Calamaria banggaiensis
Calamaria battersbyi
Calamaria bicolor
Calamaria bitorques

Calamaria boesemani
Calamaria borneensis
Calamaria brongersmai
Calamaria buchi
Calamaria butonensis
Calamaria ceramensis
Calamaria concolor
Calamaria crassa
Calamaria curta
Calamaria doederleini
Calamaria eiselti
Calamaria everetti
Calamaria forcarti
Calamaria gervaisii
Calamaria gialaiensis
Calamaria grabowskyi
Calamaria gracillima
Calamaria griswoldi
Calamaria hilleniusi
Calamaria ingeri
Calamaria javanica
Calamaria joloensis
Calamaria lateralis
Calamaria lautensis
Calamaria leucogaster
Calamaria linnaei
Calamaria longirostris
Calamaria lovii
Calamaria lumbricoidea
Calamaria lumholtzi
Calamaria margaritophora
Calamaria mecheli
Calamaria melanota
Calamaria modesta
Calamaria muelleri
Calamaria nuchalis
Calamaria palawanensis
Calamaria pavimentata
Calamaria pfefferi
Calamaria prakkei
Calamaria rebentischi
Calamaria sangi
Calamaria schlegeli
Calamaria schmidti
Calamaria septentrionalis
Calamaria suluensis
Calamaria sumatrana
Calamaria thanhi
Calamaria ulmeri
Calamaria virgulata
Calamaria yunnanensis

GENUS: CALAMORHABDIUM

- 2
- Very small
- The Celebes (Sulawesi and Bacan)
- Unknown
- Unknown
- Unknown
- A third, unnamed species is known from a single specimen. It was taken from the stomach of a snake belonging to the cobra family (*Maticora bivirgata*) on the Indonesian island of Sumatra in 1940

SPECIES:
Calamorhabdium acuticeps
Calamorhabdium kuekenthali

GENUS: COLLORHABDIUM

- 1
- Small
- The Cameron Highlands, Malaysia
- Montane forest
- Unknown

- Unknown
- A secretive snake that has been found only on a few occasions

SPECIES:
Collorhabdium williamsoni

GENUS: ETHERIDGEUM

- 1
- Small
- Sumatra
- Unknown
- Unknown
- Unknown
- Known from only a single specimen described in 1924

SPECIES:
Etheridgeum pulchrum

GENUS: MACROCALAMUS
Mountain Reed Snakes

- 7
- Small
- Malay Peninsula
- Montane forests
- Thought to be worms and slugs
- Egg-layers

SPECIES:
Macrocalamus chanardi
Macrocalamus gentingensis
Macrocalamus jasoni
Macrocalamus lateralis
Macrocalamus schulzi
Macrocalamus tweediei
Macrocalamus vogeli

GENUS: PSEUDORABDION

- 14
- Small
- Southeast Asia
- Forests, in leaf-litter and other debris
- Thought to be earthworms and other soft-bodied invertebrates
- Thought to be egg-layers

SPECIES:
Pseudorabdion albonuchalis
Pseudorabdion ater
Pseudorabdion collaris
Pseudorabdion eiselti
Pseudorabdion longiceps
Pseudorabdion mcnamarae
Pseudorabdion modiglianii
Pseudorabdion montanum
Pseudorabdion oxycephalum
Pseudorabdion sarasinorum
Pseudorabdion saravacense
Pseudorabdion sirambense
Pseudorabdion talonuran
Pseudorabdion taylori

GENUS: RABDION

- 1
- Small
- Sulawesi
- Unknown
- Unknown

⚥ Unknown
✎ Rare and poorly known

SPECIES:
Rabdion forsteni

....

SUBFAMILY: COLUBRINAE
100 GENERA CONTAINING 729 SPECIES

The colubrines constitute a very large subfamily found throughout the world and their collective description is much the same as that of the family as a whole. They may be small or large, slender or stout, and occupy a wide range of habitats. There are aquatic, burrowing, terrestrial, and arboreal species. Their diet and reproductive behaviour is equally diverse, although most are egg-layers.

GENUS: AELUROGLENA

〰 1
↔ Small
🌐 Ethiopia and northern Somalia
🏠 Desert and semi-desert
🍴 Unknown
⚥ Unknown
✎ Described in 1898 and seldom collected since

SPECIES:
Aeluroglena cucullata

GENUS: AHAETULLA

Asian Vine Snakes or Long-nosed Tree Snakes

〰 8
↔ Long, to 2 m (6 ft 6 in), and very slender
🌐 Sri Lanka, India, China, and Southeast Asia
🏠 Forests, plantations, and cultivated places; completely arboreal
🍴 Mainly lizards, but also small mammals and birds
⚥ Live-bearers
✎ Green or brown, with elongated heads and pointed snouts. The eyes have horizontally elliptical pupils, which are useful for judging distance. Rear-fanged, but not particularly dangerous to humans. They were previously placed in the genus *Dryophis*

SPECIES:
Ahaetulla dispar
Ahaetulla fasciolata
Ahaetulla fronticincta
Ahaetulla mycterizans
Ahaetulla nasuta
Ahaetulla perroteti
Ahaetulla prasina
Ahaetulla pulverulenta

GENUS: APROSDOKETOPHIS

〰 1
↔ Unknown
🌐 Somalia
🏠 Unknown
🍴 Unknown
⚥ Unknown
✎ A very poorly known species, only described in 2010

SPECIES:
Aprosdoketophis andreonei

GENUS: ARCHELAPHE

〰 1
↔ Medium
🌐 China, Myanmar, and Vietnam
🏠 Montane forests
🍴 Small mammals and possibly, frogs and lizards
⚥ Egg-layer
✎ The single species has been variously known as *Elaphe bella* and *Elaphe leonardi* among other names

SPECIES:
Archelaphe bella

GENUS: ARGYROGENA

〰 2
↔ Medium and slender
🌐 India
🏠 Open countryside
🍴 Mainly lizards
⚥ Thought to be egg-layers
✎ Diurnal and fast-moving

SPECIES:
Argyrogena fasciolata
Argyrogena vittacaudata

GENUS: ARIZONA

〰 1
↔ Moderately large
🌐 North America
🏠 Deserts and dry places
🍴 Lizards, other snakes, and small mammals
⚥ Egg-layer, producing 20 or more eggs

SPECIES:
Arizona elegans,
Glossy Snake

GENUS: BAMANOPHIS

〰 1
↔ Small
🌐 West Africa
🏠 Desert and arid scrub
🍴 Unknown, probably lizards
⚥ Presumably an egg-layer
✎ Poorly known

SPECIES:
Bamanophis dorri

GENUS: BOGERTOPHIS

Ratsnakes

〰 2
↔ Medium to large
🌐 North America (southern USA and northern Mexico)
🏠 Rocky deserts, in gulleys, gorges, and relatively humid micro-habitats
🍴 Mainly small mammals
⚥ Egg-layers, producing up to 20 eggs
✎ Powerful, constricting species with large eyes and heavily keeled scales. Active mostly at night. Formerly placed in the genus *Elaphe*

SPECIES:
Bogertophis rosaliae
• *Bogertophis subocularis,*
Trans-pecos Ratsnake (pp.76–77)

GENUS: BOIGA

〰 33
↔ Moderately large
🌐 Africa, southern Asia, Southeast Asia, the Philippines, the Indonesian archipelago, and northern Australia
🏠 Varied, including forests, lightly wooded places, and mangrove forests. All species are highly arboreal
🍴 Mainly arboreal lizards and mammals, including bats
⚥ Egg-layers
✎ Rear-fanged, but unlikely to pose a serious threat to humans. One species, the Brown Tree Snake, *Boiga irregularis*, has been accidentally introduced to several islands, notably Guam, where it has become a menace through its depredations of native birdlife and domestic animals

SPECIES:
Boiga andamanensis
Boiga angulata
Boiga barnesii
Boiga beddomei
Boiga bengkuluensis
Boiga bourreti
Boiga ceylonensis
• *Boiga cyanea,*
Green Catsnake (p.79)
Boiga cynodon,
Dog-toothed Catsnake
• *Boiga dendrophila,*
Mangrove Snake (p.78)
Boiga dightoni
Boiga drapiezii,
White-spotted Catsnake
Boiga flaviviridis
Boiga forsteni
Boiga gokool
Boiga guangxiensis
Boiga hoeseli
Boiga irregularis,
Brown Tree Snake
Boiga jaspidea
Boiga kraepelini
Boiga multifasciata
Boiga multomaculata
Boiga nigriceps
Boiga nuchalis
Boiga ochracea
Boiga philippina
Boiga quincunciata
Boiga saengsomi
Boiga schultzei
Boiga siamensis
Boiga tanahjampeana
Boiga trigonata
Boiga wallachi

GENUS: CEMOPHORA

〰 1
↔ Small
🌐 Southeastern North America
🏠 Burrowing in the ground and hiding under bark
🍴 Smaller snakes and lizards
⚥ Egg-layer, producing up to six elongated eggs
✎ Brightly coloured red, black, and white

SPECIES:
Cemophora coccinea,
Scarlet Snake

GENUS: CHAPINOPHIS

〰 1
↔ Small
🌐 Central America (Honduras)
🏠 Forest floor, among leaf-litter
🍴 Unknown
⚥ Unknown, but probably an egg-layer
✎ Poorly known

SPECIES:
Chapinophis xanthocheilus

GENUS: CHILOMENISCUS

Sand Snakes

〰 2
↔ Small
🌐 The Sonoran Desert of southwestern North America, and on islands in the Gulf of California (*C. savagei*)
🏠 Dry, sandy places
🍴 Invertebrates, including scorpions
⚥ Egg-layers
✎ The flattened heads and smooth, shiny scales are adaptations for "sand swimming"

SPECIES:
Chilomeniscus savagei
Chilomeniscus stramineus

GENUS: CHIONACTIS

Shovel-nosed Snakes

〰 3
↔ Small
🌐 Southwestern North America
🏠 Gravelly or sandy deserts, where they "swim" through the sand just below the surface
🍴 Invertebrates and insect larvae
⚥ Egg-layers, producing one to three small, elongated eggs

Brightly coloured false coral snakes with flattened heads and smooth, shiny scales

SPECIES:

Chionactis annulata
    Colorado Desert Shovel-nosed Snake
Chionactis occipitalis,
    Shovel-nosed Snake
Chionactis palarostris,
    Organ Pipe Shovel-nosed Snake

GENUS: **CHIRONIUS**

- 21
- Small to medium, and slender
- Central and northern South America
- In forests and lightly wooded areas, where they live on the ground and in low vegetation
- Lizards, birds, and small rodents
- Egg-layers

SPECIES:

Chironius bicarinatus
Chironius carinatus
Chironius challenger
Chironius diamantina
Chironius exoletus
Chironius flavolineatus
Chironius flavopictus
Chironius foveatus
Chironius fuscus
Chironius grandisquamis
Chironius laevicollis
Chironius laurenti
Chironius leucometapus
Chironius maculoventris
Chironius monticola
Chironius multiventris
Chironius quadricarinatus
Chironius scurrulus
Chironius septentrionalis
Chironius spixii
Chironius vincenti

GENUS: **CHRYSOPELEA**

Flying Snakes or Tree Snakes

- 5
- Moderately large snakes with slender bodies
- India, Sri Lanka, Myanmar, Malaysia, southern China, the Indonesian archipelago, and the Philippines
- Forests and plantations, where they are arboreal
- Arboreal lizards, frogs, and mammals
- Egg-layers
- They can flatten their undersurfaces to create a highly wind-resistant shape, enabling them to glide from treetops. Rear-fanged, but not considered particularly dangerous to humans

SPECIES:

Chrysopelea ornata
Chrysopelea paradisi,
    Paradise Tree Snake
Chrysopelea pelias
Chrysopelea rhodopleuron
Chrysopelea taprobanica

GENUS: **COELOGNATHUS**

- 7
- Medium
- India, Southeast Asia, and the Philippines
- Varied, from forests to land cleared for agriculture
- Small mammals, especially rodents
- Egg-layers
- Previously included in the genus *Elaphe*

SPECIES:

Coelognathus enganensis
Coelognathus erythrurus
Coelognathus flavolineatus,
    Yellow-striped Ratsnake
Coelognathus helena,
    Trinket Snake
Coelognathus philippinus
Coelognathus radiatus,
    Radiated Ratsnake
Coelognathus subradiatus

GENUS: **COLUBER**

Whipsnakes and Racers

- 12
- Medium to large, mostly slender
- North America
- Varied
- Lizards and small mammals. They hunt mainly on the ground, but will sometimes climb into low vegetation in pursuit of prey
- Egg-layers
- They defend themselves vigorously by biting, although they are harmless to humans. Diurnal. The genus will probably be divided into several smaller ones at a later date

SPECIES:

Coluber anthonyi
Coluber aurigulus,
    Cape Whipsnake
Coluber barbouri
Coluber bilineatus,
    Sonoran Whipsnake
Coluber constrictor,
    Racer
Coluber flagellum,
    Coachwhip Snake
Coluber fuliginosus
Coluber lateralis,
    Striped Racer
Coluber mentovarius
Coluber schotti,
    Schott's Whipsnake
Coluber slevini
Coluber taeniatus,
    Striped Whipsnake

GENUS: **COLUBROELAPS**

- 1
- Small and extremely thin
- Vietnam
- Terrestrial or burrowing, in primary and secondary forests
- Unknown
- Unknown, but probably an egg-layer

Described in 2009 and known from only two specimens so far

SPECIES:

Colubroelaps nguyenvansangi

GENUS: **CONOPSIS**

- 6
- Small
- North America (Mexico)
- Arid places and a variety of forest habitats. They live beneath leaf-litter and other forest debris
- Invertebrates, frogs, and small reptiles
- Live-bearers
- Previously included in more than one other genera

SPECIES:

Conopsis acuta
Conopsis amphisticha
Conopsis biserialis
Conopsis lineata
Conopsis megalodon
Conopsis nasus

GENUS: **CORONELLA**

Smooth Snakes

- 3
- Small
- Europe, North Africa, and central India (*C. brachyura*)
- Varied; dry to damp places, from mountains to sea-level
- Mainly lizards, but also nestling rodents
- *C. austriaca* is a live-bearer, *C. girondica* lays eggs, but the reproductive method of *C. brachyura* is unknown

SPECIES:

Coronella austriaca,
    Smooth Snake
Coronella brachyura
Coronella girondica,
    Southern Smooth Snake

GENUS: **CROTAPHOPELTIS**

- 6
- Medium
- Southern half of Africa
- Damp, marshy places
- Frogs and toads
- Egg-layers
- They have fangs towards the back of their mouths, but are not considered dangerous to humans

SPECIES:

Crotaphopeltis barotseensis,
    Barotse Water Snake
Crotaphopeltis braestrupi
Crotaphopeltis degeni
Crotaphopeltis hippocrepis
Crotaphopeltis hotamboeia,
    Herald Snake or Red-lipped Snake
Crotaphopeltis tornieri

GENUS: **CYCLOPHIOPS**

- 6
- Medium and slender
- Southeast Asia
- Unknown
- Thought to feed mostly on invertebrates
- Egg-layers

SPECIES:

Cyclophiops doriae
Cyclophiops hamptoni
Cyclophiops herminae
Cyclophiops major
Cyclophiops multicinctus
Cyclophiops semicarinatus

GENUS: **DASYPELTIS**

Egg-eating Snakes

- 12
- Medium, to about 1 m (3 ft 3 in)
- Central and southern Africa
- Varied, from arid semi-deserts to forests
- Birds' eggs, which they engulf whole, then crush in their throats
- Egg-layers
- They often mimic the appearance and behaviour of venomous adders from the same region. They have several adaptations in connection with their specialized diet

SPECIES:

Dasypeltis abyssina
Dasypeltis atra
Dasypeltis confusa
Dasypeltis fasciata
Dasypeltis gansi
Dasypeltis inornata,
    Southern Brown Egg-eater
Dasypeltis latericia
Dasypeltis medici,
    East African Egg-eater
Dasypeltis palmarum
Dasypeltis parascabra
Dasypeltis sahelensis
- *Dasypeltis scabra,*
    Common Egg-eater or
    Rhombic Egg-eater (pp.80–81)

GENUS: **DENDRELAPHIS**

- 44
- Medium to large, with slender bodies
- India, Sri Lanka, Myanmar, southern China, Southeast Asia, the Indonesian archipelago, and northern Australia
- Forests, where they are highly arboreal, although they also enter water
- Mainly lizards and amphibians, but also fish
- Egg-layers

SPECIES:

Dendrelaphis andamanensis
Dendrelaphis ashoki
Dendrelaphis bifrenalis
Dendrelaphis biloreatus
Dendrelaphis calligastra,
    Northern Tree Snake
Dendrelaphis caudolineatus

Dendrelaphis caudolineolatus
Dendrelaphis chairecacos
Dendrelaphis cyanochloris
Dendrelaphis flavescens
Dendrelaphis formosus
Dendrelaphis fuliginosus
Dendrelaphis gastrostictus
Dendrelaphis girii
Dendrelaphis grandoculis
Dendrelaphis grismeri
Dendrelaphis haasi
Dendrelaphis hollinrakei
Dendrelaphis humayuni
Dendrelaphis inornatus
Dendrelaphis keiensis
Dendrelaphis kopsteini
Dendrelaphis levitoni
Dendrelaphis lineolatus
Dendrelaphis lorentzii
Dendrelaphis luzonensis
Dendrelaphis macrops
Dendrelaphis marenae
Dendrelaphis modestus
Dendrelaphis ngansonensis
Dendrelaphis nigroserratus
Dendrelaphis oliveri
Dendrelaphis papuensis
Dendrelaphis philippinensis
Dendrelaphis pictus
Dendrelaphis punctulatus,
   Common Tree Snake
Dendrelaphis schokari
Dendrelaphis striatus
Dendrelaphis striolatus
Dendrelaphis subocularis
Dendrelaphis terrificus
Dendrelaphis tristis
Dendrelaphis underwoodi
Dendrelaphis walli

GENUS: **DENDROPHIDION**

Forest Racers

- ~ 15
- ↔ Small and very slender
- 🌐 Central and South America (Mexico to northern Bolivia)
- 🏠 Humid lowland forests, where they are mainly terrestrial, but may also climb
- ⊂ Rodents, lizards, and frogs
- ⚥ Thought to be egg-layers

SPECIES:
Dendrophidion apharocybe
Dendrophidion atlantica
Dendrophidion bivittatus
Dendrophidion boshelli
Dendrophidion brunneum
Dendrophidion clarkii
Dendrophidion crybelum
Dendrophidion dendrophis
Dendrophidion graciliverpa
Dendrophidion nuchale
Dendrophidion paucicarinatum
Dendrophidion percarinatum
Dendrophidion prolixum
Dendrophidion rufiterminorum
Dendrophidion vinitor

GENUS: **DIPSADOBOA**

- ~ 10
- ↔ Small and slender
- 🌐 Africa
- 🏠 Forests, where they are arboreal
- ⊂ Geckos and frogs
- ⚥ Egg-layers
- ☑ Rear-fanged, though not dangerous to humans; active at night

SPECIES:
Dipsadoboa aulica
Dipsadoboa brevirostris
Dipsadoboa duchesnii
Dipsadoboa flavida
Dipsadoboa shrevei
Dipsadoboa underwoodi
Dipsadoboa unicolor
Dipsadoboa viridis
Dipsadoboa weileri
Dipsadoboa werneri

GENUS: **DISPHOLIDUS**

- ~ 1
- ↔ Large, but slender
- 🌐 Throughout Africa, south of the Sahara
- 🏠 Forests, where it is arboreal
- ⊂ Hunting by day, it specializes in chameleons, but also takes other lizards. It kills its prey by grasping and chewing, using its venom fangs
- ⚥ Egg-layer, producing clutches of up to 25 eggs
- ☑ One of the few rear-fanged snakes that have caused human fatalities

SPECIES:
- Dispholidus typus,
   Boomslang (pp.82–83)

GENUS: **DOLICHOPHIS**

Old World Whipsnakes

- ~ 4
- ↔ Medium to large
- 🌐 Southeastern Europe and parts of the Middle East
- 🏠 Dry fields and hillsides
- ⊂ Small mammals and reptiles
- ⚥ Egg-layers
- ☑ Previously included in the genus Coluber

SPECIES:
Dolichophis caspius
Dolichophis cypriensis
Dolichophis jugularis
Dolichophis schmidti

GENUS: **DRYMARCHON**

- ~ 5
- ↔ Large, sometimes to 2.5 m (8 ft 2 in)
- 🌐 North, Central, and northern South America
- 🏠 Varied, dry pine hammocks and palmetto scrub to tropical forests
- ⊂ Fish, frogs, other reptiles, birds, and mammals
- ⚥ Egg-layers

SPECIES:
Drymarchon caudomaculatus
Drymarchon corais,
   Indigo Snake or Cribo
- Drymarchon couperi,
   Eastern Indigo Snake (pp.84–85)
Drymarchon margaritae
Drymarchon melanurus,
   Black-tailed Cribo

GENUS: **DRYMOBIUS**

Tropical Racers

- ~ 4
- ↔ Fairly long, and slender
- 🌐 North America (southern Texas) through Central America and into South America
- 🏠 Varied
- ⊂ Mainly amphibians
- ⚥ Egg-layers
- ☑ Active in the day

SPECIES:
Drymobius chloroticus
Drymobius margaritiferus
Drymobius melanotropis
Drymobius rhombifer

GENUS: **DRYMOLUBER**

- ~ 3
- ↔ Long and slender
- 🌐 North, Central, and South America (southern Texas to Peru)
- 🏠 Varied
- ⊂ Mainly lizards
- ⚥ Egg-layers

SPECIES:
Drymoluber apurimacensis
Drymoluber brazili
Drymoluber dichrous

GENUS: **DRYOCALAMUS**

- ~ 6
- ↔ Small
- 🌐 Sri Lanka, India, Southeast Asia, and the Philippines
- 🏠 Forests, where they are arboreal
- ⊂ Thought to be invertebrates, frogs, and lizards
- ⚥ Unknown
- ☑ Poorly known. Nocturnal

SPECIES:
Dryocalamus davisonii
Dryocalamus gracilis
Dryocalamus nympha
Dryocalamus philippinus
Dryocalamus subannulatus
Dryocalamus tristrigatus

GENUS: **DRYOPHIOPS**

- ~ 2
- ↔ Small (D. philippina) to medium
- 🌐 Southeast Asia and the Philippines
- 🏠 Forests, where they are aboreal
- ⊂ Small lizards
- ⚥ D. rubescens is a live-bearer, but the reproductive method of the other species is unknown

SPECIES:
Dryophiops philippina
Dryophiops rubescens

GENUS: **EIRENIS**

- ~ 19
- ↔ Small
- 🌐 From North Africa, throughout Turkey and the Middle East, and into northwestern India
- 🏠 Among rocks and other debris
- ⊂ Invertebrates and small lizards
- ⚥ Egg-layers, where known
- ☑ Secretive. Some species are very poorly known and others are only recently described

SPECIES:
Eirenis africana
Eirenis aurolineatus
Eirenis barani
Eirenis collaris
Eirenis coronella
Eirenis coronelloides
Eirenis decemlineatus
Eirenis eiselti
Eirenis hakkariensis
Eirenis kermanensis
Eirenis levantinus
Eirenis lineomaculatus
Eirenis medus
Eirenis modestus
Eirenis persicus
Eirenis punctatolineatus
Eirenis rechingeri
Eirenis rothii
Eirenis thospitis

GENUS: **ELACHISTODON**

- ~ 1
- ↔ Small
- 🌐 India
- 🏠 Unknown
- ⊂ Birds' eggs, paralleling the African Dasypeltis
- ⚥ Thought to be an egg-layer
- ☑ Very rare and poorly known

SPECIES:
Elachistodon westermanni,
   Indian Egg-eating Snake

GENUS: **ELAPHE**

- ~ 11
- ↔ Medium to large
- 🌐 Europe, Central Asia, and China
- 🏠 Varied, from dry rocky hillsides to grasslands and mountains
- ⊂ Small mammals and reptiles
- ⚥ Egg-layers
- ☑ The genus was previously much larger but has been split into several new genera recently. Of the remaining species, E. zoigeensis has only recently been described, from the Tibetan Plateau

SPECIES:
Elaphe anomala
Elaphe bimaculata
Elaphe carinata
Elaphe climacophora
Elaphe davidi
Elaphe dione
Elaphe quadrivirgata

Elaphe quatuorlineata
Elaphe sauromates
Elaphe schrenckii
Elaphe zoigeensis

GENUS: **EUPREPIOPHIS**

- 3
- Medium
- Southeast Asia, southern China, Japan
- Moist forests, often in foothills
- Small mammals and reptiles
- Egg-layers
- Previously included in the genus *Elaphe*

SPECIES:

Euprepiophis conspicillata,
  Japanese Wood Snake
- *Euprepiophis mandarinus,*
  Mandarin Ratsnake (pp.86–87)
Euprepiophis perlacea,
  Pearl-banded Ratsnake

GENUS: **FICIMIA**

Hook-nosed Snakes

- 7
- Small
- North and Central America
  (southern Texas to northern Honduras)
- Varied, from arid semi-deserts to forests
- Mainly spiders and centipedes
- Egg-layers
- Rear-fanged, though not dangerous to humans. Two species are each known from only a single specimen

SPECIES:

Ficimia hardyi
Ficimia olivacea
Ficimia publia,
  Yucatan Hook-nosed Snake
Ficimia ramirezi
Ficimia ruspator
Ficimia streckeri,
  Mexican Hook-nosed Snake
Ficimia variegata

GENUS: **GEAGRAS**

- 1
- Small
- Mexico
- Unknown, but thought to burrow
- Unknown
- Unknown
- Rare and poorly known

SPECIES:

Geagras redimitus

GENUS: **GONYOSOMA**

Ratsnakes or Racers

- 6
- Large
- Southeast Asia
- Forests, where they are highly arboreal
- Frogs, lizards, birds, and small mammals
- Egg-layers
- Mostly bright green in colour. Previously included in the genus *Elaphe*

SPECIES:

Gonyosoma boulengeri
Gonyosoma frenatus
Gonyosoma jansenii,
  Celebes Black-tailed Ratsnake
  or Celebes Black-tailed Racer
Gonyosoma margaritatus
- *Gonyosoma oxycephalum,*
  Red-tailed Racer (pp.88–89)
Gonyosoma prasinus,
  Green Bush Ratsnake or
  Green Bush Racer

GENUS: **GYALOPION**

Hook-nosed Snakes

- 2
- Small
- Central and northern South America
- Dry places
- Mainly spiders
- Egg-layers
- *G. quadrangulare* is bright red, and mimics the black and white coral snake. Both species are nocturnal. They are closely related to the *Ficimia* species, also known as hook-nosed snakes

SPECIES:

Gyalopion canum
Gyalopion quadrangulare

GENUS: **HAPSIDOPHRYS**

- 3
- Medium, and slender
- Tropical Africa
- Forests, where they are highly arboreal
- Frogs
- Unknown

SPECIES:

Hapsidophrys lineatus
Hapsidophrys principis
Hapsidophrys smaragdina

GENUS: **HEMEROPHIS**

- 2
- Medium
- Socotra Island, Yemen
- Dry, rocky hillsides
- Probably small mammals and reptiles
- Egg-layer
- The single species has previously been called *Zamenis socotrana* and *Coluber socotrae*

SPECIES:

Hemerophis socotrae,
  Socotran Racer
Hemerophis zebrinus

GENUS: **HEMORRHOIS**

- 4
- Medium to large
- Southern Europe, North Africa, the Middle East, and Central Asia
- Dry, scrubby and rocky hillsides, and cultivated fields
- Lizards, small rodents
- Egg-layers
- Previously included in the genus *Coluber*

SPECIES:

Hemorrhois algirus,
  Algerian Whipsnake
Hemorrhois hippocrepis,
  Horseshoe Snake
Hemorrhois nummifer
Hemorrhois ravergieri,
  Spotted Whipsnake

GENUS: **HIEROPHIS**

Whipsnakes

- 3
- Medium
- South and Southeast Europe, Cyprus, Iran
- Dry Mediterranean scrub and rocky hillsides
- Small mammals and reptiles
- Egg-layers
- Previously included in the genus *Coluber*

SPECIES:

Hierophis andreanus
Hierophis gemonensis,
  Balkan Whipsnake
Hierophis viridiflavus,
  Western Whipsnake

GENUS: **LAMPROPELTIS**

Kingsnakes

- 21
- Small to fairly large
- North, Central, and South America
- Deserts, mountains, and forests
- Lizards, other snakes, birds, and mammals
- Egg-layers
- Several are brightly coloured false coral snakes, with rings of red, black, and white. Species may be active during the day or night, depending on their habitat. Several species were formerly subspecies of *L. getula* and *L. triangulum*, but have now been elevated to full species

SPECIES:

Lampropeltis abnorma,
  Honduran Milksnake
- *Lampropeltis alterna,*
  Grey-banded Kingsnake (p.92)
Lampropeltis annulata,
  Texas Milksnake
- *Lampropeltis californiae,*
  California Kingsnake

Lampropeltis calligaster,
  Prairie Kingsnake
Lampropeltis elapsoides,
  Scarlet Kingsnake
Lampropeltis extenuata
Lampropeltis gentilis,
  Common Kingsnake
Lampropeltis getula,
  Common Kingsnake
Lampropeltis holbrooki,
  Speckled Kingsnake
Lampropeltis knoblochi,
  Chihuahan Mountain Kingsnake
- *Lampropeltis mexicana,*
  Mexican Kingsnake (p.93)
Lampropeltis micropholis,
  Ecuadorian Milksnake
Lampropeltis nigra,
  Black Kingsnake
- *Lampropeltis polyzona,*
  Atlantic Central
  American Kingsnake (pp.98–99)
- *Lampropeltis pyromelana,*
  Sonoran Mountain Kingsnake
  (pp.96–97)
Lampropeltis ruthveni,
  Queretaro Kingsnake
Lampropeltis splendida,
  Desert Kingsnake
Lampropeltis triangulum,
  Milksnake
Lampropeltis webbi
Lampropeltis zonata,
  California Mountain Kingsnake

GENUS: **LEPTODRYMUS**

- 1
- Fairly large
- Central America
- Montane rainforests
- Unknown
- Unknown
- Rare, its natural history is unknown

SPECIES:

Leptodrymus pulcherrimus

GENUS: **LEPTOPHIS**

Parrot Snakes

- 11
- Long and slender
- Central and South America
  (northwestern Mexico to Argentina and Paraguay)
- Varied, including uplands. Partially arboreal
- Amphibians, lizards, snakes, small birds (and their eggs), and small mammals
- Egg-layers
- The upper surfaces are often bright green. Rear-fanged, though not dangerous to humans. When alarmed they open their mouths widely to display bright blue inner parts. Active during the day

SPECIES:

Leptophis ahaetulla
Leptophis coeruleodorsus
Leptophis cupreus
Leptophis depressirostris
Leptophis diplotropis
Leptophis haileyi
Leptophis mexicanus

Leptophis modestus
Leptophis nebulosus
Leptophis riveti
Leptophis stimsoni

GENUS: **LEPTUROPHIS**

- 🐍 1
- ↔ Large
- 🌍 Indonesia, Malaysia (including Borneo), and Thailand
- 🏠 Lowland rainforests, often close to streams and in dense vegetation
- 🍴 Frogs, lizards, and birds
- ⚲ Thought to be an egg-layer

SPECIES:

Lepturophis albofuscus

GENUS: **LIOPELTIS**

- 🐍 6
- ↔ Small and slender
- 🌍 South and Southeast Asia
- 🏠 Mostly terrestrial, living in tropical rainforests, cultivated fields, and plantations
- 🍴 Thought to feed on invertebrates, amphibians, and lizards
- ⚲ Egg-layers
- ✏ There is some confusion over the validity of some of the species listed

SPECIES:

Liopeltis calamaria
Liopeltis frenatus
Liopeltis philippinus
Liopeltis rappi
Liopeltis stoliczkae
Liopeltis tricolor

GENUS: **LYCODON**

- 🐍 51
- ↔ Small to medium
- 🌍 Asia
- 🏠 Varied, including villages and farms. Terrestrial or slightly arboreal
- 🍴 Lizards and snakes, although other prey may be taken
- ⚲ Egg-layers, where known
- ✏ The taxonomy of the genus is confused: the number of species listed here may be greatly exaggerated

SPECIES:

Lycodon alcalai
Lycodon aulicus
Lycodon bibonius
Lycodon butleri
Lycodon capucinus
Lycodon cardamomensis
Lycodon carinatus
Lycodon cavernicolus
Lycodon chrysoprateros
Lycodon davidi
Lycodon dumerilii
Lycodon effraenis
Lycodon fasciatus
Lycodon fausti
Lycodon ferroni
Lycodon flavicollis
Lycodon flavomaculatus
Lycodon flavozonatus
Lycodon futsingensis

Lycodon gammiei
Lycodon gongshan
Lycodon hypsirhinoides
Lycodon jara
Lycodon kundui
Lycodon laoensis
Lycodon liuchengchaoi
Lycodon mackinnoni
Lycodon meridionale
Lycodon muelleri
Lycodon multifasciatus
Lycodon multizonatus
Lycodon odishii
Lycodon ophiophagus
Lycodon orientalis
Lycodon osmanhilli
Lycodon paucifasciatus
Lycodon rosozonatus
Lycodon rufozonatus
Lycodon ruhstrati
Lycodon semicarinatus
Lycodon septentrionalis
Lycodon solivagus
Lycodon stormi
Lycodon striatus
Lycodon subcinctus
Lycodon synaptor
Lycodon tessellatus
Lycodon tiwarii
Lycodon travancoricus
Lycodon zawi
Lycodon zoosvictoriae

GENUS: **LYTORHYNCHUS**

Leaf-nosed Snakes

- 🐍 6
- ↔ Small
- 🌍 North Africa, the Middle East, and Central Asia
- 🏠 Dry places, including sand dunes and gravel deserts
- 🍴 Geckos and other lizards
- ⚲ Egg-layers
- ✏ The rostral scale is enlarged and has a similar shape to that of North American leaf-nosed snakes (*Phyllorhynchus*), which live in similar habitats and are thought to have a similar diet

SPECIES:

Lytorhynchus diadema
Lytorhynchus gasperetti
Lytorhynchus kennedyi
Lytorhynchus maynardi
Lytorhynchus paradoxus
Lytorhynchus ridgewayi

GENUS: **MACROPROTODON**

- 🐍 4
- ↔ Small
- 🌍 Western Europe, North Africa, and parts of the Middle East
- 🏠 Dry and rocky places
- 🍴 Lizards, which they catch while they are asleep
- ⚲ Egg-layers
- ✏ Rear-fanged, though not dangerous to humans. Completely nocturnal

SPECIES:

Macroprotodon abubakeri
Macroprotodon brevis
Macroprotodon cucullatus,
   Cowled Snake or False Smooth Snake
Macroprotodon mauritanicus

GENUS: **MASTIGODRYAS**

- 🐍 14
- ↔ Medium with slender bodies
- 🌍 Central and South America (Mexico to Argentina)
- 🏠 Varied, but usually open country
- 🍴 Amphibians, lizards, snakes, birds, and small mammals
- ⚲ Egg-layers
- ✏ Active by day

SPECIES:

Mastigodryas alternatus
Mastigodryas amarali
Mastigodryas bifossatus
Mastigodryas boddaerti
Mastigodryas bruesi
Mastigodryas cliftoni
Mastigodryas danieli
Mastigodryas dorsalis
Mastigodryas heathii
Mastigodryas melanolomus
Mastigodryas moratoi
Mastigodryas pleei
Mastigodryas pulchriceps
Mastigodryas reticulatus

GENUS: **MEIZODON**

- 🐍 5
- ↔ Small
- 🌍 Tropical Africa
- 🏠 Unknown
- 🍴 Lizards and frogs
- ⚲ Egg-layers

SPECIES:

Meizodon coronatus
Meizodon krameri
Meizodon plumbiceps
Meizodon regularis
Meizodon semiornatus

GENUS: **OLIGODON**

Kukri Snakes

- 🐍 74
- ↔ Small to medium, with chunky bodies
- 🌍 Asia (the Middle East, through Central Asia and India, Myanmar, southern China, and into the Malay Peninsula)
- 🏠 Varied
- 🍴 Varied, including amphibians, small mammals and, especially, the eggs of reptiles
- ⚲ All the known species are egg-layers
- ✏ The snouts are slightly upturned. Long, curved fangs at the back of the mouths (similar to the kukri knives used by the Gurkha soldiers from the same part of the world) are used for slashing the shells of reptiles' eggs and for defence, although they are harmless to humans. The species may be nocturnal or diurnal

SPECIES:

Oligodon affinis
Oligodon albocinctus
Oligodon ancorus
Oligodon annamensis
Oligodon annulifer

Oligodon arnensis
Oligodon barroni
Oligodon bitorquatus
Oligodon booliati
Oligodon brevicauda
Oligodon calamarius
Oligodon catenatus
Oligodon cattiensis
Oligodon chinensis
Oligodon cinereus
Oligodon cruentatus
Oligodon cyclurus
Oligodon deuvei
Oligodon dorsalis
Oligodon eberhardti
Oligodon erythrogaster
Oligodon erythrorhachis
Oligodon everetti
Oligodon fasciolatus
Oligodon forbesi
Oligodon formosanus
Oligodon hamptoni
Oligodon inornatus
Oligodon jintakunei
Oligodon joynsoni
Oligodon juglandifer
Oligodon kampucheaensis
Oligodon kheriensis
Oligodon lacroixi
Oligodon lungshenensis
Oligodon macrurus
Oligodon maculatus
Oligodon mcdougalli
Oligodon melaneus
Oligodon melanozonatus
Oligodon meyerinkii
Oligodon modestus
Oligodon moricei
Oligodon mouhoti
Oligodon nagao
Oligodon nikhili
Oligodon notospilus
Oligodon ocellatus
Oligodon octolineatus
Oligodon ornatus
Oligodon perkinsi
Oligodon petronellae
Oligodon planiceps
Oligodon praefrontalis
Oligodon propinquus
Oligodon pseudotaeniatus
Oligodon pulcherrimus
Oligodon purpurascens
Oligodon saintgironsi
Oligodon signatus
Oligodon splendidus
Oligodon sublineatus
Oligodon taeniatus
Oligodon taeniolatus
Oligodon theobaldi
Oligodon torquatus
Oligodon travancoricus
Oligodon trilineatus
Oligodon unicolor
Oligodon venustus
Oligodon vertebralis
Oligodon waandersi
Oligodon wagneri
Oligodon woodmasoni

GENUS: **OOCATOCHUS**

- 🐍 1
- ↔ Small
- 🌍 Eastern Russia, southeastern China, Taiwan, and parts of Southeast Asia
- 🏠 Semi-aquatic, in marshes and rice-paddies
- 🍴 Frogs
- ⚲ Live-bearer
- ✏ The single species was previously known as *Elaphe rufodorsatus*

SPECIES:

Oocatochus rufodorsatus

GENUS: **OPHEODRYS**

Green Snakes

- 🐍 2
- ↔ Small and very slender
- 🌐 North America
- 🏠 Grasses and other low vegetation, where they are terrestrial
- ◀ Invertebrates, including spiders and caterpillars
- ⚥ Both species are egg-layers, but the eggs of *O. vernalis* hatch after a very short period of incubation and the species may even be a live-bearer in parts of its range
- 📝 Diurnal. *O. vernalis* is sometimes placed in a separate genus, *Liochlorophis*. Two additional species, from Mexico, are sometimes recognized

SPECIES:

- *Opheodrys aestivus*, Rough Green Snake (pp.104–05)
- *Opheodrys vernalis*, Smooth Green Snake

GENUS: **OREOCRYPTOPHIS**

Red Bamboo Ratsnake, Red Mountain Racer

- 🐍 1
- ↔ Medium
- 🌐 India, southern China, Southeast Asia
- 🏠 Moist forests, including montane rainforest
- ◀ Small mammals and, possibly, reptiles
- ⚥ Egg-layer
- 📝 The single species was previously known as *Elaphe porphyracea* or *Oreophis porphyraceus*. It occurs in many forms, often brightly coloured with bands or stripes of red and black. Several subspecies are recognized and it is possible that some of these are, in fact, separate species

SPECIES:

Oreocryptophis porphyraceus

GENUS: **ORIENTOCOLUBER**

- 🐍 1
- ↔ Medium
- 🌐 Central Asia
- 🏠 Steppe
- ◀ Small mammals and reptiles
- ⚥ Egg-layer
- 📝 The single species has been placed in various genera in the past, including *Coluber*

SPECIES:

Orientocoluber spinalis

GENUS: **ORTHRIOPHIS**

Asiatic Ratsnakes, Beauty Snakes

- 🐍 4
- ↔ Medium to large
- 🌐 India, China, Southeast Asia
- 🏠 Forests, hillsides, and cultivated land
- ◀ Small mammals
- ⚥ Egg-layers
- 📝 Previously included in a number of other ratsnake genera in the past. The largest and most widespread species, *Orthriophis taeniurus*, occurs in a number of distinct subspecies, including the well-known Cave Racer, *O. t. ridleyi*

SPECIES:

Orthriophis cantoris, Eastern Trinket Snake
Orthriophis hodgsoni
Orthriophis moellendorffi, Flower Snake or Moellendorf's Ratsnake
Orthriophis taeniurus, Beauty Snake

GENUS: **OXYBELIS**

Vine Snakes

- 🐍 4
- ↔ Long and slender
- 🌐 North, Central, and South America (Texas to Bolivia and Peru)
- 🏠 Forests, where they are arboreal
- ◀ Mainly lizards
- ⚥ Egg-layers
- 📝 They have rear fangs and bite readily, though they are not considered dangerous to humans

SPECIES:

Oxybelis aeneus, Brown Vine Snake
Oxybelis brevirostris
Oxybelis fulgidus
Oxybelis wilsoni

GENUS: **PANTHEROPHIS**

American Ratsnakes

- 🐍 9
- ↔ Medium to large
- 🌐 North America
- 🏠 Varied: farmland, wetlands, prairies, forests, and rocky deserts
- ◀ Small mammals, predominantly rodents
- ⚥ Egg-layers
- 📝 Well-known snakes previously included in the genus *Elaphe*. Several are colourful and easily managed snakes and are very popular among amateur snake-breeders

SPECIES:

Pantherophis alleghaniensis, Eastern Ratsnake
- *Pantherophis bairdi*, Baird's Ratsnake (pp.106–07)

Pantherophis emoryi, Great Plains Ratsnake
- *Pantherophis guttatus*, Corn Snake or Red Ratsnake (pp.108–09)
Pantherophis obsoletus, Western Ratsnake
Pantherophis ramspotti, Western Fox Snake
Pantherophis slowinskii, Slowinski's Corn Snake
Pantherophis spiloides, Gray Ratsnake
Pantherophis vulpinus, Eastern Fox Snake

GENUS: **PHILOTHAMNUS**

Green Snakes, Bush Snakes

- 🐍 20
- ↔ Small and slender
- 🌐 Southern half of Africa
- 🏠 Varied, but always well-vegetated
- ◀ Mainly frogs
- ⚥ Egg-layers

SPECIES:

Philothamnus angolensis, Western Bush Snake
Philothamnus battersbyi
Philothamnus bequaerti
Philothamnus carinatus
Philothamnus dorsalis
Philothamnus girardi
Philothamnus heterodermus
Philothamnus heterolepidotus
Philothamnus hoplogaster, Green Bush Snake
Philothamnus hughesi
Philothamnus irregularis
Philothamnus macrops
Philothamnus natalensis, Natal Green Snake
Philothamnus nitidus
Philothamnus ornatus, Ornate Bush Snake
Philothamnus pobeguini
Philothamnus punctatus
Philothamnus ruandae
Philothamnus semivariegatus, Spotted Bush Snake
Philothamnus thomensis

GENUS: **PHRYNONAX**

- 🐍 4
- ↔ Medium
- 🌐 Central America
- 🏠 Forests
- ◀ Birds and their eggs. Also, small mammals and reptiles
- ⚥ Egg-layer
- 📝 The single species was previously known as *Pseustes poecilonotus*

SPECIES:

Phrynonax poecilonotus
Phrynonax polylepis
Phrynonax sexcarinatus
Phrynonax shropshirei

GENUS: **PHYLLORHYNCHUS**

Leaf-nosed Snakes

- 🐍 2
- ↔ Small

- 🌐 Western North America (Sonoran Desert)
- 🏠 Dry places
- ◀ Small lizards, especially geckos, and their eggs
- ⚥ Egg-layers
- 📝 The common name is derived from the modified scale found at the tip of the snout

SPECIES:

Phyllorhynchus browni, Saddled Leaf-nosed Snake
Phyllorhynchus decurtatus, Spotted Leaf-nosed Snake

GENUS: **PITUOPHIS**

Gopher, Pine, and Bull Snakes

- 🐍 6
- ↔ Medium to large, with stout, muscular bodies
- 🌐 North and Central America
- 🏠 Varied, from deserts to pinewoods and cultivated fields
- ◀ Small mammals, up to the size of squirrels and rabbits
- ⚥ Egg-layers
- 📝 They hiss loudly if threatened and some forms bite viciously. The Louisiana Pine Snake, *P. ruthveni*, is one of the rarest snakes in North America

SPECIES:

Pituophis catenifer, Gopher Snake or Bull Snake
Pituophis deppei, Mexican Gopher Snake
Pituophis lineaticollis, Central American Gopher Snake
- *Pituophis melanoleucus*, Pine Snake (pp.110–11)
Pituophis ruthveni, Louisiana Pine Snake
Pituophis vertebralis, Cape Gopher Snake

GENUS: **PLATYCEPS**

- 🐍 24
- ↔ Small to medium
- 🌐 North Africa, southeastern Europe, Arabia, the Middle East, and Central Asia up to India
- 🏠 Varied, but mostly dry, rocky places
- ◀ Small lizards and snakes
- ⚥ Egg-layers
- 📝 Previously included in the genus *Coluber*

SPECIES:

Platyceps afarensis
Platyceps bholanathi
Platyceps brevis
Platyceps collaris
Platyceps elegantissimus
Platyceps florulentus
Platyceps gracilis
Platyceps insulanus
Platyceps karelini
Platyceps ladacensis
Platyceps largeni
Platyceps messanai

Platyceps najadum
Platyceps noeli
Platyceps rhodorachis
Platyceps scortecci
Platyceps sinai
Platyceps sindhensis
Platyceps somalicus
Platyceps taylori
Platyceps tessellata
Platyceps thomasi
Platyceps variabilis
Platyceps ventromaculatus

GENUS: PLIOCERCUS

- 3
- Medium
- South America (Amazon basin)
- Lowland rainforests
- Mainly frogs
- Egg-layers

SPECIES:
Pliocercus elapoides
Pliocercus euryzonus
Pliocercus wilmarai

GENUS: PSEUDELAPHE

Central American Ratsnake

- 1
- Medium
- Central America
- Forests and dry scrub
- Small mammals and reptiles
- Egg-layer
- The single species was previously known as *Elaphe flavirufa*

SPECIES:
Pseudelaphe flavirufa

GENUS: PSEUDOFICIMIA

- 1
- Small
- Mexico
- Unknown
- Unknown
- Unknown
- A rare snake about which almost nothing is known. Presumed to be similar in habits to the hook-nosed snakes, *Ficimia* species, which it resembles

SPECIES:
Pseudoficimia frontalis

GENUS: PTYAS

Asian Ratsnakes

- 8
- Large to very large, and powerful
- Asia
- Varied, often found around villages and towns
- Rodents, amphibians, lizards, snakes, and birds
- Egg-layers

- Active during the day. They are killed in massive numbers for the skin trade and are disappearing from many of the places where they were formerly abundant

SPECIES:
Ptyas carinata,
    Keeled Ratsnake
Ptyas dhumnades
Ptyas dipsas
Ptyas fusca
Ptyas korros
Ptyas luzonensis
Ptyas mucosa
Ptyas nigromarginata

GENUS: RHAMNOPHIS

- 2
- Small
- West and Central Africa
- Tropical forests
- Unknown
- Unknown
- Very rare and poorly known

SPECIES:
Rhamnophis aethiopissa
Rhamnophis batesii

GENUS: RHINECHIS

Ladder Snake

- 1
- Medium
- Spain, southern France
- Rocky hillsides, dry forest clearings, and cleared agricultural land, especially with dry stone walls
- Small mammals
- Egg-layer
- The single species was previously known as *Elaphe scalaris*

SPECIES:
Rhinechis scalaris,
    Ladder Snake

GENUS: RHINOBOTHRYUM

- 2
- Large and slender, with blunt heads
- Central and South America
- Forests, where they are arboreal
- Unknown
- Unknown
- Brightly banded, like the coral snake, *Micrurus alleni*, which lives in the same region. Nocturnal

SPECIES:
Rhinobothryum bovallii
Rhinobothryum lentiginosum

GENUS: RHINOCHEILUS

- 1
- Medium, to nearly 1 m (3 ft 3 in)

- North America and northern Mexico
- Dry places, where it is terrestrial
- Mostly lizards but also snakes, small mammals, and birds
- Egg-layer
- Largely nocturnal. A second form, *R. lecontei antoni*, may be a separate species

SPECIES:
Rhinocheilus lecontei,
    Long-nosed Snake

GENUS: RHYNCHOCALAMUS

- 3
- Small and slender
- Middle East
- Dry places
- Invertebrates and small reptiles
- Thought to be egg-layers

SPECIES:
Rhynchocalamus arabicus
Rhynchocalamus barani
Rhynchocalamus melanocephalus

GENUS: SALVADORA

Patch-nosed Snakes

- 6
- To about 1 m (3 ft 3 in) in length, with slender bodies
- North and Central America
- Dry, sandy, and rocky places
- Mainly lizards and snakes
- Egg-layers
- Fast-moving, diurnal hunters

SPECIES:
Salvadora bairdi
Salvadora grahamiae,
    Mountain Patch-nosed Snake
Salvadora hexalepis,
    Western Patch-nosed Snake
Salvadora intermedia
Salvadora lemniscata
Salvadora mexicana

GENUS: SCAPHIOPHIS

- 2
- To 1 m (3 ft 3 in)
- Central and West Africa
- Unknown
- Unknown
- Egg-layers

SPECIES:
Scaphiophis albopunctatus
Scaphiophis raffreyi

GENUS: SCOLECOPHIS

- 1
- Small and slender
- Central America
- Forests
- Centipedes
- Egg-layer

- A brightly marked false coral snake

SPECIES:
Scolecophis atrocinctus

GENUS: SENTICOLIS

- 1
- Long, to 2 m (6 ft 6 in), but quite slender
- North and Central America
- Forests, where it is semi-arboreal
- Lizards, birds, and small mammals
- Egg-layer
- Formerly placed in the genus *Elaphe*

SPECIES:
Senticolis triaspis,
    Neotropical Ratsnake

GENUS: SIMOPHIS

- 1
- Small and slender
- Brazil
- Fields and clearings
- Unknown
- Unknown

SPECIES:
Simophis rhinostoma

GENUS: SONORA

Ground Snakes

- 4
- Small
- North America and Mexico
- Dry places
- Insects, spiders, and scorpions
- Egg-layers
- The markings are extremely variable and various colour forms have sometimes been regarded as separate species

SPECIES:
Sonora aemula
Sonora michoacanensis
Sonora mutabilis
Sonora semiannulata

GENUS: SPALEROSOPHIS

- 6
- Fairly large, to more than 1 m (3 ft 3 in)
- North Africa and the Middle East
- Deserts and scrub
- Rodents, birds, and probably lizards
- Egg-layers

SPECIES:
Spalerosophis arenarius
Spalerosophis atriceps
Spalerosophis diadema
Spalerosophis dolichospilus
Spalerosophis josephscorteccii
Spalerosophis microlepis

GENUS: **SPILOTES**

- 🐍 2
- ↔ Large, to over 2 m (6 ft 6 in)
- 🌐 Central and South America, from Mexico to Argentina
- 🏠 Varied, but often dry forests, where they are highly arboreal. Often associated with human dwellings
- 🍴 Amphibians, reptiles, birds, birds' eggs, bats, and other mammals
- ♀ Egg-layers
- 📝 Brightly marked snakes that have prominent ridges down their backs. Common species that defend themselves vigorously by biting, but they are not harmful to humans

SPECIES:
Spilotes pullatus,
    Tiger Snake, Chicken Snake, or
    Thunder Snake
Spilotes sulphureus

GENUS: **STEGONOTUS**

- 🐍 10
- ↔ Medium to large
- 🌐 Southeast Asia, the Philippines, New Guinea, and northern Australia
- 🏠 Varied
- 🍴 Fish, frogs, and tadpoles
- ♀ Egg-layers

SPECIES:
Stegonotus batjanensis
Stegonotus borneensis
Stegonotus cucullatus,
    Slaty-grey Snake
Stegonotus diehli
Stegonotus florensis
Stegonotus guentheri
Stegonotus heterurus
Stegonotus modestus
Stegonotus muelleri
Stegonotus parvus

GENUS: **STENORRHINA**

- 🐍 2
- ↔ Medium, with stout bodies
- 🌐 Central and northern South America, from Mexico to Ecuador
- 🏠 Lowland forests and grasslands
- 🍴 Invertebrates, especially spiders and scorpions
- ♀ Egg-layers

SPECIES:
Stenorrhina degenhardtii
Stenorrhina freminvillei

GENUS: **STICHOPHANES**

- 🐍 1
- ↔ Small
- 🌐 Central China
- 🏠 Damp places
- 🍴 Slugs and snails
- ♀ Unknown
- 📝 Described from a single specimen in 1983, no more were discovered until 2006

SPECIES:
Stichophanes ningshaanensis

GENUS: **SYMPHIMUS**

- 🐍 2
- ↔ Small, to about 50 cm (1 ft 6 in), and slender
- 🌐 Mexico
- 🏠 Dry and moist forests
- 🍴 Insects, especially grasshoppers and crickets
- ♀ Thought to be egg-layers
- 📝 Partially arboreal

SPECIES:
Symphimus leucostomus
Symphimus mayae

GENUS: **SYMPHOLIS**

- 🐍 1
- ↔ Small
- 🌐 Mexico
- 🏠 Dry forests and scrub, where it lives in burrows
- 🍴 Thought to be lizards
- ♀ Unknown
- 📝 Very little is known about this secretive species

SPECIES:
Sympholis lippiens

GENUS: **TANTILLA**

Black-headed Snakes and
Crowned Snakes

- 🐍 62
- ↔ Very small and slender
- 🌐 North, Central, and South America, from central USA to Argentina
- 🏠 Varied, from deserts to forests
- 🍴 Insects and their larvae
- ♀ Egg-layers, producing from one to three eggs
- 📝 The many species are all very similar, usually brown with a black "cap" on the top of the heads. Several have small geographic ranges. Secretive snakes, which are active mainly at night and hide under stones, logs, and debris by day

SPECIES:
Tantilla albiceps
Tantilla alticola
Tantilla andinista
Tantilla armillata
Tantilla atriceps,
    Mexican Black-headed Snake
Tantilla bairdi
Tantilla bocourti
Tantilla boipiranga
Tantilla brevicauda
Tantilla briggsi
Tantilla calamarina
Tantilla capistrata
Tantilla cascadae
Tantilla ceboruca
Tantilla coronadoi
Tantilla coronata,
    Southeastern Crowned Snake
Tantilla cucullata
Tantilla cuniculator
Tantilla deppei
Tantilla flavilineata
Tantilla gracilis,
    Flat-headed Snake
Tantilla hendersoni
Tantilla hobartsmithi,
    South-western Black-headed Snake
Tantilla impensa
Tantilla insulamontana
Tantilla jani
Tantilla johnsoni
Tantilla lempira
Tantilla marcovani
Tantilla melanocephala
Tantilla miyatai
Tantilla moesta
Tantilla nigra
Tantilla nigriceps,
    Plains Black-headed Snake
Tantilla oaxacae
Tantilla olympia
Tantilla oolitica,
    Rim Rock Crowned Snake
Tantilla petersi
Tantilla planiceps,
    Californian Black-headed Snake
Tantilla psittaca
Tantilla relicta,
    Peninsula Crowned Snake
Tantilla reticulata
Tantilla robusta
Tantilla rubra
Tantilla ruficeps
Tantilla schistosa
Tantilla semicincta
Tantilla sertula
Tantilla shawi
Tantilla slavensi
Tantilla striata
Tantilla supracincta
Tantilla taeniata
Tantilla tayrae
Tantilla tecta
Tantilla trilineata
Tantilla triseriata
Tantilla tritaeniata
Tantilla vermiformis
Tantilla vulcani
Tantilla wilcoxi,
    Chihuahuan Black-headed Snake
Tantilla yaquia,
    Yaqui Black-headed Snake

GENUS: **TANTILLITA**

- 🐍 3
- ↔ Very small
- 🌐 Central America
- 🏠 Lowland forests
- 🍴 Invertebrates
- ♀ Egg-layers
- 📝 Closely related to the *Tantilla* species, which they resemble

SPECIES:
Tantillita brevissima
Tantillita canula
Tantillita lintoni

GENUS: **TELESCOPUS**

Tiger Snakes, Catsnakes

- 🐍 14
- ↔ Medium, but slender
- 🌐 Africa, the Balkan region of Europe (*T. fallax*), and the Near East
- 🏠 Varied, but usually in dry, rocky places
- 🍴 Lizards and small rodents
- ♀ Egg-layers
- 📝 Rear-fanged, though not dangerous to humans. Thoroughly nocturnal

SPECIES:
Telescopus beetzi,
    Namib Tiger Snake
Telescopus dhara
Telescopus fallax,
    European Catsnake
Telescopus finkeldeyi
Telescopus gezirae
Telescopus hoogstraali
Telescopus nigriceps
Telescopus obtusus
Telescopus pulcher
Telescopus rhinopoma
Telescopus semiannulatus,
    Eastern Tiger Snake
Telescopus tessellatus
Telescopus tripolitanus
Telescopus variegatus

GENUS: **THELOTORNIS**

Twig Snakes

- 🐍 4
- ↔ Long, up to nearly 2 m (6 ft 6 in), and extremely slender and twig-like
- 🌐 Africa, south of the Sahara
- 🏠 Rainforests and shrubby grasslands, where they are totally arboreal
- 🍴 Lizards and birds
- ♀ Egg-layers
- 📝 The heads are elongated and pointed, and the large eyes have keyhole-shaped pupils. Active by day

SPECIES:
Thelotornis capensis,
    Twig Snake or Bird Snake
Thelotornis kirtlandii,
    Kirtland's Twig Snake
Thelotornis mossambicanus
Thelotornis usambaricus

GENUS: **THRASOPS**

Tree Snakes

- 🐍 4
- ↔ Large
- 🌐 Tropical Africa
- 🏠 Forests, where they are arboreal
- 🍴 Frogs, lizards, and small mammals
- ♀ Egg-layers

SPECIES:
Thrasops flavigularis
Thrasops jacksonii,
    Jackson's Tree Snake
Thrasops occidentalis
Thrasops schmidti

GENUS: **TOXICODRYAS**

- 2
- Unknown
- West and Central Africa
- Unknown
- Unknown
- Unknown
- Extremely rare and poorly known

SPECIES:

Toxicodryas blandingii
Toxicodryas pulverulenta

GENUS: **TRIMORPHODON**

Lyre Snakes

- 7
- Medium, to about 1 m (3 ft 3 in), with slender bodies
- North and Central America
- Dry, scrubby places, frequently among rocks
- Mainly lizards, although snakes and small mammals, including bats, are sometimes taken
- Egg-layers
- Rear-fanged, though not dangerous to humans

SPECIES:

Trimorphodon biscutatus
Trimorphodon lambda,
    Sonoran Lyre Snake
Trimorphodon lyrophanes
Trimorphodon paucimaculatus
Trimorphodon quadruplex
Trimorphodon tau
Trimorphodon vilkinsonii

GENUS: **XENELAPHIS**

- 2
- Large, to 2 m (6 ft 6 in) or more
- Thailand, the Malay Peninsula, Borneo, and Java
- Semi-aquatic, in swamps
- Mainly frogs
- Egg-layers
- Poorly known

SPECIES:

Xenelaphis ellipsifer
Xenelaphis hexagonotus,
    Malaysian Brown Snake

GENUS: **XYELODONTOPHIS**

- 1
- Medium
- East Africa (Uluguru Mountains, Tanzania)
- Arboreal, in tropical forest
- Unknown, probably lizards
- Presumably an egg-layer
- Described in 2002, this is a rear-fanged snake with similarities to the Boomslang and the twig snakes; possibly dangerous to humans

SPECIES:

Xyelodontophis uluguruensis

GENUS: **ZAMENIS**

European Ratsnakes

- 5
- Medium
- Europe and the Middle East
- Varied but usually dry fields, hillsides and cultivated areas
- Small mammals, especially rodents
- Egg-layers
- Previously included in the genus *Elaphe*

SPECIES:

Zamenis hohenackeri,
    Transcaucasian Ratsnake
Zamenis lineatus,
    Striped Aesculapian Ratsnake
Zamenis longissimus,
    Aesculapian Snake
Zamenis persicus,
    Persian Ratsnake
- *Zamenis situla,*
    Leopard Snake (pp.116–17)

SUBFAMILY: **GRAYIINAE**
1 GENUS CONTAINING 4 SPECIES

This subfamily consists of four African snakes that live in and around streams and ponds, feeding on fish, frogs, and tadpoles.

GENUS: **GRAYIA**

- 4
- Large
- West Africa
- Semi-aquatic
- Thought to be fish
- Thought to be egg-layers
- Poorly known

SPECIES:

Grayia caesar
Grayia ornata
Grayia smithii
Grayia tholloni

SUBFAMILY: **SIBYNOPHIINAE**
2 GENERA CONTAINING 11 SPECIES

This is a disjunct group of snakes, with two species occurring in Central America and nine small species, sometimes known as many-toothed snakes, from India, China, and Southeast Asia. Some are rare and all are poorly known.

GENUS: **SCAPHIODONTOPHIS**

- 2
- Small
- Central and South America
- Forests
- Thought to be lizards and snakes
- Egg-layers

SPECIES:

Scaphiodontophis annulatus
Scaphiodontophis venustissimus

GENUS: **SIBYNOPHIS**

- 9 species
- Small and slender
- India, Sri Lanka, southern China, and Southeast Asia
- Forests
- Unknown
- Egg-layers
- Secretive and poorly known

SPECIES:

Sibynophis bistrigatus
Sibynophis bivittatus
Sibynophis chinensis
Sibynophis collaris
Sibynophis geminatus
Sibynophis melanocephalus
Sibynophis sagittarius
Sibynophis subpunctatus
Sibynophis triangularis

GENERA CURRENTLY UNASSIGNED TO ANY SUBFAMILY

GENUS: **BLYTHIA**

- 1
- Small
- Northern India, Myanmar, Tibet, and southern China
- Unknown, but thought to burrow
- Unknown
- Unknown

SPECIES:

Blythia reticulata

GENUS: **CYCLOCORUS**

- 2
- Small
- Philippines
- Under rotting logs and vegetation
- Thought to eat other snakes
- Unknown
- Rare and poorly known

SPECIES:

Cyclocorus lineatus
Cyclocorus nuchalis

GENUS: **ELAPOIDIS**

- 1
- Small
- Borneo, Sumatra, and Java
- Hills and mountains, in wet and damp places, where it burrows
- Unknown
- Egg-layer

SPECIES:

Elapoidis fusca

GENUS: **GONGYLOSOMA**

- 5
- Small
- Indonesia, the Malay Peninsula, and Thailand
- Hilly countryside, often close to water
- Invertebrates, amphibians, and lizards
- Thought to be egg-layers
- Previously included in the genus *Liopeltis*

SPECIES:

Gongylosoma baliodeirus
Gongylosoma longicauda
Gongylosoma mukutense
Gongylosoma nicobariensis
Gongylosoma scripta

GENUS: **HELOPHIS**

- 1
- Unknown
- Zaïre
- Unknown
- Unknown
- Unknown
- Rarely collected

SPECIES:

Helophis schoutedeni

GENUS: **MYERSOPHIS**

- 1
- Moderately large
- Banaue in the Philippines
- Unknown
- Unknown
- Unknown
- Rare and known from only a few specimens

SPECIES:

Myersophis alpestris

GENUS: **OREOCALAMUS**

- 1
- Small
- Borneo, and a small area in the Malay peninsula at 1,000–1,800 m (3,300–6,000 ft)
- Unknown
- Unknown
- Unknown
- A rare snake that has only been collected on a few occasions and about which almost nothing is known

SPECIES:

Oreocalamus hanitschi

GENUS: **POECILOPHOLIS**

- 1
- Small
- West Africa (Cameroon)
- Unknown
- Unknown
- Unknown
- Very rare and poorly known

SPECIES:

Poecilopholis cameronensis

GENUS: **RHABDOPS**

- 2
- Small
- India, northern Myanmar, and China
- Unknown
- Thought to be invertebrates
- Unknown

SPECIES:

Rhabdops bicolor
Rhabdops olivaceus

GENUS: **TETRALEPIS**

- 1
- Small
- Java
- Cool, montane forests
- Unknown
- Unknown
- Rare and poorly known

SPECIES:

Tetralepis fruhstorferi

DIPSADIDAE
96 GENERA CONTAINING 753 SPECIES

Sometimes considered to be a subfamily of the Colubridae, all the dipsadid snakes occur in the Americas, except the genus *Thermophis*, which occurs in China and Tibet. Most are small to medium-sized – less than 1 m (3 ft 3 in) – and they may be long and slender, as in the blunt-headed snakes, *Imantodes*, or heavy-bodied, such as the hog-nosed snakes, *Heterodon*, and false vipers, *Xenodon*. Between these extremes are many slender, fast-moving, diurnal "racer-like" species as well as many generalists. Most are dull-coloured, but a significant number are bright green, or banded in black, white, and red (often known as false coral snakes). Collectively, they occupy a full range of habitats, from forests to streams, and eat a great diversity of prey; some, such as the *Dipsas* and *Sibon* species specialize in slugs and snails. They include nocturnal and diurnal species. Most are egg-layers, although a few give birth to live young.

GENUS: **ADELPHICOS**

- 6
- Small
- Central America (Guatemala and Chiapas, Mexico)
- Pine, oak, and cloud forests, where they are semi-fossorial (adapted for digging)
- Earthworms
- Egg-layers

SPECIES:

Adelphicos daryi
Adelphicos ibarrorum
Adelphicos latifasciatum
Adelphicos nigrilatum
Adelphicos quadrivirgatum
Adelphicos veraepacis

GENUS: **ALSOPHIS**

- 9
- Moderately long, and slender
- West Indies, South America, and the Galapagos Islands
- Varied
- Lizards
- Thought to be egg-layers
- Fast-moving snakes, which are active by day

SPECIES:

Alsophis antiguae
Alsophis antillensis
Alsophis danforthi
Alsophis manselli
Alsophis rijgersmaei
Alsophis rufiventris
Alsophis sajdaki
Alsophis sanctonum
Alsophis sibonius

GENUS: **AMASTRIDIUM**

- 2
- Small, to a maximum of 72 cm (2 ft 4 in)
- Central America (Mexico to Panama)
- Forests, where they are terrestrial
- Thought to be frogs
- Unknown

SPECIES:

Amastridium sapperi
Amastridium veliferum

GENUS: **AMNESTEOPHIS**

- 1
- Unknown
- Brazil
- Forests
- Unknown
- Unknown, but presumably an egg-layer
- Rare and very poorly known

SPECIES:

Amnesteophis melanauchen

GENUS: **APOSTOLEPIS**

- 31
- Small
- South America
- Forests, where they spend most of their time underground
- Invertebrates, small frogs, and lizards
- Unknown

SPECIES:

Apostolepis albicollaris
Apostolepis ambiniger
Apostolepis ammodites
Apostolepis arenaria
Apostolepis assimilis
Apostolepis borellii
Apostolepis breviceps
Apostolepis cearensis
Apostolepis cerradoensis
Apostolepis christineae
Apostolepis dimidiata
Apostolepis dorbignyi
Apostolepis flavotorquata
Apostolepis gaboi
Apostolepis goiasensis
Apostolepis intermedia
Apostolepis longicaudata
Apostolepis multicincta
Apostolepis nelsonjorgei
Apostolepis niceforoi
Apostolepis nigrolineata
Apostolepis nigroterminata
Apostolepis parassimilis
Apostolepis phillipsae
Apostolepis polylepis
Apostolepis pymi
Apostolepis quirogai
Apostolepis serrana
Apostolepis striata
Apostolepis tenuis
Apostolepis vittata

GENUS: **ARRHYTON**

- 8
- Small
- West Indies and Cuba
- Varied
- Amphibians and their eggs, and lizards
- Thought to be egg-layers
- Rear-fanged, though not dangerous to humans. Otherwise poorly known

SPECIES:

Arrhyton ainictum
Arrhyton dolichura
Arrhyton procerum
Arrhyton redimitum
Arrhyton supernum
Arrhyton taeniatum
Arrhyton tanyplectum
Arrhyton vittatum

GENUS: **ATRACTUS**

- 138
- Very small
- Central and South America
- Rainforests, among leaf-litter
- Mainly invertebrates
- Egg-layers
- Most species are dark, and some have a brighter collar marking. Some species are known from only one or two specimens and have very localized distributions; others are only recently described

SPECIES:

Atractus acheronius
Atractus albuquerquei
Atractus alphonsehogei
Atractus altagratiae
Atractus alytogrammus
Atractus andinus
Atractus apophis
Atractus arangoi
Atractus atratus
Atractus attenuates
Atractus avernus
Atractus ayeush
Atractus badius
Atractus balzani
Atractus biseriatus
Atractus bocki
Atractus bocourti
Atractus boettgeri
Atractus boulengerii
Atractus caete
Atractus careolepis
Atractus carrioni
Atractus caxiuana
Atractus charitoae
Atractus chthonius
Atractus clarki
Atractus collaris
Atractus crassicaudatus
Atractus darienensis
Atractus depressiocellus
Atractus duboisi
Atractus duidensis
Atractus dunni
Atractus echidna
Atractus ecuadorensis
Atractus edioi
Atractus elaps
Atractus emigdioi
Atractus emmeli
Atractus eriki
Atractus erythromelas
Atractus favae
Atractus flammigerus
Atractus franciscopaivai
Atractus francoi
Atractus fuliginosus
Atractus gaigeae
Atractus gigas
Atractus guentheri
Atractus heliobelluomini
Atractus hoogmoedi
Atractus hostilitractus
Atractus imperfectus
Atractus indistinctus
Atractus insipidus
Atractus iridescens
Atractus lancinii
Atractus lasallei
Atractus latifrons
Atractus lehmanni
Atractus limitaneus
Atractus loveridgei
Atractus macondo
Atractus maculatus
Atractus major
Atractus manizalesensis
Atractus mariselae
Atractus matthewi
Atractus medusa
Atractus melanogaster
Atractus melas
Atractus meridensis
Atractus micheleae
Atractus microrhynchus
Atractus mijaresi
Atractus modestus
Atractus multicinctus
Atractus multidentatus
Atractus nasutus
Atractus natans
Atractus nicefori
Atractus nigricaudus
Atractus nigriventris
Atractus obesus
Atractus obtusirostris
Atractus occidentalis
Atractus occipitoalbus
Atractus ochrosetrus
Atractus oculotemporalis
Atractus orcesi
Atractus paisa
Atractus pamplonensis
Atractus pantostictus
Atractus paraguayensis
Atractus paravertebralis
Atractus paucidens
Atractus pauciscutatus
Atractus peruvianus
Atractus poeppigi
Atractus potschi
Atractus punctiventris
Atractus resplendens
Atractus reticulatus
Atractus riveroi
Atractus ronnie
Atractus roulei
Atractus sanctaemartae
Atractus sanguineus

Atractus savagei
Atractus schach
Atractus serranus
Atractus snethlageae
Atractus spinalis
Atractus steyermarki
Atractus surucucu
Atractus taeniatus
Atractus tamaensis
Atractus tamessari
Atractus taphorni
Atractus thalesdelemai
Atractus titanicus
Atractus torquatus
Atractus touzeti
Atractus trihedrurus
Atractus trilineatus
Atractus trivittatus
Atractus turikensis
Atractus typhon
Atractus univittatus
Atractus variegatus
Atractus ventrimaculatus
Atractus vertebralis
Atractus vertebrolineatus
Atractus vittatus
Atractus wagleri
Atractus werneri
Atractus zebrinus
Atractus zidoki

GENUS: **BOIRUNA**

- 🐍 2
- ↔ Large
- 🌎 South America
- 🏠 Forests and clearings
- ◖ Probably amphibians, reptiles, and small mammals
- ♀ Egg-layers
- ☑ Previously included in the genus *Clelia*

SPECIES:
Boiruna maculata
Boiruna sertaneja

GENUS: **BORIKENOPHIS**

- 🐍 3
- ↔ Medium
- 🌎 West Indies
- 🏠 Rocky hillsides and fields
- ◖ Lizards
- ♀ Egg-layers
- ☑ Previously included in the genus *Alsophis*

SPECIES:
Borikenophis portoricensis
Borikenophis sanctaecrucis
Borikenophis variegatus

GENUS: **CAAETEBOIA**

- 🐍 1
- ↔ Small
- 🌎 Brazil
- 🏠 Forest floor
- ◖ Unknown, but probably lizards
- ♀ Egg-layer
- ☑ Previously included in the genus *Liophis*

SPECIES:
Caaeteboia amarali

GENUS: **CALAMODONTOPHIS**

- 🐍 2
- ↔ Small
- 🌎 Southern Brazil
- 🏠 Unknown
- ◖ Unknown
- ♀ Unknown
- ☑ Rear-fanged, but otherwise poorly known

SPECIES:
Calamodontophis paucidens
Calamodontophis ronaldoi

GENUS: **CARAIBA**

Cuban Racer

- 🐍 1
- ↔ Medium
- 🌎 Cuba
- 🏠 Dry scrub, forests, fields, and plantations
- ◖ Probably lizards
- ♀ Egg-layer
- ☑ Only recently placed in the genus *Caraiba*. At least six subspecies are recognized from offshore islands

SPECIES:
Caraiba andreae

GENUS: **CARPHOPHIS**

Worm Snakes

- 🐍 2
- ↔ Very small
- 🌎 Eastern North America
- 🏠 Damp places, where they are found under debris
- ◖ Mainly earthworms and other soft-bodied invertebrates
- ♀ Egg-layers
- ☑ They are black or dark brown above, pink below. *C. vermis* is sometimes considered a subspecies of *C. amoenus*

SPECIES:
Carphophis amoenus
Carphophis vermis,
    Worm Snake

GENUS: **CERCOPHIS**

- 🐍 1
- ↔ Medium
- 🌎 Southeast Asia
- 🏠 Forests, where it is highly arboreal
- ◖ Mainly lizards
- ♀ Egg-layer

SPECIES:
Cercophis auratus

GENUS: **CHERSODROMUS**

- 🐍 2
- ↔ Small
- 🌎 Mexico
- 🏠 Unknown
- ◖ Unknown
- ♀ Unknown

SPECIES:
Chersodromus liebmanni
Chersodromus rubriventris

GENUS: **CLELIA**

Mussuranas

- 🐍 7
- ↔ Large
- 🌎 Central and South America
- 🏠 Forests
- ◖ Other snakes, including venomous ones, and mammals, which they constrict
- ♀ Egg-layers
- ☑ Active mainly at night

SPECIES:
Clelia clelia
Clelia equatoriana
Clelia errabunda
Clelia hussami
Clelia langeri
Clelia plumbea
Clelia scytalina

GENUS: **CONIOPHANES**

- 🐍 17
- ↔ Small
- 🌎 North, Central, and South America (southern Texas to Peru)
- 🏠 Varied, they live on the ground
- ◖ Invertebrates, frogs, and lizards
- ♀ Egg-layers
- ☑ Rear-fanged, although not normally considered dangerous to humans. The fragile tails, which are easily broken, have been found in the stomachs of coral snakes

SPECIES:
Coniophanes alvarezi
Coniophanes andresensis
Coniophanes bipunctatus
Coniophanes dromiciformis
Coniophanes fissidens
Coniophanes imperialis
Coniophanes joanae
Coniophanes lateritius
Coniophanes longinquus
Coniophanes melanocephalus
Coniophanes meridanus
Coniophanes michoacanensis
Coniophanes piceivittis
Coniophanes quinquevittatus
Coniophanes sarae
Coniophanes schmidti
Coniophanes taylori

GENUS: **CONOPHIS**

Road Guarders

- 🐍 3
- ↔ Moderately large, to about 1 m (3 ft 3 in) in length
- 🌎 Central America
- 🏠 Dry forests and clearings, including beaches
- ◖ They chase and eat lizards and snakes. They also eat frogs, toads, and small mammals
- ♀ Egg-layers
- ☑ They have enlarged rear fangs and potent venom; the bites can be painful to humans and may cause localized swelling. They are active, diurnal species

SPECIES:
Conophis lineatus
Conophis morai
Conophis vittatus

GENUS: **CONTIA**

- 🐍 2
- ↔ Small, to about 45 cm (1 ft 5 in)
- 🌎 Western North America
- 🏠 Open woodland and grassy places, usually near water
- ◖ Slugs
- ♀ Egg-layers

SPECIES:
Contia longicaudae
Contia tenuis,
    Sharp-tailed Snake

GENUS: **CORONELAPS**

- 🐍 1
- ↔ Medium
- 🌎 Brazil
- 🏠 Unknown
- ◖ Probably lizards
- ♀ Egg-layer
- ☑ Thought to be venomous

SPECIES:
Coronelaps lepidus

GENUS: **CRISANTOPHIS**

- 🐍 1
- ↔ Medium and slender
- 🌎 Mexico
- 🏠 Dry forests
- ◖ Unknown
- ♀ Thought to be an egg-layer

SPECIES:
Crisantophis nevermanni

GENUS: **CRYOPHIS**

- 🐍 1
- ↔ Medium
- 🌎 Mexico
- 🏠 Unknown
- ◖ Unknown
- ♀ Unknown
- ☑ Rare and poorly known

SPECIES:
Cryophis hallbergi

GENUS: **CUBOPHIS**

- ⬗ 6
- ↔ Medium to large
- 🌍 Caribbean region, including Cuba
- 🏠 Forest clearings, fields, and plantations
- ◀ Lizards, possibly also small mammals
- ♂ Egg-layers
- ✎ Previously included in the genus *Alsophis*

SPECIES:

Cubophis brooksi
Cubophis cantherigerus
Cubophis caymanus
Cubophis fuscicauda
Cubophis ruttyi
Cubophis vudii

GENUS: **DIADOPHIS**

- ⬗ 1
- ↔ Highly variable; small to medium depending on the subspecies
- 🌍 North America
- 🏠 Varied: it occurs in dry and moist habitats, and is often found under rocks, logs, and rubbish
- ◀ Earthworms, slugs, and other invertebrates, small amphibians, and small reptiles. Large forms sometimes eat nestling rodents
- ♂ Egg-layer

SPECIES:

Diadophis punctatus,
  Ring-necked Snake

GENUS: **DIAPHOROLEPIS**

- ⬗ 2
- ↔ Moderately large snakes
- 🌍 Panama, Colombia, and Ecuador
- 🏠 Unknown, but thought to be terrestrial
- ◀ Unknown
- ♂ Thought to be egg-layers

SPECIES:

Diaphorolepis laevis
Diaphorolepis wagneri

GENUS: **DIPSAS**

Thirst Snakes, Snail-eaters,
or Snail-suckers

- ⬗ 35
- ↔ Long and slender
- 🌍 Central and South America (Mexico to Brazil)
- 🏠 Rainforests, where they are mainly arboreal
- ◀ They feed only on snails and slugs, for which they have special adaptations to their jaws, resulting in squarish heads
- ♂ Egg-layers
- ✎ The bodies are flattened from side to side as an adaptation to an arboreal lifestyle. Some species are brightly coloured

SPECIES:

Dipsas albifrons
Dipsas alternans
Dipsas andiana
Dipsas articulata
Dipsas baliomelas
Dipsas bicolor
Dipsas brevifacies
Dipsas bucephala
Dipsas catesbyi
Dipsas chaparensis
Dipsas copei
Dipsas elegans
Dipsas ellipsifera
Dipsas gaigeae
Dipsas gracilis
Dipsas incerta
Dipsas indica
Dipsas maxillaris
Dipsas neivai
Dipsas nicholsi
Dipsas oreas
Dipsas pakaraima
Dipsas pavonina
Dipsas peruana
Dipsas praeornata
Dipsas pratti
Dipsas sanctijoannis
Dipsas sazimai
Dipsas schunkii
Dipsas temporalis
Dipsas tenuissima
Dipsas trinitatis
Dipsas variegata
Dipsas vermiculata
Dipsas viguieri

GENUS: **DITAXODON**

- ⬗ 1
- ↔ Unknown
- 🌍 Brazil
- 🏠 Unknown
- ◀ Unknown
- ♂ Unknown
- ✎ Extremely rare and poorly known

SPECIES:

Ditaxodon taeniatus

GENUS: **DREPANOIDES**

- ⬗ 1
- ↔ Small
- 🌍 South America
- 🏠 Forests, where it lives on the ground and in leaf-litter
- ◀ Unknown
- ♂ Unknown
- ✎ Brightly coloured, similar to a coral snake

SPECIES:

Drepanoides anomalus

GENUS: **ECHINANTHERA**

- ⬗ 6
- ↔ Small
- 🌍 South America
- 🏠 Unknown
- ◀ Unknown
- ♂ Unknown
- ✎ Contains several species that formerly belonged to the genus *Rhadinea*

SPECIES:

Echinanthera amoena
Echinanthera cephalomaculata
Echinanthera cephalostriata
Echinanthera cyanopleura
Echinanthera melanostigma
Echinanthera undulata

GENUS: **ELAPOMORPHUS**

- ⬗ 2
- ↔ Small
- 🌍 South America
- 🏠 Varied; a secretive, burrowing species
- ◀ Thought to be earthworms and other invertebrates
- ♂ Unknown
- ✎ Poorly known

SPECIES:

Elapomorphus quinquelineatus
Elapomorphus wuchereri

GENUS: **EMMOCHLIOPHIS**

- ⬗ 2
- ↔ Small
- 🌍 Ecuador
- 🏠 Forested Andean slopes
- ◀ Unknown
- ♂ Unknown
- ✎ The few details are known from only one specimen of each species

SPECIES:

Emmochliophis fugleri
Emmochliophis miops

GENUS: **ENULIOPHIS**

- ⬗ 1
- ↔ Small
- 🌍 Mexico, Central, and South America
- 🏠 Forest floor
- ◀ Unknown, probably frogs, lizards, and invertebrates
- ♂ Egg-layer
- ✎ The single species was previously known as *Enulius sclateri*. It is unusual among snakes in that its tail can be voluntarily discarded if grasped

SPECIES:

Enuliophis sclateri

GENUS: **ENULIUS**

- ⬗ 4
- ↔ Small and slender
- 🌍 Central and northern South America
- 🏠 Dry and moist forests, where they are burrowers
- ◀ Unknown, but thought to be invertebrates
- ♂ Unknown
- ✎ Poorly known

SPECIES:

Enulius bifoveatus
Enulius flavitorques
Enulius oligostichus
Enulius roatanensis

GENUS: **ERYTHROLAMPRUS**

False Coral Snakes

- ⬗ 48
- ↔ Small
- 🌍 Central and South America
- 🏠 Forests, where they are terrestrial
- ◀ Other reptiles
- ♂ Egg-layers
- ✎ Brightly banded, like a coral snake. Rear-fanged, though not dangerous to humans. This genus has been greatly expanded in recent years

SPECIES:

Erythrolamprus aesculapii
Erythrolamprus albertguentheri
Erythrolamprus almadensis
Erythrolamprus andinus
Erythrolamprus atraventer
Erythrolamprus bizona
Erythrolamprus breviceps
Erythrolamprus carajasensis
Erythrolamprus ceii
Erythrolamprus cobella
Erythrolamprus cursor
Erythrolamprus dorsocorallinus
Erythrolamprus epinephelus
Erythrolamprus festae
Erythrolamprus frenatus
Erythrolamprus guentheri
Erythrolamprus ingeri
Erythrolamprus jaegeri
Erythrolamprus janaleeae
Erythrolamprus juliae
Erythrolamprus longiventris
Erythrolamprus maryellenae
Erythrolamprus melanotus
Erythrolamprus mertensi
Erythrolamprus miliaris
Erythrolamprus mimus
Erythrolamprus mossoroensis
Erythrolamprus ocellatus
Erythrolamprus ornatus
Erythrolamprus perfuscus
Erythrolamprus poecilogyrus
Erythrolamprus problematicus
Erythrolamprus pseudocorallus
Erythrolamprus pyburni
Erythrolamprus pygmaeus
Erythrolamprus reginae
Erythrolamprus sagittifer
Erythrolamprus semiaureus
Erythrolamprus subocularis
Erythrolamprus taeniogaster
Erythrolamprus taeniurus
Erythrolamprus torrenicola
Erythrolamprus trebbaui
Erythrolamprus triscalis
Erythrolamprus typhlus
Erythrolamprus viridis
Erythrolamprus vitti
Erythrolamprus williamsi

GENUS: **EUTRACHELOPHIS**

- ⬗ 2
- ↔ Small
- 🌍 Peru and Bolivia
- 🏠 Unknown
- ◀ Probably lizards
- ♂ Egg-layers
- ✎ Poorly known snakes. *Eutrachelophis steinbachi* has been placed in a number of different genera at various times, while *E. bassleri* has been recently described

SPECIES:

Eutrachelophis bassleri
Eutrachelophis steinbachi

GENUS: **FARANCIA**

- 2
- Large, occasionally to 2 m (6 ft 6 in)
- North America (Florida and adjoining states)
- Semi-aquatic, in or near swamps, ditches, and lakes, often where there is plenty of cover
- Frogs, tadpoles, eels, and the eel-like salamanders belonging to the genus *Amphiuma*
- Egg-layers, depositing the eggs in an underground chamber

SPECIES:

Farancia abacura,
Mud Snake
Farancia erytrogramma,
Rainbow Snake

GENUS: **GEOPHIS**

Earth Snakes

- 49
- Small, slender snakes
- Central and northern South America (northern Mexico to Colombia)
- Varied, on the ground
- Earthworms and other soft-bodied invertebrates
- Egg-layers, where known
- Active mainly at night. Although 49 species are listed it is likely that many of these are mere variants and that the correct total of species is significantly less than this

SPECIES:

Geophis anocularis
Geophis bellus
Geophis betaniensis
Geophis bicolor
Geophis blanchardi
Geophis brachycephalus
Geophis cancellatus
Geophis carinosus
Geophis chalybeus
Geophis championi
Geophis damiani
Geophis downsi
Geophis dubius
Geophis duellmani
Geophis dugesii
Geophis dunni
Geophis fulvoguttatus
Geophis godmani
Geophis hoffmanni
Geophis immaculatus
Geophis incomptus
Geophis isthmicus
Geophis juarezi
Geophis juliai
Geophis laticinctus
Geophis laticollaris
Geophis latifrontalis
Geophis maculiferus
Geophis mutitorques
Geophis nasalis
Geophis nephodrymus
Geophis nigroalbus

Geophis nigrocinctus
Geophis occabus
Geophis omiltemanus
Geophis petersii
Geophis pyburni
Geophis rhodogaster
Geophis rostralis
Geophis russatus
Geophis ruthveni
Geophis sallaei
Geophis semidoliatus
Geophis sieboldi
Geophis talamancae
Geophis tarascae
Geophis tectus
Geophis turbidus
Geophis zeledoni

GENUS: **GOMESOPHIS**

- 1
- Small
- Brazil
- Unknown
- Unknown
- Unknown

SPECIES:

Gomesophis brasiliensis

GENUS: **HAITIOPHIS**

- 1
- Medium to large
- Hispaniola
- Forests, clearings, and cultivated areas
- Lizards
- Egg-layer
- The single species has been placed in at least five different genera in the past

SPECIES:

Haitiophis anomalus

GENUS: **HELICOPS**

- 16
- Small
- South America
- Aquatic and semi-aquatic
- Thought to be fish
- Live-bearers, although *H. angulatus* may sometimes lay eggs

SPECIES:

Helicops angulatus
Helicops apiaka
Helicops carinicaudus
Helicops danieli
Helicops gomesi
Helicops hagmanni
Helicops infrataeniatus
Helicops leopardinus
Helicops modestus
Helicops pastazae
Helicops petersi
Helicops polylepis
Helicops scalaris
Helicops tapajonicus
Helicops trivittatus
Helicops yacu

GENUS: **HETERODON**

Hog-nosed Snakes

- 5
- Small to medium, nearly 1 m (3 ft 3 in), with stocky bodies
- North America
- Varied, but often dry places with sandy soil
- Mainly toads, but also ground-nesting birds and small mammals
- Egg-layers
- When alarmed they flatten their bodies, hiss, make mock strikes, and, as a last resort, may pretend to be dead

SPECIES:

Heterodon gloydi
Heterodon kennerlyi
- *Heterodon nasicus,*
Plains Hognose Snake
(pp.90–91)
Heterodon platirhinos,
Eastern Hog-nosed Snake
Heterodon simus,
Southern Hog-nosed Snake

GENUS: **HYDRODYNASTES**

- 3
- Large, heavy-bodied
- South America
- Semi-aquatic
- Frogs and toads; also small mammals
- Egg-layers

SPECIES:

Hydrodynastes bicinctus
Hydrodynastes gigas,
False Water Cobra
Hydrodynastes melanogigas

GENUS: **HYDROMORPHUS**

- 2
- Small
- Central America
- Unknown
- Unknown
- Thought to be egg-layers
- Secretive and poorly known

SPECIES:

Hydromorphus concolor
Hydromorphus dunni

GENUS: **HYDROPS**

- 3
- Medium
- Northern South America, to the east of the Andes
- Highly aquatic
- Amphibians and fish
- Thought to be egg-layers

SPECIES:

Hydrops caesurus
Hydrops martii
Hydrops triangularis

GENUS: **HYPSIGLENA**

Night Snakes

- 9
- Small
- North and Central America
- Varied, but usually dry and rocky places.
- Lizards, which they hunt at night. Also small snakes and mammals
- Egg-layers

SPECIES:

Hypsiglena affinis
Hypsiglena catalinae
Hypsiglena chlorophaea
Hypsiglena jani
Hypsiglena ochrorhyncha
Hypsiglena slevini,
Baja California Night Snake
Hypsiglena tanzeri
Hypsiglena torquata,
Spotted Night Snake
Hypsiglena unaocularis

GENUS: **HYPSIRHYNCHUS**

- 8
- Medium and heavy-bodied
- Haiti
- Unknown
- Lizards, especially those of the genus *Anolis*
- Unknown

SPECIES:

Hypsirhynchus ater,
Jamaican Racer
Hypsirhynchus callilaemus
Hypsirhynchus ferox
Hypsirhynchus funereus
Hypsirhynchus melanichnus
Hypsirhynchus parvifrons
Hypsirhynchus polylepis
Hypsirhynchus scalaris

GENUS: **IALTRIS**

- 4
- Medium and slender
- Hispaniola (Haiti and the Dominican Republic)
- Unknown
- Unknown
- Thought to be egg-layers
- Rear-fanged, though not dangerous to humans

SPECIES:

Ialtris agyrtes
Ialtris dorsalis
Ialtris haetianus
Ialtris parishi

GENUS: **IMANTODES**

Blunt-headed Vine Snakes

- 8
- To about 1 m (3 ft 3 in) in length but exceedingly elongated
- Central and South America

- Totally arboreal, hiding in bromeliad plants during the day and hunting at night
- Lizards and frogs that rest or sleep on the extreme tips of leaves and twigs
- Egg-layers, producing small clutches of elongated eggs
- Rear-fanged, though not dangerous to humans. The heads are wide, with blunt snouts and huge eyes. Some species have a row of greatly enlarged dorsal scales running along the centre of the back

SPECIES:

Imantodes cenchoa
Imantodes chocoensis
Imantodes gemmistratus
Imantodes guane
Imantodes inornatus
Imantodes lentiferus
Imantodes phantasma
Imantodes tenuissimus

GENUS: **LEPTODEIRA**

Cat-eyed Snakes

- 12
- Mostly small, and slender
- North, Central, and South America (Texas to northern Argentina and Paraguay)
- Varied. They occur mainly on the ground but also climb into low vegetation
- Lizards, frogs, toads, and tadpoles. *L. septentrionalis* (and possibly others) specializes in eating the eggs of leaf-nesting tree frogs
- Egg-layers
- Rear-fanged, though not dangerous to humans

SPECIES:

Leptodeira annulata
Leptodeira bakeri
Leptodeira frenata
Leptodeira maculata
Leptodeira nigrofasciata
Leptodeira polysticta
Leptodeira punctata
Leptodeira rhombifera
Leptodeira rubricata
Leptodeira septentrionalis,
    Northern Cat-eyed Snake
Leptodeira splendida
Leptodeira uribei

GENUS: **LIOHETEROPHIS**

- 1
- Small
- Brazil
- Damp places
- Frogs
- Unknown

SPECIES:

Lioheterophis iheringi

GENUS: **LYGOPHIS**

- 8
- Medium
- South America, extending into southern Central America
- Varied
- Probably lizards and frogs
- Egg-layers
- Several species are marked with bold longitudinal stripes

SPECIES:

Lygophis anomalus
Lygophis dilepis
Lygophis elegantissimus
Lygophis flavifrenatus
Lygophis lineatus
Lygophis meridionalis
Lygophis paucidens
Lygophis vanzolinii

GENUS: **MAGLIOPHIS**

- 2
- Small
- Puerto Rico
- Forests and scrub
- Probably *Anolis* lizards
- Egg-layers

SPECIES:

Magliophis exiguum
Magliophis stahli

GENUS: **MANOLEPIS**

- 1
- Small
- Mexico
- Unknown
- Unknown
- Unknown

SPECIES:

Manolepis putnami

GENUS: **MUSSURANA**

- 3
- Medium to large
- South America
- Forests, scrub, and grasslands
- Probably lizards, snakes, and small mammals
- Egg-layers
- Previously included in the genus *Clelia*

SPECIES:

Mussurana bicolor
Mussurana montana
Mussurana quimi

GENUS: **NINIA**

Coffee Snakes

- 10
- Small
- Central and South America
- Leaf-litter
- Invertebrates, small lizards, and frogs

- Egg-layers
- Only six species are recognized by some authorities

SPECIES:

Ninia atrata
Ninia celata
Ninia diademata
Ninia espinali
Ninia franciscoi
Ninia hudsoni
Ninia maculata
Ninia pavimentata
Ninia psephota
Ninia sebae

GENUS: **NOTHOPSIS**

- 1
- Small
- Central America
- Humid forests, where it is possibly aquatic or semi-aquatic
- Unknown
- Unknown

SPECIES:

Nothopsis rugosus

GENUS: **OMOADIPHAS**

- 3
- Unknown
- Honduras
- Forests
- Probably lizards
- Egg-layers
- Poorly known, recently described species

SPECIES:

Omoadiphas aurula
Omoadiphas cannula
Omoadiphas texiguatensis

GENUS: **OXYRHOPUS**

- 14
- Medium, with fairly slender bodies
- Central and South America (Mexico to Peru)
- Lowland forests, where they are terrestrial
- Amphibians, lizards, snakes, and small mammals
- Egg-layers
- Boldly banded in red and black, or red, black, and white, and thought to mimic the venomous coral snakes from the region. Mainly nocturnal

SPECIES:

Oxyrhopus clathratus
Oxyrhopus doliatus
Oxyrhopus erdisii
Oxyrhopus fitzingeri
Oxyrhopus formosus
Oxyrhopus guibei
Oxyrhopus leucomelas
Oxyrhopus marcapatae
Oxyrhopus melanogenys
Oxyrhopus occipitalis
Oxyrhopus petolarius
Oxyrhopus rhombifer
Oxyrhopus trigeminus
Oxyrhopus vanidicus

GENUS: **PARAPHIMOPHIS**

- 1
- Large
- South America
- Forests
- Probably lizards and snakes
- Egg-layer
- The single species was previously known as *Clelia rustica*

SPECIES:

Paraphimophis rusticus

GENUS: **PHALOTRIS**

- 15
- Small
- South America
- Forest floors; leaf-litter
- Probably invertebrates
- Egg-layers
- Previously placed in the genus *Elapomorphus*

SPECIES:

Phalotris bilineatus
Phalotris concolor
Phalotris cuyanus
Phalotris labiomaculatus
Phalotris lativittatus
Phalotris lemniscatus
Phalotris matogrossensis
Phalotris mertensi
Phalotris multipunctatus
Phalotris nasutus
Phalotris nigrilatus
Phalotris punctatus
Phalotris reticulatus
Phalotris sansebastiani
Phalotris tricolor

GENUS: **PHILODRYAS**

- 22
- Moderately long, but slender
- South America
- Forests, where they are arboreal
- Frogs, lizards, snakes, birds, and bats
- Egg-layers
- Active by day. *P. livida* was previously placed in the genus *Platyinion*

SPECIES:

Philodryas aestiva
Philodryas agassizii
Philodryas amaru
Philodryas argentea
Philodryas arnaldoi
Philodryas baroni
Philodryas boliviana
Philodryas chamissonis
Philodryas cordata
Philodryas georgeboulengeri
Philodryas laticeps
Philodryas livida
Philodryas mattogrossensis
Philodryas nattereri
Philodryas olfersii
Philodryas patagoniensis
Philodryas psammophidea
Philodryas simonsii
Philodryas tachymenoides
Philodryas trilineata
Philodryas varia
Philodryas viridissima

GENUS: PHIMOPHIS

- 🐍 3
- ↔ Small
- 🌎 Central and South America
- 🏠 Burrowers
- 🍴 Thought to be mainly invertebrates
- ⚥ Egg-layers
- 📝 They have modified, upturned snouts, the purpose of which is unclear

SPECIES:

Phimophis guerini
Phimophis guianensis
Phimophis vittatus

GENUS: PLESIODIPSAS

- 🐍 1
- ↔ Medium, highly slender
- 🌎 Northern South America
- 🏠 Forests
- 🍴 Snails and slugs
- ⚥ Egg-layer
- 📝 The single species was previously known as *Dipsas perijanensis*

SPECIES:

Plesiodipsas perijanensis

GENUS: PSEUDALSOPHIS

- 🐍 6
- ↔ Medium
- 🌎 Disjunct distribution: five of the six species are restricted to the Galapagos Islands, whereas *P. elegans* occurs in Ecuador, Peru, and Chile
- 🏠 Dry, rocky places
- 🍴 Lizards, where known, including young marine and land iguanas
- ⚥ Egg-layers
- 📝 Previously placed in the genera *Alsophis* and *Dromicus*

SPECIES:

Pseudalsophis biserialis
Pseudalsophis dorsalis
Pseudalsophis elegans
Pseudalsophis hoodensis
Pseudalsophis slevini
Pseudalsophis steindachneri

GENUS: PSEUDOBOA

- 🐍 6
- ↔ Medium
- 🌎 Central and South America
- 🏠 Rainforests, where they live mostly on the ground
- 🍴 Lizards, snakes, and small mammals
- ⚥ Egg-layers, sometimes laying their eggs in ant nests
- 📝 Rear-fanged, though not dangerous to humans. Active at night

SPECIES:

Pseudoboa coronata
Pseudoboa haasi
Pseudoboa martinsi
Pseudoboa neuwiedii
Pseudoboa nigra
Pseudoboa serrana

GENUS: PSEUDOERYX

- 🐍 2
- ↔ Fairly large
- 🌎 Brazil and Paraguay
- 🏠 Aquatic
- 🍴 Thought to eat fish and amphibians
- ⚥ Unknown
- 📝 Their natural history is practically unknown

SPECIES:

Pseudoeryx plicatilis
Pseudoeryx relictualis

GENUS: PSEUDOLEPTODEIRA

- 🐍 1
- ↔ Small
- 🌎 Mexico
- 🏠 Terrestrial, otherwise unknown
- 🍴 Thought to be lizards and frogs
- ⚥ Egg-layer

SPECIES:

Pseudoleptodeira latifasciata

GENUS: PSEUDOTOMODON

- 🐍 1
- ↔ Medium
- 🌎 Western Argentina
- 🏠 Unknown
- 🍴 Unknown
- ⚥ Live-bearer
- 📝 Very rare and poorly known

SPECIES:

Pseudotomodon trigonatus

GENUS: PSOMOPHIS

- 🐍 3
- ↔ Small
- 🌎 Central and South America
- 🏠 Forests, especially in leaf-litter and decaying logs
- 🍴 Earthworms
- ⚥ Egg-layers
- 📝 Described in 1994; formerly placed in the genus *Rhadinaea*

SPECIES:

Psomophis genimaculatus
Psomophis joberti
Psomophis obtusus

GENUS: PTYCHOPHIS

- 🐍 1
- ↔ Small
- 🌎 Brazil
- 🏠 Damp places, where it is semi-aquatic
- 🍴 Frogs and fish
- ⚥ Live-bearer
- 📝 Rear-fanged and potentially harmful to humans

SPECIES:

Ptychophis flavovirgatus

GENUS: RHACHIDELUS

- 🐍 1
- ↔ Fairly large, over 1 m (3 ft 3 in) long, and stocky
- 🌎 Brazil and Argentina
- 🏠 Forests, where it is terrestrial
- 🍴 Mainly birds
- ⚥ Egg-layer
- 📝 Active by day

SPECIES:

Rhachidelus brazili

GENUS: RHADINAEA

- 🐍 21
- ↔ Small
- 🌎 North, Central, and South America, from North Carolina (*R. flavilata*) to Argentina
- 🏠 Varied but often damp, wooded places, under logs and forest debris
- 🍴 Earthworms and other invertebrates, frogs, frogs' eggs, and small reptiles
- ⚥ Egg-layers, producing small clutches of eggs
- 📝 Secretive. There is some doubt over the validity of certain species

SPECIES:

Rhadinaea bogertorum
Rhadinaea calligaster
Rhadinaea cuneata
Rhadinaea decorata
Rhadinaea flavilata
Rhadinaea forbesi
Rhadinaea fulvivittis
Rhadinaea gaigeae
Rhadinaea hesperia
Rhadinaea laureata
Rhadinaea macdougalli
Rhadinaea marcellae
Rhadinaea montana
Rhadinaea myersi
Rhadinaea omiltemana
Rhadinaea pulveriventris
Rhadinaea quinquelineata
Rhadinaea sargenti
Rhadinaea stadelmani
Rhadinaea taeniata
Rhadinaea vermiculaticeps

GENUS: RHADINELLA

- 🐍 16
- ↔ Small
- 🌎 Mexico and Central America
- 🏠 Montane forests
- 🍴 Unknown
- ⚥ Presumably egg-layers
- 📝 Poorly known

SPECIES:

Rhadinella anachoreta
Rhadinella donaji
Rhadinella godmani
Rhadinella hannsteini
Rhadinella hempsteadae
Rhadinella kanalchutchan
Rhadinella kinkelini
Rhadinella lachrymans
Rhadinella montecristi
Rhadinella pegosalyta
Rhadinella pilonaorum
Rhadinella posadasi
Rhadinella rogerromani
Rhadinella schistosa
Rhadinella serperaster
Rhadinella tolpanorum

GENUS: RHADINOPHANES

- 🐍 1
- ↔ Small
- 🌎 South America
- 🏠 Unknown
- 🍴 Unknown
- ⚥ Unknown
- 📝 Rare and poorly known

SPECIES:

Rhadinophanes monticola

GENUS: RODRIGUESOPHIS

- 🐍 3
- ↔ Small
- 🌎 Brazil
- 🏠 Forest floors, living among leaf-litter
- 🍴 Thought to be mainly invertebrates
- ⚥ Egg-layers
- 📝 Poorly known snakes

SPECIES:

Rodriguesophis chui
Rodriguesophis iglesiasi
Rodriguesophis scriptorcibatus

GENUS: SAPHENOPHIS

- 🐍 5
- ↔ Small
- 🌎 South America (Colombia, Ecuador, and Peru)
- 🏠 Humid forests
- 🍴 Unknown
- ⚥ Unknown
- 📝 Rare and poorly known. Some species have been included in *Lygophis* in the past

SPECIES:

Saphenophis antioquiensis
Saphenophis atahuallpae
Saphenophis boursieri
Saphenophis sneiderni
Saphenophis tristriatus

GENUS: SIBON

South American Slug-eaters

- 🐍 16
- ↔ Small: often quite long, but very slender and with rounded heads
- 🌎 Central and South America
- 🏠 Forests, where they are highly arboreal
- 🍴 Slugs and snails, for which they have specially modified jaws
- ⚥ Egg-layers

SPECIES:

Sibon annulatus
Sibon anthracops
Sibon argus
Sibon carri
Sibon dimidiatus
Sibon dunni

Sibon lamari
Sibon linearis
Sibon longifrenis
Sibon manzanaresi
Sibon merendonensis
Sibon miskitus
Sibon nebulatus
Sibon noalamina
Sibon perissostichon
Sibon sanniolus

GENUS: **SIBYNOMORPHUS**

- 🐍 11
- ↔ Small
- 🌐 South America
- 🏠 Forests and clearings
- ◖ Slugs and snails
- ♀ Thought to be egg-layers

SPECIES:

Sibynomorphus lavillai
Sibynomorphus mikanii
Sibynomorphus neuwiedi
Sibynomorphus oligozonatus
Sibynomorphus oneilli
Sibynomorphus petersi
Sibynomorphus turgidus
Sibynomorphus vagrans
Sibynomorphus vagus
Sibynomorphus ventrimaculatus
Sibynomorphus williamsi

GENUS: **SIPHLOPHIS**

- 🐍 7
- ↔ Small to medium
- 🌐 Central and South America
- 🏠 Forests, where they are arboreal
- ◖ Frogs and lizards
- ♀ Egg-layers
- ✎ Rear-fanged and capable of causing
  localized pain and swellings
  in humans. Active at night

SPECIES:

Siphlophis ayauma
Siphlophis cervinus
Siphlophis compressus
Siphlophis leucocephalus
Siphlophis longicaudatus
Siphlophis pulcher
Siphlophis worontzowi

GENUS: **SORDELLINA**

- 🐍 1
- ↔ Small
- 🌐 Brazil
- 🏠 Damp places, near water
- ◖ Frogs and tadpoles
- ♀ Egg-layer

SPECIES:

Sordellina punctata

GENUS: **SYNOPHIS**

- 🐍 4
- ↔ Small to medium
- 🌐 Colombia and Ecuador
- 🏠 Damp places
- ◖ Thought to be lizards
- ♀ Egg-layers

SPECIES:

Synophis bicolor
Synophis calamitus
Synophis lasallei
Synophis plectovertebralis

GENUS: **TACHYMENIS**

- 🐍 6
- ↔ Small
- 🌐 Northwestern South America
- 🏠 Dry situations
- ◖ Thought to be lizards
- ♀ Live-bearers

SPECIES:

Tachymenis affinis
Tachymenis attenuata
Tachymenis chilensis
Tachymenis elongata
Tachymenis peruviana
Tachymenis tarmensis

GENUS: **TAENIOPHALLUS**

- 🐍 9
- ↔ Small
- 🌐 South America
- 🏠 Unknown
- ◖ Unknown
- ♀ Unknown
- ✎ Poorly known; some species are
  only recently described

SPECIES:

Taeniophallus affinis
Taeniophallus bilineatus
Taeniophallus brevirostris
Taeniophallus nebularis
Taeniophallus nicagus
Taeniophallus occipitalis
Taeniophallus persimilis
Taeniophallus poecilopogon
Taeniophallus quadriocellatus

GENUS: **TANTALOPHIS**

- 🐍 1
- ↔ Small
- 🌐 Southcentral Mexico
- 🏠 Pine and cloud forests at high altitudes
- ◖ Unknown
- ♀ Unknown
- ✎ Rare and poorly known

SPECIES:

Tantalophis discolor

GENUS: **THAMNODYNASTES**

- 🐍 19
- ↔ Small to medium-sized, and stocky
- 🌐 South America
- 🏠 Forests, where they are terrestrial
  or arboreal
- ◖ Thought to be lizards
- ♀ Live-bearers
- ✎ Rear-fanged; the bites can cause
  local pain and swelling in humans.
  Active mainly at night

SPECIES:

Thamnodynastes almae

Thamnodynastes ceibae
Thamnodynastes chaquensis
Thamnodynastes chimanta
Thamnodynastes corocoroensis
Thamnodynastes dixoni
Thamnodynastes duida
Thamnodynastes gambotensis
Thamnodynastes hypoconia
Thamnodynastes lanei
Thamnodynastes longicaudus
Thamnodynastes marahuaquensis
Thamnodynastes pallidus
Thamnodynastes paraguanae
Thamnodynastes ramonriveroi
Thamnodynastes rutilus
Thamnodynastes sertanejo
Thamnodynastes strigatus
Thamnodynastes yavi

GENUS: **THERMOPHIS**

- 🐍 3
- ↔ Fairly small
- 🌐 Tibet and China
- 🏠 Mountains at about 4,500 m (14,700 ft)
- ◖ Fish
- ♀ Unknown
- ✎ They occur at very high altitudes,
  where they can survive the cold
  temperatures only because they live
  in the vicinity of hot springs

SPECIES:

Thermophis baileyi
Thermophis shangrila
Thermophis zhaoermii

GENUS: **TOMODON**

- 🐍 3
- ↔ Small
- 🌐 Brazil and Argentina
- 🏠 Forests
- ◖ Unknown
- ♀ Unknown

SPECIES:

Tomodon dorsatum
Tomodon ocellatus
Tomodon orestes

GENUS: **TRETANORHINUS**

Central American Swamp Snakes

- 🐍 4
- ↔ Small
- 🌐 Central America to northern
  South America, and the West Indies
- 🏠 Shallow, heavily weeded bodies
  of water. *T. nigroluteus* has been
  found swimming in the sea
- ◖ Fish, frogs, and tadpoles
- ♀ Egg-layers
- ✎ Nocturnal

SPECIES:

Tretanorhinus mocquardi
Tretanorhinus nigroluteus
Tretanorhinus taeniatus
Tretanorhinus variabilis

GENUS: **TRIMETOPON**

- 🐍 6
- ↔ Small
- 🌐 Central America
- 🏠 Rainforests
- ◖ Unknown
- ♀ Unknown

SPECIES:

Trimetopon barbouri
Trimetopon gracile
Trimetopon pliolepis
Trimetopon simile
Trimetopon slevini
Trimetopon viquezi

GENUS: **TROPIDODIPSAS**

- 🐍 7
- ↔ Small to medium, these snakes
  are slender
- 🌐 Mexico and Central America
- 🏠 Varied
- ◖ Snails
- ♀ Egg-layers
- ✎ Previously placed in the genus *Sibon*

SPECIES:

Tropidodipsas annuliferus
Tropidodipsas fasciata
Tropidodipsas fischeri
Tropidodipsas philippii
Tropidodipsas repleta
Tropidodipsas sartorii
Tropidodipsas zweifeli

GENUS: **TROPIDODRYAS**

- 🐍 2
- ↔ Medium, to about 1 m (3 ft 3 in)
- 🌐 Southern Brazil
- 🏠 Forests, where they are thought
  to be arboreal
- ◖ Frogs, lizards, birds, and
  small mammals
- ♀ Unknown

SPECIES:

Tropidodryas serra
Tropidodryas striaticeps

GENUS: **UROMACER**

- 🐍 3
- ↔ Medium to large, and slender
- 🌐 Hispaniola and surrounding islands
- 🏠 Forests
- ◖ Lizards, especially *Anolis* species
- ♀ Thought to be egg-layers

SPECIES:

Uromacer catesbyi
Uromacer frenatus
Uromacer oxyrhynchus

GENUS: **UROMACERINA**

- 🐍 1
- ↔ Medium and slender
- 🌐 Brazil
- 🏠 Forests, where they are thought
  to be arboreal

- Arboreal lizards
- Thought to be an egg-layer
- Poorly known

SPECIES:

Uromacerina ricardinii

GENUS: UROTHECA

- 8
- Small
- Central and South America
- Forest floors, grassland
- Probably invertebrates, frogs, and lizards
- Egg-layers
- Previously placed in the genus *Rhadinaea*

SPECIES:

Urotheca decipiens
Urotheca dumerilii
Urotheca fulviceps
Urotheca guentheri
Urotheca lateristriga
Urotheca multilineata
Urotheca myersi
Urotheca pachyura

GENUS: XENODON

False Vipers

- 12
- Medium to large, with stout bodies
- Central and South America (Mexico to Argentina)
- Rainforests, especially alongside water courses
- Toads
- Egg-layers
- Bad tempered and rear-fanged. Their bites are painful, though not thought to be especially dangerous

SPECIES:

Xenodon dorbignyi
Xenodon guentheri
Xenodon histricus
Xenodon matogrossensis
Xenodon merremi
Xenodon nattereri
Xenodon neuwiedii
Xenodon pulcher
Xenodon rabdocephalus
Xenodon semicinctus
Xenodon severus
Xenodon werneri

GENUS: XENOPHOLIS

- 3
- Small and slender
- South America, in the Amazon basin
- Damp forests
- Mainly frogs
- Unknown, but likely to be egg-layers

SPECIES:

Xenopholis scalaris
Xenopholis undulatus
Xenopholis werdingorum

LAMPROPHIIDAE
56 GENERA CONTAINING 309 SPECIES

The Lamprophiidae is a new family that brings together a number of species previously classified with the colubrids. The members of this family are grouped into a number of subfamilies and it seems likely that further research will eventually result in more changes. They are mostly terrestrial, but some are burrowers and a few are arboreal. They are small to medium-sized, mostly moderately slender, but with some very slender species as well as some that are thickset, correlating with their lifestyle; arboreal species are thin whereas burrowing species tend to be cylindrical and heavy-bodied. Some are colourful but most have subdued, cryptic, colours and markings. Their diet varies but usually includes small vertebrates. Most lay eggs. A number of species, including the stiletto snakes and mole vipers (subfamily Atractaspidinae), are venomous, some of them dangerously so, and human fatalities have occurred.

GENUS: BUHOMA

- 3
- Medium
- East and West Africa
- Forests
- Unknown
- Unknown
- Formerly placed in the genus *Geodipsas*

SPECIES:

Buhoma depressiceps
Buhoma procterae
Buhoma vauerocegae

GENUS: MONTASPIS

- 1
- Small
- South Africa, in the Natal Drakensberg mountains
- Wetlands above the tree line at nearly 3,000 m (9,850 ft) altitude
- Frogs
- Unknown
- Only recently described from a small number of specimens

SPECIES:

Montaspis gilvomaculata

GENUS: OXYRHABDIUM

- 2
- Moderately large
- Philippines
- Burrowing species, often found in rotting wood or leaf-litter
- Unknown
- Unknown
- Although common, almost nothing is known of their natural history

SPECIES:

Oxyrhabdium leporinum
Oxyrhabdium modestum

GENUS: PSAMMODYNASTES

Mock Vipers

- 2
- Small
- Southeast Asia, the Indonesian archipelago, and the Philippines
- Forests
- Lizards and frogs
- Live-bearers
- They have deep, angular heads, large eyes, and vertical pupils, very much like vipers; nocturnal

SPECIES:

Psammodynastes pictus
Psammodynastes pulverulentus

SUBFAMILY: APARALLACTINAE
Centipede-eaters and their relatives

9 GENERA CONTAINING 47 SPECIES

These are small snakes from sub-Saharan Africa, most of which eat invertebrates. They have enlarged fangs at the back of their mouth, below their eyes. They live on the ground or beneath the surface, often under rocks and debris, where their prey is most numerous. The quill-snouted snakes, *Xenocalamus* species, are burrowers and feed almost exclusively on amphisbaenians (worm lizards). The aparallactines include egg-layers and live-bearers.

GENUS: AMBLYODIPSAS

Purple-glossed Snakes

- 9
- Small
- Africa south of the Sahara
- Varied; burrowing in loose soil
- Burrowing reptiles, amphibians, and small mammals
- All egg-layers except *A. concolor*, which may be a live-bearer under certain circumstances
- Venomous, with a pair of grooved, venom-delivering fangs below the eyes, but not dangerous to humans

SPECIES:

Amblyodipsas concolor,
    Natal Purple-glossed Snake
Amblyodipsas dimidiata
Amblyodipsas katangensis
Amblyodipsas microphthalma,
    Eastern Purple-glossed Snake
Amblyodipsas polylepis
Amblyodipsas rodhaini
Amblyodipsas teitana
Amblyodipsas unicolor
Amblyodipsas ventrimaculata,
    Kalahari Purple-glossed Snake

GENUS: APARALLACTUS

Centipede-eaters

- 11
- Small, to about 60 cm (2 ft)
- Africa south of the Sahara
- Burrowers in sandy soil, rotting logs, abandoned termite nests, and other debris
- Centipedes
- Egg-layers, producing small clutches
- Venomous, but of no danger to humans

SPECIES:

Aparallactus capensis,
    Cape Centipede-eater
Aparallactus guentheri,
    Black Centipede-eater
Aparallactus jacksonii
Aparallactus lineatus
Aparallactus lunulatus,
    Reticulated Centipede-eater
Aparallactus modestus
Aparallactus moeruensis
Aparallactus niger
Aparallactus nigriceps,
    Mozambique Centipede-eater
Aparallactus turneri
Aparallactus werneri

GENUS: BRACHYOPHIS

- 1
- Small
- Kenya and Somalia
- Unknown
- Unknown
- Unknown
- Poorly known. Its relationships with other colubrids are unclear

SPECIES:

Brachyophis revoili

GENUS: CHILORHINOPHIS

Black and Yellow Burrowing Snakes

- 2
- Small
- Central Africa
- Forests, where they live in burrows
- Thought to feed on amphisbaenians (worm lizards) and other burrowing reptiles
- Unknown
- They have venom fangs near the front of their upper jaw

SPECIES:

Chilorhinophis butleri,
    Butler's Black and Yellow
    Burrowing Snake
Chilorhinophis gerardi,
    Gerard's Black and Yellow
    Burrowing Snake

GENUS: HYPOPTOPHIS

- 1
- Small
- Central Africa

🏠 Unknown
🍴 Unknown
⚥ Unknown

SPECIES:
Hypoptophis wilsonii

GENUS: **MACRELAPS**

🐍 1
↔ Medium
🌍 South Africa
🏠 Coastal bush, where it burrows in leaf-litter
🍴 Reptiles, amphibians, and small mammals
⚥ Egg-layer
📋 It has a potentially dangerous bite

SPECIES:
Macrelaps microlepidotus,
    Natal Black Snake

GENUS: **MICRELAPS**

🐍 5
↔ Small
🌍 Central Africa
🏠 Burrowing species, but otherwise unknown
🍴 Thought to feed on other burrowing reptiles and their eggs
⚥ Thought to be egg-layers

SPECIES:
Micrelaps bicoloratus
Micrelaps boettgeri
Micrelaps muelleri
Micrelaps tchernovi
Micrelaps vaillanti

GENUS: **POLEMON**

🐍 12
↔ Small
🌍 West and Central Africa
🏠 Burrowers
🍴 Unknown
⚥ Unknown
📋 Rare and secretive snakes, whose natural history – including their relationships with other snakes – is poorly known. Various species have been placed in the genera *Cyanodontophis*, *Elapocalamus*, and *Miodon* in the past

SPECIES:
Polemon acanthias
Polemon barthii
Polemon bocourti
Polemon christyi
Polemon collaris
Polemon fulvicollis
Polemon gabonensis
Polemon gracilis
Polemon griseiceps
Polemon neuwiedi
Polemon notatus
Polemon robustus

GENUS: **XENOCALAMUS**

Quill-snouted Snakes

🐍 5
↔ Small, to about 80 cm (2 ft 6 in), and very slender
🌍 Central and Southern Africa
🏠 Burrowers in sandy soil
🍴 Amphisbaenians (worm lizards)
⚥ Egg-layers
📋 Technically venomous but not known to bite and of no danger to humans

SPECIES:
Xenocalamus bicolor,
    Bicoloured Quill-snouted Snake
Xenocalamus mechowii,
    Elongated Quill-snouted Snake
Xenocalamus michelii,
    Mitchell's Quill-snouted Snake
Xenocalamus sabiensis,
    Sabi Quill-snouted Snake
Xenocalamus transvaalensis,
    Transvaal Quill-snouted Snake

SUBFAMILY: **ATRACTASPIDINAE**

Stiletto Snakes and Mole Vipers

2 GENERA CONTAINING 23 SPECIES

Members of the Atractaspidinae are all African apart from one species that occurs in the Middle East. *Atractaspis* species are highly venomous burrowing species and have long, hollow, venom-delivering fangs in their upper jaw. They can bring these into play by rotating them sideways so that they emerge from the side of their mouth. They strike by jabbing one of the fangs backward into prey and can successfully strike in the restricted space of a burrow. They have smooth, shiny scales and cylindrical bodies. As far as is known, they all lay eggs. Two species of *Homoroselaps* are known as harlequin snakes because of their colourful markings. Harlequin snakes are venomous but they are docile and rarely bite.

GENUS: **ATRACTASPIS**

Stiletto Snakes, Burrowing Asps

🐍 21
↔ Small to medium
🌍 Africa and the Middle East (*A. engaddensis*)
🏠 Varied, burrowing in loose or sandy soil
🍴 Small vertebrates: lizards, especially skinks, snakes, and nestling rodents
⚥ Egg-layers
📋 They have large, partially hinged fangs and powerful venoms. They can bite without opening their mouths, by moving their fangs sideways and using them to stab their prey; this makes them very difficult to handle safely and there have been human fatalities. All the species look similar and the number of species may be greater than those listed

SPECIES:
Atractaspis andersonii
Atractaspis aterrima,
    Slender Stiletto Snake
Atractaspis battersbyi,
    Battersby's Stiletto Snake
Atractaspis bibronii,
    Bibron's Stiletto Snake
Atractaspis boulengeri,
    Central African Stiletto Snake
Atractaspis congica,
    Congo Stiletto Snake
Atractaspis corpulenta,
    Fat Stiletto Snake
Atractaspis dahomeyensis,
    Dahomey Stiletto Snake
Atractaspis duerdeni,
    Duerden's Stiletto Snake
Atractaspis engaddensis
Atractaspis engdahli,
    Engdahl's Stiletto Snake
Atractaspis fallax
Atractaspis irregularis,
    Variable Stiletto Snake
Atractaspis leucomelas,
    Ogaden Stiletto Snake
Atractaspis magrettii
Atractaspis microlepidota,
    Small-scaled Stiletto Snake
Atractaspis micropholis
Atractaspis phillipsi
Atractaspis reticulata,
    Reticulated Stiletto Snake
Atractaspis scorteccii,
    Somali Stiletto Snake
Atractaspis watsoni

GENUS: **HOMOROSELAPS**

Harlequin Snakes

🐍 2
↔ Small, to 55 cm (1 ft 8 in)
🌍 Southern Africa
🏠 Often found in termite mounds
🍴 Legless skinks, thread snakes, blind snakes, and other small snakes
⚥ Egg-layers
📋 Brightly coloured. Not considered dangerous to humans, because of their small size. Formerly classified as members of the Elapidae and then the Atractaspidae before being moved, at least for the time being, to the Lamprophiidae. *H. dorsalis* is rare and its natural history is hardly known

SPECIES:
Homoroselaps dorsalis,
    Striped Harlequin Snake
Homoroselaps lacteus,
    Spotted Harlequin Snake

SUBFAMILY: **LAMPROPHIINAE**
12 GENERA CONTAINING 72 SPECIES

Members of this subfamily are restricted to sub-Saharan Africa. The house snakes, genera *Boaedon* and *Lamprophis*, are powerful constrictors with long teeth that eat rodents and lizards; some species are associated with rural houses and barns. Many species are brown but a few are olive green. The Aurora House Snake is lime green with an orange mid-dorsal stripe when it first hatches, but it later becomes duller. Most lamprophine snakes are terrestrial and nocturnal, living in a variety of habitats, including deserts and grasslands, but some, such as *Lycodonomorphus*, are semi-aquatic, and these eat fish and frogs. All are egg-layers as far as is known.

GENUS: **BOAEDON**

House Snakes

🐍 8
↔ Small to medium
🌍 Sub-Saharan Africa
🏠 Varied, from open country to forests and even deserts
🍴 Small mammals, typically rodents, and lizards
⚥ Egg-layers
📋 Species have been placed in *Lamprophis* in the past

SPECIES:
Boaedon capensis,
    Cape House Snake
● *Boaedon fuliginosus,*
    Brown House Snake (pp.74–75)
Boaedon lineatus,
    Lined House Snake
Boaedon maculatus,
    Spotted House Snake
Boaedon olivaceus,
    Olive House Snake
Boaedon radfordi
Boaedon upembae
Boaedon virgatus,
    Hallowell's House Snake

GENUS: **BOTHROLYCUS**

🐍 1
↔ Small
🌍 Central Africa
🏠 Unknown
🍴 Unknown
⚥ Unknown

SPECIES:
Bothrolycus ater

GENUS: **BOTHROPHTHALMUS**

🐍 2
↔ Small
🌍 Central and West Africa
🏠 Moist montane forests
🍴 Unknown
⚥ Unknown

SPECIES:
Bothrophthalmus brunneus
Bothrophthalmus lineatus

GENUS: **CHAMAELYCUS**

🐍 4
↔ Small
🌍 West Africa
🏠 Forests, where they live in burrows
🍴 Unknown
⚥ Unknown

SPECIES:

Chamaelycus christyi
Chamaelycus fasciatus
Chamaelycus parkeri
Chamaelycus werneri

GENUS: **DENDROLYCUS**

- 🐍 1
- ↔ Unknown
- 🌐 Zaïre
- 🏠 Forests
- ⌇ Unknown
- ⚲ Unknown

SPECIES:

Denrolycus elapoides

GENUS: **GONIONOTOPHIS**

- 🐍 15
- ↔ Small
- 🌐 West Africa
- 🏠 Rainforests
- ⌇ Thought to be frogs
- ⚲ Unknown

SPECIES:

Gonionotophis brussauxi
Gonionotophis capensis
Gonionotophis chanleri
Gonionotophis crossi
Gonionotophis egbensis
Gonionotophis gabouensis
Gonionotophis grantii
Gonionotophis guirali
Gonionotophis klingi
Gonionotophis laurenti
Gonionotophis nyassae
Gonionotophis poensis
Gonionotophis savorgnani
Gonionotophis stenophthalmus
Gonionotophis vernayi

GENUS: **HORMONOTUS**

- 🐍 1
- ↔ Unknown
- 🌐 West Africa
- 🏠 Unknown
- ⌇ Unknown
- ⚲ Unknown

SPECIES:

Hormonotus modestus

GENUS: **INYOKA**

- 🐍 1
- ↔ Small
- 🌐 Southern Africa
- 🏠 Rocky outcrops
- ⌇ Small mammals and lizards
- ⚲ Egg-layer
- 📝 The single species was known as *Lamprophis swazicus* until recently

SPECIES:

Inyoka swazicus,
    Swaziland House Snake

GENUS: **LAMPROPHIS**

House Snakes

- 🐍 7
- ↔ Small to medium
- 🌐 Africa and the Seychelles (*L. geometricus*)
- 🏠 Varied, from rocky deserts to forests
- ⌇ Lizards and small mammals. They are powerful constrictors
- ⚲ Egg-layers

SPECIES:

Lamprophis abyssinicus
Lamprophis aurora,
    Aurora House Snake
Lamprophis erlangeri
Lamprophis fiskii,
    Fisk's House Snake
Lamprophis fuscus,
    Yellow-bellied House Snake
Lamprophis geometricus,
    Seychelles House Snake
Lamprophis guttatus,
    Spotted House Snake

GENUS: **LYCODONOMORPHUS**

- 🐍 8
- ↔ Medium
- 🌐 Africa
- 🏠 Semi-aquatic
- ⌇ Fish, frogs, and tadpoles
- ⚲ Egg-layers

SPECIES:

Lycodonomorphus bicolor
Lycodonomorphus inornatus
Lycodonomorphus laevissimus
Lycodonomorphus leleupi
Lycodonomorphus obscuriventris
Lycodonomorphus rufulus
Lycodonomorphus subtaeniatus
Lycodonomorphus whytii

GENUS: **LYCOPHIDION**

Wolf Snakes

- 🐍 20
- ↔ Small
- 🌐 Africa
- 🏠 Unknown
- ⌇ Lizards and snakes
- ⚲ Egg-layers
- 📝 The name derives from the elongated front fangs

SPECIES:

Lycophidion acutirostre
Lycophidion albomaculatum
Lycophidion capense
Lycophidion depressirostre
Lycophidion hellmichi
Lycophidion irroratum
Lycophidion laterale
Lycophidion meleagris
Lycophidion multimaculatum
Lycophidion namibianum
Lycophidion nanus
Lycophidion nigromaculatum
Lycophidion ornatum
Lycophidion pembanum
Lycophidion pygmaeum
Lycophidion semiannule
Lycophidion semicinctum

Lycophidion taylori
Lycophidion uzungwense
Lycophidion variegatum

GENUS: **PSEUDOBOODON**

- 🐍 4
- ↔ Small to medium
- 🌐 The highlands of Ethiopia
- 🏠 Unknown
- ⌇ Unknown
- ⚲ Unknown
- 📝 Apparently closely related to the house snakes, *Lamprophis*, but rare and poorly known

SPECIES:

Pseudoboodon boehmei
Pseudoboodon gascae
Pseudoboodon lemniscatus
Pseudoboodon sandfordorum

SUBFAMILY: **PSAMMOPHIINAE**

Sand Snakes and their relatives

8 GENERA CONTAINING 52 SPECIES

Many members of the Psammophiinae are fast-moving, diurnal species, such as the 34 species of sand snakes (*Psammophis* species), the skaapstekers (*Psammophylax*), and the *Malpolon* species. They occur over the whole of Africa and into the Middle East and southern Europe. *Mimophis mahfalensis* is the only Madagascan species. The remaining species include the bark snakes, *Hemirhagerrhis*, which live under loose bark and feed mainly on geckos, and the beaked snakes, *Rhamphiopus*, which are stout-bodied terrestrial snakes with downturned snouts that they use to root out rodents from their burrows. Psammophine snakes have enlarged rear fangs and some, including *Malpolon* and *Psammophis*, produce toxic saliva which may be harmful to humans.

GENUS: **DIPSINA**

- 🐍 1
- ↔ Small and slender
- 🌐 Southern and Southwestern Africa
- 🏠 Dry sandy areas with rocks
- ⌇ Lizards
- ⚲ Egg-layer
- 📝 The head has a hooked snout and large eyes

SPECIES:

Dipsina multimaculata,
    Dwarf Beaked Snake

GENUS: **HEMIRHAGERRHIS**

Bark Snakes

- 🐍 4
- ↔ Small
- 🌐 Africa
- 🏠 Wooded grasslands, where they are arboreal
- ⌇ Lizards
- ⚲ Egg-layers

- 📝 Nocturnal, hiding beneath loose bark during the day

SPECIES:

Hemirhagerrhis hildebrandtii
Hemirhagerrhis kelleri
Hemirhagerrhis nototaenia,
    Bark Snake or Mopane Snake
Hemirhagerrhis viperina

GENUS: **MALPOLON**

- 🐍 2
- ↔ Large, growing to 2 m (6 ft 6 in) or more
- 🌐 Southern Europe, North Africa, and the Middle East
- 🏠 Varied, but often dry, scrubby hillsides and semi-arid deserts
- ⌇ Lizards and other snakes, which they hunt during the day
- ⚲ Egg-layers
- 📝 Rear-fanged snakes that bite readily. Although not life-threatening, the bites can cause nausea, localized pain, and swelling

SPECIES:

Malpolon insignitus
Malpolon monspessulanus,
    Montpellier Snake

GENUS: **MIMOPHIS**

- 🐍 1
- ↔ Small and slender
- 🌐 Madagascar
- 🏠 On the ground in forests and more open habitats
- ⌇ Thought to be lizards
- ⚲ Unknown, but thought to be an egg-layer

SPECIES:

Mimophis mahfalensis

GENUS: **PSAMMOPHIS**

Sand Snakes

- 🐍 34
- ↔ Small to moderately large, with slender bodies
- 🌐 Africa and the Middle East; one species (*P. condanarus*) is found in Myanmar and Thailand and another (*P. lineolatus*) in western China
- 🏠 Varied but usually open grasslands, deserts, and cultivated places
- ⌇ Mainly lizards, which they pursue with great speed
- ⚲ Egg-layers
- 📝 Rear-fanged; bites from some of the larger species can result in localized pain and swelling in humans

SPECIES:

Psammophis aegyptius
Psammophis angolensis,
    Dwarf Sand Snake
Psammophis ansorgii

Psammophis biseriatus
Psammophis brevirostris
Psammophis condanarus
Psammophis crucifer,
　　Cross-marked Sand Snake
Psammophis elegans
Psammophis indochinensis
Psammophis jallae,
　　Jalla's Sand Snake
Psammophis leightoni,
　　Cape Sand Snake
Psammophis leithii
Psammophis leopardinus
Psammophis lineatus
Psammophis lineolatus
Psammophis longifrons
Psammophis mossambicus
Psammophis namibensis
Psammophis notostictus,
　　Karoo Sand Snake
Psammophis occidentalis
Psammophis orientalis
Psammophis phillipsi,
　　Olive Sand Snake
Psammophis praeornatus
Psammophis pulcher
Psammophis punctulatus
Psammophis rukwae
Psammophis schokari
Psammophis sibilans,
　　Hissing Sand Snake
Psammophis subtaeniatus,
　　Stripe-bellied Sand Snake
Psammophis sudanensis
Psammophis tanganicus
Psammophis trigrammus,
　　Western Sand Snake
Psammophis trinasalis
Psammophis zambiensis

GENUS: **PSAMMOPHYLAX**

Skaapstekers

- 6
- Small to medium
- Southern Africa
- Grasslands and scrub
- Frogs, lizards, and small mammals
- Various: *P. tritaeniatus* and *P. rhombeatus* are egg-layers, but some populations of *P. variabilis* lay eggs, while others are live-bearers
- Rear-fanged. They produce small amounts of very potent venom, but are not considered dangerous to humans (nor to sheep, despite their name, which means "sheep killer" in Afrikaans)

SPECIES:
Psammophylax acutus
Psammophylax multisquamis
Psammophylax rhombeatus,
　　Spotted Skaapsteker or
　　Rhombic Skaapsteker
Psammophylax togoensis
Psammophylax tritaeniatus,
　　Striped Skaapsteker
Psammophylax variabilis,
　　Grey-bellied Grass Snake

GENUS: **RHAGERHIS**

- 1
- Medium
- North Africa, Arabia, and parts of the Middle East
- Deserts and other arid regions
- Mammals and reptiles
- Egg-layer
- A very aggressive snake that flattens its neck into a narrow hood if disturbed. The single species was previously known as *Malpolon moilensis*

SPECIES:
Rhagerhis moilensis

GENUS: **RHAMPHIOPHIS**

Beaked Snakes

- 3
- Medium to large, and stocky
- Africa
- Dry, scrubby countryside
- Reptiles, birds, and small mammals
- Egg-layers

SPECIES:
Rhamphiophis oxyrhynchus
Rhamphiophis rostratus
Rhamphiophis rubropunctatus

SUBFAMILY: **PROSYMNINAE**
1 GENUS CONTAINING 16 SPECIES

The shovel-snout snakes live in burrows or rock cracks, feeding almost exclusively on reptile eggs; they first puncture the egg before swallowing it whole. If disturbed they may coil up tightly like a watch-spring, with their head in the centre of the coil, and thrash about wildly if touched. They are egg-layers.

GENUS: **PROSYMNA**

Shovel-snouted Snakes

- 16
- Small and slender
- Southern half of Africa
- Varied; usually dry places, where they burrow in loose, sandy soil
- Reptile eggs
- Egg-layers, producing small numbers of elongated eggs
- Active at night

SPECIES:
Prosymna ambigua,
　　East African Shovelsnout
Prosymna angolensis,
　　Angolan Shovelsnout
Prosymna bivittata,
　　Two-striped Shovelsnout
Prosymna frontalis,
　　South-western Shovelsnout
Prosymna greigerti
Prosymna janii,
　　Mozambique Shovelsnout
Prosymna lineata
Prosymna meleagris
Prosymna ornatissima
Prosymna pitmani
Prosymna ruspolii
Prosymna semifasciata
Prosymna somalica
Prosymna stuhlmanni
Prosymna sundevalli,
　　Sundevall's Shovelsnout
Prosymna visseri,
　　Visser's Shovelsnout

SUBFAMILY: **PSEUDASPIDINAE**
Shovel-nosed Snakes

2 GENERA CONTAINING 2 SPECIES

A group of just two species: the Mole Snake, *Pseudaspis cana*, which feeds mainly on burrowing mammals and is live-bearing, and the Western Keeled Snake, from the Namib Desert, that eats mostly geckos, and is thought to be an egg-layer.

GENUS: **PSEUDASPIS**

- 1
- Large, to over 2 m (6 ft 6 in)
- Southern Africa
- Open country: grassland, scrub, deserts, and hillsides
- Small mammals
- Live-bearer. Young can number up to 100 in exceptional cases

SPECIES:
Pseudaspis cana,
　　Mole Snake

GENUS: **PYTHONODIPSAS**

- 1
- Small, to about 60 cm (2 ft)
- Namibia and Angola
- Rocky deserts
- Small lizards and rodents
- Unknown
- It is unusual among colubrids because the head is covered with many small, fragmented scales. The nostrils point upwards. It has large rear fangs but is not considered dangerous to humans. It shelters by day in sand and is often found at the base of the equally unusual Welwischia plants

SPECIES:
Pythonodipsas carinata,
　　Western Keeled Snake

SUBFAMILY: **PSEUDOXYRHOPHIINAE**
22 GENERA CONTAINING 89 SPECIES

Most members of the Pseudoxyrhophiinae occur in Madagascar and they account for the majority of snakes there. Many are nocturnal, arboreal snakes, feeding on geckos and frogs, and have slender bodies and larges eyes. The strange Madagascan vine snakes, *Langaha*, have unique structures on their snouts; these are leaf-like in females and pointed in males; the sexes are also coloured differently. They are hard to find, because they are cryptically marked and remain motionless if disturbed. They feed on lizards. Four species of African slug-eaters, genus *Duberria*, come from the African mainland and are small terrestrial snakes that live in damp places and feed on slugs and snails. They give birth to live young.

GENUS: **ALLUAUDINA**

- 2
- Small, typically to 40 cm (1 ft 3 in)
- Madagascar
- Forests
- Unknown
- Thought to be egg-layers
- Rare and poorly known. *A. mocquardi* is known from only two specimens, both taken in caves at the same locality

SPECIES:
Alluaudina bellyi
Alluaudina mocquardi

GENUS: **AMPLORHINUS**

- 1
- Small
- Southern Africa
- Damp places
- Frogs and lizards
- Live-bearer
- Rear-fanged, though not dangerous to humans

SPECIES:
Amplorhinus multimaculatus

GENUS: **BRYGOPHIS**

- 1
- Large
- Madagascar
- Unknown
- Essentially unknown
- Unknown
- Known from only a single specimen, which was reddish brown with white spots. It had previously eaten a large chameleon

SPECIES:
Brygophis coulangesi

GENUS: **COMPSOPHIS**

- 7
- Small
- Madagascar
- Unknown
- Unknown
- Unknown
- *C. albiventris* is known from only a single juvenile specimen that was brown with a dark stripe along its back. Nothing is known about its natural history and all attempts to find additional specimens have so far failed. The other six species were previously included in the genus *Geodipsas*

SPECIES:
Compsophis albiventris
Compsophis boulengeri
Compsophis fatsibe
Compsophis infralineatus
Compsophis laphystius
Compsophis vinckei
Compsophis zeny

GENUS: DITYPOPHIS

- 1
- Small
- The isolated island of Socotra, off the Arabian Peninsula
- The island is dry. Details of the snake's preferences are unknown
- Unknown
- Unknown
- Rare and poorly known

SPECIES:
Ditypophis vivax

GENUS: DROMICODRYAS

- 2
- Small and slender
- Madagascar
- Forests
- Thought to be lizards
- Thought to be egg-layers
- Active during the day

SPECIES:
Dromicodryas bernieri
Dromicodryas quadrilineatus

GENUS: DUBERRIA

Slug-eating Snakes

- 4
- Small, to about 40 cm (1 ft 3 in).
- Southern Africa
- Among grass and under logs, in damp situations
- Slugs and snails
- Live-bearers
- Secretive

SPECIES:
Duberria lutrix,
   Common Slug-eater
Duberria rhodesiana
Duberria shirana
Duberria variegata,
   Variegated Slug-eater or
   Spotted Slug-eater

GENUS: ELAPOTINUS

- 1
- Small
- Tropical Africa
- Unknown
- Unknown
- Unknown
- Rare and almost completely unknown. Its relationships with other snakes are still unclear

SPECIES:
Elapotinus picteti

GENUS: HETEROLIODON

- 3
- Small
- Madagascar
- Unknown

- Unknown
- Unknown

SPECIES:
Heteroliodon fohy
Heteroliodon lava
Heteroliodon occipitalis

GENUS: ITHYCYPHUS

- 5
- Fairly large, to about 1.5 m (5 ft)
- Madagascar
- Forests, where they are highly arboreal
- Frogs and lizards, including chameleons
- Egg-layers
- Rear-fanged, though not dangerous to humans

SPECIES:
Ithycyphus blanci
Ithycyphus goudoti
Ithycyphus miniatus
Ithycyphus oursi
Ithycyphus perineti

GENUS: LANGAHA

Madagascan Vine Snakes

- 3
- Long and extremely slender
- Madagascar
- Rainforests, where they are totally arboreal
- Lizards, especially geckos
- Egg-layers, producing small clutches of eggs
- An appendage on the tip of the snouts is flattened like a leaf in females, but is more elongated and pointed in males. Females of two species also have enlarged scales jutting out above their eyes. Active mainly in the early morning

SPECIES:
Langaha alluaudi
Langaha madagascariensis
Langaha pseudoalluaudi

GENUS: LEIOHETERODON

Madagascan Hog-nosed Snakes

- 3
- Large and robust
- Madagascar
- Dry and forested areas
- Amphibians, which they sometimes dig up using their upturned snouts
- Egg-layers

SPECIES:
Leioheterodon geayi
Leioheterodon madagascariensis
Leioheterodon modestus

GENUS: LIOPHIDIUM

- 10
- Small
- Madagascar (seven species) and the Comoros (*L. mayottensis*)
- Sandy places or on forest floors
- Unknown
- Unknown
- Poorly known: there is only one recorded specimen of *L. apperti* and two of *L. therezieni*

SPECIES:
Liophidium apperti
Liophidium chabaudi
Liophidium maintikibo
Liophidium mayottensis
Liophidium pattoni
Liophidium rhodogaster
Liophidium therezieni
Liophidium torquatum
Liophidium trilineatum
Liophidium vaillanti

GENUS: LIOPHOLIDOPHIS

- 8
- Long and slender
- Madagascar
- Varied, from swamps to forests and clearings
- Mainly frogs
- Egg-layers
- Several species were only recently discovered

SPECIES:
Liopholidophis baderi
Liopholidophis dimorphus
Liopholidophis dolicocercus
Liopholidophis grandidieri
Liopholidophis oligolepis
Liopholidophis rhadinaea
Liopholidophis sexlineatus
Liopholidophis varius

GENUS: LYCODRYAS

- 10
- Long and slender
- Indian Ocean region
- Unknown
- Lizards and frogs
- Thought to be egg-layers
- Several Madagascan species that used to be in this genus have recently been moved to the genus *Stenophis*

SPECIES:
Lycodryas carleti
Lycodryas citrinus
Lycodryas cococola
Lycodryas gaimardi
Lycodryas granuliceps
Lycodryas guentheri
Lycodryas inopinae
Lycodryas inornatus
Lycodryas maculatus
Lycodryas pseudogranuliceps

GENUS: MADAGASCAROPHIS

- 4
- Medium, with thickset bodies
- Madagascar
- Varied: on the ground and in trees and bushes
- Frogs, lizards, including chameleons, other snakes, and birds
- Egg-layers, producing small clutches of eggs
- Most active after rain

SPECIES:
Madagascarophis colubrinus
Madagascarophis fuchsi
Madagascarophis meridionalis
Madagascarophis ocellatus

GENUS: MICROPISTHODON

- 1
- Medium and slender
- Madagascar
- Unknown, but thought to be arboreal
- Thought to eat lizards and frogs
- Egg-layer
- Known from only a few specimens. Thought to be diurnal

SPECIES:
Micropisthodon ochraceus

GENUS: PARARHADINAEA

- 1
- Small
- Northern Madagascar
- Rainforest
- Unknown, possibly invertebrates
- Egg-layer
- Poorly known

SPECIES:
Pararhadinaea melanogaster

GENUS: PARASTENOPHIS

- 1
- Medium
- Madagascar
- Terrestrial, in rainforest and cleared areas
- Lizards, including chameleons
- Egg-layer
- The single species was previously known as *Stenophis betsileanus*

SPECIES:
Parastenophis betsileanus

GENUS: PHISALIXELLA

- 4
- Medium, very slender
- Madagascar
- Arboreal, in rainforests and cleared areas, including villages
- Lizards and possibly frogs
- Egg-layers

📝 Previously placed in the genus
Stenophis

SPECIES:
Phisalixella arctifasciata
Phisalixella iarakaensis
Phisalixella tulearensis
Phisalixella variabilis

GENUS: **PSEUDOXYRHOPUS**

🐍 11
↔ Small
🌐 Madagascar
🏠 Unknown; thought to be a burrowing species, often turning up beneath rotting logs and other debris
🍴 Some species may feed on frogs
⚥ Unknown

SPECIES:
Pseudoxyrhopus ambreensis
Pseudoxyrhopus analabe
Pseudoxyrhopus ankafinaensis
Pseudoxyrhopus heterurus
Pseudoxyrhopus imerinae
Pseudoxyrhopus kely
Pseudoxyrhopus microps
Pseudoxyrhopus oblectator
Pseudoxyrhopus quinquelineatus
Pseudoxyrhopus sokosoko
Pseudoxyrhopus tritaeniatus

GENUS: **THAMNOSOPHIS**

🐍 6
↔ Medium
🌐 Madagascar
🏠 Terrestrial, in rainforests, secondary forests, and cultivated areas
🍴 Frogs
⚥ Egg-layers

SPECIES:
Thamnosophis epistibes
Thamnosophis infrasignatus
Thamnosophis lateralis
Thamnosophis martae
Thamnosophis mavotenda
Thamnosophis stumpffi

NATRICIDAE
38 GENERA CONTAINING 226 SPECIES

Sometimes included as a subfamily within the Colubridae, the natricids are small to medium-sized, semi-aquatic "water" snakes from North and Central America, Europe, Asia, and Africa. Most eat fish or frogs but smaller species eat slugs, snails, and earthworms. One species, the Queen Snake, *Regina septemvittata*, eats newly-moulted crayfish. Species from the New World are live-bearers whereas those from the Old World are mostly egg-layers.

GENUS: **ADELOPHIS**

🐍 2
↔ Small
🌐 Mexico
🏠 Damp places
🍴 Earthworms
⚥ Live-bearers
📝 Poorly known

SPECIES:
Adelophis copei
Adelophis foxi

GENUS: **AFRONATRIX**

🐍 1
↔ Medium
🌐 Africa
🏠 Varied, but always close to water
🍴 Frogs and possibly fish
⚥ Thought to be an egg-layer
📝 Poorly known

SPECIES:
Afronatrix anoscopus

GENUS: **AMPHIESMA**

🐍 1
↔ Small
🌐 Southeast Asia, India, Sri Lanka, China, and Japan
🍴 Swamps, marshes, lakes, and slow-moving rivers, as well as damp forests. Some species are semi-aquatic
🍴 Amphibians and fish
⚥ Egg-layer

SPECIES:
Amphiesma stolatum

GENUS: **AMPHIESMOIDES**

🐍 1
↔ Small
🌐 China
🏠 Semi-aquatic
🍴 Unknown
⚥ Unknown
📝 Rare and poorly known

SPECIES:
Amphiesmoides ornaticeps

GENUS: **ANOPLOHYDRUS**

🐍 1
↔ Small, 43 cm (1 ft 4 in)
🌐 Sumatra
🏠 Wet forests. Thought to be semi-aquatic
🍴 Unknown
⚥ Unknown
📝 Known from only a single specimen described in 1909

SPECIES:
Anoplohydrus aemulans

GENUS: **ASPIDURA**

🐍 7
↔ Small
🌐 Sri Lanka
🏠 Forests, among leaf-litter
🍴 Mostly earthworms
⚥ Egg-layers
📝 Nocturnal

SPECIES:
Aspidura brachyorrhos
Aspidura ceylonensis
Aspidura copei
Aspidura deraniyagalae
Aspidura drummondhayi
Aspidura quentheri
Aspidura trachyprocta

GENUS: **ATRETIUM**

🐍 2
↔ Small to medium
🌐 India and Sri Lanka (*A. schistosum*) and China (*A. yunnanensis*)
🏠 Wet and damp places, where they are aquatic or semi-aquatic
🍴 Fish and frogs
⚥ Thought to be egg-layers
📝 The Chinese species is rare and hardly known

SPECIES:
Atretium schistosum
Atretium yunnanensis

GENUS: **BALANOPHIS**

🐍 1
↔ Small
🌐 Sri Lanka
🏠 Forests, living among leaf-litter
🍴 Frogs
⚥ Egg-layer

SPECIES:
Balanophis ceylonensis

GENUS: **CLONOPHIS**

🐍 1
↔ Small, to about 60 cm (2 ft)
🌐 North America
🏠 Damp places, including swamps
🍴 Earthworms and slugs
⚥ Live-bearer

SPECIES:
Clonophis kirtlandii,
Kirtland's Water Snake

GENUS: **HALDEA**

Rough Earth Snake

🐍 1
↔ Small, 18–25 cm (7–10 in)
🌐 North America (USA)
🏠 Grasslands and forest clearings, under stones
🍴 Earthworms and similar
⚥ Live-bearers
📝 Previously known as *Virginia striatula*

SPECIES:
Haldea striatula,
Rough Earth Snake

GENUS: **HEBIUS**

Keelbacks

🐍 41
↔ Medium
🌐 India, Southeast Asia, and China
🏠 Damp places near pools, lakes, and rivers
🍴 Frogs and fish
⚥ Egg-layers
📝 Previously placed in the genus *Amphiesma*

SPECIES:
Hebius andreae
Hebius arquus
Hebius atemporale
Hebius beddomei
Hebius bitaeniatum
Hebius boulengeri
Hebius celebicum
Hebius clerki
Hebius concelarum
Hebius craspedogaster
Hebius deschauenseei
Hebius flavifrons
Hebius frenatum
Hebius groundwateri
Hebius inas
Hebius ishigakiense
Hebius johannis
Hebius kerinciense
Hebius khasiense
Hebius leucomystax
Hebius metusium
Hebius miyajimae
Hebius modestum
Hebius monticola
Hebius nicobariense
Hebius octolineatum
Hebius optatum
Hebius parallelum
Hebius pealii
Hebius petersii
Hebius popei
Hebius pryeri
Hebius sanguineum
Hebius sarasinorum
Hebius sarawacense
Hebius sauteri
Hebius taronense
Hebius venningi
Hebius vibakari
Hebius viperinum
Hebius xenura

GENUS: **HERPETOREAS**

🐍 3
↔ Medium
🌐 India, Pakistan, Bangladesh, Nepal, Myanmar, and China
🏠 Forests and fields, often near villages
🍴 Frogs, lizards, fish, and small mammals
⚥ Egg-layers
📝 Previously placed in the genus *Amphiesma*

SPECIES:
Herpetoreas burbrinki
Herpetoreas platyceps
Herpetoreas sieboldii

GENUS: HOLOGERRHUM

- ~ 2
- ↔ Small
- 🌐 The island of Luzon, Philippines
- 🏠 Unknown
- ◀ Unknown
- ♂ Unknown

SPECIES:

Hologerrhum dermali
Hologerrhum philippinum

GENUS: HYDRABLABES

- ~ 2
- ↔ Small
- 🌐 Borneo
- 🏠 Forests, where they burrow
- ◀ Unknown
- ♂ Unknown
- ☑ Rare and poorly known

SPECIES:

Hydrablabes periops
Hydrablabes praefrontalis

GENUS: HYDRAETHIOPS

- ~ 2
- ↔ Small
- 🌐 Central Africa
- 🏠 Semi-aquatic
- ◀ Thought to be amphibians and fish
- ♂ Unknown
- ☑ Related to *Afronatrix*, but otherwise poorly known

SPECIES:

Hydraethiops laevis
Hydraethiops melanogaster

GENUS: IGUANOGNATHUS

- ~ 1
- ↔ Small
- 🌐 Sumatra
- 🏠 Unknown
- ◀ Unknown
- ♂ Unknown
- ☑ A rare snake that has been collected only a few times

SPECIES:

Iguanognathus werneri

GENUS: ISANOPHIS

- ~ 1
- ↔ Medium
- 🌐 Northeastern Thailand
- 🏠 Aquatic, in streams
- ◀ Presumably fish and frogs
- ♂ Unknown
- ☑ Formerly placed in the genus *Opisthotrophis*. Known from only a handful of specimens

SPECIES:

Isanophis boonsongi

GENUS: LIMNOPHIS

- ~ 2
- ↔ Small, to about 60 cm (2 ft)
- 🌐 Southern Africa
- 🏠 Semi-aquatic, in marshy places
- ◀ Fish and amphibians
- ♂ Egg-layers

SPECIES:

Limnophis bangweolicus
Limnophis bicolor

GENUS: LIODYTES

American Swamp Snakes

- ~ 3
- ↔ Small, 25–50 cm (10–20 in)
- 🌐 North America (southeastern USA)
- 🏠 Swamps, sphagnum bogs, and drainage ditches
- ◀ Crayfish, frogs, and aquatic salamanders
- ♂ Live-bearers
- ☑ Previously placed in the genera *Regina* and *Seminatrix*

SPECIES:

Liodytes alleni,
    Striped Crayfish Snake
Liodytes pygaea,
    Black Swamp Snake
Liodytes rigida,
    Glossy Crayfish Snake

GENUS: LYCOGNATHOPHIS

- ~ 1
- ↔ Medium
- 🌐 Seychelles
- 🏠 Apparently terrestrial
- ◀ Unknown
- ♂ Unknown
- ☑ Very poorly known

SPECIES:

Lycognathophis seychellensis

GENUS: MACROPISTHODON

- ~ 4
- ↔ Medium
- 🌐 India, Sri Lanka, southern China, and parts of Southeast Asia
- 🏠 Fields and grasslands
- ◀ Mainly frogs
- ♂ Egg-layers
- ☑ Rear-fanged, but innocuous. The broad heads and markings mimic those of the dangerously venomous pit vipers belonging to the genus *Gloydius* from the same region

SPECIES:

Macropisthodon flaviceps
Macropisthodon plumbicolor
Macropisthodon rhodomelas
Macropisthodon rudis

GENUS: NATRICITERES

Marsh Snakes

- ~ 5
- ↔ Small and slender
- 🌐 Tropical Africa
- 🏠 Swamps and marshes
- ◀ Frogs
- ♂ Egg-layers
- ☑ They can discard the tail if it is grasped by a predator

SPECIES:

Natriciteres bipostocularis
Natriciteres fuliginoides
Natriciteres olivacea
Natriciteres sylvatica
Natriciteres variegata

GENUS: NATRIX

Eurasian Water Snakes

- ~ 3
- ↔ Medium to large
- 🌐 Europe, Western Asia, and North Africa
- 🏠 Water and damp places
- ◀ Mainly amphibians and fish, but the Grass Snake also takes small mammals and birds
- ♂ Egg-layers, the eggs of the Grass Snake often being deposited in communal sites
- ☑ *N. megalocephala* is now considered to be a subspecies of *N. natrix*

SPECIES:

Natrix maura,
    Viperine Snake
- *Natrix natrix*,
    Grass snake (pp.100–01)
Natrix tessellata,
    Dice Snake or Tessellated Snake

GENUS: NERODIA

American Water Snakes

- ~ 10
- ↔ Medium to large, and stocky
- 🌐 Southeastern North America and Baja California, Mexico
- 🏠 Aquatic and semi-aquatic, in swamps, lakes, and coastal marshes
- ◀ Mostly amphibians and fish
- ♂ Live-bearers. The young can number nearly 100 in some species
- ☑ Some species are divided into several subspecies, some of which are sometimes regarded as full species

SPECIES:

Nerodia clarkii,
    Salt Marsh Snake
Nerodia cyclopion,
    Green Water Snake
Nerodia erythrogaster,
    Plain-bellied Water Snake
- *Nerodia fasciata*,
    Banded Water Snake or Southern
    Water Snake (pp.102–03)
Nerodia floridana,
    Florida Green Water Snake
Nerodia harteri,
    Harter's Water Snake
Nerodia paucimaculata,
    Concho Water Snake
Nerodia rhombifer,
    Diamondback Water Snake
Nerodia sipedon,
    Northern Water Snake
Nerodia taxispilota,
    Brown Water Snake

GENUS: OPISTHOTROPIS

- ~ 21
- ↔ Small to medium
- 🌐 Southern China, Southeast Asia, and the Philippines
- 🏠 Aquatic or semi-aquatic
- ◀ Fish, amphibians, freshwater shrimps, and earthworms
- ♂ Thought to be egg-layers
- ☑ Very rare and poorly known

SPECIES:

Opisthotropis alcalai
Opisthotropis andersonii
Opisthotropis atra
Opisthotropis balteata
Opisthotropis cheni
Opisthotropis cucae
Opisthotropis daovantieni
Opisthotropis durandi
Opisthotropis guangxiensis
Opisthotropis jacobi
Opisthotropis kikuzatoi
Opisthotropis kuatunensis
Opisthotropis lateralis
Opisthotropis latouchii
Opisthotropis laui
Opisthotropis maculosa
Opisthotropis maxwelli
Opisthotropis rugosa
Opisthotropis spenceri
Opisthotropis tamdaoensis
Opisthotropis typica

GENUS: PARAHELICOPS

- ~ 1
- ↔ Small
- 🌐 Thailand and Vietnam
- 🏠 Unknown
- ◀ Unknown
- ♂ Unknown
- ☑ Very rare and poorly known

SPECIES:

Parahelicops annamensis

GENUS: PARARHABDOPHIS

- ~ 1
- ↔ Medium
- 🌐 Southeast Asia
- 🏠 Unknown
- ◀ Unknown
- ♂ Unknown

SPECIES:

Pararhabdophis chapaensis

GENUS: **PARATAPINOPHIS**

- 1
- Medium
- Southeast Asia
- Aquatic, in streams
- Fish, frogs, tadpoles, freshwater shrimps, and earthworms
- Egg-layer
- The single species was previously known as *Opisthotrophis praemaxillaris*. Its appearance is remarkably similar to that of the North American *Nerodia* species

SPECIES:
Paratapinophis praemaxillaris

GENUS: **REGINA**

Crayfish Snakes

- 2
- Small to medium
- North America
- Invariably found near water
- Crustaceans and the aquatic larvae of insects. *R. septemvittata* has one of the most specialized diets of any snake: it only eats newly moulted crayfish
- Live-bearers
- Closely related to the *Nerodia* species, to which they bear a resemblance

SPECIES:
Regina grahamii,
  Graham's Water Snake
Regina septemvittata,
  Queen Snake

GENUS: **RHABDOPHIS**

- 21
- Medium, usually less than 1 m (3 ft 3 in)
- Central and Southeast Asia, India, China, and Japan
- Ponds, swamps, flooded areas, and slow-moving rivers
- Fish and frogs
- Egg-layers
- Rear-fanged and dangerous; at least one species, *R. tigrinus*, has caused human fatalities

SPECIES:
Rhabdophis adleri
Rhabdophis akraios
Rhabdophis angeli
Rhabdophis auriculata
Rhabdophis barbouri
Rhabdophis callichroma
Rhabdophis callistus
Rhabdophis chrysargoides
Rhabdophis chrysargos
Rhabdophis conspicillatus
Rhabdophis guangdongensis
Rhabdophis himalayanus
Rhabdophis leonardi
Rhabdophis lineatus
Rhabdophis murudensis
Rhabdophis nigrocinctus
Rhabdophis nuchalis

Rhabdophis spilogaster
Rhabdophis subminiatus
Rhabdophis swinhonis
Rhabdophis tigrinus

GENUS: **SINONATRIX**

- 4
- Fairly large, to about 1 m (3 ft 3 in)
- China and Vietnam
- Swamps, marshes, and pools
- Fish and amphibians
- Live-bearers, where known

SPECIES:
Sinonatrix aequifasciata
Sinonatrix annularis
Sinonatrix percarinata
Sinonatrix yunnanensis

GENUS: **STORERIA**

- 4
- Small
- North and Central America, from Canada to Honduras
- Damp places, including gardens, parks, fields, and hillsides
- Invertebrates such as slugs, snails, and insects
- Live-bearers

SPECIES:
Storeria dekayi,
  Brown Snake
Storeria hidalgoensis
Storeria occipitomaculata,
  Red-bellied Snake
Storeria storerioides

GENUS: **THAMNOPHIS**

Garter Snakes and Ribbon Snakes

- 34
- Small to fairly large, to over 1 m (3 ft 3 in) in some cases, with slender bodies
- North and Central America
- Usually damp places, often near water
- Earthworms, fish, amphibians and their tadpoles, and, sometimes, small mammals
- Live-bearers, with litters of up to 100 young in some species
- Active by day

SPECIES:
Thamnophis angustirostris
Thamnophis atratus
Thamnophis bogerti
Thamnophis brachystoma,
  Short-headed Garter Snake
Thamnophis butleri,
  Butler's Garter Snake
Thamnophis chrysocephalus
Thamnophis conanti
Thamnophis couchii,
  Western Aquatic Garter Snake
Thamnophis cyrtopsis,
  Black-necked Garter Snake
Thamnophis elegans,
  Terrestrial Garter Snake
Thamnophis eques,
  Mexican Garter Snake

Thamnophis exsul
Thamnophis fulvus
Thamnophis gigas
Thamnophis godmani
Thamnophis hammondii,
  Two-striped Garter Snake
Thamnophis lineri
Thamnophis marcianus,
  Chequered Garter Snake
  (pp.112–13)
Thamnophis melanogaster
Thamnophis mendax
Thamnophis nigronuchalis
Thamnophis ordinoides,
  Northwestern Garter Snake
Thamnophis postremus
Thamnophis proximus,
  Western Ribbon Snake
Thamnophis pulchrilatus
Thamnophis radix,
  Plains Garter Snake
Thamnophis rossmani
Thamnophis rufipunctatus,
  Narrow-headed Garter Snake
Thamnophis sauritus,
  Eastern Ribbon Snake
Thamnophis scalaris
Thamnophis scaliger
Thamnophis sirtalis,
  Eastern Garter Snake (pp.114–15)
Thamnophis sumichrasti
Thamnophis valida,
  Baja Garter Snake

GENUS: **TRACHISCHIUM**

- 5
- Small
- Northern India and Myanmar
- Forests. Thought to be terrestrial
- Unknown
- Unknown
- Thought to be nocturnal

SPECIES:
Trachischium fuscum
Trachischium guentheri
Trachischium laeve
Trachischium monticola
Trachischium tenuiceps

GENUS: **TROPIDOCLONION**

- 1
- Small
- North America
- Varied, in grassland, gardens, parks, and fields
- Earthworms
- Live-bearer

SPECIES:
Tropidoclonion lineatum,
  Lined Snake

GENUS: **TROPIDONOPHIS**

Australasian Keelbacks

- 19
- Medium, to about 1.2 m (4 ft)
- New Guinea and Borneo. One species (*T. mairii*) also occurs in northern Australia
- Semi-aquatic, such as swamps, marshes, pools, and ditches

- Mainly fish and frogs, but occasionally small lizards
- Egg-layers
- A complex genus. Certain species are sometimes known under the older name of *Macropophis*, which is here reserved for four species from the Philippine Islands

SPECIES:
Tropidonophis aenigmaticus
Tropidonophis dahlii
Tropidonophis dendrophiops
Tropidonophis dolasii
Tropidonophis doriae
Tropidonophis elongatus
Tropidonophis halmahericus
Tropidonophis hypomelas
Tropidonophis mairii,
  Keelback or Freshwater Snake
Tropidonophis mcdowelli
Tropidonophis montanus
Tropidonophis multiscutellatus
Tropidonophis negrosensis
Tropidonophis novaeguineae
Tropidonophis parkeri
Tropidonophis picturatus
Tropidonophis punctiventris
Tropidonophis statisticus
Tropidonophis truncatus

GENUS: **VIRGINIA**

Earth Snakes

- 1
- Small, to about 30 cm (12 in) or less
- Southeastern North America
- Under rocks and debris, usually in damp places
- Earthworms
- Live-bearer
- Secretive

SPECIES:
Virginia valeriae,
  Smooth Earth Snake

GENUS: **XENOCHROPHIS**

Asian Keelbacks

- 13
- Medium, to over 1 m (3 ft 3 in) in some species
- From Afghanistan, through to Southeast Asia and the Indonesian archipelago. One species, *X. piscator*, is found throughout the genus' range; the others have more limited distributions
- Damp places, usually near open water
- Fish and amphibians
- Egg-layers
- Rear-fanged; capable of giving a painful, but not serious, bite

SPECIES:
Xenochrophis asperrimus
Xenochrophis bellula
Xenochrophis cerasogaster
Xenochrophis flavipunctatus
Xenochrophis maculatus,
  Spotted Keelback
Xenochrophis melanzostus
Xenochrophis piscator,
  Asian Keelback

Xenochrophis punctulatus
Xenochrophis sanctijohannis
Xenochrophis schnurrenbergeri
Xenochrophis trianguligerus,
   Red-sided Keelback
Xenochrophis tytleri
Xenochrophis vittatus,
   Striped Keelback

PSEUDOXENODONTIDAE
2 GENERA CONTAINING 11 SPECIES

This is a small family of snakes from Southern China and Southeast Asia, previously included in the Colubridae. They are small, terrestrial species, living in a variety of habitats. They are thought to feed on soft-bodied invertebrates and frogs, but much remains to be discovered.

GENUS: **PLAGIOPHOLIS**

- ⬛ 5
- ↔ Small
- 🌐 China, Myanmar, and Thailand
- 🏠 Terrestrial; otherwise unknown
- ◀ Unknown
- ♂ Unknown

SPECIES:

Plagiopholis blakewayi
Plagiopholis delacouri
Plagiopholis nuchalis
Plagiopholis styani
Plagiopholis unipostocularis

GENUS: **PSEUDOXENODON**

- ⬛ 6
- ↔ Small to medium
- 🌐 China and Southeast Asia
- 🏠 Terrestrial
- ◀ Lizards and frogs
- ♂ Thought to be egg-layers

SPECIES:

Pseudoxenodon bambusicola
Pseudoxenodon baramensis
Pseudoxenodon inornatus
Pseudoxenodon karlschmidti
Pseudoxenodon macrops
Pseudoxenodon stejnegeri

ELAPIDAE
Cobras, Kraits, Mambas, Coral Snakes, and Sea Snakes

2 SUBFAMILIES CONTAINING 55 GENERA AND 358 SPECIES

Superficially, the members of the cobra family resemble many of the colubrids, to which they are undoubtedly closely related. They differ mostly in their dentition: cobras and their relatives have a pair of hollow, fixed, front fangs through which they deliver their venom.

Apart from the typical hooded cobras, which are familiar if only through films and cartoons of snake-charmers, this family contains a number of brightly coloured snakes, often known as coral snakes in America, Africa, and Australia, where they occur, as well as several nondescript, dark-coloured members, mostly from Australia. Their taxonomic relationships with the marine cobras (sea snakes) is still the subject of much speculation.

The mambas, kraits, taipans, brown snakes, Australian copperheads, and tiger snakes are further examples of highly venomous species within the family. The sea snakes and sea kraits (which are sometimes placed in separate families) are also dangerously venomous, although they rarely find themselves in conflict with humans. A number of genera of small, generally inoffensive and secretive snakes make up the rest of the family.

Cobras are found over much of the world but are more common in the southern hemisphere. Australia has a particularly rich selection of species, making up for its lack of vipers and near lack of colubrids.

Here, the land cobras are dealt with first, followed by the marine species.

SUBFAMILY: **ELAPINAE**
47 GENERA CONTAINING 293 SPECIES

The Elapinae includes all the terrestrial elapids (cobras, kraits, coral snakes, death adders, taipans, and others) plus the sea kraits, genus *Laticauda*, but these latter eight species are sometimes placed in a separate subfamily, the Laticaudinae.

GENUS: **ACANTHOPHIS**

Death Adders

- ⬛ 8
- ↔ Medium, but very heavy-bodied
- 🌐 Australasia (Australia and New Guinea)
- 🏠 Various
- ◀ Lizards, birds, and small mammals
- ♂ Live-bearers
- ☑ Very dangerous species that are the ecological counterparts of vipers, which are not found in the same region

SPECIES:

Acanthophis antarcticus,
   Common Death Adder
Acanthophis ceramensis
Acanthophis hawkei
Acanthophis laevis
• *Acanthophis praelongus*,
   Northern Death Adder (pp.118–19)
Acanthophis pyrrhus,
   Desert Death Adder
Acanthophis rugosus
Acanthophis wellsi

GENUS: **ANTAIOSERPENS**

- ⬛ 1
- ↔ Small
- 🌐 Australia (Queensland)
- 🏠 Tropical forests, where it lives under leaf-litter and debris
- ◀ Lizards (small skinks)
- ♂ Egg-layer
- ☑ Venomous, but probably too small to be of danger to humans

SPECIES:

Antaioserpens warro

GENUS: **ASPIDELAPS**

- ⬛ 2
- ↔ Small, to about 80 cm (2 ft 6 in)
- 🌐 Southern Africa
- 🏠 Dry places, usually those with sandy soil
- ◀ Amphibians, lizards, snakes, and small mammals
- ♂ Egg-layers
- ☑ Deaths from bites are very rare

SPECIES:

Aspidelaps lubricus,
   (African) Coral Snake
Aspidelaps scutatus,
   Shield-nosed Snake

GENUS: **ASPIDOMORPHUS**

New Guinea Crowned Snakes

- ⬛ 3
- ↔ Small, to about 40 cm (1 ft 3 in)
- 🌐 New Guinea and the Moluccas
- 🏠 Forests; in decaying wood and vegetation, and other debris
- ◀ Unknown
- ♂ Unknown, but thought to be egg-layers
- ☑ Rare, secretive snakes, whose natural history and the effects of their venom, are poorly known

SPECIES:

Aspidomorphus lineaticollis
Aspidomorphus muelleri
Aspidomorphus schlegelii

GENUS: **AUSTRELAPS**

Australian Copperheads

- ⬛ 3
- ↔ Large, to about 1.7 m (5 ft 6 in)
- 🌐 Southeastern Australia, including Tasmania
- 🏠 Damp places
- ◀ Amphibians and reptiles
- ♂ Live-bearers
- ☑ Very dangerous, though not usually aggressive. Sometimes the three species are regarded as forms of a single species

SPECIES:

Austrelaps labialis,
   Kangaroo Island Copperhead
Austrelaps ramsayi,
   Northern Copperhead
Austrelaps superbus,
   Southern Copperhead

GENUS: **BRACHYUROPHIS**

- ⬛ 7
- ↔ Small
- 🌐 Australia
- 🏠 Dry places; burrowers
- ◀ Reptile eggs or small skinks, depending on species
- ♂ Egg-layers
- ☑ Previously included in the genus *Simoselaps*. Venomous, but probably too small to be of danger to humans

SPECIES:

Brachyurophis approximans
Brachyurophis australis
Brachyurophis fasciolatus
Brachyurophis incinctus
Brachyurophis morrisi
Brachyurophis roperi
Brachyurophis semifasciatus

GENUS: **BUNGARUS**

Kraits

- ⬛ 14
- ↔ Medium to large; slender, with cylindrical, compressed, or triangular bodies
- 🌐 Asia (India and Sri Lanka to southern China and Southeast Asia)
- 🏠 Varied, often around human dwellings; terrestrial
- ◀ Other snakes
- ♂ Egg-layers
- ☑ Highly venomous and potentially lethal to humans. Nocturnal

SPECIES:

Bungarus andamanensis,
   Andaman Krait
Bungarus bungaroides
Bungarus caeruleus,
   Indian Krait
Bungarus candidus
Bungarus ceylonicus,
   Sri Lankan Krait
Bungarus fasciatus
Bungarus flaviceps
Bungarus lividus
Bungarus magnimaculatus
Bungarus multicinctus
Bungarus niger,
   Black Krait
Bungarus persicus
Bungarus sindanus
Bungarus slowinskii

GENUS: **CACOPHIS**

Crowned Snakes

- ⬛ 4
- ↔ Small, to about 75 cm (2 ft 5 in)
- 🌐 Eastern Australia
- 🏠 Various, under leaves or debris
- ◀ Unknown
- ♂ Egg-layers
- ☑ Secretive and poorly known. The venom is thought to be too mild to be dangerous to humans

SPECIES:

Cacophis churchilli
Cacophis harriettae,
   White-crowned Snake
Cacophis krefftii,
   Dwarf-crowned Snake
Cacophis squamulosus,
   Golden-crowned Snake

GENUS: **CALLIOPHIS**

- 🐍 10
- ↔ Small and slender
- 🌐 Southern and Southeast Asia
- 🏠 Forests
- 🍴 Other reptiles, especially burrowing species
- ⚥ Thought to be egg-layers
- ☑ Secretive; their relationships are poorly understood. The venom is not thought to be dangerous to humans

SPECIES:
Calliophis beddomei
Calliophis bibroni
Calliophis bivirgata
Calliophis castoe
Calliophis gracilis
Calliophis haematoetron
Calliophis intestinalis
Calliophis maculiceps
Calliophis melanurus
Calliophis nigrescens

GENUS: **CRYPTOPHIS**

- 🐍 5
- ↔ Small
- 🌐 Australia and New Guinea
- 🏠 Woodlands and rock outcrops
- 🍴 Frogs, skinks, and other snakes
- ⚥ Egg-layers
- ☑ Venomous but too small to be of danger to humans

SPECIES:
Cryptophis boschmai
Cryptophis incredibilis
Cryptophis nigrescens
Cryptophis nigrostriatus
Cryptophis pallidiceps

GENUS: **DEMANSIA**

Australian Whipsnakes

- 🐍 14
- ↔ Small to medium, and slender
- 🌐 Australia and southern New Guinea
- 🏠 Varied, from deserts to rainforests
- 🍴 Frogs, lizards, and reptile eggs
- ⚥ Egg-layers
- ☑ Considered too small to be of any great danger to humans. Diurnal and fast-moving

SPECIES:
Demansia angusticeps
Demansia calodera
Demansia flagellatio
Demansia olivacea
Demansia papuensis
Demansia psammophis,
    Yellow-faced Whipsnake
Demansia quaesitor
Demansia reticulata
Demansia rimicola
Demansia rufescens
Demansia shinei
Demansia simplex
Demansia torquata,
    Collared Whipsnake
Demansia vestigiata

GENUS: **DENDROASPIS**

Mambas

- 🐍 4
- ↔ Medium to large, sometimes reaching 4 m (13 ft), with slender bodies
- 🌐 Tropical and southern Africa
- 🏠 Forests and lightly-wooded grassland. Three species, which are green, are arboreal; the fourth (the Black Mamba) lives on the ground
- 🍴 Birds and small mammals
- ⚥ Egg-layers
- ☑ Extremely dangerous to humans, though not usually aggressive. Active during the day

SPECIES:
Dendroaspis angusticeps,
    Eastern Green Mamba
Dendroaspis jamesoni,
    Jameson's Mamba
Dendroaspis polylepis,
    Black Mamba
• Dendroaspis viridis,
    West African Green Mamba
    (pp.120–121)

GENUS: **DENISONIA**

- 🐍 2
- ↔ Small, to 60 cm (2 ft), and stocky
- 🌐 Eastern Australia
- 🏠 Lightly wooded places
- 🍴 Mainly frogs
- ⚥ D. maculata is a live-bearer, D. devisi is unknown
- ☑ Dangerous to humans, though probably not lethal. Secretive and nocturnal

SPECIES:
Denisonia devisi,
    De Vis' Banded Snake
Denisonia maculata,
    Ornamental Snake

GENUS: **DRYSDALIA**

- 🐍 3
- ↔ Small and slender
- 🌐 Southern Australia
- 🏠 Unknown
- 🍴 Lizards, including skinks
- ⚥ Live-bearers, where known
- ☑ Not considered dangerous to humans. Secretive and nocturnal

SPECIES:
Drysdalia coronoides,
    White-lipped Snake
Drysdalia mastersii,
    Masters' Snake
Drysdalia rhodogaster

GENUS: **ECHIOPSIS**

- 🐍 1
- ↔ Small
- 🌐 Southern Australia
- 🏠 Dry places
- 🍴 Frogs, lizards, birds, and small mammals
- ⚥ E. curta is a live-bearer, E. atriceps is unknown
- ☑ Not considered dangerous to humans. E. atriceps is rare and hardly known. Nocturnal

SPECIES:
Echiopsis curta,
    Bardick

GENUS: **ELAPOGNATHUS**

- 🐍 2
- ↔ Small, to 40 cm (1 ft 3 in)
- 🌐 Southwestern Australia
- 🏠 Edges of swamps
- 🍴 Unknown
- ⚥ Thought to be live-bearers
- ☑ Not considered dangerous to humans

SPECIES:
Elapognathus coronatus
Elapognathus minor,
    Little Brown Snake

GENUS: **ELAPSOIDEA**

African Garter Snakes

- 🐍 10
- ↔ Small to medium, but to over 1 m (3 ft 3 in) in one form
- 🌐 Africa, south of the Sahara
- 🏠 Varied, from arid places to woodland
- 🍴 Mainly other reptiles, but also amphibians and small mammals
- ⚥ Egg-layers
- ☑ Not considered dangerous to humans. Juveniles are often brightly coloured "coral" snakes. E. chelazziorum, from Somalia, is known from only two specimens, and E. broadleyi was only described in 1997

SPECIES:
Elapsoidea boulengeri
Elapsoidea broadleyi,
    Broadley's Garter Snake
Elapsoidea chelazziorum,
    Southern Somali Garter Snake
Elapsoidea guentherii,
    Gunther's Garter Snake
Elapsoidea laticincta,
    Central African Garter Snake
Elapsoidea loveridgei,
    East African Garter Snake
Elapsoidea nigra,
    Usumbara Garter Snake
Elapsoidea semiannulata,
    Half-banded Garter Snake
Elapsoidea sundevallii,
    Sundevall's Garter Snake
Elapsoidea trapei

GENUS: **FURINA**

- 🐍 5
- ↔ Small, exceptionally up to 1 m (3 ft 3 in) (F. tristis)
- 🌐 Australia and New Guinea (F. tristis)
- 🏠 Varied, from deserts to gardens
- 🍴 Thought to be small lizards
- ⚥ Egg-layers, where known
- ☑ Not considered dangerous to humans

SPECIES:
Furina barnardi,
    Yellow-naped Snake
Furina diadema,
    Red-naped Snake
Furina dunmalli,
    Dunmall's Snake
Furina ornata,
    Orange-naped Snake
Furina tristis,
    Brown-headed Snake

GENUS: **HEMACHATUS**

- 🐍 1
- ↔ Medium, to 1.5 m (5 ft)
- 🌐 Southern Africa
- 🏠 Grassland
- 🍴 Mainly toads
- ⚥ Live-bearer
- ☑ A very dangerous spitter, potentially causing blindness, but rarely lethal

SPECIES:
Hemachatus haemachatus
Rinkhals or Spitting Cobra

GENUS: **HEMIASPIS**

- 🐍 2
- ↔ Small, to 60 cm (2 ft)
- 🌐 Eastern Australia
- 🏠 Wet and dry forests
- 🍴 Frogs and lizards, especially skinks
- ⚥ Live-bearers
- ☑ Not considered dangerous to humans. Active at night and by day

SPECIES:
Hemiaspis damelii,
    Grey Snake
Hemiaspis signata,
    Black-bellied Swamp Snake

GENUS: **HEMIBUNGARUS**

- 🐍 1
- ↔ Small
- 🌐 Philippines
- 🏠 Forests, among leaf-litter
- 🍴 Thought to be lizards and snakes
- ⚥ Egg-layer
- ☑ A brightly coloured "coral snake"

SPECIES:
Hemibungarus calligaster

GENUS: **HOPLOCEPHALUS**

- 🐍 3
- ↔ Small to medium, the largest to 90 cm (3 ft)
- 🌐 Eastern Australia
- 🏠 Varied, often in forests. H. bungaroides is restricted to rocky outcrops, where it lives underneath flaking slabs
- 🍴 Frogs, lizards, birds, and mammals

- Live-bearers
- Aggressive, with painful, though fairly innocuous, bites

SPECIES:
Hoplocephalus bitorquatus,
Pale-headed Snake
Hoplocephalus bungaroides,
Broad-headed Snake
Hoplocephalus stephensii,
Stephen's Banded Snake

GENUS: **LATICAUDA**

Sea Kraits

- 8
- Medium to large, to about 1.5 m (5 ft)
- Southeast Asia and northern Australian coasts
- Rocky shores, mudflats, and reefs. *L. crockeri* is confined to the land-locked Lake Te-Nggano in the Solomon Islands
- Fish, especially eels
- Egg-layers, but there is some evidence that *L. crockeri* gives birth to live young
- Partially terrestrial, sea kraits come ashore to drink and to lay their eggs in sea caves. Sometimes considered to be part of a separate subfamily, or even family, from other sea snakes

SPECIES:
Laticauda colubrina
Laticauda crockeri
Laticauda frontalis
Laticauda guineai
Laticauda laticaudata
Laticauda saintgironsi
Laticauda schistorhynchus
Laticauda semifasciata

GENUS: **LOVERIDGELAPS**

- 1
- Medium, to about 80 cm (2 ft 6 in)
- Solomon Islands
- Forests, often near streams
- Frogs, lizards, and worm snakes
- Unknown
- Rare and poorly known. Boldly banded in black and white. Its bite is potentially dangerous to humans

SPECIES:
Loveridgelaps elapoides,
Solomons Small-eyed Snake or
Shark of the Jungle

GENUS: **MICROPECHIS**

- 1
- Large, to 2 m (6 ft 6 in), and stocky
- New Guinea and some of its satellite islands
- Rainforests, swamps, and plantations
- Frogs, lizards, snakes, and small mammals
- Unknown

- Highly dangerous, with several recorded fatalities

SPECIES:
Micropechis ikaheka,
Small-eyed Snake

GENUS: **MICRUROIDES**

- 1
- Small, to about 50 cm (1 ft 6 in), and slender
- North America (Arizona and northwestern Mexico)
- Arid deserts and scrub
- Lizards and snakes
- Egg-layer
- Brightly banded in red, black, and white; dangerous

SPECIES:
Micruroides euryxanthus,
Western Coral Snake

GENUS: **MICRURUS**

Coral Snakes

- 80
- Small to moderately large, with some species reaching 1.5 m (5 ft)
- North, Central, and South America
- Varied, from dry deserts to humid rainforests. Invariably terrestrial
- Other reptiles, especially burrowing forms, such as amphisbaenians (worm lizards)
- Egg-layers
- The slender bodies are brightly coloured with red, black, and white or yellow bands. Some tropical species also have blue bands. Despite having small mouths and short fangs, all coral snakes are potentially dangerous and there have been many human fatalities. Usually nocturnal. The list of species includes a number that are sometimes regarded as subspecies

SPECIES:
Micrurus albicinctus
Micrurus alleni,
Allen's Coral Snake
Micrurus altirostris
Micrurus ancoralis,
Regal Coral Snake
Micrurus annellatus
Micrurus averyi,
Black-headed Coral Snake
Micrurus baliocoryphus
Micrurus bernadi,
Blotched Coral Snake
Micrurus bocourti,
Ecuadorian Coral Snake
Micrurus bogerti,
Bogert's Coral Snake
Micrurus brasiliensis
Micrurus browni,
Brown's Coral Snake
Micrurus camilae
Micrurus catamayensis
Micrurus circinalis
Micrurus clarki,
Clark's Coral Snake
Micrurus collaris

Micrurus corallinus,
Painted Coral Snake
Micrurus decoratus,
Brazilian Coral Snake
Micrurus diana
Micrurus diastema,
Variable Coral Snake
Micrurus dissoleucus,
Pygmy Coral Snake
Micrurus distans,
West Mexican Coral Snake
Micrurus dumerilii,
Dumeril's Coral Snake
Micrurus elegans,
Elegant Coral Snake
Micrurus ephippifer,
Oaxacan Coral Snake
Micrurus filiformis,
Slender Coral Snake
Micrurus frontalis,
Southern Coral Snake
Micrurus fulvius,
Eastern Coral Snake
Micrurus hemprichii,
Hemprich's Coral Snake
Micrurus hippocrepis,
Mayan Coral Snake
Micrurus ibiboboca,
Caatinga Coral Snake
Micrurus isozonus,
Venezuelan Coral Snake
Micrurus langsdorffi,
Langsdorff's Coral Snake
Micrurus laticollaris
Micrurus latifasciatus,
Broad-ringed Coral Snake
Micrurus lemniscatus,
South American Coral Snake
Micrurus limbatus,
Tuxtlan Coral Snake
Micrurus margaritiferus,
Speckled Coral Snake
Micrurus medemi
Micrurus meridensis
Micrurus mertensi,
Merten's Coral Snake
Micrurus mipartitus,
Red-tailed Coral Snake
Micrurus mosquitensis
Micrurus multifasciatus,
Many-banded Coral Snake
Micrurus multiscutatus,
Cauca Coral Snake
Micrurus narduccii
Micrurus nattereri
Micrurus nebularis
Micrurus nigrocinctus,
Central American Coral Snake
Micrurus obscurus
Micrurus oligoanellatus
Micrurus ornatissimus
Micrurus pacaraimae
Micrurus pachecogili
Micrurus paraensis
Micrurus peruvianus,
Peruvian Coral Snake
Micrurus petersi,
Peters' Coral Snake
Micrurus potyguara
Micrurus proximans
Micrurus psyches,
Carib Coral Snake
Micrurus putumayensis
Micrurus pyrrhocryptus
Micrurus remotus
Micrurus renjifoi
Micrurus ruatanus,
Roatán Coral Snake
Micrurus sangilensis,
Santander Coral Snake
Micrurus scutiventris
Micrurus serranus
Micrurus silviae
Micrurus spixii,
Amazonian Coral Snake

Micrurus spurrelli,
Colombian Coral Snake
Micrurus steindachneri,
Steindachner's Coral Snake
Micrurus stewarti,
Panamanian Coral Snake
Micrurus stuarti,
Stuart's Coral Snake
Micrurus surinamensis,
Aquatic Coral Snake
Micrurus tamaulipensis
Micrurus tener
Micrurus tikuna
Micrurus tschudii,
Desert Coral Snake

GENUS: **NAJA**

Cobras

- 29
- Medium to large, reaching over 2 m (6 ft 6 in) in some cases, and fairly stout
- Africa, and southern and Southeast Asia
- Varied, from deserts to forests, and including fields, plantations, and human dwellings
- Highly adaptable, eating fish, amphibians, lizards, snakes, birds, and mammals
- Egg-layers
- All cobras are dangerous and capable of giving a lethal bite. Several species in Africa and in Asia also spit venom. Hoods are spread only when the snakes are alarmed. Active by day and night depending on species. The Asian species were formerly regarded as different forms of one widespread species

SPECIES:
Naja anchietae,
Anchieta's Cobra
Naja annulata,
Ringed Water Cobra
Naja annulifera
Naja arabica
Naja ashei,
Ash's Spitting cobra
- *Naja atra*,
Chinese Cobra (p.122)
Naja christyi
Naja crawshayi
Naja haje,
Egyptian Cobra
- *Naja kaouthia*,
Monocled Cobra (p.123)
Naja katiensis,
West African Brown Spitting Cobra
Naja mandalayensis
Naja melanoleuca,
Forest Cobra
Naja mossambica,
Mozambique Spitting Cobra
Naja multifasciata
Naja naja,
Asiatic Cobra
Naja nigricincta
Naja nigricollis,
Black-necked Spitting Cobra
Naja nivea,
Cape Cobra
Naja nubiae
Naja oxiana

- *Naja pallida*,
    Red Spitting Cobra (pp.124–25)
  Naja philippinensis
  Naja sagittifera
  Naja samarensis
  Naja senegalensis
  Naja siamensis
  Naja sputatrix
  Naja sumatrana

GENUS: **NOTECHIS**

Tiger Snakes

- 🐍 1
- ↔ Moderately large, to 1.5 m (5 ft),
  and stocky
- 🌏 Southern Australia, including Tasmania
- 🏠 Varied, from marshes to dry,
  rocky places
- 🦎 Mainly frogs and small mammals,
  but the population of *N. s. ater*
  living on small islands depends
  almost entirely on the seasonally
  abundant mutton bird chicks
- ♀ Live-bearer
- 📋 Highly venomous, responsible for
  a large proportion of human deaths
  from snakebite in Australia

SPECIES:
Notechis scutatus,
    Eastern Snake or Mainland Tiger Snake

GENUS: **OGMODON**

- 🐍 1
- ↔ Small
- 🌏 Vitu Levi, one of the Fijian Islands
- 🏠 Mountain valleys, where it is burrowing
  and secretive
- 🦎 Thought to be earthworms and
  other soft-bodied invertebrates
- ♀ Unknown
- 📋 A rare species whose natural history
  is poorly known. Not likely to be
  dangerous to humans

SPECIES:
Ogmodon vitianus

GENUS: **OPHIOPHAGUS**

- 🐍 1
- ↔ Very large, to over 5 m (16 ft),
  and therefore the world's longest
  venomous snake
- 🌏 India, Southeast Asia,
  and the Philippines
- 🏠 Humid woods and forests; occasionally
  in fields and near human dwellings
- 🦎 Other snakes
- ♀ Egg-layer; the female stays near
  the eggs throughout their incubation
- 📋 Highly venomous, but not
  normally aggressive

SPECIES:
Ophiophagus hannah,
    King Cobra

GENUS: **OXYURANUS**

Taipans

- 🐍 3
- ↔ Large, to 2.5 m (8 ft 2 in)
  and therefore the largest venomous
  snake in Australia
- 🌏 Australia and New Guinea
- 🏠 Varied, mainly in lightly wooded places
  and grasslands, including gardens
- 🦎 Small mammals, especially rats
- ♀ Egg-layers
- 📋 Rare. Extremely dangerous,
  with powerful venom and
  an erratic temperament

SPECIES:
Oxyuranus microlepidotus,
    Fierce Snake or Inland Taipan
Oxyuranus scutellatus,
    Taipan
Oxyuranus temporalis,
    Western Desert Taipan

GENUS: **PARAPISTOCALAMUS**

- 🐍 1
- ↔ Small, to about 50 cm (1 ft 6 in),
  and slender
- 🌏 Bougainville Island, New Guinea
- 🏠 Forests
- 🦎 Unknown
- ♀ Unknown
- 📋 Rare and poorly known. Not
  likely to be dangerous to humans,
  on account of its small size

SPECIES:
Parapistocalamus hedigeri,
    Bougainville Coral Snake

GENUS: **PARASUTA**

Hooded Snakes

- 🐍 6
- ↔ Small
- 🌏 Australia
- 🏠 Dry places, where they live in soil
  cracks, burrows, and under debris
- 🦎 Lizards
- ♀ Live-bearers
- 📋 Venomous, but not considered
  life-threatening to humans

SPECIES:
Parasuta dwyeri
Parasuta flagellum
Parasuta gouldii
Parasuta monachus
Parasuta nigriceps
Parasuta spectabilis

GENUS: **PAROPLOCEPHALUS**

- 🐍 1
- ↔ Small
- 🌏 Western Australia
- 🏠 Arid places
- 🦎 Unknown, probably lizards
- ♀ Thought to be a live-bearer

- 📋 Potentially dangerous

SPECIES:
Paroplocephalus atriceps

GENUS: **PSEUDECHIS**

Brown Snakes

- 🐍 9
- ↔ Large, to 2 m (6 ft 6 in)
- 🌏 Australia and New Guinea
- 🏠 Varied, from tropical forests to deserts
- 🦎 Frogs, lizards, snakes,
  and small mammals
- ♀ Egg-layers
- 📋 Dangerously venomous

SPECIES:
Pseudechis australis,
    Mulga Snake or King Brown Snake
Pseudechis butleri
- *Pseudechis colletti*,
    Collett's Snake (pp.126–27)
Pseudechis guttatus,
    Spotted Black Snake
Pseudechis pailsei
Pseudechis papuanus,
    Papuan Black Snake
Pseudechis porphyriacus,
    Red-bellied Black Snake
Pseudechis rossignolii
Pseudechis weigeli

GENUS: **PSEUDOHAJE**

Tree Cobras

- 🐍 2
- ↔ Large, to 2.5 m (8 ft 2 in)
- 🌏 Central and West Africa
- 🏠 Forests, where they are highly arboreal
- 🦎 Amphibians and possibly
  small mammals
- ♀ Egg-layers
- 📋 Both species are poorly known
  and no bites have been recorded.
  Potentially dangerous to humans

SPECIES:
Pseudohaje goldii,
    Gold's Tree Cobra
Pseudohaje nigra,
    Black Tree Cobra

GENUS: **PSEUDONAJA**

- 🐍 9
- ↔ Moderately large, up to
  1.5 m (5 ft)
- 🌏 Australia and New Guinea
- 🏠 Mainly open places, including dunes
  and grasslands, but sometimes in
  lightly wooded places
- 🦎 Frogs, small lizards, and mammals
- ♀ Egg-layers
- 📋 Very dangerous to humans,
  with highly potent venom

SPECIES:
Pseudonaja affinis,
    Dugite
Pseudonaja aspidorhyncha
Pseudonaja guttata

Pseudonaja inframacula,
    Peninsula Brown Snake
Pseudonaja ingrami,
    Ingram's Brown Snake
Pseudonaja mengdeni
Pseudonaja modesta,
    Ringed Brown Snake
Pseudonaja nuchalis,
    Western Brown Snake
Pseudonaja textilis,
    Eastern Brown Snake

GENUS: **RHINOPLOCEPHALUS**

- 🐍 1
- ↔ Small, to about 50 cm (1 ft 6 in)
- 🌏 Australia and New Guinea
- 🏠 Forests, woodlands, grassy places,
  and among rocks
- 🦎 Thought to be small lizards
- ♀ Live-bearer, where known
- 📋 Secretive and nocturnal, rarely
  encountered. Unlikely to be
  dangerous to humans

SPECIES:
Rhinoplocephalus bicolor

GENUS: **SALOMONELAPS**

- 🐍 1
- ↔ Medium, to just over 1 m (3 ft 3 in)
- 🌏 Solomon Islands and Bougainville
  Island, New Guinea
- 🏠 Forests
- 🦎 Mainly lizards, especially skinks,
  but also frogs and snakes
- ♀ Egg-layer
- 📋 Poorly known. Bites may be dangerous
  to humans

SPECIES:
Salomonelaps par,
    Solomons Coral Snake

GENUS: **SIMOSELAPS**

Australian Coral Snakes

- 🐍 5
- ↔ Small, up to about
  60 cm (2 ft) long
- 🌏 Australia
- 🏠 Mostly dry, sandy places, where
  they live beneath the surface
- 🦎 Lizards, especially burrowing skinks
- ♀ Egg-layers
- 📋 Most species are boldly banded.
  Not considered dangerous to humans

SPECIES:
Simoselaps anomalus
Simoselaps bertholdi,
    Desert Banded Snake
Simoselaps bimaculatus,
    Western Black-naped Snake
Simoselaps littoralis
Simoselaps minimus

GENUS: SINOMICRURUS

- 5
- Small to medium
- South China, Taiwan, Japan, and Southeast Asia
- Varied; terrestrial in forests, fields, etc
- Probably lizards and snakes
- Egg-layers
- Venomous and potentially dangerous to humans, though not aggressive

SPECIES:

Sinomicrurus hatori
Sinomicrurus japonicus
Sinomicrurus kelloggi
Sinomicrurus macclellandi
Sinomicrurus sauteri

GENUS: SUTA

- 4
- Small, mostly to 40 cm (1 ft 3 in), but *S. ordensis* grows to 75 cm (2 ft 5 in)
- Australia and southern New Guinea
- Dry places, including heaths and woodlands
- Lizards, especially skinks, and frogs
- Live-bearers, where known
- Not likely to be dangerous to humans because of their small size, but the bites of certain species are painful

SPECIES:

Suta fasciata,
Rosen's Snake
Suta ordensis
Suta punctata,
Little Spotted Snake
Suta suta,
Curl Snake

GENUS: TOXICOCALAMUS

New Guinea Forest Snakes

- 12
- Small to medium, from about 50 cm (1 ft 6 in) to nearly 1 m (3 ft 3 in)
- New Guinea
- Lowland and montane rainforest, grasslands, and gardens. Secretive and burrowing species, living beneath leaf-litter and other forest debris
- Earthworms and other soft-bodied invertebrates and their larvae; perhaps also frogs
- Egg-layers, where known
- Very poorly known, but thought to be innocuous to humans

SPECIES:

Toxicocalamus buergersi
Toxicocalamus ernstmayri
Toxicocalamus grandis
Toxicocalamus holopelturus
Toxicocalamus longissimus
Toxicocalamus loriae
Toxicocalamus mintoni
Toxicocalamus misimae
Toxicocalamus pachysomus
Toxicocalamus preussi
Toxicocalamus spilolepidotus
Toxicocalamus stanleyanus

GENUS: TROPIDECHIS

- 1
- Medium, occasionally to about 1 m (3 ft 3 in)
- Eastern Australia
- Forests
- Frogs, reptiles, birds, and small mammals
- Live-bearer
- Aggressive and dangerous to humans

SPECIES:

Tropidechis carinatus,
Rough-scaled Snake

GENUS: VERMICELLA

Bandy-bandies

- 6
- Small, to 60 cm (2 ft), and slender
- Australia
- Varied; burrowers
- Blind snakes
- Egg-layers
- Boldly banded black and white. Too small to be considered dangerous to humans. *V. intermedia* and *V. vermiformis* are not always considered distinct species

SPECIES:

Vermicella annulata,
Bandy-bandy
Vermicella calonotus
Vermicella intermedia
Vermicella multifasciata,
Northern Bandy-bandy
Vermicella snelli
Vermicella vermiformis

GENUS: WALTERINNESIA

- 2
- Medium, to just over 1 m (3 ft 3 in), and thickset
- North Africa (Sinai) and the Middle East
- Deserts
- Lizards, especially dabb lizards (*Uromastyx*), and possibly small mammals
- Egg-layers
- Dangerous; although they rarely bite, fatalities are known

SPECIES:

Walterinnesia aegyptia,
Desert Black Snake
Walterinnesia morgani

SUBFAMILY: HYDROPHIINAE
8 GENERA CONTAINING 62 SPECIES

All the marine elapids, apart from the sea kraits, *Laticauda* species, are placed in this subfamily.

Some authorities consider that the marine species of the Elapidae should be placed in a separate family, the Hydropheidae. Others consider that this family should also include the Australian terrestrial elapids and that it should be sub-divided to separate the sea snakes from the terrestrial species. Here they are treated as part of the cobra family, while accepting that there are several important differences between the terrestrial elapids and the marine ones, and that there are also differences between the sea kraits, *Laticauda*, and the other sea snakes.

Although sea snakes are extremely venomous, they are generally inoffensive and there are relatively few cases of human deaths through their bites. Most of them feed on fish, including eels, but some are specialists, feeding only on fish eggs.

All species live completely aquatic lives and give birth to live young.

Marine species of the Elapidae are found in the Indian and Pacific Oceans and are most abundant around the coasts of northern Australia. Most species are associated with coral reefs, but the Pelagic Sea Snake, *Pelamis platurus*, is an ocean-going wanderer, with large shoals drifting right across the Pacific as far as the shores of Central America. There have been fears that this species would eventually find its way through the Panama Canal to populate the so-far sea-snake-free Caribbean region.

GENUS: AIPYSURUS

- 8
- Medium to large; mostly under 1 m (3 ft 3 in), but *A. laevis* can grow to 2 m (6 ft 6 in)
- Coasts of northern Australia, New Guinea, and New Caledonia
- Mostly found near reefs, although some frequent deeper water
- Thought to be fish
- Live-bearers, producing small litters of young
- Some species are rarely seen and poorly known

SPECIES:

Aipysurus apraefrontalis
Aipysurus duboisii
Aipysurus eydouxii
Aipysurus foliosquama
Aipysurus fuscus
Aipysurus laevis,
Olive Sea Snake
Aipysurus mosaicus
Aipysurus tenuis

GENUS: EMYDOCEPHALUS

Turtle-headed Sea Snakes

- 3
- Small, to less than 1 m (3 ft 3 in)
- South China Sea and northern Australia
- Reefs, often in shallow water
- Fish eggs
- Live-bearers
- They have no teeth or associated venom apparatus

SPECIES:

Emydocephalus annulatus
Emydocephalus ijimae
Emydocephalus szczerbaki

GENUS: EPHALOPHIS

- 1
- Small, to 50 cm (1 ft 6 in)
- Coasts of Western Australia, around Broome
- Mangroves and estuarine mudflats
- Unknown, probably fish
- Live-bearer

SPECIES:

Ephalophis greyae

GENUS: HYDRELAPS

- 1
- Small, to 50 cm (1 ft 6 in)
- Coasts of northern Australia and southern Papua New Guinea
- Mudflats, especially near mangroves
- Probably fish
- Live-bearer

SPECIES:

Hydrelaps darwiniensis

GENUS: HYDROPHIS

- 46
- Small to large; from about 50 cm (1 ft 6 in) to more than 1.5 m (5 ft)
- Widespread, from the Persian Gulf to the northern coasts of Australia and north to the Philippines
- Mainly shallow coastal waters, although some have occasionally been trawled from deeper waters. *H. semperi* is unique among sea snakes because it lives only in the freshwater Lake Taal on Luzon Island, Philippines
- Fish, especially eels
- Live-bearers
- This large genus is likely to be divided into several smaller ones in the near future

SPECIES:

Hydrophis atriceps
Hydrophis belcheri
Hydrophis bituberculatus
Hydrophis brookii
Hydrophis caerulescens
Hydrophis cantoris
Hydrophis coggeri
Hydrophis curtus
Hydrophis cyanocinctus
Hydrophis czeblukovi
Hydrophis donaldi
Hydrophis elegans
Hydrophis fasciatus
Hydrophis gracilis
Hydrophis hardwickii
Hydrophis hendersoni
Hydrophis inornatus
Hydrophis jerdonii
Hydrophis kingii
Hydrophis klossi
Hydrophis laboutei

Hydrophis lamberti
Hydrophis lapemoides
Hydrophis macdowelli
Hydrophis major
Hydrophis mamillaris
Hydrophis melanocephalus
Hydrophis melanosoma
Hydrophis nigrocinctus
Hydrophis obscurus
Hydrophis ornatus
Hydrophis pachycercos
Hydrophis pacificus
Hydrophis parviceps
Hydrophis peronii
Hydrophis platurus
Hydrophis schistosus
Hydrophis semperi
Hydrophis sibauensis
Hydrophis spiralis
Hydrophis stokesii
Hydrophis stricticollis
Hydrophis torquatus
Hydrophis viperinus
Hydrophis vorisi
Hydrophis zweifeli

GENUS: **KOLPOPHIS**

- 1
- Unknown
- South China Sea, from Thailand to Indonesia
- Coastal waters
- Probably fish
- Thought to be a live-bearer
- Only recently discovered and still poorly known

SPECIES:
Kolpophis annandalei

GENUS: **PARAHYDROPHIS**

- 1
- Small, to about 50 cm (1 ft 6 in)
- Coasts of northern Australia
- Coastal and estuarine mangroves and mudflats
- Small fish
- Live-bearer

SPECIES:
Parahydrophis mertoni

GENUS: **THALASSOPHIS**

- 1
- Medium
- Coasts of Thailand and Indonesia
- Coastal waters
- Fish
- Live-bearer

SPECIES:
Thalassophis anomalus

HOMALOPSIDAE
28 GENERA CONTAINING 53 SPECIES

Previously included in the Colubridae, the homalopsid snakes are small to medium-sized aquatic species with valvular, crescent-shaped nostrils and small eyes positioned on top of their heads. They are back-fanged and do not appear to pose any threat to humans. They eat frogs, tadpoles, and fish, but *Fordonia leucobalia* eats crabs. All the species give birth to live young. Until recently, a large proportion were included in the genus *Enhydris*, but many have now been removed and placed in several new genera containing only one or two species each.

GENUS: **BITIA**

- 1
- Small
- Myanmar, Thailand, and the Malay peninsula
- Estuaries and river mouths
- Fish
- Live-bearer
- The narrow head and compressed tail help the snake to swim

SPECIES:
Bitia hydroides

GENUS: **BRACHYORRHOS**

- 4
- Small
- The Indonesian archipelago
- Unknown
- Unknown
- Unknown

SPECIES:
Brachyorrhus albus
Brachyorrhos gastrotaenius
Brachyorrhos raffrayi
Brachyorrhos wallacei

GENUS: **CALAMOPHIS**

- 4
- Small to medium, 22–75 cm (9–30 in)
- West Papua New Guinea
- Semi-aquatic
- Fish, frogs, and tadpoles
- Live-bearers
- *Calamophis jobiensis*, from New Guinea, apparently lives in soil and feeds on earthworms

SPECIES:
Calamophis jobiensis
Calamophis katesandersae
Calamophis ruuddelangi
Calamophis sharonbrooksae

GENUS: **CANTORIA**

- 1
- Small
- The coasts of India, the Malay peninsula, Indonesia, and the Andaman Islands
- Coastal waters and estuaries. Semi-aquatic
- Mainly fish
- Live-bearer

SPECIES:
Cantoria violacea

GENUS: **CERBERUS**

- 5
- Medium
- Southeast Asia, the Indonesian archipelago, New Guinea, and tropical Australia
- Estuaries, mangrove swamps, and mudflats, where they are totally aquatic
- Fish and marine crustaceans
- Live-bearers
- Rear-fanged, but not considered dangerous to humans

SPECIES:
Cerberus australis
Cerberus dunsoni
Cerberus microlepis
Cerberus rynchops,
  Bockadam
Cerberus schneiderii

GENUS: **DIEUROSTUS**

- 1
- Small to medium, 60–92 cm (2–3 ft)
- Southwestern India (Kerala)
- Aquatic, in lakes, swamps, paddy-fields, and floodplains
- Fish
- Live-bearer
- The single species was previously known as *Enhydris dussumieri*

SPECIES:
Dieurostus dussumieri,
  Kerala Mud Snake

GENUS: **DJOKOISKANDARUS**

- 1
- Small, 30–60 cm (1–2 ft)
- New Guinea
- Aquatic, estuarine and marine waters
- Crabs
- Live-bearer
- The single species was previously known as *Cantoria annulata*

SPECIES:
Djokoiskandarus annulata

GENUS: **ENHYDRIS**

- 6
- Small
- India, China, Southeast Asia, New Guinea, and northern Australia
- Totally aquatic, found in ponds, marshes, and hill streams
- Fish, and frogs and their larvae (tadpoles)
- Live-bearers; the young are born in the water
- The cylindrical bodies have smooth glossy scales, and the eyes point upwards. Many more species were previously included in this genus, but they have now been moved to new genera

SPECIES:
Enhydris chanardi
Enhydris enhydris
Enhydris innominata
Enhydris jagorii
Enhydris longicauda
Enhydris subtaeniata

GENUS: **ERPETON**

- 1
- Medium
- Southeast Asia
- Totally aquatic
- Fish. It rests among dense aquatic vegetation waiting to ambush its prey
- Live-bearer. The young are born underwater
- The body is almost rectangular in cross-section, the head is flattened, and there are two strange, fleshy appendages projecting from the snout. The ventral scales are reduced to a thin, raised ridge

SPECIES:
Erpeton tentaculatum,
  Tentacled Snake, Fishing Snake

GENUS: **FERANIA**

- 1
- Small to medium, 50–78 cm (1 ft 6 in–2 ft 5 in)
- India, Bangladesh, and Nepal
- Aquatic, in muddy estuaries and rivers
- Fish
- Live-bearer
- The single species was previously known as *Enhydris sieboldii*

SPECIES:
Ferania sieboldii

GENUS: **FORDONIA**

- 1
- Small
- Around the coasts of Southeast Asia, the Philippines, New Guinea, and northern Australia
- Coastal mudflats and mangrove forests
- Crabs, which it constricts, then eats piece by piece
- Live-bearer
- A highly specialized species

SPECIES:
Fordonia leucobalia,
  White-bellied Mangrove Snake

GENUS: **GERARDA**

- 1
- Small
- Around the coasts and estuaries of Sri Lanka, India, Myanmar, and Thailand
- Mangrove forests; highly aquatic
- Unknown; thought to be fish
- Live-bearer

SPECIES:
Gerarda prevostiana

GENUS: **GYIOPHIS**

Mud Snakes

- 2
- Medium
- Myanmar
- Muddy river deltas
- Fish
- Live-bearers
- Included in the genus *Enhydris* until recently

SPECIES:
Gyiophis maculosa
Gyiophis vorisi

GENUS: **HEURNIA**

- 1
- Small, less than 1 m (3 ft 3 in)
- New Guinea
- Semi-aquatic
- Fish
- Live-bearer
- Closely related to the *Enhydris* species

SPECIES:
Heurnia ventromaculata

GENUS: **HOMALOPHIS**

- 2
- Small, 65 cm (2 ft)
- Borneo, Kalimantan
- Swamps and muddy rivers
- Probably fish and frogs
- Live-bearers
- Included in the genus *Enhydris* until recently

SPECIES:
Homalophis doriae
Homalophis gyii

GENUS: **HOMALOPSIS**

- 5
- Medium
- India and Southeast Asia
- Fresh and brackish water
- Fish and frogs. Can become pests in fisheries
- Live-bearers

SPECIES:
Homalopsis buccata,
  Puff-faced Water Snake
Homalopsis hardwickii
Homalopsis mereljcoxi
Homalopsis nigroventralis
Homalopsis semizonata

GENUS: **HYPSISCOPUS**

- 2
- Small, 50 cm (1 ft 6 in)
- India, Southeast Asia, southern China, and Indonesia
- Swamps, drainage ditches, and rice fields
- Frogs and tadpoles
- Live-bearers
- Included in the genus *Enhydris* until recently

SPECIES:
Hypsiscopus matannensis
Hypsiscopus plumbea

GENUS: **KARNSOPHIS**

- 1
- Less than 1 m (3 ft 3 in)
- Sumatra, Indonesia
- Unknown, presumably similar to other homalopsid snakes
- A frog was found in the stomach of a preserved specimen
- Presumably a live-bearer
- Only described in 2012 from a single preserved specimen collected in 1937

SPECIES:
Karnsophis siantaris

GENUS: **KUALATAHAN**

- 1
- Medium
- West Malaysia (Pahang)
- Aquatic, in freshwater rivers
- Unknown, but probably fish and frogs
- Presumably a live-bearer
- The single species was known as *Enhydris pahangensis* until recently

SPECIES:
Kualatahan pahangensis

GENUS: **MINTONOPHIS**

- 1
- Medium
- Pakistan (Lower Indus River)
- Aquatic, in shallow pools
- Fish and frogs
- Live-bearer
- The single species was known as *Enhydris pakistanica* until recently

SPECIES:
Mintonophis pakistanicus

GENUS: **MIRALIA**

- 1
- Medium
- Indonesia, East Malaysia (Borneo)
- Muddy rivers and lakes
- Fish and frogs
- Live-bearer
- The single species was known as *Enhydris alternans* until recently

SPECIES:
Miralia alternans

GENUS: **MYRON**

- 3
- Small
- New Guinea and extreme northern Australia
- Mudflats and mangrove forests
- Crabs and small fish
- Live-bearers

SPECIES:
Myron karnsi
Myron resetari
Myron richardsonii,
  Richardson's Mangrove Snake

GENUS: **MYRROPHIS**

- 2
- Medium
- Southeast China, Taiwan, and Southeast Asia
- Freshwater (*M. chinensis*) and brackish estuarine and marine waters (*M. bennettii*)
- Mainly fish
- Live-bearers
- Included in the genus *Enhydris* until recently

SPECIES:
Myrrophis bennettii
Myrrophis chinensis

GENUS: **PHYTOLOPSIS**

- 1
- Medium
- Indonesia and Borneo
- Muddy rivers and lakes
- Fish and frogs
- Live-bearers
- The single species was known as *Enhydris punctata* until recently

SPECIES:
Phytolopsis punctata

GENUS: **PSEUDOFERANIA**

- 1
- Medium, 80 cm (2 ft 6 in)
- Australia and New Guinea
- Freshwater streams and swamps
- Fish and frogs
- Live-bearer
- The single species was known as *Enhydris polylepis* until recently

SPECIES:
Pseudoferania polylepis

GENUS: **RACLITIA**

- 1
- Medium
- West Malaysia
- Muddy rivers and estuaries
- Fish and frogs
- Live-bearer
- The single species was known as *Enhydris indica* until recently

SPECIES:
Raclitia indica

GENUS: **SUBSESSOR**

- 1
- Medium
- Southeast Asia
- Muddy rivers and estuaries
- Frogs and fish
- Live-bearer
- The single species was known as *Enhydris bocourti* until recently

SPECIES:
Subsessor bocourti

GENUS: **SUMATRANUS**

- 1
- Medium
- Indonesia
- Muddy freshwater swamps and rivers
- Fish and frogs
- Live-bearer
- The single species was known as *Enhydris albomaculata* until recently

SPECIES:
Sumatranus albomaculata

PAREATIDAE
Asian Slug- and Snail-eating Snakes

3 GENERA CONTAINING 20 SPECIES

These are slender snakes with wide heads and large eyes; the Montane Slug-eating Snake has deep red eyes. Arboreal and semi-arboreal species are included and all are nocturnal, apparently tracking snails and slugs by following slime-trails. Their long sharp teeth help them to pull snails from their shells.

GENUS: **APLOPELTURA**

- 1
- Medium
- Southeast Asia
- Rainforests, in vegetation and on the ground
- Snails

- ⚥ Thought to be an egg-layer
- 📝 It is very elongated, with a square head and mottled brown and black markings. Closely parallels the *Dipsas* species from Central and South America

SPECIES:

Aplopeltura boa

GENUS: **ASTHENODIPSAS**

- 🐍 5
- ↔ Medium, 45–90 cm (1 ft 5 in–3 ft) but very slender
- 🌏 Southeast Asia, Borneo, and Celebes
- 🏠 Rainforests
- 🍴 Slugs and snails
- ⚥ Egg-layers
- 📝 Like *Aplopeltura Boa*, these snakes closely parallel the American slug-eaters, *Dipsadidae*, both in appearance and behaviour

SPECIES:

Asthenodipsas laevis
Asthenodipsas lasgalenensis
Asthenodipsas malaccanus
Asthenodipsas tropidonotus
Asthenodipsas vertebralis,
  Montane Slug-eating Snake

GENUS: **PAREAS**

Asian Slug-eaters

- 🐍 14
- ↔ Small
- 🌏 Southern China and Southeast Asia, including the island of Borneo
- 🏠 Humid forests and plantations
- 🍴 Slugs and snails; the skulls and jaws are modified for extracting them from their shells
- ⚥ Egg-layers

SPECIES:

Pareas atayal
Pareas boulengeri
Pareas carinatus
Pareas chinensis
Pareas formosensis
Pareas hamptoni
Pareas iwasakii
Pareas komaii
Pareas margaritophorus
Pareas monticola
Pareas nigriceps
Pareas nuchalis
Pareas stanleyi
Pareas vindumi

XENODERMATIDAE
Odd-scaled Snakes

6 GENERA CONTAINING 18 SPECIES

These are poorly understood snakes that used to be included in the Colubridae. They may, in fact, be more closely related to the file snakes but for the time being, they are tentatively grouped within the Colubroidea superfamily.

The type species, *Xenodermus javanicus*, known as the Javanese Dragon Snake, has

a broad head covered with small granular scales and a double row of enlarged tubercles running the length of its back. Other species vary in their appearance.

GENUS: **ACHALINUS**

- 🐍 9
- ↔ Small
- 🌏 China and Southeast Asia
- 🏠 Unknown
- 🍴 Thought to eat worms and slugs
- ⚥ Egg-layers
- 📝 Poorly known, secretive snakes

SPECIES:

Achalinus ater
Achalinus formosanus
Achalinus hainanus
Achalinus jinggangensis
Achalinus meiguensis
Achalinus niger
Achalinus rufescens
Achalinus spinalis
Achalinus werneri

GENUS: **FIMBRIOS**

- 🐍 2
- ↔ Small
- 🌏 Southeast Asia
- 🏠 Thought to be forests, where they are terrestrial
- 🍴 Unknown
- ⚥ Unknown
- 📝 Rare and poorly known. They have a patch of spiky scales on the lower jaw, the function of which is unknown. Nocturnal

SPECIES:

Fimbrios klossi
Fimbrios smithi

GENUS: **PARAFIMBRIOS**

- 🐍 1
- ↔ Unknown
- 🌏 Laos
- 🏠 Unknown
- 🍴 Unknown
- ⚥ Unknown
- 📝 A new species, discovered only in 2015

SPECIES:

Parafimbrios lao

GENUS: **STOLICZKIA**

- 🐍 2
- ↔ Small
- 🌏 India (*S. khasiensis*) and Borneo
- 🏠 Montane species
- 🍴 Unknown
- ⚥ Unknown
- 📝 Rare snakes whose natural history and relationships are poorly known

SPECIES:

Stoliczkia borneensis
Stoliczkia khasiensis

GENUS: **XENODERMUS**

- 🐍 1
- ↔ Small, to about 70 cm (2 ft 3 in)
- 🌏 The Malay Peninsula, Java, Sumatra, and Borneo
- 🏠 Damp forests, marshes, paddy fields, and irrigation ditches. Semi-aquatic and semi-burrowing
- 🍴 Frogs
- ⚥ Egg-layer
- 📝 An unusual, sluggish species

SPECIES:

Xenodermus javanicus,
  Javanese Dragon Snake

GENUS: **XYLOPHIS**

- 🐍 3
- ↔ Small
- 🌏 Southern India
- 🏠 Thought to be semi-burrowing
- 🍴 Unknown
- ⚥ Unknown
- 📝 Secretive snakes about which little is known

SPECIES:

Xylophis captaini
Xylophis perroteti
Xylophis stenorhynchus

VIPERIDAE
Vipers and Pit Vipers

3 SUBFAMILIES CONTAINING 35 GENERA AND 331 SPECIES

Most vipers are short and stout, with wide, triangular heads, and most have keeled scales, although there are exceptions in each case. The family is considered to be the most advanced of all snakes, with many features that are not found in any other families. These include the long, folding fangs with which they envenomate their prey and, in the group known as pit vipers, a pair of heat pits in their face that are more sensitive than those of the pythons, and which must therefore have evolved independently.

Vipers are found throughout much of the world but are absent from Australasia and Madagascar. They have several adaptations that enable them to live in cold places, and the family includes the snakes that are found furthest north (*Vipera berus*) and furthest south (*Bothrops ammodytoides*), as well as the snake (*Gloydius himalayanus*) that is found at the highest altitude, at 4,900 m (16,000 ft) in the Himalayas.

There are three subfamilies, which are all well defined.

SUBFAMILY: **AZEMIOPINAE**
1 GENUS CONTAINING 2 SPECIES

Just two species, considered to be the most primitive vipers, are placed under this subfamily. The species, *A. feae*, is banded orange on dark grey or black and has a

yellow or buff head with large, plate-like scales but no heat pits. Its natural history is virtually unknown but its venom is believed to be mild. The other species, *A. kharini*, is recently described from northern Vietnam and eastern China.

GENUS: **AZEMIOPS**

- 🐍 2
- ↔ Medium, to just under 1 m (3 ft 3 in), and slender
- 🌏 Myanmar, northern Vietnam, southern and central China, and southeastern Tibet
- 🏠 Cool, montane habitats to 2,000 m (6,500 ft)
- 🍴 Small mammals
- ⚥ Unknown
- 📝 Very rare, with only a few known specimens. *A. kharini* was only discovered in 2013

SPECIES:

Azemiops feae,
  Fea's Viper
Azemiops kharini

SUBFAMILY: **CROTALINAE**
Pit Vipers

21 GENERA CONTAINING 231 SPECIES

Superficially, many pit vipers resemble the vipers in the Viperinae subfamily, but they all possess heat-sensitive organs in the form of a pair of deep and conspicuous facial pits between their eyes and nostrils.

Pit vipers may be terrestrial or arboreal, dull or bright in colour, and live-bearers or egg-layers – they have explored a number of evolutionary options. These vipers are best equipped to hunt warm-blooded animals, which make up the majority of their food.

Pit vipers are found in the New World (North, Central, and South America) and the Old, in Africa and Asia.

GENUS: **AGKISTRODON**

- 🐍 6
- ↔ Medium, to about 1 m (3 ft 3 in), and stocky
- 🌏 North America, including Mexico
- 🏠 Varied, from swamps to high, rocky mountain slopes
- 🍴 Mainly small birds and mammals, but a variety of other prey is taken by some species, including fish, frogs, and carrion by *A. piscivorus*
- ⚥ Live-bearers
- 📝 The bites are dangerous to humans, though they rarely prove to be fatal

SPECIES:

Agkistrodon bilineatus,
  Cantil
- *Agkistrodon contortrix*,
  Copperhead (pp.128–29)
Agkistrodon howardgloydi

Agkistrodon piscivorus,
Cottonmouth
Agkistrodon russeolus
Agkistrodon taylori

GENUS: **ATROPOIDES**

- 6
- Small to medium, to just over 1 m (3 ft 3 in), but extremely stout
- Central America
- Rain and cloud forests
- Amphibians, reptiles, and small mammals
- Live-bearers
- Venomous, but bites are unlikely to prove fatal. Previously placed in the genus *Porthidium*

SPECIES:

Atropoides indomitus
Atropoides mexicanus
Atropoides nummifer,
Jumping Pit Viper
Atropoides occiduus
Atropoides olmec,
Olmec Pit Viper
Atropoides picadoi,
Picado's Pit Viper

GENUS: **BOTHRIECHIS**

Palm Pit Vipers

- 10
- Medium, sometimes over 1 m (3 ft 3 in), but usually less
- Central America. *B. schlegelii* extends into South America as far as Ecuador
- Forests, where they are arboreal
- Amphibians, reptiles, small birds, and mammals
- Live-bearers
- Bites are painful and have resulted in fatalities

SPECIES:

Bothriechis aurifer,
Yellow-blotched Palm Pit Viper
Bothriechis bicolor,
Guatemalan Palm Pit Viper
Bothriechis guifarroi
Bothriechis lateralis,
Side-striped Palm Pit Viper
Bothriechis marchi,
March's Palm Pit Viper
Bothriechis nigroviridis,
Black-speckled Palm Pit Viper
Bothriechis rowleyi,
Rowley's Palm Pit Viper
Bothriechis schlegelii,
Eyelash Viper
Bothriechis supraciliaris
Bothriechis thalassinus

GENUS: **BOTHROCOPHIAS**

- 6
- About 1 m (3 ft 3 in)
- South America, including the Andean foothills
- Rainforests and grasslands
- Amphibians, lizards, birds, and mammals

- Live-bearers
- Some species were formerly included in the genus *Bothrops*

SPECIES:

Bothrocophias andianus,
Andean Lancehead
Bothrocophias campbelli
Bothrocophias colombianus,
Colombian Lancehead
Bothrocophias hyoprora
Bothrocophias microphthalmus,
Small-eyed Lancehead
Bothrocophias myersi

GENUS: **BOTHROPS**

Lance-headed Pit Vipers or
Fer-de-Lances

- 44
- Small to large, with some species reaching 2.5 m (8 ft 2 in) in length
- Central and South America (Mexico to Argentina)
- Highly varied: rainforests, forest clearings, hillsides, grasslands, plantations, and fields, and even the Atacama Desert (*B. pictus*). Forest species are often encountered alongside streams and rivers
- Amphibians, lizards, birds, and mammals
- Live-bearers
- Certain species are very dangerous on account of their association with human habitation, excellent camouflage, and the potent venom. *B. asper, B. atrox,* and *B. jararaca* are responsible for most of the snakebite fatalities recorded in Central and South America. Two additional species, *B. colombiensis* and *B. isabelae,* are usually considered to be forms of *B. atrox*

SPECIES:

Bothrops alcatraz
Bothrops alternatus,
Urutu
Bothrops ammodytoides,
Patagonian Lancehead
Bothrops asper,
Terciopelo or Velvet Snake
Bothrops atrox,
Common Lancehead
Bothrops ayerbei
Bothrops barnetti,
Barnett's Lancehead
Bothrops bilineata
Bothrops brazili,
Brazil's Lancehead
Bothrops caribbaeus,
Saint Lucia Lancehead
Bothrops chloromelas
Bothrops cotiara,
Cotiara
Bothrops diporus
Bothrops erythromelas,
Caatinga Lancehead
Bothrops fonsecai,
Fonseca's Lancehead
Bothrops insularis,
Golden Lancehead

Bothrops itapetiningae,
São Paulo Lancehead
- *Bothrops jararaca,*
Jararaca (pp.134–35)
Bothrops jararacussu,
Jararacussu
Bothrops jonathani
Bothrops lanceolatus,
Martinique Lancehead
Bothrops leucurus,
White-tailed Lancehead
Bothrops lojanus,
Lojan Lancehead
Bothrops lutzi
Bothrops marajoensis,
Marajó Lancehead
Bothrops marmoratus
Bothrops matogrossensis
Bothrops medusa
Bothrops moojeni,
Brazilian Lancehead
Bothrops muriciensis
Bothrops neuwiedi,
Neuwied's Lancehead
Bothrops oligolepis
Bothrops osbornei
Bothrops otavioi
Bothrops pauloensis
Bothrops pictus,
Desert Lancehead
Bothrops pirajai,
Piraja's Lancehead
Bothrops pubescens
Bothrops pulchra,
Dusky Lancehead
Bothrops punctatus
Bothrops rhombeatus
Bothrops sanctaecrucis,
Bolivian Lancehead
Bothrops taeniata
Bothrops venezuelensis,
Venezuelan Lancehead

GENUS: **CALLOSELASMA**

- 1
- Large
- Malaysian Peninsula and some Indonesian islands
- Forests
- Lizards, snakes, small birds, and mammals
- Egg-layer. There is evidence that females coil around and guard their eggs
- Bad-tempered and strongly inclined to bite, although bites are rarely serious

SPECIES:

Calloselasma rhodostoma,
Malaysian Pit Viper

GENUS: **CERROPHIDION**

- 5
- Small, 50–75 cm (1 ft 6 in– 2 ft 5 in) in length
- Central America
- Montane forests of pine-oak, and cloud forests up to about 3,000 m (9,800 ft). Terrestrial
- Lizards and small mammals
- Live-bearers
- Sometimes included in the genus *Porthidium*

SPECIES:

Cerrophidion godmani
Cerrophidion petlalcensis
Cerrophidion sasai
Cerrophidion tzotzilorum
Cerrophidion wilsoni

GENUS: **CROTALUS**

Rattlesnakes

- 41
- Small to large, from 50 cm (1 ft 6 in) to over 2 m (6 ft 6 in) in exceptional circumstances
- North, Central, and South America
- Extremely varied: including temperate and tropical forests, grasslands, rocky and sandy deserts, and mountainsides
- Lizards, birds, and small mammals
- Live-bearers

SPECIES:

Crotalus adamanteus,
Eastern Diamondback Rattlesnake
Crotalus angelensis
Crotalus aquilus,
Queretaran Dusky Rattlesnake
Crotalus armstrongi,
Mexican Dusky Rattlesnake
- *Crotalus atrox,*
Western Diamondback Rattlesnake (pp.146–47)
Crotalus basiliscus,
Mexican West Coast Rattlesnake
Crotalus campbelli
Crotalus catalinensis,
Santa Catalina Rattlesnake or Rattleless Rattlesnake
- *Crotalus cerastes,*
Sidewinder (p.150)
Crotalus cerberus
Arizona Black Rattlesnake
Crotalus culminatus
- *Crotalus durissus,*
Neotropical Rattlesnake (pp.148–49)
Crotalus enyo,
Baja Rattlesnake
Crotalus ericsmithi
Crotalus horridus,
Timber Rattlesnake or Canebrake Rattlesnake
Crotalus intermedius,
Mexican Small-headed Rattlesnake
Crotalus lannomi,
Autlan Rattlesnake
Crotalus lepidus,
Rock Rattlesnake
Crotalus mitchellii,
Speckled Rattlesnake
Crotalus molossus,
Black-headed Rattlesnake
Crotalus oreganus,
Western Rattlesnake
Crotalus ornatus
Crotalus polystictus,
Mexican Lance-headed Rattlesnake
Crotalus pricei,
Twin-spotted Rattlesnake
Crotalus pusillus,
Tancitaran Rattlesnake
Crotalus pyrrhus
Crotalus ravus,
Mexican Pygmy Rattlesnake
Crotalus ruber,
Red Diamond Rattlesnake
Crotalus scutulatus,
Mojave Rattlesnake
Crotalus simus
Crotalus stejnegeri,
Long-tailed Rattlesnake

Crotalus stephensi
Crotalus tancitarensis
Crotalus tigris,
  Tiger Rattlesnake
Crotalus tlaloci
Crotalus totonacus
Crotalus transversus,
  Cross-banded Mountain Rattlesnake
Crotalus triseriatus,
  Mexican Dusky Rattlesnake
Crotalus tzabcan
Crotalus viridis,
  Pacific Rattlesnake
Crotalus willardi,
  Ridge-nosed Rattlesnake

GENUS: **DEINAGKISTRODON**

- ꙮ 1
- ↔ Large
- 🌐 Southeastern China and Taiwan
- 🏠 Wooded mountains and hills
- ◄ Amphibians, lizards, snakes, and mammals
- ⚥ Egg-layer
- ▥ Common and highly dangerous, with a bite that often proves fatal. The common name refers to the supposed distance that a victim travels before succumbing

SPECIES:

Deinagkistrodon acutus,
  Hundred-pace Snake

GENUS: **GARTHIUS**

- ꙮ 1
- ↔ Small, 65 cm (2 ft)
- 🌐 Sabah, Borneo. Known from only five specimens, four of them from Mount Kinabalu
- 🏠 Montane rainforest
- ◄ Unknown; probably lizards, frogs, and small mammals
- ⚥ Egg-layer
- ▥ Previously placed in the genus *Ovophis*

SPECIES:

Garthius chaseni,
  Kinabalu Brown Pit Viper

GENUS: **GLOYDIUS**

- ꙮ 13
- ↔ Small, to 75 cm (2 ft 5 in) at most
- 🌐 Central Asia
- 🏠 Mountain slopes, often at high altitude (to nearly 5,000 m [16,400 ft] in *G. himalayanus*)
- ◄ Lizards, snakes, and small mammals
- ⚥ Live-bearers
- ▥ Previously included in the genus *Agkistrodon*

SPECIES:

Gloydius blomhoffii,
  Mamushi
Gloydius brevicaudus
Gloydius halys,
  Siberian Pit Viper
Gloydius himalayanus,
  Himalayan Pit Viper
Gloydius intermedius

Gloydius lijianlii
Gloydius liupanensis
Gloydius monticola
Gloydius saxatilis
Gloydius shedaoensis
Gloydius strauchi
Gloydius tsushimaensis
Gloydius ussuriensis

GENUS: **HYPNALE**

Hump-nosed Vipers

- ꙮ 3
- ↔ Small; among the smallest pit vipers at 30–55 cm (1 ft–1 ft 8 in), depending on species
- 🌐 Southwestern India (Western Ghats) and Sri Lanka
- 🏠 Forests, including rainforests, hillsides, plantations, and fields, often near human habitation
- ◄ Frogs, lizards, snakes (including their eggs), and small mammals
- ⚥ Live-bearers
- ▥ Venomous, although not aggressive

SPECIES:

Hypnale hypnale,
  Hump-nosed Viper
Hypnale nepa,
  Sri Lankan Hump-nosed Viper
Hypnale zara

GENUS: **LACHESIS**

- ꙮ 4
- ↔ Very large, occasionally to over 3 m (9 ft 8 in) and longer
- 🌐 Central and South America
- 🏠 Wet tropical forests and recently cleared land
- ◄ Mammals
- ⚥ Egg-layers
- ▥ The largest pit vipers, with a fearsome reputation. Highly dangerous, though quite rare and secretive

SPECIES:

Lachesis acrochorda
Lachesis melanocephala,
  Black-headed Bushmaster
Lachesis muta,
  Bushmaster
Lachesis stenophrys,
  Central American Bushmaster

GENUS: **MIXCOATLUS**

- ꙮ 3
- ↔ Small, to 55 cm (1 ft 8 in)
- 🌐 Mexico
- 🏠 Montane forests and scrub, where they are mostly diurnal
- ◄ Probably frogs, lizards, and small mammals
- ⚥ Live-bearers
- ▥ Previously placed in the genus *Porthidium*

SPECIES:

Mixcoatlus barbouri
Mixcoatlus browni
Mixcoatlus melanurus

GENUS: **OPHRYACUS**

- ꙮ 1
- ↔ Small, to about 70 cm (2 ft 3 in)
- 🌐 Central Mexico
- 🏠 Pine-oak and cloud forests
- ◄ Unknown, but probably lizards and small mammals
- ⚥ Live-bearer
- ▥ The effects of the venom are not known, although the bites are unlikely to be life-threatening

SPECIES:

Ophryacus undulatus,
  Mexican Horned Viper

GENUS: **OVOPHIS**

- ꙮ 6
- ↔ Small to medium
- 🌐 Southeast Asia, Borneo, and the Ryukyu Islands (Japan)
- 🏠 Forests
- ◄ Lizards and small mammals
- ⚥ Egg-layers
- ▥ Sometimes included in the genus *Trimeresurus*

SPECIES:

Ovophis convictus
Ovophis makazayazaya
Ovophis monticola,
  Mountain Pit Viper
Ovophis okinavensis
Ovophis tonkinensis
Ovophis zayuensis

GENUS: **PORTHIDIUM**

Hog-nosed Vipers

- ꙮ 9
- ↔ Small, rarely more than 70 cm (2 ft 3 in)
- 🌐 Central and South America
- 🏠 Humid and dry tropical forests, where they are terrestrial
- ◄ Frogs, lizards, and small mammals
- ⚥ Live-bearers
- ▥ Venomous, though not usually considered to be very dangerous, except in the case of *P. nasutum*, which has caused human fatalities. Several snakes have been removed from this genus and placed in *Atropoides* and *Cerrophidion*

SPECIES:

Porthidium arcosae
Porthidium dunni,
  Dunn's Hog-nosed Viper
Porthidium hespere,
  Western Hog-nosed Viper
Porthidium lansbergii,
  Lansberg's Hog-nosed Viper
Porthidium nasutum,
  Rainforest Hog-nosed Viper
Porthidium ophryomegas,
  Slender Hog-nosed Viper
Porthidium porrasi
Porthidium volcanicum
Porthidium yucatanicum,
  Yucatán Hog-nosed Viper

GENUS: **PROTOBOTHROPS**

- ꙮ 14
- ↔ Large, to 1.5 m (5 ft), exceptionally to 2.5 m (8 ft 2 in) in the case of the Habu, *Protobothrops flavoviridis*
- 🌐 China, India, Southeast Asia, and Japan
- 🏠 Varied, from montane grasslands and forests to lowland fields and plantations
- ◄ Frogs, lizards, and small mammals
- ⚥ Egg-layers, where known
- ▥ Previously placed in the genus *Trimeresurus*, although some species are recently described

SPECIES:

Protobothrops cornutus
Protobothrops dabieshanensis
Protobothrops elegans
Protobothrops flavoviridis
Protobothrops himalayanus
Protobothrops jerdonii
Protobothrops kaulbacki
Protobothrops mangshanensis
Protobothrops maolanensis
Protobothrops mucrosquamatus
Protobothrops sieversorum
Protobothrops tokarensis
Protobothrops trungkhanhensis
Protobothrops xiangchengensis

GENUS: **SISTRURUS**

Pygmy Rattlesnakes

- ꙮ 2
- ↔ Small to medium, from 50 cm (1 ft 6 in) to nearly 1 m (3 ft 3 in) occasionally
- 🌐 Northeastern North America to northern Mexico
- 🏠 Swamps and marshes, grasslands, pine woods, meadows, and forest clearings
- ◄ Lizards and small mammals
- ⚥ Live-bearers
- ▥ Capable of giving painful bites, but which are unlikely to have serious long-term effects on humans

SPECIES:

Sistrurus catenatus,
  Massassauga
Sistrurus miliarius,
  Pygmy Rattlesnake

GENUS: **TRIMERESURUS**

Bamboo Vipers and Asian Pit Vipers

- ꙮ 50
- ↔ Small to medium
- 🌐 Asia, from Sri Lanka and India through southern China and into Southeast Asia, the Indonesian archipelago, the Philippines, and Japan
- 🏠 Varied: typically forests and thickets, but not all species are arboreal
- ◄ Frogs, lizards, and small mammals
- ⚥ Mostly live-bearers though some species are egg-layers

✎ The genus is poorly studied. Many new species have been described recently, others have been removed to the genus *Ovophis*, and there are likely to be more changes in the near future

SPECIES:

● *Trimeresurus albolabris*,
　White-lipped Tree Viper
　(pp.140–41)
Trimeresurus andalasensis
Trimeresurus andersonii
Trimeresurus barati
Trimeresurus borneensis,
　Bornean Pit Viper
Trimeresurus brongersmai
Trimeresurus buniana
Trimeresurus cantori
Trimeresurus cardamomensis
Trimeresurus erythrurus
Trimeresurus fasciatus
Trimeresurus flavomaculatus
Trimeresurus fucatus
Trimeresurus gracilis
Trimeresurus gramineus
Trimeresurus gumprechti
Trimeresurus gunaleni
Trimeresurus hageni
Trimeresurus honsonensis
Trimeresurus insularis
Trimeresurus kanburiensis
Trimeresurus labialis
Trimeresurus macrolepis
Trimeresurus macrops
Trimeresurus malabaricus
Trimeresurus malcolmi
Trimeresurus mcgregori
Trimeresurus medoensis
Trimeresurus mutabilis
Trimeresurus nebularis
Trimeresurus phuketensis
Trimeresurus popeiorum,
　Pope's Pit Viper
Trimeresurus puniceus,
　Leaf-nosed Pit Viper
Trimeresurus purpureomaculatus,
　Shore Pit Viper
Trimeresurus rubeus
Trimeresurus sabahi
Trimeresurus schultzei
Trimeresurus septentrionalis
Trimeresurus sichuanensis
Trimeresurus stejnegeri
Trimeresurus strigatus
Trimeresurus sumatranus,
　Sumatran Pit Viper
Trimeresurus tibetanus
Trimeresurus toba
Trimeresurus trigonocephalus
Trimeresurus truongsonensis
Trimeresurus venustus
Trimeresurus vogeli
Trimeresurus wiroti
Trimeresurus yunnanensis

GENUS: **TROPIDOLAEMUS**

🐍 5
↔ Medium, to about 1 m (3 ft 3 in)
🌐 Southeast Asia
🏠 Forests and mangroves, where they are highly arboreal
🍴 Lizards, small birds, and mammals
⚥ Live-bearers
✎ Formerly included in the genus *Trimeresurus*

SPECIES:

Tropidolaemus huttoni
Tropidolaemus laticinctus

Tropidolaemus philippensis
Tropidolaemus subannulatus
Tropidolaemus wagleri,
　Wagler's Pit Viper

SUBFAMILY: **VIPERINAE**
Old World vipers without pits

13 GENERA CONTAINING 98 SPECIES

The vipers in this subfamily are mostly small to medium-sized, heavily built snakes, with wide heads covered in small, fragmented scales. They typically have a dorsal pattern of blotches, often joined and sometimes forming a continuous zigzag. Many species, especially those belonging to the genus *Bitis*, appear to have colourful, even garish, patterns when seen out of habitat, but these markings disrupt the outline of the snakes to provide them with exceptional camouflage when they are resting on the appropriate substrates.

They are mostly terrestrial, with the exception of members of the African genus *Atheris*, which are known as bush vipers, although several of the European vipers also climb into low vegetation and bushes in search of nestling birds. Most species give birth to live young, but some lay eggs, and the reproduction of others is unknown.

This subfamily is restricted to Europe, Africa, and Asia.

GENUS: **ATHERIS**

Bush Vipers

🐍 16
↔ Small to medium, to about 75 cm (2 ft 5 in), and relatively slender
🌐 West, Central, and East Africa
🏠 Forests and swamps. All except two species are arboreal
🍴 Frogs, lizards, and small mammals
⚥ Live-bearers
✎ Dangerous to humans, although only *A. squamigera* has caused fatalities. Several species have extremely small geographic ranges and are known from only a few specimens

SPECIES:

Atheris acuminata
Atheris anisolepis
Atheris barbouri
Atheris broadleyi
Atheris ceratophora,
　Usambara Bush Viper
Atheris chlorechis,
　Western Bush Viper
Atheris desaixi,
　Mount Kenya Bush Viper
Atheris hirsuta
Atheris hispida,
　Rough-scaled Bush Viper or Hairy Bush Viper
Atheris katangensis,
　Shaba Bush Viper
Atheris mabuensis
Atheris matildae
Atheris nitschei,
　Great Lakes Bush Viper

Atheris rungweensis
Atheris squamigera,
　Green Bush Viper
Atheris subocularis

GENUS: **BITIS**

African Adders

🐍 17
↔ Small to large: from a maximum of 27 cm (10½ in) in *B. schneideri*, to over 2 m (6 ft 6 in) in *B. gabonica*. Invariably stout with wide heads
🌐 Africa
🏠 Varied, from rainforests and grasslands to the most arid deserts
🍴 Lizards and small mammals
⚥ Live-bearers
✎ Species that live on dunes, for example *B. peringueyi*, move by sidewinding. The larger species, notably the common Puff Adder, are among the most dangerous snakes in Africa. Small species give relatively innocuous bites. Several species (*B. heraldica*, *B. parviocula*, and *B. worthingtoni*, for example) have rarely been collected and their natural history is relatively unknown. *B. rubida* was described only in 1997

SPECIES:

Bitis albanica
● *Bitis arietans*,
　Puff Adder (pp.130–31)
Bitis armata,
　Southern Adder
Bitis atropos,
　Berg Adder
Bitis caudalis,
　Horned Adder
Bitis cornuta,
　Many-horned Adder
● *Bitis gabonica*,
　Gaboon Viper or Adder (pp.132–33)
Bitis heraldica,
　Angolan Adder
Bitis inornata,
　Plain Mountain Adder
Bitis nasicornis,
　Rhinoceros Viper
Bitis parviocula,
　Ethiopian Mountain Adder
Bitis peringueyi,
　Peringuey's Adder
Bitis rhinoceros,
　Horned Gaboon Viper
Bitis rubida
Bitis schneideri,
　Dwarf Adder
Bitis worthingtoni,
　Kenyan Horned Viper
Bitis xeropaga,
　Desert Mountain Adder

GENUS: **CAUSUS**

Night Adders

🐍 7
↔ Small, 60–70 cm (2–2 ft 3 in), and slender
🌐 Africa, south of the Sahara

🏠 Varied, including grasslands, forests, and swamps. Often associated with damp places
🍴 Amphibians, especially toads
⚥ Egg-layers
✎ They inject large amounts of venom, but their bites are unlikely to lead to serious consequences

SPECIES:

Causus bilineatus,
　Two-striped Night Adder
Causus defilippii,
　Snouted Night Adder
Causus lichtensteinii,
　Forest Night Adder
Causus maculatus,
　West African Night Adder
Causus rasmusseni
Causus resimus,
　Green Night Adder
Causus rhombeatus,
　Rhombic Night Adder

GENUS: **CERASTES**

North African desert vipers

🐍 4
↔ Short, to about 60 cm (2 ft), but very stout
🌐 North Africa and the Middle East
🏠 Sandy and rocky deserts
🍴 Small lizards and mammals
⚥ Egg-layers
✎ Very heavily keeled scales. Capable of painful, though rarely fatal, bites. They move by sidewinding

SPECIES:

Cerastes boehmei
● *Cerastes cerastes*,
　Desert Horned Viper (pp.136–37)
Cerastes gasperettii,
　Arabian Horned Viper
Cerastes vipera,
　Sahara Horned Viper

GENUS: **DABOIA**

🐍 5
↔ Large, to well over 1 m (3 ft 3 in), and very heavily built
🌐 India, Sri Lanka, Myanmar, Thailand, Bangladesh, Cambodia, southern China, Taiwan, Java, Komodo, and Flores
🏠 Varied; found in most habitats except dense forests
🍴 Mammals
⚥ Live-bearers
✎ Sometimes retained in the genus *Vipera*

SPECIES:

Daboia deserti
Daboia mauritanica
Daboia palaestinae,
　Palestinian Viper
Daboia russelii,
　Russell's Viper
Daboia siamensis

GENUS: **ECHIS**

Saw-scaled, or Carpet, Vipers

🐍 11
↔ Small, all under 1 m (3 ft 3 in)
🌍 West and North Africa, through the Middle East and into India and Sri Lanka
🏠 Dry grasslands and lightly wooded places
🦎 Varied, including spiders, scorpions, lizards, snakes, birds, and small mammals
⚥ Egg-layers
📝 Responsible for the majority of fatal snakebites where they occur, partly because they are numerous and well camouflaged and therefore easily trodden on. They make a characteristic coil when disturbed, rubbing their scales together to produce a rasping sound. The identification of the various species is difficult and their taxonomy is not completely fixed at present

SPECIES:
Echis borkini
Echis carinatus,
Saw-scaled Viper (pp.138–39)
Echis coloratus,
Burton's Viper or Painted Saw-scaled Viper
Echis hughesi,
Hughes' Saw-scaled Viper
Echis jogeri,
Joger's Saw-scaled Viper
Echis khosatzkii
Echis leucogaster,
White-bellied Saw-scaled Viper
Echis megalocephalus
Echis ocellatus,
West African Saw-scaled Viper
Echis omanensis
Echis pyramidum,
Northeast African Saw-scaled Viper

GENUS: **ERISTICOPHIS**

🐍 1
↔ Small
🌍 Afghanistan and northern Pakistan
🏠 Sand deserts
🦎 Lizards and small mammals
⚥ Unknown
📝 Rarely collected and poorly known

SPECIES:
Eristicophis macmahoni,
MacMahon's Viper

GENUS: **MACROVIPERA**

🐍 2
↔ Large, 1–2 m (3 ft 3 in–6 ft 6 in)
🌍 North Africa, southeastern Europe, and western Asia
🏠 Deserts, rocky hillsides, and scrub
🦎 Small birds and mammals
⚥ Egg-layers

📝 Dangerous, with serious, though rarely fatal, bites. Previously placed in the genus *Vipera*. The species *M. schweizeri* is endangered

SPECIES:
Macrovipera lebetina,
Levant Viper
Macrovipera schweizeri,
Milos Viper

GENUS: **MONTATHERIS**

🐍 1
↔ Small, 30 cm (12 in)
🌍 East Africa. Restricted to a small area around Mount Kenya and the Aberdare mountains
🏠 Montane moorland
🦎 Probably lizards and frogs
⚥ Live-bearer
📝 The single species was previously known as *Atheris hindii*

SPECIES:
Montatheris hindii,
Kenya Montane Viper

GENUS: **MONTIVIPERA**

🐍 8
↔ Small to medium, 50–130 cm (1 ft 6 in–4 ft 2 in)
🌍 Southeast Europe, Turkey, and the Middle East
🏠 Rocky hillsides and grasslands
🦎 Lizards and small mammals
⚥ Live-bearers
📝 Several species are endangered due to habitat destruction and illegal collecting

SPECIES:
Montivipera albizona
Montivipera bornmuelleri,
Lebanon Viper
Montivipera bulgardaghica
Montivipera kuhrangica
Montivipera latifii,
Latifi's Viper
Montivipera raddei,
Caucasus Viper
Montivipera wagneri,
Wagner's Viper
Montivipera xanthina,
Ottoman Viper

GENUS: **PROATHERIS**

🐍 1
↔ Small, 50–60 cm (1 ft 6 in–2 ft)
🌍 East Africa
🏠 Marshes and floodplains
🦎 Small rodents
⚥ Live-bearer
📝 The single species was previously known as *Atheris superciliaris*

SPECIES:
Proatheris superciliaris,
Lowland Swamp Viper

GENUS: **PSEUDOCERASTES**

🐍 3
↔ Medium, occasionally up to 1 m (3 ft 3 in)
🌍 Middle East
🏠 Sandy and rocky deserts
🦎 Lizards and small mammals
⚥ Thought to be live-bearers
📝 They move by sidewinding

SPECIES:
Pseudocerastes fieldi
Pseudocerastes persicus,
Iranian Horned Viper
Pseudocerastes urarachnoides

GENUS: **VIPERA**

🐍 22
↔ Small to moderately large
🌍 Europe, western Asia, the Middle East, and North Africa
🏠 Extremely varied, from mountainsides, meadows, and lightly wooded areas to rocky deserts, scree slopes, and high valleys
🦎 Insects, lizards, birds, and small mammals
⚥ Live-bearers
📝 Many new species have been recently described, especially from Turkey and neighbouring territories

SPECIES:
Vipera altaica
Vipera ammodytes,
Nose-horned Viper or Sand Viper (pp.142–43)
Vipera anatolica,
Anatolian Meadow Viper
Vipera aspis,
Asp or Aspic Viper
Vipera barani
Vipera berus,
Adder or Northern Viper (pp.144–45)
Vipera darevskii,
Darevski's Viper
Vipera dinniki
Vipera eriwanensis
Vipera kaznakovi
Vipera latastei,
Lataste's Viper
Vipera lotievi
Vipera magnifica
Vipera monticola
Vipera olguni
Vipera orlovi
Vipera pontica,
Pontic Viper
Vipera renardi,
Steppe Viper
Vipera seoanei,
Spanish Viper
Vipera shemakhensis
Vipera transcaucasiana
Vipera ursinii,
Orsini's Viper or Meadow Viper

GLOSSARY

The terms below are defined as they apply to snakes and may have alternative or slightly different meanings in other contexts. Words in italics within an entry have their own entry in the glossary.

Advanced The term used to refer to characteristics that evolved relatively recently, and the *species*, *families*, etc. that display these characteristics. For example, hinged fangs are advanced characteristics and, therefore, vipers, which have hinged fangs, are members of an advanced family. The opposite of *primitive*.

Amphisbaenian A member of a group of reptiles that is closely allied to snakes and lizards. They live below ground and (apart from three species) have no legs. Often known as worm lizards.

Arboreal Tree-dwelling.

Balling A defensive response in which the snake rolls into a ball and hides its head inside its coils (see p.32).

Caecilian A group of legless, worm-like amphibians that live in damp soil or water and are found in tropical countries.

Cloud forest Tropical forest that is frequently cloaked in mist, usually located on hills or the flanks of mountains. This is the popular term for Tropical Montane forest.

Colubrid A snake that belongs to the *family* Colubridae.

Described species Any species for which a scientific description, including a scientific, or Latin, name, has been published in a reputable journal. Each new species must be recorded in this way.

Diurnal Active during the day.

Dorsal Relating to the back. Dorsal scales, for instance, are the tile-like scales that cover the back and flanks of a snake's body.

Ectothermic Relying on outside sources, usually the sun, for body heat.

Elapid Belonging to the *family* Elapidae, whose members include the cobras, coral snakes, mambas, sea snakes, and taipans.

False coral snake A term sometimes applied to certain brightly coloured, harmless snakes that seem to mimic the appearance of venomous coral snakes, which are members of the cobra family (see p.31).

Family A scientific category containing *genera* considered to be closely related.

Some snake families contain only one genus, but most have more than one. In zoology, family names always end in the suffix -idae.

Form A group of organisms differing from others within the same *species* in, for example, pattern or colouring. Each variation is known as a separate form, for example, "striped form". See also *polymorphism*.

Generalist A species that operates over a wide ecological niche. For example, a species that feeds on a variety of prey and lives in different habitats. The opposite of *specialist*.

Genus (plural **genera**) A scientific category consisting of one or more closely related species. All members of the same genus have the same generic name, for example, *Lampropeltis* (a genus of kingsnakes).

Heat pits Facial pits, found in some boas and pythons and in all pit vipers, that detect small differences in temperature, such as those radiating from warm-blooded animals (see p.23).

Hood The area immediately behind the head of certain cobras. The snake can spread the hood by moving its ribs. The main purpose of the hood is to intimidate potential predators.

Interstitial skin The area of tissue between the scales. Interstitial skin is common to snakes and other reptiles. Also known as interscalar skin (see p.16).

Jacobson's organ A supplementary organ of smell situated in the roof of a snake's mouth. The tongue transfers scent particles to the Jacobson's organ, which connects to the brain via nerves (see p.22).

Keeled scales Those scales with one or (rarely) two longitudinal ridges running down the centre (see p.17).

Live-bearing See *viviparous*.

Montane forest A type of rainforest, usually at least 1,000 m (3,200 ft) above sea level. Characterized by high rainfall and/or frequent mists, and by an abundance of plants, such as mosses, that are epiphytic (growing on other plants). Often cool in comparison with other habitats at the same latitude, this type of forest is frequently inhabited by *specialist* snake species.

Nocturnal Active during the night.

Opisthoglyphous Rear-fanged. Applied to snakes with enlarged fangs, often grooved, towards the rear of the mouth (see p.21).

Oviparous Egg-laying.

Ovo-viviparous Retaining fertilized eggs inside the body until just before or immediately after they hatch.

Parthenogenesis The process whereby an unfertilized egg develops into an embryo. Parthenogenetic species can reproduce without mating and can thus consist only of females. Only one snake species, the Brahminy Blind Snake, *Indotyphlops braminus*, is parthenogenetic.

Pelagic Inhabiting the middle and upper layers of the oceans.

Polymorphism The occurrence of two or more distinct *forms* within a single population of the same species (see p.31).

Primitive The term used to refer to characteristics that reflect an early ancestral evolutionary line and the *species*, *families*, etc. that are part of that line. For example, thread snakes share many characteristics with some of the earliest known snakes and are therefore members of a primitive family. The opposite of *advanced*.

Proteroglyphous Front-fanged. Applied to snakes that have enlarged, *venom*-delivering fangs in their upper jaw, including elapids, vipers, and some burrowing asps (Lamprophiidae) (see p.21).

Relic (or **relict**) Surviving populations of a *species* or *family* that once had a large distribution but now has only a fragmented or localized one.

Rostral scale The scale at the very tip of a snake's snout (see p.17).

Secondary forest Forest that has recolonized a cleared area.

Sidewinding A method of locomotion, practised by some snakes living among sand dunes, in which the body moves forward at an angle of about 45 degrees (see p.19).

Specialist A *species* that operates over a narrow ecological niche. For example, a species that feeds on one or two other species or lives in a restricted habitat. The opposite of *generalist*.

Species (plural and singular) A basic category of classification comprising a group of related organisms differing from others in the same *genus*. The most important classification in biology. A species' name consists of two Latin words: the generic name, followed by

the specific name. *Crotalus atrox*, for example, is a species of rattlesnake. Traditionally, species are reproductively isolated; they can interbreed with each other, but not with individuals of other species. This is not always so, however, and hybrids occasionally occur.

Stridulation The production of a sound by the rubbing together of two surfaces, such as the specialized, rough flank scales of several *species* of snake.

Sub-caudal scales The scales underneath a snake's tail (see p.17).

Subocular scales Those scales immediately behind the eye. Found only in some snake *species* (see p.17).

Subspecies A scientific category below the level of *species*. Used to denote differences in size, colour, pattern, etc. between populations within a *species* that are found over a wide geographical area or on islands.

Substrate The ground or surface on which a *species* rests or lives.

Taxonomy The science and practice of classification, in which organisms are arranged and named according to their relationships with one another.

Terrestrial Living mostly on the ground.

Tubercles Small raised swellings or pimples (see p.23).

Understorey Vegetated habitat below the forest canopy, usually consisting of shrubs, bushes, and grasses.

Venom Modified saliva, the main purpose of which is to incapacitate prey (see p.28).

Ventral scales Those scales on a snake's underside (see p.17).

Vertebrates Animals with backbones (mammals, birds, reptiles, amphibians, and fish). All other animals are invertebrates.

Vestigial limbs Undeveloped limbs that have diminished in size due to natural selection and are no longer functional.

Viviparous Giving birth to live young. The majority of snakes are not truly viviparous in the same way as mammals, since the embryos do not receive nourishment from their mothers. Instead, the eggs (without shells) remain in the female's oviducts during development and hatch just before or after birth. Strictly speaking, such snakes are *ovo-viviparous* (see p.37).

INDEX

A

Acanthophis:
  praelongus, 118
  pyrrhus, 119
Acrantophis dumerili, 60–61
Acrochordidae family, 155
  classification, 40, 155
Acrochordoidea superfamily, 40
Acrochordus species, 36
adaptation to habitats, 9
Adder, 29, 144–45
African Mole Snake, 37
African Rock Python, 25, 37, 54
African Saw-scaled Viper, 139
Agkistrodon:
  contortrix, 129
  piscivorus, 24
Ahaetulla, 22
Alsophis antigua, 39
amelanistic forms, 109
American Ratsnake, 17
Amphisbaenia suborder, 40
amphisbaenians, 8
anacondas, 70–71
anatomy, 18–19
Aniliidae family, 154
  classification, 40, 154
Anomalepididae family, 151
  classification, 40, 151
anomalepids, 13, 22
Anomochilidae family, 155
  classification, 40, 155
Antaresia:
  childreni, 46
  maculosa, 47
Antiguan Racer, 39
Aplopeltura boa, 105
aquatic/marine snakes, 11
  body shape, 13
  live-bearing, 37
  locomotion, 19
  right lung, 18
  types of prey, 24
  see also sea snakes
arboreal snakes:
  body shape, 13
  evolutionary convergence, 9
  live-bearing, 37
Argentine Rainbow Boa, 69
arid regions, adapting to, 10
Arizona Mountain Kingsnake, 96
articulation of skull bones, 20
Asian Sunbeam Snake, 45, 157
Asian Tentacled Snake, 17
Atlantic Central American Milksnake, 98–99
audible warnings, 33
Australian Inland Taipan, 28

B

Baird, Spencer Fullerton, 106
Baird's Ratsnake, 17, 106–107
Ball Python, 32
balling, 32
Banded Krait, 78
Banded Water Snake, 102–103
basking, 10, 11
binocular vision, 22, 83
Bitis:
  arietans, 130–131
  gabonica, 133
Black Adder, 144
Black-banded Snake, 105
Black Mamba, 28, 120

Black Pine Snake, 110
black snakes, 120
blind snakes, 8, 37, 151–54
  classification, 151, 153
Blood Python, 56–57
Blunt-headed Slug Snake, 105
Boa constrictor, 62
Boa Constrictor, 62
Boaedon:
  fuliginosus, 74
  fuliginosus mentalis, 75
boas, 60–73, 157–59
  classification, 40, 157
  dispersal of, 9
  fossils, 8
  heat pits, 23
  hunting methods, 24, 25
  scales, 17
  size of, 12
body shape, 13
body temperature/heat, regulating, 10, 11
body triads, 96
Bogertophis subocularis, 76–77
Boidae family, 60–72, 157–59
  classification, 40, 157
Boiga:
  cyanea, 79
  dendrophila, 78
Bolyeriidae family, 38, 155
  classification, 40, 155
bones of skull, 20, 21
Booidea superfamily, 40
Boomslang, 29, 32, 82–83
Bothrops:
  asper, 135
  jararaca, 134
Brahminy Blind Snake, 37
Brazilian Rainbow Boa, 68
breathing, *see* respiratory system
Brown House Snake, 74–75
  desert form, 75
Bull Snake, 111
bulls-eye markings, 86
Burmese Python, 54–55
  albino form, 54
burrowing, 8, 10, 11
burrowing asps, 21, 29, 177
  classification, 40
  side strike, 29
burrowing snakes:
  body shape, 13
  dorsal scales, 16
  seeing, 22
  tail, 17

C

Calabar Ground Python, 32, 64–65
Calabaria reinhardtii, 65
California Kingsnake, 31, 94–95
California Mountain Kingsnake, 97
camouflage, 30
  Copperhead, 128
  Cribo, 85
  Desert Horned Viper, 137
  Dumeril's Ground Boa, 60
  Gaboon Viper, 30, 133
  Reticulated Python, 48
  Rough Green Snake, 105
Candoia aspera, 31
captive breeding programmes, 39
  Dumeril's Ground Boa, 60
Carpet Python, 50–51
Casarea dussumieri, 38
Cascabel, 148

catsnakes, 13, 79
Central Australian Carpet Python, 51
Central Baja Rosy Boa, 72
Cerastes cerastes, 137
Chappel Island Tiger Snake, 127
Charina bottae, 12
Chequered Garter Snake, 112–13
Children, JG, 46
Children's Python, 46
chin, 20
chin groove, 60
Chinese Cobra, 122
Chionactis occipitalis, 105
circulatory system, 18
classification, 40, 151
climbing snakes:
  body shape, 13
Coastal Rosy Boa, 72
cobras, 122–27, 184–89
  fangs, 20, 21
  large head scales, 17
  venom, 21, 28, 29
  warning coloration, 30
coiling:
  brooding eggs, 46
  minimizing water loss, 11
cold conditions, adapting to, 10, 11
Collett's Snake, 126–27
coloration, 17
  defensive, 31
  warning, 30, 31
colour change:
  Emerald Tree Boa, 17
  Haitian Dwarf Boa, 42
colour scheme for venomous
  snakes, 30
Colubroidea superfamily, 40
Colubridae family, 74–117, 159–69
  classification, 40, 159
colubrids, 25, 74–117, 159–69
  fangs, 21
  large head scales, 17
  pupil shape, 22
  skull, 20
  venom, 21, 28, 29
Common Boa, 12, 22, 62–63
  swallowing prey, 25
Common Egg-eater, 80–81
Common Garter Snake, 37, 114
Common Pipe Snake, 32
compound bone, 20, 21
concealment, 31
concertina movement, 19
conditions, extreme living, 10–11
conservation, 38–39
constrictors, 25
continental land masses, 8
Copperhead, 128–29
copulatory organs, *see* hemipenes
Coral Snake, 99
coral snakes, 30, 31, 99
Corallus:
  caninus, 67
  enhydris, 31
  hortulanus, 23
Corn Snake, 108–109
Cottonmouth, 24, 102
courtship, 36
Cribo, 85
Crocodylia order, 40
Crotalus:
  atrox, 146
  cerastes, 150
  durissus, 148
  durissus vegrandis, 149

Crotalus (cont.):
  ruber, 23
  scutulatus, 29
  willardi, 36
cuatro natrices (four nostrils), 23
Cuban Dwarf Boa, 43
Cyclades Blunt-nosed Viper, 39
Cylindrophiidae family, 155–56
  classification, 40, 155
Cylindrophis ruffus, 32

D

Dasypeltis scabra, 81
day hunters,
  see diurnal (day) hunters
Death Adder, 9
death adders, 118–19
death, feigning, 32
defence:
  active, 28, 32–35
  passive, 30–31
  protection from scales, 16
defensive displays, 32
defensive posture:
  Calabar Ground Python, 65
  saw-scaled vipers, 139
  Common Egg-eater, 81
  Grass Snake, 101
  Red-tailed Racer, 89
  Royal Python, 58
  see also mimicry/mimics
deforestation, 38
  Madagascar, 61
dehydration, resisting, 11
Dendroaspis, 120
  polylepis, 28, 120
  viridis, 120–21
dentary bone, 20, 21
desert, adapting to the, 10
Desert Carpet Python, 51
Desert Death Adder, 119
Desert Horned Viper, 31, 33, 136–37
desert species, 11, 16, 31
desert vipers, 33
diamondbacks, 146–47
digestive system, 18, 19
dimorphic sexes:
  Nose-horned Viper, 142–43
Dipsadidae family, 169–76
  classification, 40, 169
Dispholidus typus, 83
diurnal (day) hunters, 25
  pupil shape, 22
dorsal scales, 16, 17
Drymarchon couperi, 85
Dumeril's Ground Boa, 10, 17, 60–61
Duvernoy's glands, 29
Dwarf boas, 32, 42–43, 155
dwarf pipe snakes, 155

E

earliest known snake, 8
Eastern Diamondback, 146
Eastern Garter Snake, 114
Eastern Hog-nosed Snake, 90
Eastern Indigo Snake, 84–85
Echis, 139
  carinatus, 138
ecological niches, filling, 9
ectotherms, 10, 11
education, conservation, 39
egg chamber, 37
egg-eating snakes, 25, 80

egg incubation:
  Grass Snake, 101
  pythons, 46
egg-laying snakes, 37
egg-tooth, 37, 56
eggs, 37
  clutch size, 37
  development of, 36
  eating, 25, 80
Elapidae family, 30, 118–27, 184–89
  classification, 40, 184
elapids:
  land, 29
  marine, 28
  venom, 28, 29
Emerald Tree Boa, 9, 17, 66–67
endangered habitat, *see* habitat destruction
endangered snakes:
  Burmese Python, 55
  Common Boa, 62
  Dumeril's Ground Boa, 61
  San Francisco Garter Snake, 114–15
  see also skin trade
energy, saving, 11
environment, adaptation to, 9, 10–11
Epicrates:
  alvarezi, 69
  cenchria, 69
  crassus, 69
Erpeton tentaculatum, 17
Erythrolamprus ornatus, 39
Eunectes:
  murinus, 71
  notaeus, 71
Euprepiophis mandarinus, 87
evolution, 8–9
  dispersal, 8, 9
  origins, 8
  radiation, 9
evolutionary convergence, 9
excretory system, 19
extinction, 38
eyes, 22
  and hunting, 25
  binocular vision, 22, 83
  swivelling, 56
eyespots, 69, 122, 123

F

false coral snakes, 30, 31
families (classification), 40
family tree (classification), 40
fangs, 21
  fixed front, 20
  grooved, 21
  hinged front, 20, 21, 28, 144
  hollow 20, 21
  rear, 21, 29
  replacement of, 21
  sheathed, 146
  specialized front, 29
Fawcett, Sir Percy, 12
feeding, 24–25
Fer-de-Lance, 37, 135
fertilization, 36
file snakes, 17, 36, 155
flexible jaws, *see* jaws
fossil record of snakes, 8
front-fanged snakes, 21, 29

G

Gaboon Viper, 13, 30,
  132–33
Garden Tree Boa, 23, 31, 67
garter snakes, 22, 36, 112–15
  identifying, 114
  surviving the cold, 11
Gerrhopilidae family, 151
  classification, 40, 151

giant pythons, 12
giving birth, 37, 142
Glass Lizard, 8
golden pythons, 54
Gondwanaland, 8
Gonyosoma, 89
  oxycephalum, 88
gopher snakes, 111
granular dorsal scales, 17
Grass Snake, 100–101
  eating live prey, 24
Green Anaconda, 12, 70–71
Green Catsnake, 13, 79
Green Tree Python, 9,
  52–53
Green Tree Viper, 79
Green Vine Snake,14–15
Grey-banded Kingsnake, 92
ground-dwellers:
  body shape, 13

H

habitat destruction, 38
  Florida, 103
  Honduras, 62
  Madagascar, 61
  San Francisco area, 114
haemotoxic venom, 29
Haitian Dwarf Boa, 42
hatching, 37, 56
head scales, 16, 17
  modified, 16
heads, hiding, 32
hearing, 23
heart, 18
heat pits, 19, 23
heat, sensing, 23
Hemachatus haemachatus, 32
hemipenes, 19, 36
Heterodon nasicus, 90–91
hibernation, 10, 11, 36
  Adder, 145
  California Mountain Kingsnake, 97
hiding places, 42
hissing, 11, 32, 33
hog-nosed snakes, 24, 32,
  90–91
Homalopsidae family, 189–90
  classification, 40, 189
hood (Cobra), 122, 123, 124
horizontal pupil, 22
horned adders, 17
horns, 136
human deaths by snakebites, 28, 29
hunters, and pupil shape, 22
hunting methods, 24–27
  Carpet Python, 50
  Copperhead, 128

I

ice crystals, 11
Indian Python, 37
internal systems, 18–19
interscalar skin, 16
interstitial skin, 16
intimidation, 32, 33
invertebrate eaters, 105
iridescence, 17, 45, 68
Iridescent Earth Snake, 45

J, K

Jacobson's organ, 19, 22
Jararaca, 134–35
jawbones, *see* jaws
jaws, 20, 21
  evolution of flexible, 20
keeled dorsal scales, 17
killing prey, *see* prey

King Cobra, 13
  digesting prey, 28
  threatening posture, 33
  toxicity of venom, 28
kingsnakes, 31, 92–97
kraits, 13

L

labial scales, 17
Lampropeltis, 31
  alterna, 92
  californiae, 94–95
  mexicana, 93
  mexicana mexicana, 93
  mexicana thayeri, 93
  polyzona, 99
  pyromelana, 97
  zonata, 97
Lamprophiidae family, 176–81
  classification, 40, 176
  venom, 28, 29
lanceheads, 134–35
land drift, 8
land elapids, 29
Langaha madagascariensis, 16
Lapparentophis defrennei, 8
large head scales, 17
largest snakes, 12–13
  Common Boa, 12
  Green Anaconda, 12, 70
  pythons, 12
  Reticulated Python, 12, 48
Lataste's Viper, 143
lateral undulation, 19
Laurasia, 8
legislation, conservation, 39
legless lizards, 8
Leopard Snake, 31, 116–17
Leptodeira septentrionalis, 24
Leptotyphlopidae family, 153–54
  classification, 40, 153
leptotyphlopids, 13, 22
Lichanura:
  trivirgata, 72–73
  trivirgata trivirgata, 72
  trivirgata roseofusca, 72
  trivirgata saslowi, 72
  orcutti, 73
linear progression, 19
litter size, 37
live-bearing snakes, 37
lizards, 8
  as prey, 29
locomotion, 16, 19
Long-nosed Tree Snake, 22
lower jawbone, 20, 21
Loxocemidae family, 44–45, 156
  classification, 40, 156
Loxocemus bicolor, 44
lungs, 18

M

Madagascan Vine Snake, 16
Mainland Island Snake, 127
Malayopython reticulatus, 48
male-to-male combat, 36, 145
mambas, 20, 120–21
Mandarin Ratsnake, 86–87
Mangrove Snake, 78
marine elapids, 28
marine snakes, early, 8
mating, 36
mating ball, 36, 102
maxilla, 20, 21
mental groove, 60
Mexican Baird's Ratsnake, 106, 107
Mexican Kingsnake, 93
Mexican Rosy Boa, 72
Milksnake, 31, 98–99

Milos Viper, 39
mimicry/mimics, 31, 81, 99
Mississippi Green Water Snake, 37
Moccasin, 129
moisture, balancing, 11
Mojave Rattlesnake, 29
Monocled Cobra, 123
Morelia:
  bredli, 51
  spilota, 50
  viridis, 53
mountain kingsnakes, 31
movement, 19
muscles, 19
myotoxic venom, 29

N

Naja:
  atra, 122
  kaouthia, 123
  pallida, 125
Natricidae family, 181–84
  classification, 40, 181
Natriciteres species, 32
Natrix natrix, 100
natural selection, 7, 12
nature reserves, 39
Neotropical Rattlesnake, 148–49
Neotropical Sunbeam Snake, 44
Nerodia:
  cyclopion, 37
  fasciata, 103
nervous system, 19
neurotoxic venom, 29
New Mexican Ridge-nosed Rattlesnake, 36
nocturnal (night) hunters, 25
  pupil shape, 22
Northern Death Adder, 118–19
Northern Pine Snake, 110–11
Northern Rosy Boa, 73
Northern Viper, 144
Nose-horned Viper, 142–43
nostrils, 22
Notechis, 127
Nuevo Leon Kingsnake, 93

O

Opheodrys aestivus, 105
Ophiophagus hannah, 13
opistoglyphous snakes, 21
orders (classification), 40
Oreocryptophis porphyraceus, 89
organs, 18
Ornate Ground Snake, 39
ovaries, 19
Oxybelis fulgidus, 14–15
Oxyuranus:
  microlepidotus, 28
  scutellatus, 13

P

Pacific Boa, 17
paired subcaudal scales, 17
pairs (sets) of species, 9
palatine bones, 20, 21
Pangaea, 8
Pantherophis:
  bairdi, 107
  guttatus, 108
Paraguayan Rainbow Boa, 69
Pareatidae family, 190–91
  classification, 40, 190
Peringuey's Viper, 26–27
parthenogenetic (female-only) species, 37
pet trade, 38, 60
pets, domestic, 68, 108
pigments, 16, 17
Pine Snake, 110–11
pipe snakes, 8, 32, 40, 154–56

pit vipers, 140–41, 128
    heat pits, 23
    island species, 141
Pituophis melanoleucus, 111
Plains Hog-nosed Snake, 90–91
Plains Garter Snake, 113, 114
playing dead, 32
Pliocercus elapoides, 32
polymorphism, 31
pre-anal scale, 16
predators of snakes, 30
prey:
    and constriction, 25, 47
    and use of venom, 21, 29, 34–35, 83
    detecting, 23
    digesting, 28
    eating, 20, 24
    lizards as, 29
    snakes as, 29, 30, 94
    striking at, 29
    subduing, 28
    swallowing, 63
    types of, 24
primitive living snakes, 8
    size, 13
    skulls, 20
proteroglyphous snakes, 21
Psammophis species, 32
Pseudaspis cana, 37
Pseudechis, 126
    colletti, 127
Pseudoxenodontidae family, 184
    classification, 40, 184
pterygoid bones, 20, 21
Pueblan Milksnake, 98, 99
Puff Adder, 37, 130–31
    pupil shapes, 22
Pythonoidea superfamily, 40
Python:
    bivittatus, 55
    breitensteini, 57
    curtus, 57
    regius, 58–59
    sebae, 12, 37
Pythonidae family, 46–59, 156–57
    classification, 40, 156
pythons, 46–59, 156–57
    body shape, 13
    classification, 40
    clutch size, 37
    heat pits, 23
    hunting methods, 24, 25, 26–27
    jaws, 20
    size, 12
    smooth scales, 17

Q, R

quadrate bone, 23
racers, 13, 22, 88–89
Rainbow Boa, 17, 68–69
rainforest destruction, 38
rasp, warning, 33
ratsnakes, 76–77, 86–87, 89, 106–09, 116–117
    body shape, 13
    constrictors, 25
    hatching, 37
rattle, 17, 33, 147
rattlesnake roundups, 38, 146
rattlesnakes, 17, 33, 146–50
    as prey species, 94
    breeding habits, 149
rear-fanged snakes, 21, 29
Red Diamond Rattlesnake, 23, 146
Red Mountain Racer, 89
Red Ratsnake, 108
Red-sided Garter Snake, 36
Red Spitting Cobra, 124–25
Red-tailed Racer, 88–89
reproduction, 36–37

reproductive system, 19
Reptilia class, 40
reptiles, burrowing, 8
research, conservation, 39
respiratory system, 18
Reticulated Python, 12, 33, 48–49
    clutch size, 37
reticulations, 50
Rhinoceros Viper, 6
Rhynchocephalia order, 40
ribs, 18
Ring-necked Spitting Cobra, 32
Rinkhals, 32
rostral scale, 17, 90
Rosy Boa, 17, 72–73
Rough Green Snake, 22, 104–105
Round Island, 38, 39
Round Island Burrowing Boa, 38
Round Island boas, 155
round pupil, 22
Royal Python, 32, 58–59

S

salt, correcting balance of, 11
San Diego Gopher Snake, 111
San Francisco Garter Snake, 114–15
San Luis Potosí Kingsnake, 93
sand snakes, 13
Sauria suborder, 40
Saw-scaled Viper, 138–39
saw-scaled vipers, 29, 138–39
scales, 16–17, 90, 118
    characteristics, 17
    coloration, 17
    functions of, 16
    modified, 16
    specialized, 11, 17
    types of, 16, 17
Scaphiodontophis venustissimus, 32
scents, analysing, 22
Scolecophidia superfamily, 40, 151
Scolecophis atrocinctus, 105
Scrub Python, 12
sea snakes, 11, 29, 37
    classification, 40
    types of prey, 24
secretions, foul-smelling, 32
seeing, 22
selective breeding, 108
sense organs, 22–23
Serpentes suborder, 40
shape, *see* body shape
shedding skin, 13
shield-tailed snakes, 17, 156
shivering thermogenesis, 54
Short-tailed Python, 57
side strike, 29
Sidewinder, 150
sidewinding, 19, 136, 150
Simalia kinghorni, 12
Simoliophis, 8
Sinaloan Milksnake, 98
single-sex snake, 37
single subcaudal scales, 17
size, 12–13
skeleton, 18, 19
skin, 16
skin trade, 38
    Burmese Python, 55
    Royal Python, 58
skull, 18, 20–21
    evolution of, 20
    flexibility of, 21
small head scales, 17
small snakes, 13
smelling, 22
smooth dorsal scales, 17
Smooth Green Snake, 104
snail- and slug-eating snakes, 25
snake charmers, 123

snakes as prey, 29, 30, 94
snout, modified, 16
Snow Corn Snake, 109
snow corns, 109
Sonoran Mountain Kingsnake, 96–97
Southern Rubber Boa, 12
species, 8, 151
sperm, 19, 36
spine, 18–19
spitting, 33, 34–35
spitting cobras, 32, 33, 34–35
Spotted Python, 47
Squamata order, 8, 40
stapes, 23
stridulation, 11
subcaudal scales, 17
subfamilies, 151
subocular scales, 17
suborders (classification), 40
Sumatran Pit Viper, 141
sunbeam snakes, 45, 157
superfamilies (classification), 40, 151
supraocular scales, 118

T

tail:
    loss, 32
    specialized scales, 17, 33
    to lure prey, 24
    vertebrae, 32
tail imitating head:
    Calabar Ground Python, 32, 64
Taipan, 13, 28
teeth, 20–21, 28
    curved, 33
    replacement of, 21
temperature, regulating body, 10, 11
Terciopelo, 135
testes, 19
Testudines order, 40
Tetracheilostoma carlae, 13
Thamnophis:
    marcianus, 112
    sirtalis parietalis, 36
    sirtalis tetrataenia, 115
Thelotornis, 22
thermogenesis, shivering, 54
thermoreceptors, 23
thread snakes, 8, 20, 153
threatening posture, 33
tiger snakes, 127
tongue, 22
    and salt balance, 11
    blue, 89
    tracheal lung, 18
Trans-Pecos Ratsnake, 76–77
    blonde form, 76
Tree Asp, *see Dendroaspis*
tree snakes, 22
triads, 96
Trimeresurus albolabris, 141
Tropidophiidae family, 42–43, 155
    classification, 40, 155
Tropidophis:
    haetianus, 42
    melanurus, 43
tubercles (pits), 23
twig snakes, 22, 29, 33
Typhlopidae family, 151–53
    classification, 40, 151
typhlopids, 13, 22

U

upper jawbone, 20, 21
uric acid, 11
Uropeltoidea superfamily, 40
Uropeltidae family, 156
    classification, 40, 156

V

venom, 28, 29
    injecting, 29
    producing, 28
    spraying, 33, 34–35
    toxicity, 28, 29
venom duct, 21
venom gland, 21
venomous snakes, 28–29
    warning coloration, 30, 31
ventral scales, 16, 17
vertebrae, 18
vertical pupil, 22
vestigial:
    limbs, 19
    pelvic girdle, 19
vibrations, hearing, 23
Viper Boa, 31
Vipera, 143
    ammodytes, 142–43
    berus, 144
    latastei, 143
Viperidae family, 128–50, 191–95
    classification, 40, 191
vipers, 128–50, 191–95
    body shape, 13
    dispersal of, 9
    fangs, 21, 28
    hunting methods, 24
    live-bearing, 37
    pupil shape, 22
    scales, 16, 17
    skull, 21
    venom, 21, 28, 29
    see also pit vipers

W

warm climates, living in, 10
warning:
    coloration, 30, 31
    signals, 33
    sounds, 33
wart snakes, 11, 17
water snakes, 22, 102–103
West African Green Mamba, 120–21
Western Diamondback Rattlesnake, 33, 146–47
Western Shovel-nosed Snake, 105
whipsnakes, 13, 22
White-lipped Tree Viper, 140–41
    identification of, 40

X

Xenodermatidae family, 191
    classification, 40, 191
Xenopeltidae family, 45, 157
    classification, 40, 157
Xenopeltis unicolor, 45
Xenophidiidae family, 155
    classification, 40, 155
Xenotyphlopidae family, 154
    classification, 40, 154

Y, Z

Yarar, 134
Yararaca, 134
Yellow Anaconda, 71
Zamenis situla, 117

ACKNOWLEDGMENTS

FOR REVISED EDITION

Author's acknowledgments

The author would like to thank Dharini Ganesh and Kaiya Shang for their editorial work, patience, and helpful suggestions.

Dorling Kindersley would like to thank the following:

Sneha Sunder Benjamin, Arpita Dasgupta, Suefa Lee, Riji Raju, and Rupa Rao for editorial assistance; and Shanker Prasad, Pawan Kumar, and Nityanand Kumar for DTP assistance.

Mark Amey and the teams at Wrigglies Exotic Pets and Animal Actors for supplying and handling snakes for photography.

FOR FIRST EDITION

Author's acknowledgments

Over the years I have benefited enormously from the expertise and good company of a number of fellow herpetologists while on snake-hunting trips to several parts of the world. Although they are too numerous to mention individually, I hope they all realize, nevertheless, that their contributions have been important to me.

More specifically, I would also like to thank the following people, listed alphabetically, who provided many of the snakes that I photographed for this project:

John and Linda Bird (for many specimens), the staff of Birdquest, Gretchen Mattison, Richard Haigh, David Kershaw, Paul Rowley, Frank Schofield, and Cliff Stone.

In addition to loaning specimens, all these people also helped to restrain and pose the snakes. In this respect, I am especially indebted to Paul Rowley of the Liverpool School of Tropical Medicine, who helped me photograph a number of highly dangerous species, and to Gretchen Mattison, who has always been a willing helper when it comes to controlling uncooperative snakes in the studio, and who has also helped to find and photograph snakes in the field.

Finally, thanks to Hugh Schermuly, Sally McEachern, and the other designers and editors of Schermuly Design, and to Stephanie Jackson, Adèle Hayward, and the rest of the editorial team at Dorling Kindersley, not only for all their hard work but also for helping to make this book a pleasure to write.

Dorling Kindersley would like to thank the following:
Senior Editor: Adèle Hayward
Senior Art Editor: Tracy Hambleton-Miles
Production Controller: Silvia La Greca
Managing Editor: Stephanie Jackson
Managing Art Editor: Nigel Duffield

Produced by Schermuly Design Co.
The Church Hall, York Rise,
Dartmouth Park,
London NW5 1SB
Designers: Hugh Schermuly, Nick Buzzard, Masumi Higo
Editors: Sally MacEachern, Josie Bryan, Claire Calman

Dorling Kindersley would also like to thank the following for additional help:
Editors: Jane Simmonds for start-up project management; Tracey Beresford, Josephine Bryan, Claire Calman, and Nicola Munro for editorial assistance
Designers: Kate Poole for start-up project management; Tassy King as Senior Art Editor in the final stages of production
Administrative assistant: Chris Gordon

Schermuly Design Co. would like to thank the following:
Trevor Smith of Animal World for supplying and handling snakes for photography. Laura Wickenden for going lens to face with some very lively snakes. Mark O'Shea of West Midland Safari and Leisure Park for allowing us to photograph his cobras. Lynn Bresler for proof reading and indexing. Didier Chatelus and Jenny Buzzard for DTP assistance.

Picture credits
The publisher would like to thank the following for their kind permission to reproduce their photographs:
(Key: a-above; b-below/bottom; c-centre; f-far; l-left; r-right; t-top)

Alamy Images: John Cancalosi 39clb
Ardea London Ltd: 25 tc, Adrian Warren 120 bl, Francois Gohier 36 bl, McDougal 25 tc
BBC Natural History Unit: 85 tc, Andrew Cooper 11 bl, Artur Tabor 29 bl, Jeff Foott 19 br, John Cancalosi 94 b, 127 bc, Jurgen Freund 11 br, Lynn M. Stone 90 tr, Martin Holmes 127 br, Steven David Miller 102 tr
Biofotos: Slim Sreedharan 29 tl
Bruce Coleman Ltd: 29 r, Dr. Frieder Sauer 144 bc, Erwin and Peggy Bauer 108 cl
Chris Mattison: 4 br, 5 br, 6 r, 9 cl, cr, br, 10 bl, bc, br, 12 tr, 13 tr, 16 bl, bc, tr, cr, 17 tl, tcl, tcr, tr, cl, ccl, ccr, cr, 19 tc, 20 cl, 21 cr, 22 tl, cl, bl, 33 tr, 37 cl, cr, 39 tc, tr, 40 tr, 41 br, 42 t, tr, 43 bl, r, 44 cl, b, cr, 45 c, br, 46 tr, b, 47 cr, b, 49 tr, 50 c, 51 br, 53 bc, 56 bl, 57 tc, 62 c, 66 tl, 67 c, br, 69 tc, tr, cr, 70 br, 72 cr, 73 tr, 74 bl, c, 75 bl, 81 c, cra, crb, 82 tl, br, 83 tr, 88 c, 89 tr, 91 tc, 92 t, 93 cl, br, 94 cl, 95 c, 96 c, 98 bc, 103 tr, 104 tl, c, 105 bl, tr, cr, br, 106 bl, 107 c, cr, 111 br, 114 tr, br, 115 tr, c, 116 c, bl, 117 tl, 118 c, bl, 126 t, 132 cl, r, 133 br, 134 b, 135 tr, 136 cl, 138 cl, 139 br, c, 140 c, 141 r, 142 c, 143 bl, 145 tr, 148 r, 149 tr, 150 tr
Corbis: Jack Goldfarb / Design Pics 85 cb, Sebastian Kennerknecht / Minden Pictures 115 cb
Dorling Kindersley: Liberty's Owl, Raptor and Reptile Centre, Hampshire, UK 54 c
FLPA: Chris Mattison 67 tl, M. Ranjiit 28 tr, Gregory Guida / Biosphoto 39 cb, Jelger Herder, Buiten-beeld / Minden Pictures 34-35, Kevin Schafer / Minden Pictures 14-15

George McCarthy: 36 cb, 101 tr, 145 tc
Gerald Cubitt: 38 b
Getty Images: Tom Cockrem 38 tr
Jane Burton: 24 tr
Joe McDonald: endpapers, 136 bl, 137 cr, 146 tr
John Cancaloni: 97 cr
John Visser: 80 cl, 80 bl
Laura Wickenden: 5 tr, 10 tr, 12 c, 13 br, 16 br, 32 bl, 41 l, c, 52 c, 53 cr, 54 bl, 55 br, 56 c, 58 cl, bc, 59 c, 60 tr, 61 tr, 64 c, br, 70 l, c, 72 tr, cl, 73 c, 76 bl, 78 bl, 100 c, 110 c, bl, 122 c, bl, 123 c, bl, 124 c, bl
Michael and Patricia Fogden: 11 cb, 21 cb, 31 bl, 32 tr, 48 cl, 50 tr, 63 tr, 99 tr, 119 br, 141 tc
MPL: Fogden 135 br
naturepl.com: Solvin Zankl 31 tl
N.H.P.A.: Anthony Bannister 83 bl, Daniel Heuclin 32 bl, 37 tr, 125 tr, 143 tc, 149 br, E. Hanumantha Rao 33 bl, G.I. Bernard 29 br, Ken Griffiths 118 tr, Martin Wendler 41 br, 71 br, Stephen Dalton 144 cl
Oxford Scientific Films: B.P. Kent 128 bl, M. Fogden 21 tr, Steve Tisner 30 bl, Z. Leszczynski 24 bl
Papilio Photographic: 33 t
Planet Earth Pictures: Brian Kenney 111 c, 128 br, 130 cl, Carol Farneti 53 bc, Mary Clay 114 tr
Premaphotos Wildlife: K.G. Preston-Matham 31 tc
SuperStock: Animals Animals 103 cb
Warren Photographic: Kim Taylor 28 b

Maps by Masumi Higo
Illustrations by Evi Antoniou

All other images © Dorling Kindersley
For further information see:
www.dkimages.com